French Harpsichord Music
of the 17th Century

Studies in Musicology, No. 11

Other Titles in This Series

No. 10 Theories of Chromatic and Enharmonic Music
in Late 16th Century Italy   Karol Berger

No. 12 The Genesis of Schumann's DICHTERLIEBE:
A Source Study   Rufus E. Hallmark

No. 13 The Formation of Opera:
The Influence of Humanist Thought and
Italian Renaissance Poetry   Barbara Russano Hanning

No. 14 Kurt Weill in Europe   Kim H. Kowalke

No. 15 TON UND WORT: The Lieder of
Richard Strauss   Barbara A. Petersen

No. 16   Italian Opera in London, 1760-1800   Fred C. Petty

No. 17 German Music Theory in the Early 17th Century:
The Treatises of Johannes Lippius   Benito V. Rivera

No. 18 Italian Manuscript Sources of
17th Century Keyboard Music   Alexander Silbiger

French Harpsichord Music
of the 17th Century

A Thematic Catalog of the Sources with Commentary

VOLUME TWO
Catalog Inventories 1-36

---

by
Bruce Gustafson

umi
RESEARCH PRESS

Produced and distributed by
University Microfilms International
Ann Arbor, Michigan 48106

Library of Congress Cataloging in Publication Data

Gustafson, Bruce, 1945-
  French harpsichord music of the 17th century.

  (Studies in musicology ; no. 11)
  Includes bibliographies and index.
  1. Harpsichord music—Thematic catalogs. 2. Music,
French—Thematic catalogs.   I. Title. II. Series.

ML128.H35G9   016.7864'04'210944   79-23567
ISBN 0-8357-1069-6 (set)
ISBN 0-8357-1067-X v.2

INTRODUCTION

All abbreviations are explained in the *List of Abbreviations* (Volume I, pages xvii-xliii). An *Explanation of the Catalog* is found as the last chapter of the Commentary (Volume I, pages 147-154).

Provenance: Denmark?, 1626-ca. 1650 (dated ℓ. 2v, "1626, 3. Jan" and ℓ. 7v, "1639. 3. Januar").

Location: Copenhagen; Det kongelige Bibliotek, Handscrift Afd., Gl. kgl. Saml. 376 fol.

Description: 1 p.ℓ., 34 ℓ. (i.e., 33: 5 omitted in numeration); 4 quires (A^4, B^8, C^{12}, D^8, and 1 ℓ. pasted to final end paper); folio format, 32 x 20 cm. Watermark #96. 3/4 leather binding (ca. 1915-1930), 32.5 x 21 cm.

Notation: New German organ tablature (5-6 systems per page, written across facing pages).

Scribes: Several unidentified hands.

Marginalia: Miscellaneous marks and letters on several pages, including ℓ. 34r (see Fig. 1 in Commentary).

Summary:

Composers:
ABEL: #2, 3.
LA BARRE: #39, 40?.
MESANGEAU: #50.
PINEL: #48a, 51.

Contents:

#1-9	Simple dances; opening prelude added later.
10-24	Chorales, psalm tunes.
25-58	Dances and miscellaneous pieces.
59-69	Popular tune settings, Germanic dances.

Inventory:

ℓ i^r [blank, pasted to end paper]

	ℓ iᵛ	[instructional material in German, major and minor scales].
1	ℓ 1r$^{1-5}$	Praeludium /C
	ℓ 1v	[blank]
2	ℓ 2r^1-3r^1	Praeludium /ex clave G♮ / Ab Org: [ie, ABEL]
3	ℓ 2v^2-2v^5	Currant / Ab |Año 1626, 3 Jan. /fecit [G] [ABEL]
4	ℓ 3r^5-3r^6	Allamande. [d]
5	ℓ 3v^1-4r^2	Courrante. [C]
6	ℓ 3v^3-4r^4	Sarabande. [g]

CO: cf 2-Witzendorff #54
　　cf 16-Cosyn #101
　　cf 18-Ch-Ch-1236 #6
　　cf Drallius #94
　　cf Eyck I ℓ 36v′
　　cf Kabinet I ℓ 9v
　　cf Oude 731 X 8

7	ℓ 3v^5-3v^6	Tantz [F]
	ℓ 4v$^{1-2}$	Der naech /Tantz. [fragment (F)]
8	ℓ 4v$^{3-4}$	Mascharad: [fragment (c)]
9	ℓ 4v$^{5-6}$	Sarabande. [fragment (d)]

[ℓ lacking; ℓ 5 omitted in numbering system]

10	ℓ 6r$^{1-2}$	[fragment (g)]
11	ℓ 6r^4	[fragment (F)]
12	ℓ 6r^5	[fragment (G)]
13	ℓ 6v^1-7r^2	Von Himmel /Hoch da kom ich /her
14	ℓ 6v^3-6v^4	Nun kom Der /Heÿden Heÿland.
15	ℓ 6v^5-7r^6	Sarabande. [g]
16	ℓ 7v^1-8r^3	Der 3. Psalmen. /Wie Viel sind der /o

Herr. /Angefangen 1639. /3. Januar:-

17	ℓ $8v^1$-$9r^3$	Der 5. Psalmen /O Herr dein Ohren /zu mir.
18	ℓ $8v^4$-$9r^6$	Der 103 Psalmen /Nu Preiß mein /Seelen.
19	ℓ $9v^1$-$10r^3$	Der 8 Psalmen. /O Höchster /Gott.
20	ℓ $9v^4$-$10r^5$	Erstanden ist /der Heilige /Christ.
21	ℓ $9v^6$-$10r^6$	Kom Gott /Schöpffer /Heÿliger /Geist.
22	ℓ $10v^1$-$11r^3$	Der 91 Psalmen /Wer in Des aller höchsten /Hut
23	ℓ $10v^4$-$11r^4$	Intonation. [d]
24	ℓ $10v^5$-$11r^6$ $12r^6$	In dulci /Jubilo.
25	ℓ $11v^1$-$11v^4$	Allamande. [C]
26	ℓ $11v^4$-$11v^6$	Courrante. [C]
27	ℓ $12v^1$-$13r^5$	Engelendishe /Nachtigall:- [C]
28	ℓ $12v^6$-$13r^6$	Sarabande. [C]
29	ℓ $13v^{1-3}$	Engelendiesher /Galliard: [fragment (D)]
30	ℓ $13v^{4-5}$	Praeludium [fragment (D)]
31	ℓ $13v^6$	Intonation /ex G^b. [fragment]
	[ℓ lacking]	
32	ℓ $14r^{1-2}$	[allemande; fragment (g)]
33	ℓ $14r^{3-5}$	[sarabande; fragment (g)]
34	ℓ $14r^{5-6}$	2.da Sarabande. [fragment (g)]
35a	ℓ $14v^1$-$14v^4$	Courante /Lavigon [g]
35b	ℓ $14v^4$-$16r^2$	La /Duble.
36	ℓ $15v^3$-$16r^4$	Courante /Simple [d]
37	ℓ $15v^5$-$16r^6$	Courrante /La Reÿn [g]

38 | ℓ 16v^1-17r^1 Sarabande [g]

39 | [LA BARRE (arr?): <u>Allemande</u> (a)]

Allamande.
 ℓ 16v^2-17r^3 [$\frac{4}{4}$]|7|6|

CO: cf 27-Gresse #21, Almande ... L.B.$^{[d]}$
  cf 3-Berlin-40623 #72, Allmande [d]

ED: Ex 2 above, Dickinson #39, Hamburger p 138;
  cf Epstein #22a, Curtis-MMN #68.

40 | [LA BARRE?: <u>Sarabande</u> (a)]

Sarabande
 ℓ 16v^4-17r^5 C |8|10| [$\frac{3}{4}$|8|10|]

CO: cf 29-Chigi #32, Sarabanda del mS [ie, La Barre]
  cf Eyck II ℓ 22v, Lossy

ED: Ex 3 above, Dickinson #40, Hamburger p 138;
  cf Lincoln-II p 41.

41 | ℓ 16^6-17r^6 Praeludium /ex. A: [a]

42 | ℓ 17v^1-18r^2 Courrante /La Boudate. [G]

43a | ℓ 17v^3-17v^4 Allamande. [C]

43b | ℓ 18v^1-18v^4 Variatio vel Alio modo /Sequitur |Alio modo

44 | ℓ 18v^5-19r^6 Ich füle lauter /angst undt Schmerzen.

45 | ℓ 19v^1-20r^2 Courrande [D]

45a | ℓ 19v^4 Niederlendish Liedtgen [1 meas only]
CO: 1-Copenhagen-376 #60

46 | ℓ 19v^4-20r^6 Sarabande [C]

47a | ℓ 20v^1-21r^3 Courrante /La Bourbono. [d]

47b | ℓ 20v^4-21v^3 Devision.

48a | [PINEL, arr: Sarabande (d)]

Sarabande.
    ℓ 21v^4-22r^6 𝄴 [$\frac{3}{4}$]|8|8|8|

CO: cf 11-Ryge #15, Aria di D.B.H. [BUXTEHUDE]
    cf 18-Ch-Ch-1236 #38, Sarabande Mr. Ben: Rogers
    cf Drallius #128, Saraband
    cf Leningrad #22, Serbande
    cf Van-Eijl #13, Serbande Gisbert Steenwick ...
    cf Van-Eijl #16, Saraband Barend Broeckhuisen ...
    cf Faille ℓ 121v, Sarabande Pinel

ED: Ex 1 above, Dickinson #48a, Hamburger p 139;
    cf Noske #13, #16, **Bangert** p 84.

48b | ℓ 22v^1-23r^3 Duoble.

49 | Courante /La Chabotte [D]

50 | [MESANGEAU, arr: <u>Allemande</u> (a)]

Allamande /de Mr: /Meschanson

ℓ 23v^1-24r^4 [$^2_2$]|10|13|

ED: Dickinson #50, Epstein #17, Pirro #1, Souris-M
p 57.

---

51 | [PINEL, arr: <u>Allemande</u> (g)]

Allamande. /de: Mr: Pinell:

ℓ 24v^1-25r^2 [$^2_2$]|6|7|

ED: Dickinson #51.

52	ℓ 24v^3-25r^4 Sarabande [g]
53	ℓ 25v^1-26r^3 Allamande [a]
54	ℓ 25v^4-26r^5 Sarabande [D]
55	ℓ 26v^1-27r^3 Courăte /de /Delphin [d]
56	ℓ 26v^4-26v^6 Als Damon /Lang Geplaget
57	ℓ 27v^1-28r^3 Le /Vulcan
58	ℓ 27v^4-28r^5 Sarabande [G]
	ℓ 28v - 29r [blank]
59a	ℓ 29v^1-30r^2 Tantz [g]
59b	ℓ 29v^3-29v^5 Sprunckg [g]
60	ℓ 30v^1-30v^3 Niederlendish Liedtgen [g]

61	ℓ 30v^3-30v^6	Courante. /La Bour/bon [d]
62	ℓ 31v^1-32r^2	Tantz [G]
62a	ℓ 31v^5	Liester Ehder /tantz [2.meas only]
		CO: 1-Copenhagen-376 #69
63	ℓ 32v^1-32v^2	Engellendisches Liedtgen [g]
64	ℓ 32v^3-33r^4	Niederlendishes Liedtgen [d]
65	ℓ 32v^3-33r^5	[piece (C)]
66	ℓ 32v^6-44r^6	Aarie [d]
67	ℓ 33v$^{1-2}$	Lusi [C]
68a	ℓ 33v$^{3-4}$	Rondadinela [C]
68b	ℓ 33v$^{5-6}$	Davatte po den [C]
	[ℓ 34 stubbed arbitrarily at this point]	
68c	ℓ 34r^3	[fragment (C)]
69	ℓ 34r$^{4-5}$	Liester Ehder /dantze [fragment?]
		CO: 1-Copenhagen-376 #62a
	ℓ 34v	[blank, pasted to modern end paper].

2-WITZENDORFF

Provenance: Lüneburg, 1655-1659 (dated ℓ. i^r, "Franciscus Witzendorff Lüaeb: Aõ 1655. 3 Non: Jan: Incept: Anno 1659. 17 Iunÿ auffgefärrt").

Location: Lüneburg; Ratsbücherei Lüneburg, KN 148.

Description: 2 p.ℓ., 99 p. and/or ℓ. (i.e., 88 ℓ. numerated irregularly as p. and ℓ.); 12 quires (A^4, B-K^8, L^6); oblong quarto format, 15.5 x 20 cm. Watermark #98. Original vellum binding, from a chant ms, 16.5 x 21 cm.

Notation: New German organ tablature (3 systems per page, written across facing pages; except ℓ. 99v: 4 systems).

Scribe: Franciscus Witzendorff.

Marginalia: Original numeration of pages and leaves (retained below) and modern numeration of pieces (retained below).

Summary:
    Composers:
       CHAMBONNIÈRES: #94.
       MESANGEAU: #99.

    Contents:
       Miscellaneous mixture of 64 dances, 25 chorales
          and 14 songs.
       Alphabetical index, inside back cover.

Inventory:

    ℓ i^r [title page:] Siquidem maximus ingenüs
                Musicam et probtam et excultam inuenio.
                /Sic Socratem et Pythagoram, praecipuos,
                Philosophos, sumopere hac juiste delec-

ta/tos, stradiderunt uesteres. Sic
Alexander [etc.] ... Temnius. |Francis-
cus Witzendorff Lüaeb: Aõ 1655. /3 Non:
Jan: [in a different ink:] Incept: /Anno
1659. 17 Iunÿ auffgefärrt.

	ℓ i^v	[blank]
1	ℓ ii^r	[scales in organ tablature:] Ex. F ... /G ... /A ... /E ... /D
	ℓ ii^v	[blank]
2	p 1$^{1-2}$	Pargamasch.
3	p 2^2-3^2	Unlängst Ich Meine /Chloris fandt.
4	p 4$^{1-2}$	Zerspalte nicht / betrübtes Herz.
5	p 5$^{2-3}$	Curant /Der schönste /Matresse
6	p 6$^{1-3}$	O Wir Armen /Sünder.
7	p 8^1-9^3	Christ Lag in Todes /Banden.
8	p 10$^{1-2}$	Werde Munter /mein gemühter
9	p 10$^{2-3}$	Gott der du /selber bist daß /licht.
10	p 12^1-15^1	Kom heiliger /Geist, herre /Gott.
11	p 14^2-15^3	Allemand [g]
12	p 16$^{1-3}$	Curant [d]
13	p 18$^{1-2}$	Wol dem der /weit von hohen /Dingen
14	p 18$^{2-3}$	Coridon der /ging betrübet
15	p 20^1-ℓ 22r^1	Allemand |2da Variatio [G]
16	ℓ 21v$^{2-3}$	Woll dem der /feine Tagh.
16a	ℓ 22r^1-22v^1	Woll dem der /feine Tagh.
17	ℓ 22v$^{2-3}$	Waß lobes sollen /wir Dir O Vater /singen
18	ℓ 23v^1-24r^2	Curant /Frantzosich [d]

19	ℓ 24v$^{1-2}$	Saraband. /Wenn ich gedencke /der vorigen /Zeiten.
20	ℓ 24v$^{2-3}$	Wer sich auff /daß Wasser /begibt
21	ℓ 25v$^{1-2}$	Nuhn laßt uns /Gott den Herren
22	ℓ 25v^{2}-26r^{3}	Nuhn kompt der /Heiden Heilandt.
23	ℓ 26r$^{1-2}$	More Palatino
24	ℓ 26v^{2}-28r^{3}	Frantosish /Allemod |Ida /Variatio ... 8
25	ℓ 28v$^{1-3}$	In Dulci jubilo
26	ℓ 29v$^{1-2}$	Von Himmel /hoch da kom /ich her.
27	ℓ 29v$^{2-3}$	Auf Meinen /hertzen grun/de
28	ℓ 30v^{1}-31r^{2}	O Lamb Gottes /Inschuldig.
29	ℓ 31r$^{2-3}$	Ach Amarillis /hastu den
30	ℓ 31v^{1}-32r^{2}	Wie schön Leüchehtet /der Morgenstern
31	ℓ 32v$^{1-2}$	Itzund Kompt /die Nacht /herbeÿ |Proportio
32	ℓ 33r^{2}-32v^{3}	Ach Phillis /mein außer /wählter Schatz
33	ℓ 33v$^{1-3}$	Curant /Lavion
34	ℓ 34v^{1}-36r^{2}	Englisch Mascharad /oder /dass Glück gantz /wanckelmütig /ist.
35	ℓ 36v$^{1-2}$	Surrexit Christus /Dominus /od /Wir dancken dir herr Je/su Christ etcc.
36	ℓ 36v^{2}-37r^{3}	Nuhn freut /euch lieber Christen /gemein
37	ℓ 37v^{1}-38r^{3}	Nu Lob mein /Sehl den herren
38	ℓ 38v$^{1-3}$	Nuhn Bitten /wir den heiligen /Geist
39	ℓ 39v$^{1-2}$	Hertzlich thut /mich verlangen.
40	ℓ 39v$^{2-3}$	Von Gott Will /ich nicht laßen /oder Helftt mir Gottes /güte preisen

41	ℓ 40v$^{1-3}$	Englische /Nachtigall
42	ℓ 41v$^{1-2}$	Saraband [g]
43	ℓ 41v^2-42r^3	Saraband [g]
44	ℓ 42v^1-43r^3	Allemand [d]
45	ℓ 43v^1-44r^3	Ein Franzosisch /Tantz |Proportio [d]
46	ℓ 44v^1-45r^3	Tanick /Polschÿ
47	ℓ 45v$^{1-3}$	Ein Tantz /von der Fortuna |Proportio
48	p 47-ℓ 48r^3	Ballet
49	ℓ 48v^1-49r^3	Der Hamburger /Crawal. |Proportio
50	ℓ 50v^1-51r^3	Ballet
50a	ℓ 51v^1-52r^2	Curant Auff /vorhergehendes /Ballet
51	ℓ 52r$^{2-3}$	Du Priesten /fürst herr /Jesu Christ
52	ℓ 52v^1-53v^1	Curant |2da Variatio /Contra/punct [d]
53	ℓ 53v$^{2-3}$	Saraband [a]
54	ℓ 54v$^{1-2}$	Saraband [a]

CO: cf 1-Copenhagen-376 #6
    cf 16-Cosyn #101
    cf 18-Ch-Ch-1236 #6
    cf Drallius #94
    cf Eyck I ℓ 36v
    cf Kabinet I ℓ 9v
    cf Oude 731 X 8

55	ℓ 54v^2-55r^3	Saraband [a]
56	ℓ 55v^1-57r^1	Ballet |Verte
57	ℓ 56r^2-57r^3	Curant /Frantzosisch [d]
58	ℓ 57v^1-58r^2	Gelobet seistu /Jesu Christu
59	ℓ 58r^1-60r^3	Curante: |Secunda /Varia/tio |3... [a]
60	ℓ 60v^1-62r^3	Curant |Secunda /Variatio [d]
61	ℓ 62v^1-63r^3	Christus der /unß seelich /macht.
62	ℓ 63v^1-64r^2	Ballet du /Roÿ [g]
63	ℓ 64r^2-63v^3	Saraband [D]

64	ℓ 64v^1-65r^2 Allemand [d]
65	ℓ 66r$^{2-3}$ Ros Ballet
66	ℓ 66v^1-74r^2 Auffzug /der Behren Tantz |2 /Auffzug ... |16 ...
67	ℓ 74v^2-75r^3 Ballet der /helden
68	ℓ 75v^1-80r^1 Saraband |Secunda /Variatio ... |Octava ... [g]
69	ℓ 79v^2-80r^2 Aria /Gallica [d]
70	ℓ 79v^3-80r^3 Gavotte [C]
71	ℓ 80v^1-81r^1 Saraband [d]
72	ℓ 81r^1-80v^3 Saraband [G]
73	ℓ 80v$^{2-3}$ Saraband [g]
74	ℓ 81v^1-82r^1 Saraband /Mein Lieb ist /schön gnung vor /meinen augen [G]
75	ℓ 81v$^{2-3}$ Saraband [G]
76	ℓ 81v^3-82r^3 Curant [C]
77	ℓ 82v$^{1-2}$ Ein Liedt /Wiltu nicht /Von Bräutigam hören.
78	ℓ 83r^2-82v^3 Courant
79	ℓ 83v$^{1-2}$ Auff Meinen /Lieben Gott
80	ℓ 84r^2-83v^3 Ballet
81	ℓ 84v$^{1-2}$ Saraband |Variatio [C]
82	ℓ 84v$^{2-3}$ Gavotte |Variatio [d]
83	ℓ 85v^1-86r^1 Ein Liedt /Jungfräulein /ich vermeine
84	ℓ 85v^2-86r^3 Saraband /od. /Es hat Kurtz /Klotz. od. /Es ließ sich ein /Braut den alt Rock Schnelden.
85	ℓ 86v^1-87r^2 Türkische Intrada [index:] f 97

86	ℓ 87v[1]-88r[3] Curant [F]
87	ℓ 88v[1]-89r[2] Curant [F]
88	ℓ 89v[1-2] [C]urant Laroine /de /Angleterre [G]
89	ℓ 89v[2]-90r[3] Curant [d]
90	ℓ 90v[1-3] Curant [C]
91	ℓ 91v[1]-92r[3] Allemand [d]
92	ℓ 92v[1]-93r[2] 105 /Curant [a]
93	ℓ 93v[1-2] Curant [d]

94 [CHAMBONNIÈRES: Courante (a)]
Curant /Gombonier
   ℓ 94r[2]-94v[1]   [$\frac{3}{4}$]|12|17|

CO: 38-Gen-2348/53 #5, Courante
    62-Chamb-I #4, Courante
ED: cf Brunold-Tessier #4, Dart-Ch #4.

95	ℓ 94v[1-2] Ein Liedt
96	ℓ **94v[2]-95r[3]** Allemand [g]
97	ℓ 95v[1]-96r[2] Allemand [G]
98	ℓ 96v[1-2] Ein Liedt

99 | [MESANGEAU, arr: <u>Courante</u> (G)]
112 /Curant /Messau/gea
  ℓ 96r^2-97r^3 [$\frac{3}{4}$]|10|12|

100| ℓ 97v^1-98r^2 113 /Amor hat mich /Zum süßen /Possen.
101| ℓ 97v^3-99r^1 114 /Ein Lied /Im Meyen
102| ℓ 98v^2-99r^3 115 /Saraband [C]
103| ℓ 99v$^{1-4}$ 116 /Curant [d]

paste down [Alphabetical index by p or ℓ which
             is accurate, with a few omissions]

3-BERLIN-40623

Provenance: North Germany, 1678 (dated ℓ. 1).

Location: unlocated since the Second World War; formerly:
Berlin; Deutsche Staatsbibliothek, Mus. Ms. 40623.
Information based on Ernesto Epstein, Der franzö-
sische Einfluss auf die deutsche Klaviersuite im
17. Jahrhundert (Würtzburg: K. Triltsch, 1940), pp.
84-85, App. #20-24.

Description: 194 ℓ.

Notation: New German organ tablature.

Scribe: Several unidentified hands.

Marginalia: Initials "C. A. I. C." on ℓ. 1; "CLAVICOR
DIUM BUCH" on final p.

Summary:
Composers:
KRIEGER: #57.
LA BARRE: #72.
LORENTZ: #53, 61.
LULLY: #1.
SCHOP: #61-64.
STRIE: #73.
Contents:
ℓ. 1-20v Chorales
21r-130r Poems
130v-194v 29 tunes and dances, written from the
back of the volume towards the center.

Inventory:

[The following pieces are known specifi-
cally by number:]

15

1   Aria [LULLY, arr: <u>Bel</u> <u>Iris</u> from <u>Ballet</u>
    <u>de</u> <u>l'Impatience</u> (1661) (d)]

   CO: cf 11-Ryge #48
      cf 28-Brussels-926 ℓ 3r
      cf Skara #35
      cf Terburg
      cf Van-Eijl #25
      cf Rés-819-2 ℓ 72r
      cf Stockholm-228 ℓ 20v

   ED: cf Noske #25, Bangert p 78.

42 Allemande [C]
   ED: Epstein #21a

43 Courant [C]
   ED: Epstein #21b

44 Sarrabande [C]
   ED: Epstein #21c

53 Menuet Joh Laurentz [a]
   ED: Epstein #23

57 Aria [<u>Amanda</u> <u>darf</u> <u>man</u> <u>dich</u> <u>wohl</u> <u>küssen?</u>
    (KRIEGER)]

61 la Boure de Jhan Laurentz

62 la Boure A. Schop

63 Sarrabande A. Schop

64 [SCHOP: <u>Courante</u>]
   CO: Van-Eijl #18
   ED: cf Noske #18

66 Sarabande [with 2] Double[s]

72 | [LA BARRE (arr?): <u>Allemande</u> (d)]

Allemande

$[\frac{4}{4}]$ |7|6|

[after Epstein]

CO: cf 1-Copenhagen-376 #39, Allamande [a]
cf 27-Gresse #21, Almande LB

ED: Ex 2 above, Epstein #22a; cf Curtis-MMN #68,
Dickinson #39, Hamburger p 138.

73 | Courant D Strie [d]

ED: Epstein #22b

75 | Ballet oder Mühlendantz

[The following additional pieces are
known without specific number citations:]

Täntze [with] Proportio [4]

polnishce Täntze [4]

Nachtigall [English]

Englisch Boure

Ballo [2]

Balletto [1]

Damon laß das Trauern seyn

Komm Amena meine Schöne

Sarabande [7]

Courante [7]

Bourrée [6:] la Boure, Laboure, B.
Dauphin

Allemande [3]

Menuet [2]

Canarie

Galliarde

Branle de Bousche

Passe Pied de Charlotte Courante

la Cochilie [La Coquille (Air ancien)?]
CO: cf 27-Gresse #13
    cf Skara #34
    cf Vat-mus-569 p 112

Arie francoise de Schallmeÿe

Folie Span [3 variations]

Tricdrac dal Affection

die alte Lamoustarde [C]
CO: cf 7-Munich-1511f #20
    cf 27-Gresse #6
    cf Veron ℓ 21v
    cf Add-16889 ℓ 99r
ED: Epstein #24
neue lamoustarde

Marche des grands Mousquetoires

Provenance: Southern Germany?, ca. 1615-1650.

Location: East Berlin; Deutsche Staatsbibliothek, Lübbenau Tabulaturen: Lynar A-1.

Description: 1 p.ℓ., 356 p. (332-356 blank, ruled); quires in 12 except L^{10}; folio format, 31 x 19.5 cm. Watermarks #6, 22. Original vellum binding, 31.5 x 20 cm.

Notation: Keyboard score (two 6-line staves, 5 systems per page, written page by page). Clefs: $F^{3,4}$, $G^{3,4}$, $C^{1,2,5,6}$; usually F^4, G^3 duplicated with C clefs.

Scribe: 1 (?) unidentified hand for the musical notation, with the possible exception of #78-81; the same hand as Lynar-A2.

Marginalia: Sixth line added to ruled 5-line staves.

Summary:
  Composers:
    BALLARD (Robert [II]): #68.
    BULL: cf #50, 60.
    CORNET: #71-72.
    ERBACH: #2, 8-9, 17, 19.
    FARNABY (Giles): #51.
    FARNABY (Richard): #52.
    GABRIELI: #11, 13-15.
    GAULTIER: #66.
    GIBBONS: #53.
    LA BARRE: #62-65.
    LASSO: cf #41.
    MARENZIO: cf #43.
    PHILIPS: #31, 41-42, 44, 74.
    STRIGGIO: cf #42.
    SWEELINCK: #1-7, 16, 20-30, 33-40, 46-48.
    WOODSON: #61.

Contents:

#1-7   Toccatas by Sweelinck.

8-23   Free and fugal pieces by Erbach, Gabrieli
          and Sweelinck.

24-40   Chorale-based pieces, and some free
          pieces by Sweelinck and Philips.

41-45   Italianate pieces by Philips.

46-49   Secular pieces by Sweelinck, anon.

50-61   Virginalist pieces.

62-68   French pieces.

69-70   Popular tune settings.

71-74   Free pieces and intabulations by Cornet
          and Philips.

75-77   Free pieces, anon.

78-81   Anon. suite, added later (in same hand?).

Inventory: See Werner Breig, "Die Lübbenauer Tabulaturen
    Lynar A 1 und A 2," Archiv für Musikwissenschaft 25
    (1968): 102-106.

Inventory of French Section:

62   [LA BARRE: Courante with Double (D)]
     Courante /de /La barre
       p 292^1-293^3 ^{3}|15|27| [$\frac{3}{4}$|8|8|16|16|]

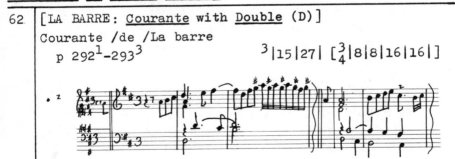

     ED: Bonfils-58 #1.

63 | [LA BARRE?: <u>Courante</u> with <u>Double</u> (d)]

Corante

　p 294^1-295^3　　　　　^{3}|4|4|16| [$^6_4$|4|4|16|]

ED: Bonfils-58 #2.

64 | [LA BARRE: <u>Courante</u> with <u>Double</u> (d)]

Auttre Corant /de la Barre |Variatio

　p 296^1-298^2　　　　　^{3}|7|7|28| [$^6_4$|7|8|30|]

ED: Bonfils-58 #3.

65 | [LA BARRE: <u>Courante</u> with <u>Double</u> (d)]

Courant /de /La /Barre |Variatio

　p 298^3-299^3　　　　^{3}|4|3|4|4|4|4| [$^6_4$|4| x 6]

CO:　16-Cosyn #44, Coranto:- Mr Tresure
　　　18-Ch-Ch-1236 #1, ... Jonas Tresure
　　　18-Ch-Ch-1236 #8, Corant La bar
　　　19-Heardson #46, (coranto) Mr Gibbons
　　　27-Gresse #22, Courante
　　　29-Chigi #30, Corante de Monsu della Bara
　　　Oxford-IB

ED: Bonfils-58 #4; cf Maas #91, Curtis-MMN #69,
    Lincoln-II p 38, Bonfils-18 #23.

---

66 | [GAULTIER, arr: <u>Courante</u> with <u>Double</u> (d)]

Courant /de /Gautier

p 300^1-302^4 ^{3}|8|8|7|7|8|8|7|6| [ie $^6_4$|:8:|:7:|:8:|:7:|]

ED: Bonfils-58 #5.

---

67 | [<u>Courante</u> with <u>Double</u> (d)]

Corante

p 302^5-303^4 ^{3}|3|2|6|6| [$^6_4$|3|3|6|6|]

ED: Bonfils-58 #6.

---

68 | [BALLARD, arr: <u>Courante de la reyne</u> with <u>Double</u> (d)]

Corant /de /Ballard

p 304^1-305^4 ^{3}[$^6_4$]|6|6|11|11|

CO: cf Ballard-1611, Courante de la Reyne
    cf Fuhrmann p 164, Courante 5

ED: Bonfils-58 #7; cf Souris-BaI p 40, 96-97.

69 | [<u>Courante</u> <u>la</u> <u>vignon</u> with <u>Double</u> (d)]

Courante /La /Vigon

   p 306¹-307⁴

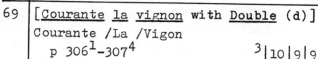

ED: Bonfils-58 #8.

<u>5-MUNICH-1503L</u>

<u>Provenance</u>: Germany or France, ca. 1660?

<u>Location</u>: Munich; Bayerische Staatsbibliothek, Mus. Mss. 1503$^\ell$.

<u>Description</u>: 19 ℓ.; 1 quire; oblong quarto format, 17.2 x 21.2 cm. Watermark #76 (same as 7-Munich-1511f). Modern paper-covered boards (original covers bound-in as ℓ. 1 and [21], latter cut away), 18 x 22.2 cm.

<u>Notation</u>: Keyboard score (two 5-line staves, 3 systems per page, written page by page). Clefs: F^3, C^1, G^2.

<u>Scribe</u>: 1 (?) unidentified French hand, the same as Munich-1503k; see "Contents," below.

<u>Marginalia</u>: Some original fingering, ℓ. 6v. Modern title (ℓ. 1r) and numeration by ℓ. and pieces, **initialed** on ℓ. 18r: J.♪. **M**['aier].

<u>Summary</u>:

    Composers:

      ARTUS: #2.

      CHAMBONNIÈRES: #1.

      DUMONT: #11-13.

      FROBERGER: cf #5.

      PINEL: #4.

    Contents:

#1-6	Dances in hand A.
7-9	Dances in rougher version of A (B?).
10	Dance in hand A.
11-15	Dances in rougher version of A (B?).

<u>Inventory</u>:

        [unnumbered binding end paper]

ℓ 1r   [modern title:] Inhalt: /15. Sarabanden,

Couranten, Allemanden, /Giguen, p.p.p.
/für /Clavier. (N.°. 4 "pour l'Espinette).

ℓ 1v   [poem, main hand:] Dans cet aymable Se-
iour /tout y rit /tout fleurit /au
poinct du Jour /dans ces rochers d'alen-
tour / dans ces bois les Sillons /les
petits oysillons /les grillons /les papil-
lons /tout y faict l'amour

---

1   [CHAMBONNIÈRES: <u>Sarabande jeunes zéphirs</u> (G)]

Sarrabande /de Mons: /Chambonnier |fin

 ℓ 2r^1-2v^3 ^{3}[$^3_3$]|8|17|]]

CO: 32-Oldham #8, Sarabande de Monsieur de Chambon-
        nieres
  33-Rés-89ter #36, Sarabande Chambonnieres ...
        Double
  35-Bauyn-I #96, Sarabande de Mr de Chambonnieres
  36-Parville #93, Sarabande Chanbonniere
  44-LaPierre p 42, Les Zephirs de Mr de Chanboniere
  45-Dart #55, Sarabande de chambonniere
  63-Chamb-II #29, Sarabande Jeunes Zephirs
  cf Philidor p 22, Jeunes Zephirs (de Mr de chan-
        boniere) [for instruments]
ED: Brunold-Tessier #59, Dart-Ch #59; cf Gilbert p 194.

---

2   [ARTUS, arr: <u>Courante royale</u> (d)]

Courante royalle /Darthus |Suitte

 ℓ 3r^1-3v^3 ^{3}|11|18| [$^3_4$|12|19|]

3 | [Sarabande (d)]

Sarabande
   ℓ 4r¹-v¹   ³[¾] |8|8|

4 | [PINEL, arr: <u>Gigue</u> (C)]

Gigues po. /L'Espinette. |Suitte |Suitte
   ℓ 5r¹-6r¹   ¢|8|16 ³|10| [²₂|8|5 ¾|11|]

CO: 7-Munich-1511f #17, Gigue
    cf Rodenegg ℓ 68v, Gigue Pinels [lute]
ED: Danckert p 160.

5 | [FROBERGER (?): <u>Allemande</u> (d)]

allemande /tres bonne |fin
   ℓ 6v¹-7r²   ¢|8|8|

CO: Stoss ℓ 37v, Froberger Allemande
ED: Epstein #14, Tessier-F p 151.

6 | [Sarabande (d)]

sarrabande |Suitte |[meas 22:] becarre |fin
ℓ 7v^1-8r^2 ^{3}[$^3_4$]|8|16|

CO: cf 16-Cosyn #102, Sellabrand
    cf 17-Rogers #19, [Sarabande]
    cf 32-Oldham # 6 , Sarabande
ED: cf Maas #103, Cofone #19, Sargent #19.

7 | [Sarabande (C)]

[corner with writing torn out]... Sarabande
ℓ 8v$^{1-3}$ ^{3}[$^3_4$]|8|8|

8 | [Allemande (G)]

Allemande |Suitte |fin
ℓ 9r^1-v^3 ¢[unmeasured] [$^2_2$|8|14|]

9 | [Gigue (C)]

Gigue |Suitte |fin
   ℓ 10r^1-v^2 ^{3}[$^3_4$]|11|14|

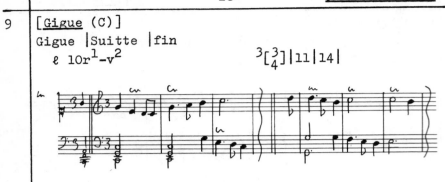

10 | [Courante (d)]

Courante |fin
   ℓ 11r^1-v^2 ^{3}|7|7| [$^3_4$|8|8|]

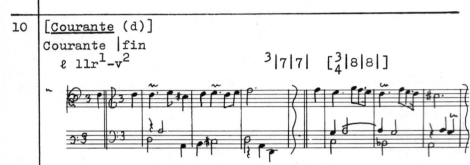

CO: 7-Munich-1511f #12, Courante
   22a-Roper #55, Courante
   44-LaPierre p 12, Courante en d la re

11 | [DUMONT: Allemande (C)]

allemande de /Du Mont |Suitte |fin
   ℓ 12r^1-v^3 ¢|7|7|

ED: Epstein #15a, Bonfils-13 #16.

12　[DUMONT: <u>Allemande</u> (a)]

belle allemande /de mons. /Du mont .|. |Suitte
|Suitte |fin.|.
　ℓ 13r^1-14v^3　　　　　　¢|8|11|

CO: 35-Bauyn-III #84, Allemande de Mr Dumont
ED: Bonfils-13 #18.

13　[DUMONT: <u>Allemande</u> <u>lente</u> (d)]

Allemande /Lante du mesme /autheur .|. |Suitte
|Suitte |fin .|.
　ℓ 15r^1-16r^2　　　　　　c|6|8|

ED: Epstein #15b, Bonfils-13 #17.

14　[<u>Sarabande</u> (d)]

Sarrabande |Reprise |fin .|.
　ℓ 16v^1-17r^2　　　　　$^3[\frac{3}{4}]$|8|8|

CO: 7-Munich-1511f #15, Sarrabande du 1r Ton

15 | [Bourrée la matelotte (C)]
La Matelotte |Reprise |fin
    ℓ 17v^1-18r^3 ¢|7|7|

ℓ 18v-19v   [blank, ruled]

[ℓ 20]   [torn out, stub remaining]

[ℓ 21]   [original cover, cut away, stub re-
             maining]

             [1 modern end paper, blank]

6-MUNICH-1511E

<u>Provenance</u>: Germany?, ca. 1660?

<u>Location</u>: Munich; Bayerische Staatsbibliothek, Mus. Mss. 1511e.

<u>Description</u>: 2 p.ℓ., 21 ℓ.; 1 quire (A^{22}, ℓ. 19 stubbed-in); oblong quarto format, 17.7 x 21.5 cm (trimmed). Watermarks #24 and 25 (end papers). Modern paper-covered boards (original covers bound-in as ℓ. i and 21), 18.2 x 22.2 cm.

<u>Notation</u>: Keyboard score and French letter score (two 5-line staves, 3 systems per page, written page by page). Clefs: F^3, C^1, G^2. French letter score consists of letters in place of notes on staves, without rhythmic signs. Cf. Ex. 7 in the Commentary; cf. 7-Munich-1511f, 32-Oldham.

<u>Scribes</u>: 2-4 hands intermixed (see "Contents" below), the primary hand perhaps the same as 7-Munich-1511f.

<u>Marginalia</u>: Original miscellaneous marks on ℓ. 20v. Modern title (ℓ. ir), bracket on first system and numeration by ℓ. and pieces, initialed on ℓ. 20v: J.J. M[aier].

<u>Summary</u>:

  Composers:

    MONNARD; #11.

  Contents:

#1-5	Dances in hand A, French letter score.
6-10	Dances in variant of A (B?), keyboard score and French letter score.
11-12	Dances in another variant of A (C?), keyboard score and French letter score.
13-15	Pieces in another hand (D), French

letter score.

Inventory:

ℓ i^r [modern title:] 15 Tänze (französiche)
für Clavier ...

ℓ i^v-ii^v [blank]

---

1 | [La Trompette (C)]
la trompette. |Reprise |Suitte |fin
   ℓ 1r^1-v^1 [unmeasured] | | |

CO: cf Veron ℓ 9r, Marche Royalle [violin]

---

2 | [Trompette (C)]
autre |[below 2nd system:] basse continue |Reprise
|fin
   ℓ 1v^2-2r^3 [unmeasure] | | |

3 | [<u>Trompette</u> (C)]

autre |Reprise |fin
   ℓ 2v^1-3r^3 [unmeasured] | | |

ED: Epstein #11 (realized).

4 | [<u>Branle</u> (C) (incomplete?)]

  Bransle |Reprise
   ℓ 3v^1-4r^3 [unmeasured] | |

5 | [<u>Branle</u> (G)]

autre bransle |Reprise |Suitte |fin
   ℓ 4v^1-5r^2 [unmeasured] | | |

6   [Courante suedoise (d)]

Suedoise /Courante. |Suite |Reprise |Suite

ℓ 5v^1-6v^2 ^{3}|11|13| [$\frac{3}{4}$|12|14|]

ED: Epstein #13a.

---

7   [Entrée de ballet (d)]

Entrée de /Ballet |Reprise

ℓ 7r^1-8r^3 ^{3}[$\frac{3}{4}$]|8|19|

---

8   [Sarabande (C)]

Sarabande |Suite |Reprise |Suite |fin

ℓ 8v^1-9v^3 ^{3}[$\frac{3}{4}$]|12|14|

ED: Epstein #13b.

9 | [Branle de Mets (d)]

Bransle de /Mets |Reprise |Suitte |Suitte |fin
ℓ 10r^1-12r^2 [unmeasured] | | | | |

10 | [Sarabande (d)]

Sarrabande. |Reprise
ℓ 12v^1-13r^3 $^3[\frac{3}{4}]$|8|8|

CO: 18-Ch-Ch-1236 #20, Sarabrand
    22a-Roper #56, Sarabande

11 | [MONNARD: Sarabande (C)]

Sarrabande |fin
ℓ 13v^1-14r^3 [unmeasured] | | |

CO: 23-Tenbury #4, Sarabande
    24-Babell #56, Sarabande
    30-Cecilia ℓ 48r, Sarabande ... redoublè
    31-Madrid-1360 #23/6, Sexta (Zarabanda)
    35-Bauyn-III #60, Sarabande De Mr. Monnard
    38-Gen-2348/53 #34, Sarabande.
    44-LaPierre p 2, [Sarabande]

ED: Ex. 7 above; cf Bonfils-18 p 6.

12   [<u>La princesse</u> (Air ancien) (d)]

La princesse |Reprise |Suitte |fin

    ℓ 14v^1-15v^3 ¢|6|8|

CO: cf 7-Munich-1511f #18, La princesse
    cf **9-Ihre-284** #51, La princes DhB
    cf 31-Madrid-1360 #24/10, Otro (Minuet)
    cf Skara #26, La Princesse [g]
    cf Berlin-40147
    cf Van-Eijl #12, #20, La Princesse
    cf Cassel "A", La Princesse Bourrée [incomplete]

13   [<u>La Diablesse</u> (C)]

La diablesse [?] |Suitte |Suitte

    ℓ 16r^1-16v^3 [unmeasured] | | |

14   [Petit Jean (C)]

petit [?] Jean |Suite

    ℓ 17r^1-17v^1 [unmeasured] | |

15 | [<u>Bergère</u> (a)]
Bergere |Suitte
ℓ 18r^1-v^2 [unmeasured]| | | |

CO: cf Celle p 162, Aria fransch

ℓ 18v^3 Fin du Liure [in ornamental script]

ℓ 19r-20r   [blank, unruled]

ℓ 20v   [blank, unruled with miscellaneous marks
               at top:] autre m m N bon [etc]

ℓ 21r-v   [original cover, blank]

<u>7-MUNICH-1511f</u>

<u>Provenance</u>: Germany?, ca. 1660?

<u>Location</u>: Munich; Bayerische Staatsbibliothek, Mus. Mss. 1511f.

<u>Description</u>: 22 ℓ.; 3 quires (A^{14}, B^6, C^2); oblong quarto format, 17.3 x 21.2 cm. Watermarks #76 (quires A and B, the same mark as 5-Munich-1503ℓ), 53 (quire C). Modern paper-covered boards, 18 x 22 cm.

<u>Notation</u>: French letter score (two 5-line staves, 3 systems per page, written page by page). Clefs: F^3, C^1, G^2. Cf. Ex. 7 in Commentary; cf 6-Munich-1511e, 32-Oldham.

<u>Scribes</u>: 1-4 hand(s), possibly the same as hand A of 6-Munich-1511e; see "Contents," below.

<u>Marginalia</u>: Modern title (front end paper), numeration by ℓ. and pieces, initialed J.J. M[aier].

<u>Summary</u>:
   Composers:
     ARTUS: #24.
     PINEL: #17.

   Contents:

#1-7	Dances in hand A.
8	Dance in another version of A (B?).
8-19	Dances in hand A.
20-28	Dances in another version of A (C?).
29	Dance (?) in another version of A (D?), perhaps from another ms (quire C).

<u>Inventory</u>:

end paper   [modern title:] 28 Tänze (französiche) für Clavier ...

1 [Moutarde nouvelle (C)]

moutarde   nouuelle

  ℓ 1r$^{1-2}$

       [unmeasured] | | |

2 [Tricottes nouveaux (Air ancien) (d)]

tricotes /Nouuaux

  ℓ 1v$^{1-3}$

       [unmeasured] | | | |

CO: cf 8-Hintze #9, Tricottes de Blois
  cf 27-Gresse #3, Tricoté
  cf Veron ℓ 21v, Tricotes [violin]
ED: cf MGG 13:661.

3 [Branle d'Orléans (C)]

bransle Dorleans |fin

  ℓ 2r^{1}-v^{2}

       [unmeasured] | | | | | |

4 | [Sarabande (C)]
sarrabande |fin
ℓ 3r$^{1-3}$ [unmeasured] | | | |

5 | [Sarabande (C)]
Sarrabande |fin
ℓ 3v$^{1-3}$ ^{3}|8|8|

6 | [Courante la duchesse (Air ancien) (a)]
La duchesse /Courante
ℓ 4r^1-v^2 ^{3}|11|8|

CO: cf 8-Hintze #17, La Duchesse [d]
    cf Celle p 166, courant LaduChesse [d]
    cf Veron ℓ 22r, La Duchesse [violin]
    cf Cassel Suite VII, La duchesse. Courante
                        figurée [instuments]
    cf Vat-mus-569 p 103, Courante La Duchesse [a]
ED: cf Écorcheville 2:97.

7 | [Gavotte (a)]

Gauotte
ℓ 5r$^{1-3}$ [unmeasured] | |

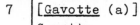

8 | [La Sisonne (Air ancien) (d)]

sissionie |fin
ℓ 5v$^{1-3}$ [unmeasured] | |

CO: cf Celle p 29, Arien fransch
    cf Veron ℓ 21v, La sisonne

9 | [Les Marionnettes (d)]

Les Marionettes |Suitte |fin
ℓ 6r^{1}-v^{3} [unmeasured] | | | |

10 | [Sarabande l'altesse (Air ancien) (C)]

Laltesse Sarabande |Suitte |Suitte |fin

ℓ 7r^1-8r^1 [unmeasured] | | |

CO: cf 8-Hintze #16, La Altesse

---

11 | [Les Barantins (d)]

Les Barantins [?] |Suitte

ℓ 8v^1-9r^3 [unmeasured] | | |

CO: cf 54-Gen-2350/57 #36, Courante
    cf 55-Redon #8 [untitled]

---

12 | [Courante (d)]

Courante |Suitte |fin

ℓ 9v^1-10r^2 [unmeasured] | |

CO: 5-Munich-1503ℓ #10, Courante
    22a-Roper #55, Courante
    44-LaPierre p 12, Courante en d la re

13 [Air nouveau (d)]

air nouueau |fin
ℓ 10v[1]-11v[2]   [unmeasured] | | | |

---

14 [Trompette (C)]

La Trompette /Batterie |Suitte |Suitte |Suitte
ℓ 12r[1]-13r[3]   [unmeasured] | | |

---

15 [Sarabande (d)]

Sarrabande /du 1[r] Ton |Suitte |fin
ℓ 13v[1]-14r[3]   [unmeasured] | | |

CO: 5-Munich-1503ℓ #14, Sarrabande

16 | [<u>Prélude</u> (d)]

Prelude /du 1 Ton |fin

     ℓ 14v$^{1-3}$ [unmeasured] | |

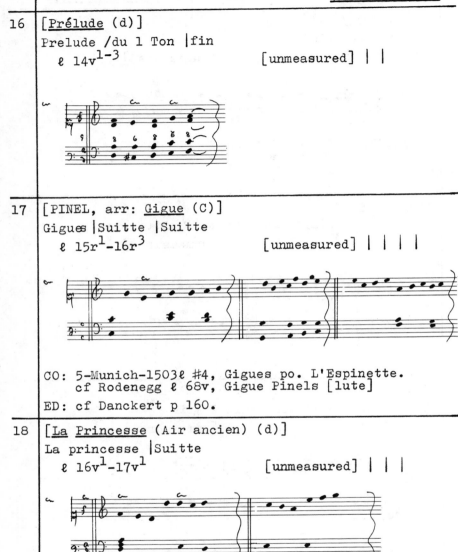

17 | [PINEL, arr: <u>Gigue</u> (C)]

Gigues |Suitte |Suitte

     ℓ 15r^{1}-16r^{3} [unmeasured] | | | |

CO: 5-Munich-1503ℓ #4, Gigues po. L'Espinette.
     cf Rodenegg ℓ 68v, Gigue Pinels [lute]

ED: cf Danckert p 160.

18 | [<u>La</u> <u>Princesse</u> (Air ancien) (d)]

La princesse |Suitte

     ℓ 16v^{1}-17v^{1} [unmeasured] | | |

CO: cf 6-Munich-1511e #12, La princesse
     cf 9-Ihre-284 #51, La princes DhB
     cf 31-Madrid-1360 #24/10, Otro (Minuet)
     cf Skara #26, La Princesse [g]
     cf Berlin-40147

cf Van-Eijl #12, #20, La Princesse
cf Cassel "A", La Princesse Bourrée [incomplete]

19	[Manssiry (C)]

manssiry [?]
ℓ 17v$^{2-3}$ [unmeasured] | |

20	[La Moutarde (Air ancien) (C)]

La Moutarde
ℓ 18r$^{1-2}$ [unmeasured] | | | |

CO: cf 3-Berlin-40623, die alte Lamoustarde
  cf 27-Gresse #6, La Moustarde
  cf Veron ℓ 21v, La Moutarde [violin]
  cf Add-16889, ℓ 99r, La Moutarde [lute, 1618]
ED: cf Epstein #24.

21	[Canarie (G)]

canarie
ℓ 18r^{3} [unmeasured] | | |

22 | [Bergère (C)]

bergere.1.

 ℓ 18v[1]   [unmeasured] | | |

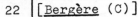

---

23 | [Gavotte royalle (Air ancien?) (C)]

gauotte Royalle

 ℓ 18v[2-3]   [unmeasured] | | |

CO: cf 8-Hintze #7, Gavotte Royale
  cf Lüneburg-1198 p 52, Gavotte
  cf Veron ℓ 9r, Gauotte Royalle [violin]

---

24 | [ARTUS, arr: Bourrée (C)]

Bouree /darthus

 ℓ 19r[1-2]   [unmeasured] | | |

CO: cf 8-Hintze #24, Petite Boureè [D]
  cf 27-Gresse.#4, la Bouré Dartus
  cf 59a-Handmaide #22, Duke of York's March [D]
  cf Celle p 18, Laure de Paris [D]

ED: cf Dart-HI #22.

25 | [A̲ l̲a̲ v̲e̲n̲u̲e̲ d̲e̲ n̲o̲ë̲l̲ (Noël) (d)]

alavenue /de noel

    ℓ 19r^3 [unmeasured] | |

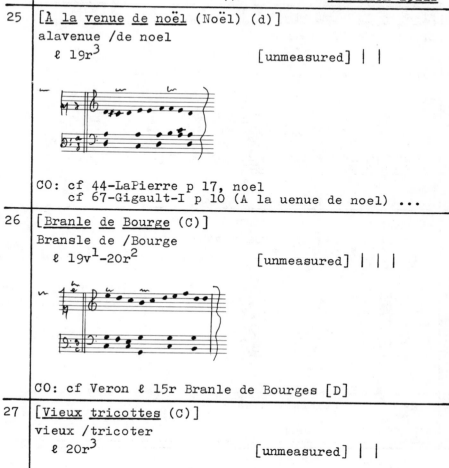

CO: cf 44-LaPierre p 17, noel
     cf 67-Gigault-I p 10 (A la uenue de noel) ...

26 | [B̲r̲a̲n̲l̲e̲ d̲e̲ B̲o̲u̲r̲g̲e̲ (C)]

Bransle de /Bourge

    ℓ 19v^1-20r^2 [unmeasured] | | |

CO: cf Veron ℓ 15r Branle de Bourges [D]

27 | [V̲i̲e̲u̲x̲ t̲r̲i̲c̲o̲t̲t̲e̲s̲ (C)]

vieux /tricoter

    ℓ 20r^3 [unmeasured] | |

28 | [Branle de Normandie (d)]
bransle de /Normandie
ℓ 20v^{1-3}   [unmeasured] | | |
   [final note(s) lacking due to trimming]

29 | [Pièce (a)]
[untitled; fragment from another ms?]
   ℓ 21r^{1}-v^{2}   [unmeasured]

ℓ 22r   [blank, ruled]

end paper   [blank]

Provenance: Dresden or Hamburg, ca. 1650-1674?

Location: New Haven, Connecticut; Yale University,
John Herrick Jackson Music Library, Ma 21 H 59;
administered by the Beinecke Library, Music Deposit
No. 3.

Description: 18 ℓ. (originally at least 20 ℓ. as two mss:
6, 14 ℓ.); 2 quires (A^5, B^{13}); folio format, 32 x
19.7 cm. Watermarks #10 (quire A) and 92 (quire B).
Unbound, modern full leather folder.

Notation: Keyboard score (two 6-line staves, 5 systems
per page, written page by page). Clefs: G^3, F^3,
duplicated with C clefs.

Scribe: 1 hand, the same as in part of Lüneburg-147 and
Lüneburg-207:6, almost certainlz that of M. WECKMANN.

Marginalia: Many corrections or alternate readings
added in organ tablature in different ink. "Geo:
Bohm" in pencil barely visible on ℓ. 1v. "Louis
Hintze /Lüneburg /Oct. 1896" in pencil, ℓ. 2r.
Modern numeration by pages in pencil, omitting
preliminary and blank pages (given in parentheses
in Inventory below).

Summary:
  Composers:
    ARTUS: #24.
    CHAMBONNIÈRES: #15.
    ERBEN: #6, 12, 13.
    FROBERGER: #5, 22.
    KERLL: #4.
    LA BARRE: #11.
    TRESURE: #1-2, 3(?).

Contents:
28 dances, some based on popular melodies, some organized in suites.

Inventory:

	ℓ 1r	Franzosche Art Instrument /Stücklein
	ℓ 1v	[pencil:] Geo: Bohm
	ℓ 2r	[blank, unruled]
1	ℓ 3r$^{1-4}$ (p 1)	Allemande plörant. Jonas Tresor [e]
2	ℓ 3v$^{1-4}$ (p 2)	Cour Jo. Tr: [e]
	[ℓ lacking]	
	ℓ 4r-5v	[blank, unruled]
3	ℓ 6r$^{1-4}$ (p 3)	Sarabande [TRESURE? (e)]
4	ℓ 6v^{1}-8r^{5} (p 4-7)	Toccata: J:C K. [KERLL] [G] ED: MGG, s.v. "Kerll" (facsim).
5	ℓ 8v^{1}-94^{4} (p 8-9)	Meditation faist sur ma Mort future la quelle se joue lentement avec /discretion /di Gio: Giu: Fro[berger] [D] ⎮NB /Memento Mori /Froberger. ⎮Hierauff Auch die Gigue hernach Courant /undt Sarab hinten in diesem buch /zu letzt gespielt. -Undt so /setzt er Nun fast Alle seine Sachen in /Solchen Ordnung. NB [The Courante, Sarabande and Gigue are lacking; cf #22] ED: cf Adler-II p 57.
6	ℓ 9v$^{1-3}$ (p 10)	Passagaglia. Balth: Erben Aus Sein Buch [C]

7	$\ell\ 9v^{4-5}$ (p 10)	Gavotte Royale [C]

CO: cf 7-Munich-1511f #23
    cf Lüneburg-1198 ℓ 52
    cf Veron ℓ 9r

8	$\ell\ 10r^{1-2}$ (p 11)	Triscottes de Paris [g]

ED: MGG 13-661 (facsim).

9	$\ell\ 10r^{3-4}$ (p 11)	Tricottes de Blois [Air ancien (d)]

CO: cf 7-Munich-1511f #2
    cf 27-Gresse #3
    cf Veron ℓ 21v

ED: MGG 13-661 (facsim).

10	$\ell\ 10r^{4-5}$ (p 11)	Amarillis [Air ancien (d)]

---

11 [LABARRE (arr?): <u>Courante</u> (d)]
Courant.
   $\ell\ 10v^{1-4}$ (p 12) $^3|9|10|\ [^6_4|8|10|]$

CO: cf Saizenay-I p 5, Courante De La barre
ED: cf Souris-V p 151, Bonfils-31 p 5.

12	$\ell\ 10v^4-11r^5$ (p 12-13)	Courante. /B. Erben [a]
13	$\ell\ 11v^{1-5}$	Sarabande d'Erben. [a]
14	$\ell\ 12r^1-v^1$	Allemande. [C]

15 | [CHAMBONNIÈRES: <u>Courante</u> <u>Iris</u> (C)]

Courante.

ℓ 12v$^{2-5}$ (p 16) $^{3}[^{6}_{4}]$|8|8|

CO: 22a-Roper #58, **Courante Chambonniere...double**
  23-Tenbury #3, (courante chambonii)
  24-Babell #58, Courante de Mr. de Chambonniere
  33-Rés-89ter #2, Courante. Chambonnieres...**Double**
  35-Bauyn-I #9, Courante de Mr De Chambonnieres
  36-Parville #61, Courante Chanbonniere
  44-LaPierre p 18, p 34A, Courante Chambonniere...**Double**
  47-Gen-2356 #12, Courante
  53-Oldham-2 **p 107, Courante de Chamboniere**
  55-Redon #23, Courante de Monsieur de Chambonniere
  62-Chamb-I #8, Courante Iris
  cf 32-Oldham #17, Double de La Courante Iris

ED: cf Brunold-Tessier #8, Dart-Ch #8, Gilbert p 148.

16 | ℓ 13r$^{1-3}$ La Altesse [Air ancien (C)]
  (p 17)   CO: cf 7-Munich-1511f #10

17 | ℓ 13r^{4}-v^{4} La Duchesse [Air ancien (d)]
  (p 17-18)   CO: cf 7-Munich-1511f #6
        cf Celle p 166
        cf Veron ℓ 22r
        cf Cassel Suite VII
        cf Vat-mus-569 p 103
      ED: cf Écorcheville 2:97.

18 | ℓ 13v^{4}-14r^{5} Sarabande [d]
  (p 18-19)

19 | ℓ 14v^{1}-15r^{1} Allemande. [G]
  (p 20-21)

20 | ℓ 15r$^{2-5}$ Courant. [G]
  (p 21)

21 | ℓ 15v$^{1-5}$ Sarabande. [G]
  (p 22)

22	ℓ 16r$^{1-4}$ (p 23)	Courante Frob[erger]: [D, cf #5] ED: cf Adler-II p 31.
23	ℓ 16v$^{1-3}$ (p 24)	Sarabande [D]
24	ℓ 16v$^{4-5}$ (p 24)	Petite Bovreè [ARTUS, arr (D)] CO: cf 7-Munich-1511f #24 [C] cf 27-Gresse #4 [C] cf 59a-Handmaide #22 cf Celle p 18 ED: cf Dart-HI #22.
25	ℓ 17r$^{1-5}$ (p 25)	Cour [D]
26	ℓ 17v$^{1-5}$ (p 26)	Covrante. ♪ E 3 /Pohlman /manier auch dabey ' ge... [?] [D]
27	ℓ 18r$^{1-5}$ (p 27)	Courante [D]
28	ℓ 18v$^{1-4}$ (p 28)	Ballo di Mantova [d]

Provenance: Visby, Sweden; ca. 1679 (dated ℓ. i^r, "MLDCL-
XXIX [1679] Die 15 calend. Febr." and p. 25, "T I 9b
[November] 1678."

Location: Uppsala; Universitetsbibliotek, Ihre 284.

Description: 1 p.ℓ., 160 p., 1 ℓ.; 11 quires (A^{12}, B^6
C^8, D^8, E^4, F^7, G^4, H^2, I^6, J-K^{12}); upright quarto
format, 20.6 x 15.6 cm. (except quire A: 20 x 15.4
cm.; and quires H-I: 19.2 x 14.7 cm.); upright
quarto format. Watermarks #18, 47 and 103. Worn
contemporary vellum binding with chant notation on it,
21.3 x 16 cm.

Notation: Mixed. Single part notation, ℓ. 1r; Keyboard
score (two 6-line staves, clefs: G^3, F^4, duplicated
with C clefs), ℓ. 1v-p. 23 (quire A); new German
organ tablature (4 systems per page, usually written
page by page), p. 24-161.

Scribes: 4-5 hands; one ("C") almost certainly that of
Thomas Ihre (b. 1659):
A: #1-19.
B: #20-28; 56-58; 60-76; 79; (same hand as C?).
C: #29-51; 90-128.
D: #52-55; 59.
E: #77-78; 81-89.
F: #129.

Marginalia: Much writing of proverbs, etc. in French
and German on ℓ. i^r; several times the name "Ihre";
poem in Swedish on ℓ. i^v; miscellaneous letters and
numbers on final ℓ.; modern numeration of pages
(retained below) and of pieces as #1-110 (not retained below).

Composers:

ARTUS: #85.

BRULLARD, #52-55.

DUMANOIR: #40-46.

GAULTIER: #98.

LA BARRE: #47(?), 48, 49(?).

LORENTZ: #23-24, 27-28, 30, 34, 37(?), 38-46, 52-55, 77-78,
          80-81, 82(?), 83, 84(?), 85-88, 89(?), 95, 97,102.

LULLY: #88.

SCHEIDEMANN; #26.

TRESURE: #76.

[unidentified initials:] H.D.: #29; dhB[?]: #51; WS: #65;
          GVB[PVB?]: #67; PB[JB?]: #69; N.D.: #90;
          JJN.: #91; R[?]D: #123.

Contents:

Originally 3 mss: #1-18   (quire A)
                     56-67   (quires H-I)
                     19-55,⎫
                     68-129⎭ (quires B-G, J-K)

#1   Melody and bass parts.

2-18   6 anon. suites in keyboard score

19-128   Miscellaneous dance pieces, some organ-
           ized in 2-3 movement suites, in new
           German organ tablature.

Inventory:

	ℓ i^{r-v}	[see "Marginalia," above]
1	p 1$^{1-6}$	[untitled melody and bass parts]
2	p 2^{1}-3^{2}	Allemande [D]
3	p 4^{1}-5^{1}	Courant [D]
4	p 5^{2}-3	Sarabande [D]
5	p 6^{1}-7^{3}	Giqve [D]
6	p 8$^{1-3}$	Allemande [c]

7	p 9^{1-3}	Courant [c]
8	p 10^{1-2}	Saraband [c]
9	p 10^3-11^3	Allemand [C]
10	p 12^{1-3}	Courant [C]
11	p 13^{1-3}	Saraband [C]
12	p 14^1-15^2	Allemand [d]
13	p 16^1-17^1	Courant [d]
14	p 17^2-18^1	Saraband [d]
15	p 18^3-19^3	Allemand [a]
16	p 20^1-21^2	Courant [a]
17	p 22^{1-3}	Sarabande [a]
18	p 23^{1-3}	Allemande [C]
		[#19 and 31-129 in organ tablature written page by page; #20-30 written across facing pages]
19	p 24^{1-4}	[Piece (a)]
20	p 25^1-26^3	1. Les Boubons /T I 9b [November] 1678.
21	p 27^1-28^2	2 B. molliter
22	p 28^3-29^4	Præludium /Ex Clave G
23	p 30^{1-4}	Præludium /Ex Clave /G. /J[ohann] L[orentz] ED: Lundgren #10.
24	p 31^{1-4}	Præludium /Ex Clave /A /J.L: ED: Lundgren #11.
25	p 32^1-33^4	Præludium [a]
26	p 34^1-39^4	Tocata /H:S:M: [SCHEIDEMANN]
27	p 40^1-44^2	Præludium /J:L: [d] ED: Lundgren #12.

28	p 44^2-45^4	Præludium /Ex Clave /F /Joh: Lorent: ED: Lundgren #13.
29	p 46^1-47^2	Allemand /von der /Lauten /gesetzt H. D. [a]
30	p 47^{2-4}	Prælud./ex cl. /D /JL. ED: Lundgren #14.
31	p 48^{1-4}	Courant /Friedrich [g]
32	p 49^{1-4}	Saraband [G]
33	p 50^1-51^3	Allemand [g]
34	p 51^{3-4}	Prælud:/ex /A /JL. [added in a different ink] ED: Lundgren #15.
35	p 52^{1-4}	Courant [G]
36	p 53^{1-4}	Sarabanda [C]
37	p 54^1-55^2	Allemand [a] [LORENTZ?] ED: Lundgren #16.
38	p 56^{1-4}	Courant. /J.L. [a] ED: Lundgren #17.
39	p 57^{1-4}	Sarabanda /JL [a] ED: Lundgren #18.
40 41	p 58^1-59^1	Brandles /du /Mons. Manoir [DUMANOIR] /en Tavol /par Jean.Lorentz: [C] ED: Lundgren #19.
42	p 59^{2-4}	Gaÿ [DUMANOIR, arr LORENTZ] ED: Lundgren #20.
43	p 60^{1-4}	Amenez [DUMANOIR, arr LORENTZ] ED: Lundgren #21.
44	p 61^{1-3}	Double [DUMANOIR, arr LORENTZ] ED: Lundgren #22.

45 | p 62^{1}-63^{1} Montirade [C] [DUMANOIR, arr LORENTZ]
             ED: Lundgren #23.

46 | p 63$^{1-3}$ Gavotte [C] [DUMANOIR, arr LORENTZ]
             ED: Lundgren #24.

47 | [LA BARRE?: Allemande (C)]
Allemand
    p 64^{1}-65^{3} [$\frac{4}{4}$] |8|9|

48 | [LA BARRE: Courante (C)]
Courant /La Bar.
    p 66$^{1-4}$ [$\frac{3}{4}$] |12|16|

49 | [LA BARRE?: Sarabande (C)]
Saraband
    p 67$^{1-3}$ [$\frac{3}{4}$] |8|8|

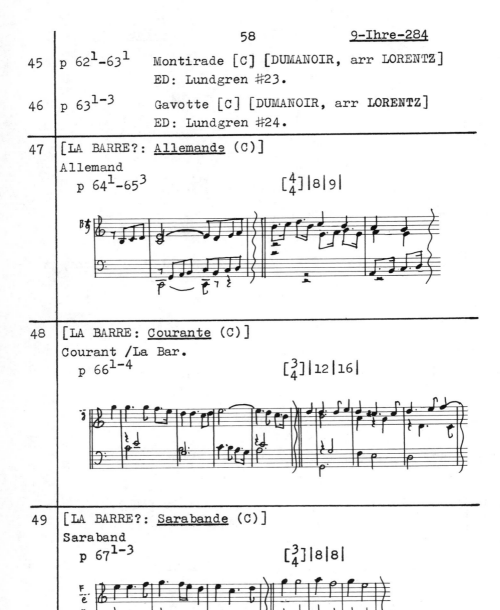

50	p 68$^{1-4}$	Courant [C]
51	p 69$^{1-4}$	La princes d h B [?] [g] [Air ancien]
		CO: cf 6-Munich-1511e #12 cf 7-Munich-1511f #18 cf 31-Madrid-1360 #24/10 cf Skara #26 cf Berlin-40147 cf Van-Eijl #12, 20 cf Cassel "A"
52	p 70^{1}-71^{3}	Brandles /de /Monsr: Brulare /In Tavolat /de /J.L. [C]
		CO: cf Cassel Suite VI
		ED: Lundgren #25, 52-55; cf Écorcheville Suite VI.
53	p 72$^{1-4}$	Gaÿ [BRULLARD, arr LORENTZ]
		ED: Lundgren #26.
54	p 73$^{1-4}$	Amenez [C] [BRULLARD, arr LORENTZ]
		ED: Lundgren #27.
55	p 74^{1}-75^{2}	Gavotte [C] [BRULLARD, arr LORENTZ]
		ED: Lundgren #28.
56	p 76$^{1-4}$	Aria [C]
57	p 77$^{1-4}$	Allemand [C]
58	p 78$^{1-4}$	Allemand [C]
59	p 79$^{1-3}$	Saraband [C]
60	p 80^{1}-81^{1}	Courant [c]
61	p 81$^{1-4}$	Saraband [c]
62	p 82^{1}-83^{1}	Ball. /Ein /Shones /bild
63	p 84^{1}-85^{2}	Courant [d]
64	p 85$^{2-5}$	Saraband [d]
65	p 86$^{1-4}$	Saraband /WS [? (I V S?)] [F]
66	p 87$^{1-3}$	Gigue [F]

67	p 88$^{1-4}$	Allemande /en Tavolatur /du /CVB [PVB?] [g]
	[1 ℓ lacking]	
68	p 89$^{1-4}$	Sarab. [G]
69	p 90^{1}-91^{1}	Allem. /Von der /Viol /In Tavol /du P.B [J B ?] [G]
70	p 91$^{1-4}$	Ballet [G]
71	p 92$^{1-4}$	Sarab: [G]
72	p 93$^{1-4}$	La Gavotte /du.Roÿ [Air ancien] [a] CO: cf Skara #29
73	p 94$^{1-3}$	Aria [G]
74	p 94$^{3-4}$	Sara/band. [G]
75	p 95$^{1-3}$	La Rene /du pree [?] [d]
75a	p 95^{3}-96^{1}	Sara/band [d]
76	p 96$^{1-4}$	Sarab./Tresor. [a] CO: 27-Gresse #33 ED: cf Curtis-MMN #78
77	p 97$^{1-4}$	Passepie Charlott /In Tavolat: Joh: Laurent: [C] ED: Lundgren #29.
78	p 98$^{1-4}$	Saraband /In Tavolat: /Joh: Laurent: [C] ED: Lundgren #30.
79	p 99$^{1-3}$	Tantz /Englishe [g]
80	p 100^{1}-101^{3}	Allemand /J:L: [a] ED: Lundgren #31.
81	p 102^{1}-103^{3}	Courant J:L: [a] ED: Lundgren #32.
82	p 104$^{1-4}$	Saraband [a] [LORENTZ?] ED: Lundgren #33.

83	p 105$^{1-4}$	Courant /Simple /In Tavolat: /Joh: Laurent: [d]
		ED: Lundgren #34
84	p 106$^{1-4}$	Saraband [d] [arr LORENTZ?]
		ED: Lundgren #35.
85	p 107$^{1-4}$	La Galliard [ARTUS] /In Tavolat: /Joh: Laurent: [d]
		CO: cf 55-Redon #12
		cf Cassel Suite XIV
		ED: Lundgren #36; cf Écorcheville 2-176.
86	p 108^{1}-109^{2}	Courant /J:L: [d]
		ED: Lundgren #37.
87	p 110$^{1-4}$	Saraband /J:L: [d]
		ED: Lundgren #38.
88	p 111$^{1-4}$	Minoit [LULLY from Ballet de flore XV (1669)] InTavolat:/de /Joh: Laurent: [C]
		CO: cf 27-Gresse #9
		cf 36-Parville #124
		ED: Lundgren #39.
89	p 112$^{1-4}$	Courant [a] [arr LORENTZ?]
		ED: Lundgren #40.
90	p 113$^{1-4}$	Courant fur /Allemande /de /N.D. [a]
91	p 114$^{1-4}$	Saraband /JJN [d]
92	p 115^{1}-116^{3}	Aria [d]
	p 117^{1}	[erroneous beginning of #93]
93	p 117$^{2-4}$	Traganer /Maesq [C]
94	p 118$^{1-3}$	Courant [d]
94a	p 119$^{1-4}$	Double [d]
95	p 120^{1}-121^{3}	La Viona [Courante la vignon (Air ancien)] InTavolat /d' /J.L.
		ED: Lundgren #41.

95a	p 122^1-123^4	La Double d' /Joh. Lor: [d] ED: Lundgren #42.
96	p 124^{1-4}	Minoit [D]
97	p 125^{1-5}	Aria /en Tav. /JL. [C] ED: Lundgren #43.
98	p 126^{1-3}	Allem /Goutier [GAULTIER] [G]
99	p 126^4-127^2	Courant [G]
100	p 127^{2-4}	Sarab. [G]
101	p 128^{1-3}	Sarab. [G]
102	p 128^4-129^1	Sarab /JL. [C] ED: Lundgren #44.
102 a	p 129^{2-4}	Variatio [C] ED: Lundgren #44.
103	p 130^1-131^1	Allemand [d]
104	p 131^{2-4}	Sar: [d]
105	p 132^{1-4}	Courant [d]
106	p 133^{1-4}	Sarab: [d]
107	p 134^{1-4}	Courant [G]
107 a	p 135^{1-4}	Le Double [G]
108	p 136^{1-4}	Courant [d]
109	p 137^{1-3}	Aria /Adoranda [d]
110	p 137^{4-5}	Sara/band [D]
111	p 138^1-139^4	Courant /Madam [Air ancien] [F] CO: cf 55-Redon #21.
112	p 140^{1-3}	Sarabanda [F]
113	p 141^{1-4}	Saraband [d]
114	p 142^1-143^3	Allemand /a /Theorb: [C]

115	p 144^1-145^1	Courant [C]
116	p 145^{1-4}	Saraband [C]
117	p 146^1-147^4	Englische /Nachtigall [C]
118	p 148^{1-4}	Courant [C]
119	p 149^{1-4}	Sarabanda [C]
120	p 150^{1-4}	Courant [G]
121	p 151^{1-4}	Sarabanda [G]
122	p 152^{1-4}	Saraband [d]
123	p 153^{1-4}	Aria [undecipherable monogram:] R [?] [D]
124	p 154^{1-2}	Courant [fragment (G)]
125	p 155^{1-4}	Saraband [G]
126	p 156^1-157^2	Allem. [C]
127	p 157^3-158^3	Courant [C]
128	p 158^3-159^3	Saraband [C]
129	p 160^{1-3}	Englishe / ... [illegible]
	final ℓ	[miscellaneous letters and numbers]

Provenance: Germany, post 1684 (transcription from
    Amadis).

Location: Schwerin, German Democratic Republic; Wissen-
    schaftliche Allgemeinbibliothek des Bezirkes Schwerin,
    Musik Hs. 617 (olim Anonyma D-2).

Description: 1, 45, 1 ℓ. (numbered A-Z, AI-TI, plus
    end papers); horizontal folio format, 23 x 37.5 cm.
    Watermarks #73 and 93 (end papers). Contemporary
    vellum binding, 23.5 x 38 cm.

Notation: Keyboard score (two 5-line staves, 4 systems
    per page, written on recto side only). Clefs: C^1,
    F^4.

Scribe: 1 unidentified hand; very careful but unskilled.

Marginalia: Original numeration of leaves; some vertical
    pencil guide lines, some dotted and some in ink.

Summary:
    Composers:
      FROBERGER: #4-7, 22-25, 29-35.
      LEBÈGUE: #10.
      LULLY: #19.
    Contents: Pieces arranged by key:
      #1-2   d
       3-13   C
      14-20   g
      21-25   d
      26-27   C
      28-32   G
      33-35   e

Inventory:

1	ℓ A^1	Prelude [d]
2	ℓ A^1-H^4	Folie d'Espagne |I. Variation ... [d]
3	ℓ I$^{1-3}$	Prelude [C]
4	ℓ K$^{1-4}$	Allemande [FROBERGER] [C]
		ED: cf Adler-II p 10.
5	ℓ L$^{1-4}$	Courante [FROBERGER] [C]
		ED: cf Adler-II p 11.
6	ℓ M$^{1-4}$	Sarabande [FROBERGER] [C]
		ED: cf Adler-II p 12.
7	ℓ N$^{1-4}$	Gique [FROBERGER] [C]
		ED: cf Adler-II p 35.
8	ℓ O$^{1-4}$	Ouverture [C]
		CO: cf Grimm ℓ 82r
9	ℓ P$^{1-4}$	Aria [C]

10 [LEBÈGUE: <u>Gavotte</u> (C)]

Gavotte
   ℓ Q$^{1-3}$ ^{C}|4|8|

CO: 13-Möllersche, [copy of Lebègue-I]
    14-Schwerin-619 #91, Gavotte
    21-Rés-1186bis #12, Gavott
    23-Tenbury #6, Gavotte Mr Le Begue
    24-Babell #60, Gavotte de Mr. le Begue
    30-Cecilia ℓ 47r, Gavotte
    35-Bauyn-III #54, (Gavotte) de Mr Lebegue
    36-Parville #68, Gauotte Mr le Begue
    45-Dart #22, [copy of Lebègue-I]
    46-Menetou #102, Gavotte
    50-Paignon #11, Balet de Mr lebegue
    64-Lebègue-I #43, Gauotte

ED: cf Dufourcq-L p 38, Brunold/Dart-Co #132.

11	ℓ R$^{1-4}$	March [C]
12	ℓ S$^{1-4}$	Menuet [C]
13	ℓ T^1-U^4	Gique |voiès la lettre U [C]
14	ℓ W^1	Prelude [g]
15	ℓ W$^{2-4}$	Allemande [g]
16	ℓ X$^{1-3}$	Sarabande [g]
16a	ℓ Y$^{1-4}$	Le Double [g]
17	ℓ Z$^{1-2}$	Gique [g]
18	ℓ Z^3	[Menuet (d)]
19	ℓ AI$^{1-4}$	Menuet [LULLY, arr, from <u>Amadis</u> (1684) II-7 (g)]
		CO: cf 36-Parville #110 cf 46-Menetou #20, 39 cf 42-Vm7-6307-2 #8 cf 49-RésF-933 #23
20	ℓ BI$^{1-4}$	Aria [g]
21	ℓ CI^1	Prelude [d]
22	ℓ CI$^{2-4}$	Allemande [FROBERGER] [d] ED: cf Adler-II p 3.
23	ℓ DI^1-EI^3	Gique |voiès la Lettre EI [d] [FROBERGER] ED: cf Adler-II p 38.
24	ℓ FI$^{1-4}$	Courante [FROBERGER] [d] ED: cf Adler-II p 4.
25	ℓ GI$^{1-4}$	Sarabande [FROBERGER] [d] ED: cf Adler-II p 4.
26	ℓ HI$^{1-2}$	Prelude [C]
27	ℓ HI$^{3-4}$	Fuga [C]
28	ℓ II$^{1-2}$	Prelude [G]

29	ℓ KI^1-LI^4	Allemande ¦voiés la lettre LI [FROBERGER] [G] ED: cf Adler-II p 46.
30	ℓ MI$^{1-4}$	Courante [FROBERGER] [G] ED: cf Adler-II p 47.
31	ℓ NI$^{1-4}$	Sarabande [FROBERGER] [G] ED: cf Adler-II p 47 (variant).
32	ℓ OI$^{1-4}$	Gique [FROBERGER] [G] ED: cf Adler-II p 48.
33	ℓ PI$^{1-4}$	Allemande [FROBERGER] [e] ED: cf Adler-II p 67.
33a	ℓ QI$^{1-4}$	Le Double [FROBERGER] [e] ED: cf Adler-II p 68.
34	ℓ RI$^{1-4}$	Courante [FROBERGER] [e] ED: cf Adler-II p 68.
34a	ℓ SI$^{1-4}$	Le Double [FROBERGER] [e] ED: cf Adler-II p 69.
35	ℓ TI$^{1-2}$	Sarabande [FROBERGER] [e] ED: cf Adler-II p 70 (variant).
35a	ℓ TI$^{3-4}$	Le Double [FROBERGER] [e] ED: cf Adler-II p 70.

11-RYGE

Provenance: Denmark, ca. 1700?

Location: Copenhagen; Kongelige Bibliotek, Musikafde-
lingen, Mu 6806.1399 (C II 49).

Description: 3 p.ℓ., 450 p., 83, 1 ℓ. (second numeration from the back of the volume, which is the musical section); oblong quarto format, 15.8 x 18.9
cm. (top and fore-edges gilted). Watermark #94.
Original gilt-tooled vellum-covered boards with monogram (tracing #109); facsimile of binding in Bangert
p. iii; 31.5 x 20 cm.

Notation: New German organ tablature (4 systems per
page, written across facing pages); facsimile tipped
into Bangert.

Scribe: Unidentified member of the Ryge family (?);
family history in several hands (members of the
Ryge family).

Marginalia: Original numeration by pages from the front
(family history); modern pencil numeration by leaves
from the back (musical section).

Summary:
   Composers:
     BUXTEHUDE: #1-8, 14-31, 33-36, 38-42, 44-48, 51-54,
          61-90.
     LEBÈGUE: #10-13, 57-60.
     LULLY: #48.
     PACHELBEL: #37, 43, 49.
     REINCKEN: #55.
   Contents:
     p.1-227   Family history
     228-450   Largely blank; some family history, etc.
     [p.451]   The end of the musical section, ℓ. 83v.

ℓ. 1-83   Music, pieces grouped by keys:

#1-8	e	51-54	g
9-13	d	55-56	G
14-15	a	57-60	g
16-20	d	61-64	A
21-26	C	65-71	C
27-32	G	72-75	a
33-37	F	76-79	g
38-43	e	80-88	C
44-50	d	89-90	D

Inventory (Suite numbers assigned by Bangert in parentheses):

1
(1)   ℓ iv^1-1r^4 E /INI /Allemanda /di D.B.H. [BUXTEHUDE] [e]
                         ED: Bangert p 31.

2   ℓ 1v$^{1-3}$ Courant [e]
                         ED: Bangert p 32.

3   ℓ 2r$^{3-4}$.   Saraband [e]
                         ED: Bangert p 33.

4   ℓ 2v$^{1-4}$ Gique [e]
                         ED: Bangert p 34.

5
(2)   ℓ 3v^1-4r^3 I.XI.I /Allemanda. /ex E /di D.B.H. [e]
                         ED: Bangert p 35.

6   ℓ 4v$^{1-3}$ Courent [e]
                         ED: Bangert p 36.

7   ℓ 4v^3-5r^4 Saraband [e]
                         ED: Bangert p 36.

8   ℓ 5v^1-6r^3 Giqve [e]
                         ED: Bangert p 37.

9
(3)   ℓ 5v^4-6r^4 Menue [d]

10 ℓ 6v^1-7r^2 D♭ /Allemanda /di /D.B.H. [LEBÈGUE:
(4)   Allemande (d)]
                        CO: 48-LaBarre-6 #36
                            65-Lebègue-II #1 [copy thereof]
                        ED: Bangert p 26; cf Dufourcq-L p 49.

11 ℓ 6v^3-7r^4 Courent [LEBÈGUE: Courante (d)]
                        CO: 48-LaBarre-6 #37
                            65-Lebègue-II #2 [copy thereof]
                        ED: Bangert p 26; cf Dufourcq-L p 50.

12 ℓ 7v^1-8r^2 Saraband [LEBÈGUE: Sarabande grave (d)]
                        CO: 65-Lebègue-II #3 [copy thereof]
                        ED: Bangert p 27; cf Dufourcq-L p 50.

13 ℓ 7v^3-8r^4 Gique [LEBÈGUE: Gigue (d)]
                        CO: 65-Lebègue-II #4 [copy thereof]
                        ED: Bangert p 28; cf Dufourcq-L p 51.

14 ℓ 8v^1-10v^2 Courent /simple /di /Di Buxtehude
(5)   [8 variations (a)]
                        ED: Bangert p 80.

15 ℓ 10v^3-13r^4 Aria /di /D.B.H. [3 variations (a)]
(6)   CO: cf 1-Copenhagen-376 #48a
                            cf 18-Ch-Ch-1236 #38
                            cf Drallius #128
                            cf Leningrad #22
                            cf Van-Eijl #13, 16
                            cf Faille ℓ 121v

                        ED: Bangert p 84; cf Ex 1 abóve, Dickin-
                            son #48a, Hamburger p 139, Noske #13,
                            #16.

16 ℓ 13v$^{1-3}$ Allemanda /d'Aour /Svitte del Signore
(7)   /di /Dieterico Buxtehuden [d]
                        ED: Bangert p 18.

17 ℓ 13v^3-14r^4 Courent [d]
                        ED: Bangert p 18.

18 ℓ 14v$^{1-2}$ Sarabande /d'Amour [d]
                            ED: Bangert p 19.

19	ℓ $14r^{2-3}$	Saraband [d]

ED: Bangert p 20.

| 20 | ℓ $14v^3$-$15r^4$ | Giqve [d] |

ED: Bangert p 20.

| 21
(8) | ℓ $15v^1$-$21v^3$ | Aria di /D: Buxtehude [10 variations (C)] |

ED: Bangert p 64.

| 22
(9) | ℓ $22v^1$-$23r^3$ | Allemand /di /Dieter. Buxtehude [C] |

ED: Bangert p 7.

| 23 | ℓ $23v^1$-$24r^3$ | Courent [C] |

ED: Bangert p 8.

| 24 | ℓ $24r^{3-4}$ | Saraband [C] |

ED: Bangert p 8.

| 25 | ℓ $24v^1$-$25r^3$ | Gique [C] |

ED: Bangert p 9.

| 26
(10) | ℓ $25v^1$-$31r^2$ | Aria /More Palatino /di /D.B.H. [12 variations (C)] |

ED: Bangert p 72.

| 27
(11) | ℓ $31v^1$-$32r^2$ | Allemand /di /D.B.H. [G] |

ED: Bangert p 54.

| 28 | ℓ $31v^3$-$32r^4$ | Courent [G] |

ED: Bangert p 55.

| 29 | ℓ $32v^{1-2}$ | Saraband [G] |

ED: Bangert p 56.

| 30 | ℓ $32v^{2-3}$ | Gique [G] |

ED: Bangert p 56.

| 31
(12) | ℓ $33v^1$-$42r^4$ | Aria /Partite diverse una Aria /d'Invention detta La Capri/ciosa del /Dieterico Buxtehude ... [32 partite (G)] |

ED: Bangert p 88.

| 32
(13) | ℓ $42v^{1-3}$ | Simphonie [G] |

ED: Bangert p 103 (as anon)

33 (14)	ℓ $43v^1$-$44r^2$	Allemand /di /D.B.H. [F] ED: Bangert p 42.
34	ℓ $43v^3$-$44r^4$	Courent [F] ED: Bangert p 43.
35	ℓ $44v^{1-2}$	Saraband [F] ED: Bangert p 44.
36	ℓ $44v^2$-$45r^3$	Giqve [F] ED: Bangert p 44.
37 (15)	ℓ $45v^1$-$46r^4$	Aria [PACHELBEL (F)] CO: Hexachordum #3 ED: Moser p 10.
38 (16)	ℓ $46v^1$-$47r^2$	Allemand /di /D.B.H. [e] ED: Bangert p 38.
39	ℓ $46v^3$-$47r^4$	Courent [e] ED: Bangert p 39.
40	ℓ $47v^1$-$48r^1$	Saraband [e] ED: Bangert p 39.
41	ℓ $47v^{2-3}$	Saraband [e] ED: Bangert p 40.
42	ℓ $47v^3$-$48r^4$	Giqve [e] ED: Bangert p 40.
43 (17)	ℓ $48v^1$-$51r^2$	Aria [5 variations; PACHELBEL (e)] ED: Moser p 6.
44 (18)	ℓ $51v^1$-$52r^4$	Allemand /di /DBH |Variatio /Le double [d] ED: Bangert p 21
45	ℓ $52v^1$-$53r^4$	Courent |Variatio /Le Double [d] ED: Bangert p 23.
46	ℓ $53v^{1-2}$	Saraband [d] ED: Bangert p 25.
47	ℓ $53v^2$-$54r^2$	Saraband [d] ED: Bangert p 25.

48　ℓ 55r^3　　Rofilis /D.B.H. [LULLY: Entrée from Ballet
(19)　　　　　de l'impatience (1661) II-1 (d), 3 varia-
　　　　　　tions by BUXTEHUDE]
　　　　　　CO: cf 3-Berlin-40623 #1
　　　　　　　　cf 28-Brussels-926 ℓ 3r
　　　　　　　　cf Rés-819-2 ℓ 72r
　　　　　　　　cf Terburg
　　　　　　　　cf Skara #35
　　　　　　　　cf Van-Eijl #25
　　　　　　　　cf Stockholm-228 ℓ 20v
　　　　　　ED: Bangert p 78; cf Noske #25.

49　ℓ 54v^4-55v^3　Aria [6 variations; PACHELBEL (d)]
　　　　　　ED: cf Moser p 2.

50　ℓ 56v^3-57r^4　Courent [d]
(21)　　　　ED: Bangert p 101 (as anon).

51　ℓ 57v^1-58r^2　Allemand. /di /D.B.H. [g]
(22)　　　　ED: Bangert p 48.

52　ℓ 57v^3-58r^4　Courent [g]
　　　　　　ED: Bangert p 49.

53　ℓ 58v^1-59r^1　Saraband [g]
　　　　　　ED: Bangert p 50.

54　ℓ 58v^2-59r^3　Giqve [g]
　　　　　　ED: Bangert p 50.

55　ℓ 59v^1-65v^2　Aria [18 variations; REINCKEN: Partite
(23)　　　　diverse sopra l'Aria "Schweigt mir von
　　　　　　Weiber nehmen," altrimente chiamate La
　　　　　　Meyerin (G)]
　　　　　　ED: cf Apel-R p 61.

56 ℓ 65v^3-66r^4 Courent [G]
(24)   ED: Bangert p 102 (as anon).

57 ℓ 66v^1-67r^2 Allemand /di /D:B:H: [LEBÈGUE: <u>Allemande</u>
(25)   (g)]
            CO: 14-Schwerin-619 #1
                65-Lebègue-II #6 [copy thereof]
            ED: Bangert p 51; cf Dufourcq-L p 53.

58 ℓ 66v^3-67r^4 Courent [LEBÈGUE: <u>Courante</u> (g)]
            CO: 14-Schwerin-619 #3
                65-Lebègue-II #8 [copy thereof]
            ED: Bangert p 52; cf Dufourcq-L p 55.

59 ℓ 67v$^{1-2}$ Saraband [LEBÈGUE: <u>Sarabande</u> (g)]
            CO: 14-Schwerin-619 #4
                65-Lebègue-II #9 [copy thereof]
            ED: Bangert p 52; cf Du**fourcq**-L p 56.

60 ℓ 67v^2-68r^4 Giqve [LEBÈGUE: <u>Gigue</u> (g)]
            CO: 14-Schwerin-619 #6
                65-Lebègue-II #11 [copy thereof]
            ED: Bangert p 53; cf Dufourcq-L p 57.

61 ℓ 68v$^{1-3}$ Allemand /di /D.B.H. [A]
(26)   ED: Bangert p 61.

62 ℓ 68v^3-69r^4 Courent [A]
            ED: Bangert p 62.

63 ℓ 69v$^{1-2}$ Saraband [A]
            ED: Bangert p 62.

64 ℓ 69v^2-70r^4 Giqve [A]
            ED: Bangert p 63.

65 ℓ 70v^1-71r^2 Allemand /D.B.H: [C]
(27)   CO: cf 22a-Roper #22
                cf 65-Lebègue-II #35
            ED: Bangert p 13; cf Dufourcq-L p 79.

66 ℓ 70v^3-71r^4 Courent [C]
            CO: cf 65-Lebègue-II #36
            ED: Bangert p 13; cf Dufourcq-L p 80.

67 ℓ 71v$^{1-2}$ Saraband [C]
                 CO: cf 65-Lebègue-II #37
                 ED: Bangert p 14; cf Dufourcq-L p 81.

68 ℓ 72v^1-73r^2 Allemand /di /D.B.H. [C]
(28)   ED: Bangert p 15.

69 ℓ 72v^3-73v^4 Courent [C]
                 ED: Bangert p 16.

70 ℓ 73v^1-74r^1 Saraband [C]
                 ED: Bangert p 16.

71 ℓ 73v^2-74r^4 Giqve [C]
                 ED: Bangert p 17.

72 ℓ 74v^1-75r^2 Allemand. /Ex A♭ /di /D.B.H. [a]
(29)   ED: Bangert p 57.

73 ℓ 74r^3-75r^4 Courent [a]
                 ED: Bangert p 58.

74 ℓ 75v^1-76r^1 Saraband [a]
                 ED: Bangert p 58.

75 ℓ 75v^2-76r^4 Giqve [a]
                 ED: Bangert p 59.

76 ℓ 76v^1-77r^2 Allemand. /ex G♭ /di /D.B.H. [g]
(30)   ED: Bangert p 45.

77 ℓ 76v^3-77r^4 Courent [g]
                 ED: Bangert p 46

78 ℓ 77v^1-78r^1 Saraband [g]
                 ED: Bangert p 47.

79 ℓ 77v$^{2-3}$ Giqve [g]
                 ED: Bangert p 47.

80 ℓ 78v^1-79r^2 Allemand. /Ex C♮ /di /D.B.H. [C]
(31)   ED: Bangert p 3.

81 ℓ $78v^3$-$79r^4$ Courent [C]
                    ED: Bangert p 4.

82 ℓ $79v^1$-$80r^1$ Saraband [C]
                    ED: Bangert p 5.

83 ℓ $79v^2$-$80r^2$ Sarabande /La Seconde [C]
                    ED: Bangert p 5.

84 ℓ $79v^3$-$80r^4$ Giqve [C]
                    ED: Bangert p 6.

85 ℓ $80v^1$-$81r^2$ Allemand /Ex C♮ /di /D.B.H. [C]
(32)   ED: Bangert p 10.

86 ℓ $80v^1$-$81r^4$ Courent [C]
                    ED: Bangert p 11.

87 ℓ $81v^1$-$82r^2$ Saraband |Double [C]
                    ED: Bangert p 11.

88 ℓ $81v^3$-$82r^4$ Giqve [C]
                    ED: Bangert p 12.

89 ℓ $82v^1$-$83r^2$ Allemande /D♮ /di /D.B.H. [D]
(33)   ED: Bangert p 29.

90 ℓ $82v^3$-$83r^4$ Courent [D]
                    ED: Bangert p 30.

    ℓ 83v   [blank, ruled; the same as (p 451)]

12-WALTHER

Provenance: Weimar, ca. 1712-post 1731.

Location: East Berlin; Deutsche Staatsbibliothek, Mus.
    Ms. Bach P 801.

Description: (various mss bound together:) ii, 520 p.
    (i.e., 522: 280 repeated), average size: 17 x 20 cm.
    Modern half leather binding, 18.1 x 20.3 cm.

Notation: Keyboard score (two 5-line staves). Clefs
    usually F^4, C^1.

Scribes: three hands intermingled:
    Johann Gottfried Walther (1684-1748), including the
        d'Anglebert and Lebègue pieces.
    Johann Tobias Krebs (1690-1762)
    Johann Ludwig Krebs (1713-1780)

Summary:
    Composers:

        d'ANGLEBERT: p 259.
        BACH (JS): passim.
        BUYSTIJN: p 227.
        BUXTEHUDE: p 333.
        CLÉRAMBAULT: p 423.
        DANDRIEU: p 239.
        DIEUPART: p 301.
        KAUFFMANN: p 513.
        KREBS: p 64, 195.
        LEBÈGUE: p 485.
        LE ROUX: p 497.
        LÜBECK: p 357, 373.
        MARCHAND: p 447.
        NEUFVILLE: p 219.
        NIVERS: p 289.

TELEMANN: p 275, 317, 325, 463.

Contents:

    Miscellaneous harpsichord and organ compositions.

Inventory:

    See Hermann Zietz, Quellenkritische Untersuchungen
den Bach-Handschriften P 801, P 802 und P 803 aus
dem "Krebs'schen Nachlass" unter besonderer Berück-
sichtigung der Choralbearbeitungen des jungen J.S.
Bach, Hamburger Beiträge zur Musikwissenschaft 1
(Hamburg: Verlag der Musikalienhandlung Karl Dieter
Wagner, 1969), pp. 38-60.

Inventory of 17th-century French harpsichord music:

p 259-273	[d'ANGLEBERT: Suite (d)]
	Allemande ... [etc]
	CO: 68-d'Anglebert #39, 41, 40, 40a, 42-45
	[copies thereof]
	33-Rés-89ter #24
	ED: Gilbert p 50, Roesgen-Champion p 76.
p 485-496	[LEBÈGUE: Suite (g/G)]
	Svite En g re sol ut /Mons Beque ... [etc]
	CO: 13-Möllersche ℓ 82v-85v
	22a-Roper #20-21
	23-Tenbury #41-42
	24-Babell #85-86
	45-Dart #8, 10, 12-13, 28-29
	64-Lebègue-I #16-27 [copies thereof]
	ED: Dufourcq-L p 13.

13-MÖLLERSCHE

<u>Provenance</u>: Köthen, 1717-1719.

<u>Location</u>: West Berlin (Dahlem); Staatsbibliothek der
    Stiftung preussischer Kulturbesitz, Mus. Ms. 40644.

<u>Description</u>: 100 ℓ., 18.4 x 32 cm. 3/4 modern leather
    binding.

<u>Notation</u>: Mixed. Instrumental score; keyboard score
    (two 5-line staves); new German organ tablature.

<u>Scribe</u>: Johann Bernard Bach.

<u>Marginalia</u>: Library stamp of Werner Wolffheim.

<u>Summary</u>:
    Composers:
        ALBINONI, Tomaso (1671-1750)
        BACH, Johann Sebastian (1685-1750)
        BÖHM, Georg (1661-1773)
        BRUHNS, Nicolaus (1605-1697)
        BUXTEHUDE, Dietrich (1637-1707)
        COBERG, Johann Anton (1650-1708)
        EDELMANN, Moritz (d. 1680)
        FABRICIUS, Werner (1633-1679)
        FLOR, Christian (1626-1697)
        HEYDORN (fl. 1693)
        KLAR, J
        LEBÈGUE, Nicolas-Antoine (ca. 1631-1702): ℓ 82v-96v.
        LULLY, Jean-Baptiste (1632-1687)
        PACHELBEL, Johann (1653-1706)
        PEZ, Johann Christoph (1664-1716)
        REINCKEN, Johann Adam (1623-1722)
        RITTER, Christian (fl. 1666-1725)
        STEFFANI, Agostino (1654-1728)
        STIL, Joh

ZACHOW, Friedrich Wilhelm (1663-1712)

Contents: 51 pieces:
   ℓ 1v-15r Instrumental pieces by Coberg, Albinoni,
           Pez.
   15v-69r Keyboard pieces by Reincken, Böhm,
           Ritter, Heydorn, Coberg, Bach, Lully
           (arr.), Buxtehude, Flor, Steffani,
           Fabricius.
   69v-70r Instrumental music by Stil.
   71v-73r Keyboard music by Klar (another hand?).
   74v-100v Keyboard pieces by Bach, Lebègue, Pachel-
           bel, Zachow, Bruhns (in organ tablature),
           Edelmann (fragment).

Inventory of 17th-century French harpsichord music:

ℓ 82v^1-85r^4 | [LEBÈGUE: Suite (g/G)]

Suite. En g re sol ut Composseès par Mons:
Le.Beque ... [etc]
CO: 12-Walther p 485-496
    22a-Roper #20-21
    23-Tenbury #41-42
    24-Babell #85-86
    45-Dart #8, 10, 12-13, 28-29
    64-Lebègue-I #16-27 [copies thereof]
ED: Dufourcq-L p 13.

ℓ 86r^1-89v^3 | [LEBÈGUE: Suite (d/D)]

Suite avec Prelude En d la re Sol Composeè
par Mons. Nicolas Le Beque ... fin de la
Suite Premier p.
CO: 22a-Roper #17, 23, 24
    45-Dart #2, 4-7, 9
    48-LaBarre-6 #26
    64-Lebègue-I #2-14 [copies thereof]
ED: Dufourcq-L p 2.

ℓ 89v^4-91v^4 | [LEBÈGUE: Suite (a/A)]

Allemande [etc] |Fine De la Suite /En a mi
la re /di Monsieur /Le Beque.
CO: 22a-Roper #10-12
    28-Brussels-926 ℓ 66r
    45-Dart #11, 15

64-Lebègue-I #29-35 [copies thereof]

ED: Dufourcq-L p 23.

ℓ 92r^1-94v^3 [LEBÈGUE: Suite (C)]

Allemande et Suite de Mons: Le Begue [etc]
|La Fin

CO: 10-Schwerin-617 #10
    14-Schwerin-619 #91
    21-Rés-1186bis #12
    22a-Roper #3-6; cf #13
    23-Tenbury #6
    24-Babell #60
    30-Cecilia ℓ 47r
    35-Bauyn-III #54
    36-Parville #68
    45-Dart #22, 26
    46-Menetou #102
    50-Pagnon #11
    64-Lebègue-I #37-44 [copies thereof]
 ED: Dufourcq-Lp 30; cf Brunold/Dart-Co #132.

ℓ 94v^4-86v^2 [LEBÈGUE: Suite (F)]

Svite auec Prelude. En.f.ut.fa. par Mons.
Le Beque [etc]
CO: 64-Lebègue-I #46-51 [copies thereof]
ED: Dufourcq-L p 41.

ℓ 96v   Demonstration des Marques [copied from
64-Lebègue-I p iii]

Provenance: Schwerin (?), ca. 1720?

Location: Schwerin, German Democratic Republic; Wissen-
schaftliches Allgemeinbibliothek des Bezirkes Schwerin,
Mus. Ms. 619.

Description: 4 p.ℓ., 105 ℓ. (i.e., 104: ℓ. 40 omitted in
numeration), 2 ℓ.; 29 quires in 4 (except A^3, BB^2,
CC^2); oblong quarto format, 20.1 x 26.2 cm. Watermarks #41 (1st section), 42 (2nd section). Original
(?) full leather binding, gilt-tooled spine and
marbled paper paste-downs, 20.7 x 27.5 cm.

Notation: Keyboard score (two 5-line staves, 4 systems
per page, written page by page). Clefs: F^4, C^1, G^2.

Scribes: 3 unidentified German hands:
A: #1-104
B: 105-123
C: 124

Marginalia: "N. 7" added in a later hand before title,
ℓ iii.

Summary:
Composers:
COLLASSE: #42.
CORELLI: #41, 87-88, 92, 103.
DANDRIEU: # 70, 93-94, 102, 106, 109-110.
GAULTIER (Pierre): #54, 57.
LEBÈGUE: #1-30, 91.
LOEILLET: cf #89.
LULLY: #42, 48-53, 55-56, 58-69, 71-78, 82-86, 111,
118, 121-123.
MARCHAND: #108.
RAMEAU: #115.
VERACINI: #47.

Contents:

#1-30   Suites by Lebègue.

31-37   Opera transcriptions, etc.

38-41   Italianate pieces.

42-47   Suite (D) by Collasse, anon., Veracini

48-86   Lully and Gaultier transcriptions, grouped
         by key.

87-92   Dances by Lebègue, Corelli, anon.

93-103   Suites by Dandrieu, Corelli, anon.

104-124   Pieces by Dandrieu, Marchand, Rameau,
         Lully, anon.

Inventory:

    ℓ i-ii   [blank]

    ℓ iii^r Clavir Buch

1   ℓ iii^{v1}-iv^{v4} Allemande [LEBÈGUE: <u>Allemande</u> (g)]
         CO: 11-Ryge #57
            65-Lebègue-II #6 [copy thereof]
         ED: Dufourcq-L p 53, **cf Bangert p 51.**

2   ℓ iv^{v1}-1r^2 Allemande [LEBÈGUE: <u>Allemande</u> (g)]
         CO: 65-Lebègue-II #7 [copy thereof]
         ED: Dufourcq-L p 54.

3   ℓ 1v^1-2r^2 Courante [LEBÈGUE: <u>Courante</u> (g)]
         CO: 11-Ryge #58
            65-Lebègue-II #8 [copy thereof]
         ED: Dufourcq-L p 55, **cf Bangert p 52.**

4   ℓ 2v$^{1-4}$ Saraband [LEBÈGUE: <u>Sarabande</u> (g)]
         CO: 11-Ryge #59
            65-Lebègue-II #9 [copy thereof]
         ED: Dufourcq-L p 56, **cf Bangert p 52.**

5   ℓ 3r$^{1-3}$ Rondeau [LEBÈGUE: <u>Rondeau</u> (g)]
         CO: 65-Lebègue-II #10 [copy thereof]
         ED: Dufourcq-L p 56.

6	ℓ 3v^1-4r^4	Gig [LEBÈGUE: <u>Gigue</u> (g)]
		CO: 11-Ryge #60
		65-Lebègue-II #11 [copy thereof]
		ED: Dufourcq-L p 57, cf Bangert p 53.
7	ℓ 4v^1-5r^4	Passacaille [LEBÈGUE: <u>Passacaille</u> (g)]
		CO: 45-Dart #14
		65-Lebègue-II #12 [copy thereof]
		ED: Dufourcq-L p 58.
8	ℓ 5v$^{1-4}$	Menuet [LEBÈGUE: <u>Menuet</u> (g)]
		CO: 45-Dart #17
		65-Lebègue-II #13 [copy thereof]
		ED: Dufourcq-L p 60.
9	ℓ 6r$^{1-3}$	Gavotte [LEBÈGUE: <u>Gavotte</u> (g)]
		CO: 45-Dart #18
		65-Lebègue-II #14 [copy. thereof]
		ED: Dufourcq-L p 60.
10	ℓ 6v$^{1-3}$	Gavotte [LEBÈGUE: <u>Gavotte</u> (B♭)]
		CO: 65-Lebègue-II #15 [copy thereof]
		ED: Dufourcq-L p 61.
11	ℓ 7r$^{1-3}$	Menuet [LEBÈGUE: <u>Menuet</u> (B♭)]
		CO: 45-Dart #19
		65-Lebègue-II #16 [copy thereof]
		ED: Dufourcq-L p 61.
	ℓ 7v^1-8r^4	Suitte Enamilare. [by LEBÈGUE]
12	ℓ 7v^1-8r^4	Allemande [LEBÈGUE: <u>Allemande</u> (a)]
		CO: 65-Lebègue-II #17 [copy thereof]
		ED: Dufoucq-L p 62.
13	ℓ 8v$^{1-4}$	Sarabande [LEBÈGUE: <u>Sarabande</u> (a)]
		CO: 65-Lebègue-II #19 [copy thereof]
		ED: Dufourcq-L p 64.
14	ℓ 9r$^{1-3}$	Gavotte [LEBÈGUE: Gavotte (a)]
		CO: 45-Dart #20
		65-Lebègue-II #20 **[copy thereof]**
		ED: Dufourcq-L p 64.

15 | ℓ 9v$^{1-3}$ Menuet [LEBÈGUE: <u>Menuet</u> (a)]
                       CO: 65-Lebègue-II #21 [copy thereof]
                       ED: Dufourcq-L p 65.

   | ℓ 10r   [blank, ruled]

   | ℓ 10v   Suitte en amilare [by LEBÈGUE]

16 | ℓ 10v^{1}-11r^{2} Allemande [LEBÈGUE: <u>Allemande</u> (A)]
                       CO: 65-Lebègue-II #22 [copy thereof]
                       ED: Dufourcq-L p 66.

17 | ℓ 11v$^{1-4}$ Courant [LEBÈGUE: <u>Courante</u> (A)]
                       CO: 48-LaBarre-6 #39
                           65-Lebègue-II #23 [copy thereof]
                       ED: Dufourcq-L p 67.

18 | ℓ 12r$^{1-4}$ forte Graue /Saraband [LEBÈGUE: <u>Sarabande</u>
                       <u>fort</u> <u>grave</u> (A)]
                       CO: **45-Dart** #23
                           65-Lebègue-II #24 [copy thereof]
                       ED: **Dufourcq-L p 68.**

19 | ℓ 12v^{1}-13r^{4} Gique [LEBÈGUE: <u>Gigue</u> (A)]
                       CO: 65-Lebègue-II #25 [copy thereof]
                       ED: Dufourcq-L p 68.

20 | ℓ 13v^{1}-14r^{4} Bouréé ... Bouréé double [LEBÈGUE: <u>Bour-
                       rée</u> with <u>Double</u> (A)]
                       CO: 65-Lebègue-II #26, 26a [copy there-
                                                        of]
                       ED: Dufourcq-L p 70.

21 | ℓ 14v$^{1-4}$ [LEBÈGUE: <u>Sarabande</u> (F)]
                       CO: 65-Lebègue-II #31 [copy thereof]
                       ED: Dufourcq-L p 74.

22 | ℓ 15r$^{1-3}$ Menuet [LEBÈGUE: <u>Menuet</u> (F)]
                       CO: **24-Babell** #9
                           65-Lebègue-II #32 [copy thereof]
                       ED: Dufourcq-L p 75.

23   ℓ 15v$^{1-4}$ Menuet [LEBÈGUE: <u>Menuet</u> (F)]

               CO: 24-Babell #8
                   45-Dart #25
                   65-Lebègue-II #33 [copy thereof]
               ED: Dufourcq-L p 75.

24   ℓ 16r$^{1-2}$ Menuet [LEBÈGUE: <u>Menuet</u> (G)]

               CO: 65-Lebègue-II #39 [copy thereof]
               ED: Dufourcq-L p 86.

25   ℓ 16v$^{1-3}$ Bouréé [LEBÈGUE: <u>Bourrée</u> (G)]

               CO: 65-Lebègue-II #41 [copy thereof]
               ED: Dufourcq-L p 87.

26   ℓ 17r$^{1-4}$ Air de Hautbois [LEBÈGUE: <u>Air de Haut-</u>
               <u>bois</u> (G)]

               CO: 45-Dart #27
                   65-Lebègue-II #42 [copy thereof]
               ED: Dufourcq-L p 88.

27   ℓ 17v^{1}-19v^{2} Chaconne Grave [LEBÈGUE: <u>Chaconne grave</u>
               (G)]

               CO: 65-Lebègue-II #38
               ED: Dufourcq-L p 82.

28   ℓ 20r^{1}-v^{4} Gavotte |Double [LEBÈGUE: <u>Gavotte</u> with
               <u>Double</u> (G)]

               CO: 65-Lebègue-II #43, 43a [copy thereof]
               ED: Dufourcq-L p 88.

    ℓ 21r   [blank, ruled]

29   ℓ 21v^{1}-22r^{4} Petitte/Chaconne [LEBÈGUE: <u>Petite Chaconne</u>
               (G)]

               CO: 65-Lebègue-II #44 [copy thereof]
               ED: Dufourcq-L p 90.

30   ℓ 22v^{1}-24r^{3} Chaconne [LEBÈGUE: <u>Chaconne</u> (F)]

               CO: 65-Lebègue-II #34 [copy thereof]
               ED: Dufourcq-L p 76.

31	ℓ 24v^1-25r^3 Aria /Da Capo .[d]
32	ℓ 25v^1-26v^4 Ouverteur [C]
33	ℓ 27r$^{1-4}$ Entree [a]
34	ℓ 27v^1-28r^4 Aria |Finis |Da Capo [B♭]
35	ℓ 28v^1-29r^2 Aria [g]
36	ℓ 29v^1-30r^3 Aria ⌊C]
37	ℓ 30v^1-31r^1 Aria |Finis |Da Capo [D]
	ℓ 31v [blank, ruled]
38	ℓ 32r$^{1-4}$ Balletto |piano |forte ⌊etc] [A]
39	ℓ 32v^1-33r^1 Courente |piano [A]
40	ℓ 33r$^{2-4}$ Air Anglois |piano |forte [etc] [A]
	CO: 14-Schwerin-619 #112
41	ℓ 33v^1-34v^2 Giga |pian [CORELLI, arr: <u>Sonata</u> IX,
	op 5 (A)]
42	ℓ 34v^3-35v^2 Ouverture /De Tetis /Et pelëe [LULLY/COL-
	LASSE, arr: from <u>Thétis</u> <u>et</u> <u>Pelée</u> (1654)
	(D)]
	CO: cf 23-Tenbury #17
	cf 48-LaBarre-6 #35
43	ℓ 35v^3-36v^3 Allemanda |piano [D]
44	ℓ 36v^4-37r^4 Corrente ⌊D]
45	ℓ 37v^1-38r^4 Bouree |Double /du /Dessus |Duble La
	Basse [D]
46	ℓ 38v^1-39r^1 Gigue [D]
	[ℓ 40] [omitted in numeration system]
47	ℓ 39v^1-41r^1 Echo /di /veracini |forte |piano [etc][D]
48	ℓ 41r$^{2-4}$ Allemande /des /fragments /de /M: Lully [D]
	CO: cf 42-Vm7-6307-2 #11
	cf Berlin-30363 ℓ 1r

49 | ℓ 41v^1-42v^2 Overture /de /Roland [LULLY (1685) (d)]
CO: cf 24-Babell #182
    cf 46-Menetou #27

50 | ℓ 42v^3-45r^3 Passacaille /de /Gallathee [LULLY from
Acis et Galathée (1686) III-9 (d)]

51 | ℓ 45v^1-46r^4 Ouverture /Disis [LULLY (1677) (g)]
CO: cf 24-Babell #128
    cf 33-Rés-89ter #42c
    cf 36-Parville #42
    cf 40-Rés-476 #35
    cf 42-Vm7-6307-2 #5
    cf 46-Menetou #85
    cf 49-RésF-933 #24
    cf Stoss ℓ 24v

ED: cf Bonfils-LP p 101, Howell #2,
    Gilbert p 199.

52 | ℓ 46v^1-47r^4 Ouverture Des Festes /de Lamour /Et
Bacchus [LULLY (1672) (g)]
CO: cf 46-Menetou #83

53 | ℓ 47v$^{1-4}$ Songes /Agreables /Datis [LULLY, arr:
Les Songes agréables from Atys (1676)
III-4]

CO: cf 24-Babell #131
    cf 33-Rés-89ter #43
    cf 36-Parville #117
    cf 46-Menetou #114
    cf 68-d'Anglebert #34

ED: cf Gilbert p 116, Roesgen-Champion p 63.

54 | ℓ 48r$^{1-4}$ Les plaisirs /de /Gautier [Pierre GAUL-
TIER, arr (g)]
CO: 14-Schwerin #57
    cf 36-Parville #138
    cf 45-Dart #44
    cf Gaultier p 35

55 | ℓ 48v^1-49r^3 Echõ /Datis |fort |fin [LULLY, arr:
Entrée des zéphirs from Atys (1676) II-4
(g)]
CO: cf 24-Babell #132

56 | ℓ 49v^1-50r^2 Ouverture/dapollon /du /Triomphe /de
Lamour [LULLY, arr: Entrée d'Apollon
from Le Triomphe de l'amour (1681) (g)]

        CO: cf 24-Babell #129
           cf 30-Cecilia ℓ 52r
           cf 36-Parville #43
           cf 46-Menetou #100
           cf 68-d'Anglebert #35
           cf Stockholm-176 ℓ 14v
           cf Saizenay-I p 222 [lute]

        ED: cf Gilbert p 118, Roesgen-Champion p 64.

57 | ℓ 50v$^{1-4}$ Les plaisirs /de /Gautier [Pierre GAUL-
TIER, arr (g)]

        CO: 14-Schwerin #54
           cf 36-Parville #138
           cf 45-Dart #44
           cf Gaultier p 35

58 | ℓ 51r$^{1-3}$ Rondeau /D'atis |Fin [LULLY, arr: Air
pour la suite de Flore from Atys (1676)
Prologue (G)]

59 | ℓ 51v^1-52r^2 Echo de La /grotte. De /Versaille [LULLY,
arr: Air des echos from La Grotte de
Versailles (1668) (G)]

60 | ℓ 52v^1-53r^1 La discorde /De /Prosperine [LULLY, arr:
Air (la discorde) from Proserpine (1680)
Prologue (G)]
        CO cf 23-Tenbury #46.

61 | ℓ 53r^2-55r^3 Chaconne /de /Phäeton [LULLY (1683) II-5
(G)]

        CO: cf 24-Babell #263
           cf 43-Gen-2354 #1
           cf 44-LaPierre p 24, 45A
           cf 46-Menetou #9
           cf 68-d'Anglebert #15

        ED: cf Gilbert p 100, Roesgen-Champion
           p 30.

62 ℓ 55v$^{1-4}$ La Mariee /De /Roland [LULLY (1685) (G)]
                CO: cf 22a-Roper #19
                    cf 36-Parville #122
                    cf 45-Dart #34, 65

63 ℓ 56r^{1}-58r^{3} Passacaille /Darmide [LULLY (1686) V-2
                (g)]
                CO: cf 24-Babell #138
                    cf 31-Madrid-1360 #27
                    cf 49-RésF-933 #1
                    cf 68-d'Anglebert #37
                    cf Minorite ℓ 44v
                ED: cf Gilbert p 108, Roesgen-Champion p 67.

64 ℓ 58v^{1}-59r^{3} Sourdinet /damide [LULLY, arr: <u>Second</u>
                <u>sourdines</u> from <u>Armide</u> (1686) II-4 (g)]
                CO: cf 23-Tenbury #49
                    cf 24-Babell #124
                    cf 36-Parville #115, 149
                    cf 49-RésF-933 #2
                    cf 68-d'Anglebert #33
                ED: cf Gilbert p 115, Roesgen-Champion p 62.

65 ℓ 59v^{1}-60r^{4} Entre /De La gloire /Et de La Sagesse
                /darmide. [LULLY (1686) Prologue (a)]

66 ℓ 60v^{1}-61r^{4} Ouverture /De /Persée [LULLY (1682) (a)]
                CO: cf 24-Babell #152
                    cf 46-Menetou #98

67 ℓ 61v^{1}-63r^{1} Passacaille /de persee [LULLY (1682) V-8
                (a)]
                CO: cf 46-Menetou #96

68 ℓ 63v^{1}-64r^{4} Ouverture /du Temple /de La paix [LULLY
                (1685) (a)]
                CO: cf 28-Brussels-926 ℓ 63v
                    cf 46-Menetou #56

69 ℓ 64v$^{1-4}$ Descente /De Mars /De Thesee |Fin
                [LULLY, arr: <u>Trompettes</u> (<u>Mars</u>) from
                <u>Thésée</u> (1675) Prologue (C)]
                CO: cf 36-Parville #131
                    cf 44-LaPierre p 44, 20A

70 | ℓ 65r^1-68r^2 Chaconne /de /M^r. Dandre [DANDRIEU] [C]
CO: Dandrieu-5 Suite 1, La figurée

71 | ℓ 68v$^{1-2}$ Menuet [LULLY, arr: <u>Haubois</u> from <u>Thésée</u>
(1675) Prologue (C)]
CO: cf 25-Bod-426 #7
cf 36-Parville #132
cf 44-LaPierre p 22A

72 | ℓ 68v^3-69r^2 Sacrifiee /de Thesee [LULLY, arr: <u>Marche</u>
from <u>Thésée</u> (1675) I-8 (C)]
CO: cf 36-Parville #133
cf 40-Rés-476 #42
cf 44-LaPierre p 23A
ED: cf Bonfils-LP p 109, Howell #9.

73 | ℓ 69v^1-70r^1 Entree des Combattans de Thesee [LULLY
(1675) I-8 (C)]

74 | ℓ 70r$^{2-4}$ Trompet /Disis [LULLY, arr: <u>Air</u> (<u>trom-
pettes</u>) from <u>Isis</u> (1677) Prologue (C)]
CO: cf 22a-Roper #28
cf 40-Rés-476 #36
ED: cf Bonfils-LP p 103, Howell #3.

75 | ℓ 70v$^{1-4}$ Sacrifice /de Mars /de /Cadmus [LULLY,
arr: <u>Marche</u> <u>des</u> <u>sacrificateurs</u> from
<u>Cadmus</u> (1673) III-6 (C)]
CO: cf 44-LaPierre p 48

76 | ℓ 71r$^{1-3}$ Entree des Basqs: /du Temple de la paix
[LULLY (1865) (C)]
CO: cf 48-LaBarre-6 #33.

77 | ℓ 71v^1-72v^3 Ouverture /De /Phaëton [LULLY (1683) (C)]
CO: cf 46-Menetou #1

78 | ℓ 72v^3-73r^4 Furie De /Cadmus [LULLY: <u>Entrée</u> <u>de</u> <u>l'en-
vie</u> from <u>Cadmus</u> (1673) Prologue-3 (C)]

79 | ℓ 73v^1-74r^2 Marche /de /Bergere [C]

80 | ℓ 74v$^{1-2}$ Pastourelle [C]

81 | ℓ 74v$^{3-4}$ 2 /Pastourelle [C]

82 | ℓ 75r^{1}-76r^{2} Ouverture /de Psiche |verte Cito [LULLY (1678) (C)]
       CO: cf 24-Babell #57

83 | ℓ 76v^{1}-77r^{4} Ouverture /de /Bellerophon [LULLY (1679) (C)]
       CO: cf 24-Babell #199
           cf 27-Gresse #53
           cf 40-Rés-476 #26
           cf 46-Menetou #87
           cf Bod-576 p 54
       ED: cf Bonfils-LP p 86, Howell #1.

84 | ℓ 77v^{1}-78v^{3} Ouverture /du /Triomp /de /Lamour [LULLY (1681) (F)]
       CO: cf 24-Babell #231
           cf 46-Menetou #94

85 | ℓ 78v^{4}-79r^{4} Air /des /Songes /funestes /daTis [LULLY, arr: Entrée des songes funestes from Atys (1676) III-4 (B♭)]
       CO: cf Grimm ℓ 80v

86 | ℓ 79v^{1}-80r^{1} 2 Air /des /Songes /funestes /Datis [LULLY, arr from Atys (1676) III-4 (B♭)]
       CO: cf 46-Menetou #115

87 | ℓ 80r^{2}-80v^{2} Allemanda /Corelli [B♭]

88 | ℓ 80v^{3}-81r^{4} Corrente /Corelli |piano |forte [etc] [b]

89 | ℓ 81v^{1}-82r^{3} Giga /Baptiste [LOEILLET?] [F]

90 | ℓ 82v^{1}-84r^{3} Chaconne [F]

91 | ℓ 84v$^{1-3}$ Gavotte [LEBÈGUE (C)]
       CO: 10-Schwerin-617 #10
           13-Mollersche
           21-Rés-1186bis #12
           23-Tenbury #6
           24-Babell #60
           30-Cecilia ℓ 47r
           35-Bauyn-III #54
           36-Parville #68

        45-Dart #22
        46-Menetou #102
        50-Paignon #11
        64-Lebègue-I #43

      ED: Dufourcq-L p 38, Brunold/Dart-Co
      #132.

91a | ℓ $84v^3$-$85r^3$ [Double (C)]

      CO: cf 13-Möllersche
          cf 23-Tenbury #6a
          cf 24-Babell #60a
          cf 35-Bauyn-III #54a
          cf 36-Parville #68a
          cf 36-Parville #146
          cf 50-Paignon #11a
          cf 64-Lebègue-I #43a

      ED: Dufourcq-L p 38, Brunold/Dart-Co
      #132[a].

92 | ℓ $85v^1$-$86v^2$ Giga /Corelli [Allegro from Op 5 III (C)]

93 | ℓ $86v^3$-$87r^1$ Bouree /En Rondeau /de Mr Dan[drieu?][C]
      CO: 14-Schwerin-619 #120

94 | ℓ $87v^1$-$88r^2$ Allemande [DANDRIEU: La Modeste (c)]
      CO: Dandrieu-6 Suite 3, La Modeste

95 | ℓ $88v^1$-$89r^1$ Courente [c]

96 | ℓ $89r^{2-4}$ Sarabande [c]

97 | ℓ $89v^1$-$90r^3$ Allemande [B♭]

98 | ℓ $90v^1$-$91r^4$ Courente |Double de la Courente [B♭]

99 | ℓ $91v^{1-3}$ Sarabande [B♭]

100 | ℓ $91v^4$-$92r^4$ Gavotte /En Rond: [B♭]

101 | ℓ $92v^{1-3}$ Bouree [B♭]

102 | ℓ $93r^1$-$94r^4$ Giga De Mr Dandriue [B♭]

103 | ℓ $94v^1$-$95r^3$ Corante /De Corelli [Corrente from Op 4
         I (C)]

104 | ℓ $95v^1$-$96r^1$ Gavotta [g]

| | ℓ 96v | [blank, ruled] |

105 | ℓ 97r$^{1-4}$ | Entree [A]

106 | ℓ 97v$^{1-3}$ | Harmonieuse |fin |Da/Capo [DANDRIEU (C)]
CO: Dandrieu-4 Suite 1, L'Harmonieuse

107 | ℓ 98r$^{1-2}$ | Giqve |fin |Da Capo [A]

108 | ℓ 98v^{1}-99r^{1} | Venitienne de Mr Marchand [F]
CO: 52-Rés-2671 #19

109 | ℓ 99r$^{2-4}$ | [DANDRIEU: Le Polichinet (F)]
CO: Dandrieu-5 Suite 2, Le Polichinet

110 | ℓ 99v$^{1-4}$ | [DANDRIEU: La Favorite (A)]
CO: Berlin-30363 ℓ 3r
Dandrieu-4 Suite 4, La Favorite

111 | ℓ 100r$^{1-3}$ | Chaconne [LULLY, arr: Chaconne from
Ballet des muses (1666) II-2 (G)]
CO: cf 36-Parville #116 [B♭]
cf 46-Menetou #116
cf 50-Paignon #12 [C]
cf Minorite ℓ 50r

112 | ℓ 100v$^{1-2}$ | Air Anglois [A]
CO: 14-Schwerin-619 #40

113 | ℓ 100v$^{3-4}$ | Menuet [DANDRIEU: Les Papillons (A)]
CO: Dandrieu-4 Suite 4 Les Papillons/1

114 | ℓ 101r$^{1-2}$ | Gavotte [C]

115 | ℓ 101r$^{3-4}$ | Menuet [RAMEAU (a)]
CO: Rameau-1706

116 | ℓ 101v$^{1-4}$ | [DANDRIEU: La Corelli (C)]
CO: Dandrieu-5 Suite 1, La Corelli

117 | ℓ 102r$^{1-4}$ | Giqve [C]

118 | ℓ 102v$^{1-4}$ | Prelude [LULLY, arr: Prélude des muses
from Isis (1677) Prologue-3 (g)]

119 | ℓ 103r$^{1-2}$ | Gavotte [A]

120 | ℓ 103$^{3-4}$ | Boure en Rondeau |Da Capo [DANDRIEU? (C)]
CO: 14-Schwerin-619 #93

121	ℓ 103v^1-104r^1	Ouverture de La Grotte de versaille [LULLY (1668) (g)]

        CO: cf 36-Parville #121
            cf 46-Menetou #118
            cf 49-RésF-933 #3
            cf Minorite ℓ 44**r**
            cf Saizenay-I p 226 [lute]
        ED: cf Strizich p 104.

122	ℓ 104r$^{2-4}$	Marche [LULLY, arr: <u>Marche des amazones</u> from <u>Bellérophon</u> (1679) I-5 (C)]

        CO: cf 46-Menetou #90

123	ℓ 104v$^{1-4}$	[C]haconne de Galothe [LULLY: <u>Chaconne</u> from <u>Acis</u> <u>et</u> <u>Galathée</u> (1686) II-5 (D)]

        CO: cf 23-Tenbury #75
            cf 24-Babell #97
            cf 36-Parville #29
            cf 49-RésF-933 #4
            cf 51-LaBarre-11 p 206
            cf 68-d'Anglebert #55
        ED: cf Gilbert p 106, Roesgen-Champion
            p 112.

124	ℓ 105r^1-105v^1	Gavotte [DANDRIEU: <u>La</u> <u>Follète</u> (g)]

        CO: Dandrieu-6 Suite **4**, La Follète

	[2 ℓ]	[binding end papers, blank]

Provenance: Germany, ca. 1750-1770.

Location: East Berlin; Deutsche Staatsbibliothek, Mus.
   Ms. 30 206.

Description: 179 p.; upright quarto format, 30 x 23.2 cm.
   Modern 3/4 buckram binding, with spine stamping:
   Klavierstücke.

Notation: Keyboard score (5-line staves).   Clefs usually
   F^4, G^2.

Scribe: One unidentified hand.

Summary:
   Composers:
     AGNESI, Maria Teresa (1720-1795)
     d'ANGLEBERT, Jean-Henri (1628-1691): p 40.
     GALUPPI, Baldassare (1706-1785)
     HILLER, Johann Adam (1728-1804)
     ORLANDI
     SCHALE, Christian Friedrich (1713-1800)
     SERINI, Giovanni Batista (ca. 1710-post 1756)
     STĚPÁN, Josef Antonín (1726-1797)
     UMSTATT, Joseph (c. 1762)
     WAGENSEIL, Georg Christoph (1715-1777)
     ZACH, Johann (1699-ca. 1773)
     ZACHARIÄ, Justus Friedrich Wilhelm (1726-1777)
   Contents: Miscellaneous keyboard works.

Inventory of French music:

p 40-44	Variations sur les Folies d'Espagne |par J. Henry Anglebert [d]
	CO: 33-Rés-89ter #21 68-d'Anglebert #49 [copy thereof]
	ED: cf Gilbert p 64, Roesgen-Champion p 93.

16-COSYN

Provenance: London, ca. 1613-1652; French pieces all
1652 (dated ℓ. 20v, "1652" incorporated into heading
of Cosyn's index).

Location: Paris; Bibliothèque nationale, département de
la musique, fonds conservatoire, Réserve 1184, 1185
(olim Conservatoire 18548).

Description: 1 p.ℓ., 21 ℓ [exemplum of Parthenia], 348
p. [ms]; folio format, 29.4 x 19.2 cm. Watermarks:
#34 (Réserve 1184); 84, 85, 90, 91, 102 (Réserve 1185).
Modern re-binding using remnants of contemporary full
leather binding, gilt tooling and gilt design with
initials M.W. [Michael Wise?], 30.2 x 20.3 cm.

Notation (ms only): Keyboard score (two 6-line staves,
4 systems per page, written page by page). Clefs:
$C^{1,3,4,6}$, G^3, $F^{1,2,4,6}$; usually F^4, G^3.

Scribes (ms only): Two main hands. The earlier (A) perhaps that of John Bull, the later (B) that of Benja-
min Cosyn. C is unidentified. B added and replaced
pages, re-copying parts of pieces by A, indicated below with parentheses:
A: #1-7, 10-37, 45-47, 50-65, 67-74, 75A-86.
B: (1), (7), 8-9, (10), 38-44, 48-49, 66-66A, 75,
87-87A, 89-122, index (ℓ. 20v) and numeration
of pieces.
C: 88.

Marginalia: ℓ. 1 (late 18th-century hand?), "This book
[Parthenia] is supposed to have been printed about
the year 1611.- See Hawkins; Hist. of Music, Vol
III p 287-. the MS. at the end [Réserve 1185] was
transcribed about the same period; the compositions

97

of Orlando Gibbons, D^r. Bull, B^n. Cossyn, W^m. Lawes,
Formilos. [in another ink:] By the Initials on the
Cover, M.W., perhaps, it might belong to Michael
Wise [ca. 1648-1687], a composer & one of the Gentle-
men of the Chapel Royal, almone [?] & Master of the
Choristers of St. Pauls: who was in great favour with
Charles II. [in another ink:] Or [smudged and not
continued]." Title page in contemporary hand (18th
century?): "a maid a/playing on /the virginalls
[beside illustration]; 1659 Q^{ry} [beside imprint]."
Miscellaneous letters, including "buttermilk," p. 300.
Beneath original "B.C." in modern pencil, "Query
Ben Cosyn who Fl. about 1600" p. 339. After Cosyn's
index, in a later contemporary hand, a selected
index, drawn from (not in addition to) the main
index, ℓ. 21r.

Summary:
    Composers:
      BULL: # 1-7, 9-30, 31, 33-37B, 45, 47, 50-55, 57-65,
            67-72, 75-86, 93.
      COSYN: #97, 106, 112, 116, 121.
      FORMILOE: #38, 40.
      GIBBONS (Orlando): #8, 32, 48, 88, 91, 104(?), 117, 119
      LA BARRE: #44, cf 66, 87, 87A, 99(?), 100-101, 114.
      LAWES (William): #104.
      TALLIS: #81(?).
      TRESURE: #(44), 89, 101(?).
      YOUNG: #95, 96, 115.

    Contents:
      ℓ. 1-20r Parthenia, exemplar of 2nd ed., ca. 1614.
        20v-21r Index to ms in hand of Cosyn.
      p. 1-348 Pieces grouped by key:
                # 1-3   d
                  4-30   G (also g, C)
                  31-37 a

38-43	F
44-49	d, a, G
50-65	a
66-66A	C
67-73	d
74-80	C
81-86	F
87-87A	a
88-102	d
103-109	a
110-117	C
118-122	a, d, G

Inventory of ms (information from Cosyn's index is given in parentheses):

1 p 1^1-4^1 The Galliard to Dr Bulles Mallankolly
           Pavin [BULL (d)]
           ED: Dart-BII #67b.

2 p 4^2-9^3 Fantasia [BULL (d)]
           ED: Dart-BI #10.

3 p 10^{1-4} Paven (A Prelude) [BULL (d)]
           ED: Dart-BII #69

4 p 11^1-14^3 In Nomine [BULL (G)]
           ED: Dart-BI #38.

5 p 14^4-17^1 Miserere [BULL? (G)]
           ED: Dart-BI #36.

6 p 17^2-25^2 Salutor Mundi Dole [BULL (G)]
           ED: Dart-BI #37.

7 p 25^3-29^3 Miserere |Finis Dr Bull: [G]
           ED: Dart-BI #34.

8 p 30^1-31^4 Allmaine: Or: Gibbons: [G]
           ED: Hendrie #27.

10	p 32^{1-3}	Dorick Musique: /A Prellude[BULL (g)] ED: Dart-BI #59.
9	p 32^4-46^2	vt-re-me-fa-sol-la- [BULL (C)] ED: Dart-BI #18.
11	p 47^1-59^4	(Dr Bulles) Quadrant paven |Variatio eiusdem[G] ED: Dart-BII #127b-c.
12	p 60^1-69^4	Quadrant Galyard [BULL (G)] ED: Dart-BII #127d.
13	p 70^1-74^1	(The Lord Lumnies) Paven ⌊BULL (G)] ED: Dart-BII #129a.
14	p 74^2-77^3	Galyard [BULL (G)] ED: Dart-BII #129b.
15	p 78^1-80^3	(The Trumpitt) Paven [BULL (G)] ED: Dart-BII #128a.
16	p 80^4-82^4	Galyard ⌊BULL (G)] ED: Dart-BII #128b.
17	p 83^1-84^4	paven [BULL (G)] ED: Dart-BII #130a.
18	p 85^1-86^2	Galyard [BULL (G)] ED: Dart-BII #130b.
19	p 86^3-93^4	Regina Galyard |Variatio eiusdem [BULL (G)] ED: Dart-BII #132b-c.
20	p 94^1-97^2	Galyard [BULL (g)] ED: Dart-BII #78.
21	p 97^3-99^3	Galyard [BULL (G)] ED: Dart-BII #133.
22	p 100^1-104^1	Bulls Goodnighte [BULL (G)] ED: Dart-BII #143

23 | p 104^2-109^4 The Kings Hunt [BULL (G)]
ED: Dart-BII #125.

24 | p 110^1-112^3 (Dr Bulles) My Juell [BULL (G)]
ED: Dart-BII #141.

25 | p 113^1-116^1 My Selfe: |variatio [BULL (G)]
ED: Dart-BII #138.

26 | p 116^2-117^2 Almaine [BULL (G)]
ED: Dart-BII #135.

27 | p 117^3-119^3 Almaine fantazia [BULL (G)]
ED: Dart-BII #134.

28 | p 120^1-121^4 Bony Pegg of Ramsey (Bonnie Pegge Ramsie)
[BULL (G)]
ED: Dart-BII #75.

29 | p 122^{1-4} (Dr. Bulles) My Greife:- [G]
ED: Dart-BII #139.

30 | p 123^1-124^1 praeludium:- [BULL (G)]
ED: Dart-BII #117.

30A | p 124^{1-4} Coranto |Finis [numbered:] 75 [G]
ED: Maas #87.

31 | p 125^1-128^4 (Dr Bulles) In Nomine [a]
ED: Dart-BI #42.

32 | p 129^1-133^4 Fantazia: [in another hand:] Orlando
Gibbons Fancy [a]
ED: Hendrie #12.

33 | p 134^1-138^4 In nomine:- /prima pars 12. [BULL (a)]
CO: 16-Cosyn #37B
ED: Dart-BI #20.

34 | p 139^1-143^1 The second way [BULL (a)]
ED: Dart-BI #21.

34A | p 143^2-146^3 Tertia Ps [BULL (a)]
ED: Dart-BI #22.

35 | p 146^4-150^4 In Noīe:- [BULL (a)]
                    ED: Dart-BI #23.

36 | p 151^1-155^4 (Orlando Gibbons) In noīe [BULL (a)]
                    ED: Dart-BI #24.

37 | p 156^1-159^1 Innoīe [BULL (a)]
                    ED: Dart-BI #25.

37A | p 159^2-166^3 In noīe [BULL]
                    ED: Dart-BI #28.

37B | p 166^4-170^4 In Noīe   [BULL (a)]
                    CO: 16-Cosyn #33
                    ED: Dart-BI #20.

38 | p 171^{1-2} Mr Formiloe /Allmaine: |Finis [F]

39 | p 171^{3-4} Coranto Finis [F]

40 | p 172^{1-2} (Serabrand) A Cuntry dance:- Mr Formiloe
                    [F]

41 | p 172^{2-4} Allmaine - an 8 hyer   in $\frac{6}{3}$ base [F]
                    ED: Maas #88.

42 | p 172^4-173^2 Coranto |Finis [F]
                    ED: Maas #89.

43 | p 173^{3-4} Sellabrand. |Finis [F]
                    ED: Maas #90.

---

44 | [LA BARRE: Courante (d)]
   Coranto:- |Finis |Mr Tresure
        p 174^{1-4} $^3[\frac{3}{4}]$|16|16|

   CO: 4-Lynar #65, Courante de La Barre

18-Ch-Ch-1236 #1, ... Jonas Tresure
18-Ch-Ch-1236 #8, Corant La bar
19-Heardson #46, (coranto) Mr Gibbons
27-Gresse #22, Courante
29-Chigi #30, Corante de Monsu della Bara
Oxford-IB
ED: Maas #91; cf Bonfils-58 #4, Curtis-MMN #69,
Lincoln-II p 38, Bonfils-18 #23.

45	p 175^1-177^4	In nole Tertia pars:- [BULL (a)]
		[cf 16-Cosyn #37B]
		ED: Dart-BI #22
46	p 178^1-179^2	Dorick musique /3. parts [a]
47	p 179^3-180^4	Voluntarie. 4.parts:- Dorick musique
		|Finis [BULL (a)]
		ED: Dart-BI #58.
48	p 181$^{1-4}$	Mr Orlando Gibbons /Coranto |Finis [mis-
		numbered:] 45 [crossed out:] |Monsier
		Beare: [d]
		[original p 181 had:] A maske [also listed
		in index]
		ED: Hendrie #39.
49	p 182$^{1-4}$	Allmaine |Finis [G]
		ED: Maas #92.
50	p 183^1-188^2	(Dr Bulles) paven chromatique [BULL (a)]
		ED: Dart-BII #87a.
51	p 188^3-192^4	Galiard [BULL (a)]
		ED: Dart-BII #87b.
52	p 193^1-199^4	(Dr Bulles) paven:- (fantastik) [BULL
		(a)]
		ED: Dart-BII #86a.
53	p 200^1-202^4	Galiard:- [BULL (a)]
		ED: Dart-BII #86b.

54 | p 203^1-208^2 (Dr Bulles) paven [BULL (a)]
           ED: Dart-BII #88a.

55 | p 208^3-211^4 (The Galliard to itt) [BULL (a)]
           ED: Dart-BII #88b.

56 | p 212^1-214^4 Galyard [a]

57 | p 215^1-216^4 (Dr Bulles dancinge) Galyard [BULL (a)]
           ED: Dart-BII #90.

58 | p 217^1-241^3 (Dr Bulles) Wallsingame [a]
           ED: Dart- BII #85.

59 | p 242^1-243^2 Germans Almaine [BULL (a)]
           ED: Dart-BII #94.

60 | p 243^3-244^2 Duch daunce:- [BULL (a)]
           ED: Dart-BII #99.

61 | p 244^3-245^4 Galyard Italiano [BULL (a)]
           ED: Dart-BII #92.

62 | p 246^1-247^1 English toy:- [BULL (a)]
           ED: Dart-BII #96.

63 | p 247^2-248^2 French Almaine:- [BULL (a)]
           ED: Dart-BII #95.

64 | p 248^3-250^1 (The Duke of Brunswike) Almaine:- [BULL
           (a)]
           ED: Dart-BII #93.

65 | p 250^2-251^1 Most sweet, and fayre:- Finis /D^r. Bull [a]
           ED: Dart-BII #97.

66 | p 251^2-252^2 A masque |Finis [C] [original p 251 had:]
           Almaine [which was listed in index as:]
           (Mr Bares Allmaine)
           ED: Maas #93 (A Masque).

66A	p 252$^{3-4}$	When $\overset{e}{y}$ kinge Inioyeth his owne againe:- |Finis [C] ED: Maas #94.
67	p 253^{1}-257^{2}	(Dr Bulles) paven:- [numbered:] 66 [BULL (d)] ED: Dart-BII #66a.
68	p 257^{3}-260^{2}	Galyard:- [BULL (d)] ED: Dart-BII #66b.
69	p 260^{3}-263^{2}	Galyard:- [BULL (d)] ED: Dart-BII #72.
70	p 263^{3}-267^{4}	Why aske ye^{e}:- [BULL (d)] ED: Dart-BII #62.
71	p 268^{1}-271^{4}	Bony sweet Robin:- [BULL (d)] ED: Dart-BII #65.
72	p 272^{1}-273^{1}	What care you:- [BULL (d)] ED: Dart-BII #116.
73	p 273^{2}-274^{4}	praeludium:- [d]
74	p 275^{1}-276^{3}	Galyard:- [C]
75	p 276^{4}-277^{4}	Dalying Almaine:- out of the Lidian musique [BULL (C)] ED: Dart-BII #104.
76	p 278^{1}-280^{1}	Galyard [BULL (C)] ED: Dart-BII #103.
77	p 280^{2}-281^{3}	French Currante:- [BULL (C)] ED: Dart-BII #105.
78	p 282$^{1-4}$	Welch daunce.- [BULL (C)] ED: Dart-BII #107.
79	p 283^{1}-284^{4}	Aurora Lucis rutilat [C] ED: cf Dart-BII p 223.

80 | p 285$^{1-4}$ prima verssus:- [C]
                ED: cf Dart-BII p 223.

81 | p 286$^{1-4}$ 2. versus:- [TALLIS? (C)]
                ED: cf Dart-BII p 223.

82 | p 287^{1}-288^{3} Battle paven:- [BULL (F)]
                ED: Dart-BII #109a.

83 | p 288^{4}-290^{2} Galyard:- [BULL (F)]
                ED: Dart-BII #109b.

84 | p 290^{3}-297^{4} A Battle, and no Battle:- /frigian musique
                [etc, with some descriptive comments
                written in] [BULL (F)]
                ED: Dart-BII #108.

85 | p 298^{1}-299^{3} Almaine Jonicke, and frigian musique:-
                [BULL (F)]
                ED: Dart-BII #110.

86 | p 300$^{1-4}$ Irish toye:- [BULL (F)]
                ED: Dart-BII #112.

87 | [LA BARRE: Allemande (a)]
(Monsier Bares) Allmaine [pasted over a] praeludium
[on the original p 301]
    p 301$^{1-3}$ $^{3}[^{4}_{4}]$ |7|7|

87A [LA BARRE: Courante (a)]
Coranto (to itt) |Finis
   p 301$^{3-4}$ $^{3}[\frac{3}{4}]$ |8|8|

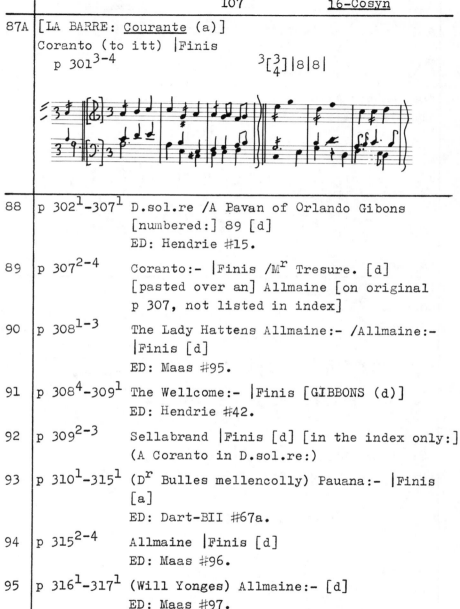

88 | p 302^{1}-307^{1} D.sol.re /A Pavan of Orlando Gibons
                  [numbered:] 89 [d]
                  ED: Hendrie #15.

89 | p 307$^{2-4}$ Coranto:- |Finis /Mr Tresure. [d]
                  [pasted over an] Allmaine [on original
                  p 307, not listed in index]

90 | p 308$^{1-3}$ The Lady Hattens Allmaine:- /Allmaine:-
                  |Finis [d]
                  ED: Maas #95.

91 | p 308^{4}-309^{1} The Wellcome:- |Finis [GIBBONS (d)]
                  ED: Hendrie #42.

92 | p 309$^{2-3}$ Sellabrand |Finis [d] [in the index only:]
                  (A Coranto in D.sol.re:)

93 | p 310^{1}-315^{1} (Dr Bulles mellencolly) Pauana:- |Finis
                  [a]
                  ED: Dart-BII #67a.

94 | p 315$^{2-4}$ Allmaine |Finis [d]
                  ED: Maas #96.

95 | p 316^{1}-317^{1} (Will Yonges) Allmaine:- [d]
                  ED: Maas #97.

96 | p 317^{1}-318^{3} Coranto (to itt) |Finis [YOUNG (d)]
                  ED: Maas #98.

97 | p 318⁴-319³ Sellabrand:- |Finis B.C. [COSYN (d)]
                 ED: Maas #99.

98 | p 319⁴   An Ayre- |Finis [d]

99 | [LA BARRE?: Allemande (d)]
     Allmaine:- |Finis
        p 320¹⁻²   ¢|6|6|

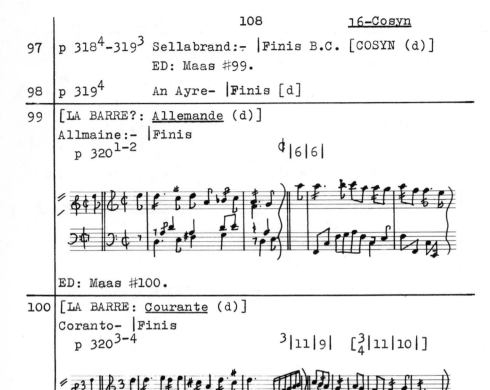

     ED: Maas #100.

100 | [LA BARRE: Courante (d)]
      Coranto- |Finis
         p 320³⁻⁴   ³|11|9| [³₄|11|10|]

      CO: 18-Ch-Ch-1236 #47, Corant Mr Bare
      ED: Maas #101, cf Bonfils-18 p 27.

101 | [LA BARRE or TRESURE?: <u>Sarabande</u> (d)]
Sellabrand:- |Finis
   p 321¹⁻² $^3[\frac{3}{4}]$|8|10|

CO: 18-Ch-Ch-1236 #6, Saraband
    cf 1-Copenhagen-376 #6, Sarabande
    cf 2-Witzendorff #54, Saraband
    cf Drallius #94, Saraband
    cf Eyck-I ℓ 36v, Philis Schoone Harderinne
    cf Oude 731 X 8, Jen ne puis éviter
    cf Kabinet I ℓ 9v, Je ne puis eviter
ED: Maas #102; cf Dickinson #6.

102 | p 321³⁻⁴   Sellabrand:- |Finis [d]
                  CO: cf 5-Munich-1503ℓ #6
                      cf 17-Rogers #19
                      cf 32-Oldham #6
                  ED: Maas #103; cf Cofone #19, Sargent
                      #19.

103 | p 322¹-327⁴ Aire:- Lachrime Pavin:- |Finis [a]
                  ED: Maas #104.

104 | p 328¹-329¹ Will: Lawes:- Allmaine:- |Finis. B:C: [a]
                  ED: Maas #105, Hendrie #34 (as Gibbons).

105 | p 329²⁻⁴   Coranto:- (to itt) [a]
                  ED: Maas #106.

106 | p 330¹⁻⁴   Sellabrand |Finis /B.C. [a]
                  CO: 59a-Handmaide #49
                  ED: Maas #107; cf Dart-HI #49.
107 | p 331¹⁻³   Fuge |Finis [a]
                  ED: Maas #108.

108 | p 332¹⁻⁴   The chessnvtt |Finis [a]
                  ED: Maas #109.

109 | p 333[1-4]   Serabrand |Finis [a]
                    ED: Maas #110.

110 | p 334[1-3]   C. fa. vt /Allmaine [C]
                    ED: Maas #111.

111 | p 334[3]-335[2] Coranto [C]
                    ED: Maas #112.

112 | p 335[2-4]   Serabrand:- |Finis /B.C: [C]
                    CO: 17-Rogers #31
                    ED: Maas #113; cf Cofone #42, Sargent
                        #42.

113 | p 336[1-4]   Allmaine |Finis [C]
                    ED: Maas #114.

---

114 | [LA BARRE: Courante with Double (C)]
     Coranto |Finis
         p 337[1-4] $^3[\frac{3}{4}]$|16|20|

     CO: 17-Rogers #23, Corrant Beare
         17-Rogers #95, [C]orant
         18-Ch-Ch-1236 #31, Corant
         59a-Handmaide #43, Coranto
         Drexel-5609 p 12 & 39 [copz of 17-Rogers]
     ED: Maas #115; cf Cofone #23, 74; Sargent #23, 62;
         Rastall #15, Dart-HI #43.

---

115 | p 338[1-4]   Serabrand |Finis M[r] Yues:- [C]
                    ED: Maas #116.

116 | p 339[1-4]   The skoch covinant:- |Finis B.C. [C]
                    ED: Maas #117.

117 | p 340[1]-341[2] Orlando: Gibbons:- /The Temple Mask:-
                    |Finis [C]
                    ED: Hendrie #45.

118	p 341$^{3-4}$	Allmaine |Finis [a]
119	p 342^{1}-343^{3}	Lincolles Jnne Mask:- Or: Gibb: **ED**: Hendrie #44.
120	p 344^{1}-347^{3}	The Ladies Daughter:- **Finis** [d] ED: Maas #118.
121	p 347$^{3-4}$	Prelludem:- |Finis /Ben: Cosyn:- [d]
122	p 348$^{1-4}$	A Maske:- |Finis (An Allmaine in Gamut:) [G] ED: Maas #119.

Provenance: England, pre 1656, with later additions (dated, hand A, ℓ. i^v, "February ye^e 27: 1656").

Location: London; British Library [British Museum], Department of Manuscripts, Additional mss 10337.

Description: 1 p.ℓ., 132 p.(i.e. 134; 2 p. omitted in numeration; originally 136: 1 ℓ. lacking); folio format, 29 x 18.8 cm. Watermarks #89 and 70 (latter section). Modern (1940) full leather binding, using remnant of contemporary leather binding; cover stamping, "E F" (Elizabeth Fayre, cf "Marginalia"), 29 x 19.7 cm.

Notation: Keyboard score (two 6-line staves, 4-5 systems per page, written page by page). Clefs: $C^{1,2}$, $G^{2,3,4}$, $F^{4,6}$; usually F^4, G^3, duplicated with C clefs.

Scribes: 2-4 hands:
  A: #1-71, except (?) 19.
  B: 72-102 (from the back of the book forward).
  C: 19 (same as A?).
  D: Titles which appear at tops of pieces (same as A?).

Marginalia: Original numeration by pages; modern pencil numeration by leaves, omitting blank leaves (ignored in Inventory below). On ℓ. i^r, the original front cover before binding, many doodles, an incomplete index, the name "Elizabeth Fayre" twice, poetry "Time and Tide /Stayes for none here /I me now and Straye /am gon" and "where love by grace hath .../ posses one the parting kiss ... /deap inpreson" "This is the dart that pearst the hart the /Constant love ... " (6 lines). In hand D, ℓ. 2r, "The names of [crossed out: all] most of these Tunes are /at the

end of each)$_\tau$" On ℓ. iA^r, 3 beginnings of the poem
"Sith hart and break thou must no longer live ..."
in same hand as ℓ. i^r. On ℓ. iA^v, "In Excesse of joy
and payne ..." On p. 1, top, "John Tillett" (later owner?).

Summary:
    Composers:
        BALES: #93.
        BREWER: cf #73-91.
        BYRD: #28.
        CAMPIAN: cf #73-91.
        GIBBONS (Orlando): #2, 4, 47.
        JOHNSON (Robert): #24, cf 47.
        LA BARRE: #21-23, 26, 27, 95.
        LANIER: cf #73-91.
        LAWES (Henry): cf #73-91.
        MERCURE (John): #66, 69.
        PORTER: #72.
        STRENGTHFIELD: #14, 15, 17, 18, 57, 64.
        WILSON: cf #73-91.

    Contents:
        #1-72   Miscellaneous harpsichord pieces in hand
                        A, by Byrd, Gibbons, Johnson, La Barre,
                        Mercure, Porter, Strengthfield and anon.
        73-92   Secular vocal pieces in hand B.

        93-101   Anonymous harpsichord pieces in hand B.

Inventory:
    ℓ i^r [see "marginalia"]
    ℓ i^v Elizabeth Roger's hir- /virginall booke.
                  February ye^e 27: 1656 [followed by a
                  complete index of pieces #1-72]

    p 1-2   [lacking; index shows contents to have
                  been:]

Preludin
An Almaine
Philena
Corrante

1	p 3$^{1-4}$	|St Tho: Fairfax Marche [C] ED: Cofone #1, Sargent #1.
2	p 4$^{1-2}$	Nanns Maske [GIBBONS (d)] ED: Cofone #2, Sargent #2, **Hendrie #41.**
3	p 4$^{3-4}$	Almayne [d] ED: Cofone #3, Sargent #3.
4	p 5$^{1-4}$	The Fairest Nimphes the valleys /or moun- taines ever bred &tc [GIBBONS (a)] ED: Cofone #4, Sargent #4, **Hendrie #43.**
5	p 6$^{1-3}$	The Scots Marche. [F] ED: Cofone #5, Sargent #5.
6	p 7$^{1-3}$	|Prince Ruperts Martch:| [C] ED: Cofone #6, Sargent #6.
7	p 8$^{1-3}$	|One of y^e symphonies[C] ED: Cofone #7, Sargent #7.
8	p 9$^{1-3}$	|One of y^e Symphonies [C] ED: Cofone #8, Sargent #8.
9	p 10$^{1-2}$	|Selebrand [g] ED: Cofone #9, Sargent #9.
10	p 10$^{3-4}$	|When the King enjoyes /his owne againe ED: Cofone #10, Sargent #10.
11	p 11$^{1-3}$	|Almaygen [g] ED: Cofone #11, Sargent #11.
12	p 12$^{1-3}$	|A Trumpett tune.[D] ED: Cofone #12, Sargent #12.

13	p 13[1]	|Essex /Last /goodnight [C] ED: Cofone #13, Sargent #13.
14	p 13[2-4]	|Almaygne per /Tho: Strengthfeild: [a] ED: Cofone #14, Sargent #14.
15	p 14[1-2]	|The Corrant to y[e] last Alm[ayne] /per Tho: Strengthfeild: [a] ED: Cofone #15, Sargent #15.
16	p 14[3-4]	|Ruperts Retraite.| [C] **ED:** Cofone #16, Sargent #16.
17	p 15[1-4]	|Almaygne per /Tho: Strenthfeild [a] ED: Cofone #17, Sargent #17.
18	p 16[1-2]	|Corrant to y[e] /former Alma[ygne] [a]/per /Tho: Strengthfeild [C] ED: Cofone #18, Sargent #18.

19	p 16[3-4]	[Sarabande (d)] [not listed in index]
		CO: cf 5-Munich-1503ℓ #6
		    cf 16-Cosyn #102
		    cf 32-Oldham #6
		ED: Cofone #19, Sargent #19; cf Maas
		    #103.

20	p 17[1-4]	The Nightingale |The Nightingale [C] ED: Cofone #20, Sargent #20.

21 [LA BARRE: _Courante_ (d)]
\|Corrant /Beare
  p 18[1-2]

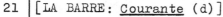

CO: 18-Ch-Ch-1236 #33, Courant
    Drexel-5609 p 11 [copy of 17-Rogers #21]
ED: Cofone #21, Sargent #21.

22 | [LA BARRE: <u>Sarabande</u> (d)]
|Selebrand /Beare .|
    p 18$^{3-4}$

$\mathrm{C}\begin{bmatrix}6\\3\end{bmatrix}$ $\begin{bmatrix}4\\3\end{bmatrix}$ |4|4|

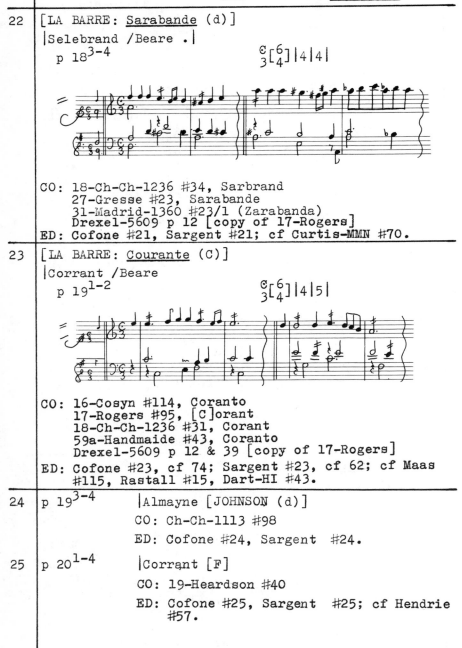

CO: 18-Ch-Ch-1236 #34, Sarbrand
    27-Gresse #23, Sarabande
    31-Madrid-1360 #23/1 (Zarabanda)
    Drexel-5609 p 12 [copy of 17-Rogers]
ED: Cofone #21, Sargent #21; cf Curtis-MMN #70.

23 | [LA BARRE: <u>Courante</u> (C)]
|Corrant /Beare
    p 19$^{1-2}$

$\mathrm{C}\begin{bmatrix}6\\3\end{bmatrix}$ |4|5|

CO: 16-Cosyn #114, Coranto
    17-Rogers #95, [C]orant
    18-Ch-Ch-1236 #31, Corant
    59a-Handmaide #43, Coranto
    Drexel-5609 p 12 & 39 [copy of 17-Rogers]
ED: Cofone #23, cf 74; Sargent #23, cf 62; cf Maas
    #115, Rastall #15, Dart-HI #43.

24 | p 19$^{3-4}$ |Almayne [JOHNSON (d)]
         CO: Ch-Ch-1113 #98
         ED: Cofone #24, Sargent #24.

25 | p 20$^{1-4}$ |Corrant [F]
         CO: 19-Heardson #40
         ED: Cofone #25, Sargent #25; cf Hendrie
            #57.

26 | [LA BARRE: <u>Courante</u> (d)]

|Corrant /Beare .|
   p 21[1-2]

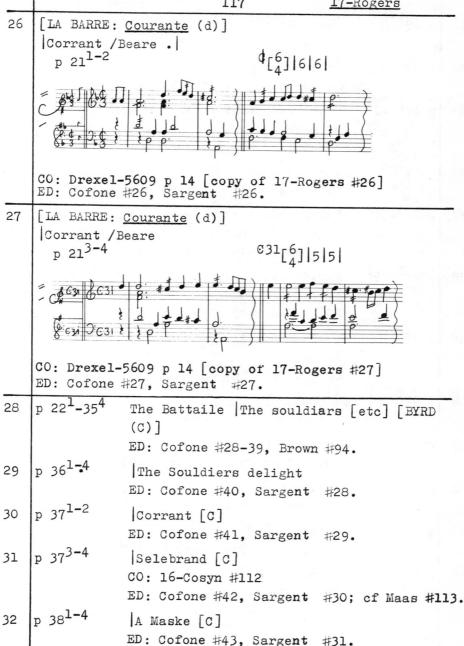

CO: Drexel-5609 p 14 [copy of 17-Rogers #26]
ED: Cofone #26, Sargent #26.

27 | [LA BARRE: <u>Courante</u> (d)]

|Corrant /Beare
   p 21[3-4]

CO: Drexel-5609 p 14 [copy of 17-Rogers #27]
ED: Cofone #27, Sargent #27.

28 | p 22[1]-35[4]   The Battaile |The souldiars [etc] [BYRD
                     (C)]
                     ED: Cofone #28-39, Brown #94.

29 | p 36[1-4] |The Souldiers delight
                  ED: Cofone #40, Sargent #28.

30 | p 37[1-2] |Corrant [C]
                  ED: Cofone #41, Sargent #29.

31 | p 37[3-4] |Selebrand [C]
                  CO: 16-Cosyn #112
                  ED: Cofone #42, Sargent #30; cf Maas #113.

32 | p 38[1-4] |A Maske [C]
                  ED: Cofone #43, Sargent #31.

33 | p 39$^{1-2}$ | |Corrant [C]
ED: Cofone #44, Sargent #32.

34 | p 39$^{3-4}$ | |Selebrand [C]
ED: Cofone #45, Sargent #33.

35 | p 40^{1}-41^{1} | [untitled; text between staves:] Ly still
my **Deare** ...
ED: Cofone #46, Sargent #34.

36 | p 41$^{2-4}$ | |The Chesnut [d]
ED: Cofone #47, Sargent #35.

37 | p 42^{1}-43^{2} | [untitled; text between staves:] Cloris
sight and songe, & wept ...
ED: Cofone #48, Sargent #36.

38 | p 44^{1}-45^{1} | [untitled; text between staves:] Now y^{e}
springe is comne ...
ED: Cofone #49, Sargent #37.

39 | p 45$^{2-4}$ | [untitled; text between staves:] O Jesu
meeke ...
ED: Cofone #50, Sargent #38.

40 | p 46$^{1-3}$ | |Corrant [C]
ED: Cofone #51, Sargent #39.

41 | p 47$^{1-3}$ | |Corrant [G]
ED: Cofone #52, Sargent #40.

42 | p 48$^{1-4}$ | |Maske [G]
ED: Cofone #53, Sargent #41.

43 | p 49$^{1-3}$ | |Corrant [d]
ED: Cofone #54, Sargent #42.

44 | p 50$^{1-4}$ | |Almaygne [D]
CO: 17-Rogers #61 [C]
ED: Cofone #55, Sargent #43; cf Cofone
#83, Sargent #69.

45	p 51$^{1-4}$	|Lupus Ayre [A] ED: Cofone #56, Sargent #44.
46	p 52^{1}-53^{1}	[untitled; text between staves:] Could thine incomparable eye ... ED: Cofone #57, Sargent #45.
	p 53^{2}	[first few notes of a piece]
47	p 54^{1}-56^{3}	|Allmaygne: Mr Johnson [GIBBONS (G)] ED: Cofone #58, Sargent #46, Hendrie #27.
48	p 57$^{1-4}$	|Mock-Nightingale .| [d] ED: Cofone #59, Sargent #47.
49	p 58$^{1-4}$	|What if the King /should come to y^{e} City ED: Cofone #60, Sargent #48.
50	p 59$^{1-4}$	|The Kings Complaint [d] ED: Cofone #61, Sargent #49.
51	p 60$^{1-2}$	|Allmaygne [d] ED: Cofone #62, Sargent #50.
52	p 60$^{3-4}$	|Corrant [d] ED: Cofone #63, Sargent #51.
53	p 61$^{1-2}$	|Selebrand [d] ED: Cofone #64, Sargent #52.
	p 61^{4}	[see p 67A]
54	p 62$^{1-3}$	|My Delyght [d] ED: Cofone #65, Sargent #53.
	p 63-75	[see p 54A-65A]
55	p 76^{1}-77^{3}	|A horn/pipe [G] ED: Cofone #77, Sargent #63.
	p 78-79	[blank, ruled]
56	p 80$^{1-4}$	|Almaygne [G] ED: Cofone #78, Sargent #64.

57 | p 81$^{1-2}$ | |Corrant per /Tho: Strengthfeild [G]
ED: Sargent #65, Cofone #79.

58 | p 81$^{3-4}$ | |Selebrand [G]
ED: Cofone #80, Sargent #66.

[#59-61: written upside down, but in hand A]

59 | p 82$^{1-3}$ | |Allmain [C]
ED: Cofone #81, Sargent #67.

60 | p 82$^{4-5}$ | |Corant [incomplete (C)]
ED: Cofone #82, Sargent #68.

61 | p 83$^{1-4}$ | |Allmaygne [C]
CO: 17-Rogers #44 [D]
ED: Cofone #83, Sargent #69; cf Cofone
      #55, Sargent #43.

62 | p 84$^{1-4}$ | [untitled; text between staves:] I wish
noe more thou shouldst Love mee...
ED: Cofone #84, Sargent #70.

63 | p 85$^{1-2}$ | [untitled (a)]
ED: Cofone #85, Sargent #71.

64 | p 85$^{3-5}$ | |Selebrand [with Double] T S [STRENGTH-
FIELD (a)]
ED: Cofone #86, Sargent #72.

65 | p 86$^{1-4}$ | |Love is strange [C]
ED: Cofone #87, Sargent #73.

66 | p 87$^{1-5}$ | Almaygne /Mercure [a]
CO: 18-Ch-Ch-1236 #44
ED: Cofone #88, Sargent #74; cf Rollin p 74.

67 | p 88$^{1-4}$ | The Glory of the North |Glory of y^e North
ED: Cofone #89, Sargent #75.

68 | p 89$^{1-3}$ | (Almaine) [d]
ED: Cofone #90, Sargent #76.

69	p 89$^{4-5}$	[Sarabande] $\natural$ Merceur: [a] CO: 18-Ch-Ch-1236 #46 ED: Cofone #91, Sargent #77; cf Rollin p 92.
70	p 90$^{1-3}$	|Corrant [G]. ED: Cofone #92, Sargent #78.
71	p 90$^{4-5}$	|Corrant .| [G] ED: Cofone #93, Sargent #79.
72	p 91$^{1-3}$	|Phill: Porters Lamentation [G] ED: Cofone #94, Sargent #80.
	p 92-132	[see ℓ iA-p 37A]
		[from the back of the book forward:]
	ℓ iA^{r}	[see "marginalia"]
	ℓ iA^{v}	[see "marginalia"; also an index in the same hand as ℓ i^{r}:] Vocal Lessons [listing contents for p 1A-24A]
73- 91	p 1A-27A	[18 sacred and secular vocal pieces, melody and bass, texts between staves, with additional verses of texts following. BREWER, CAMPIAN, LANIER, LAWES, WILSON, ANON] ED: Cofone #95-112.
	p 28A-37A	[blank, ruled]
	p 38A-53A	[see p 76-91]
92- 93	p 54A-57A	[2 vocal pieces, the second by BALES] ED: Cofone #75-76.
	p 58A	[blank, ruled]
	p 59A-60A	[blank, unruled]
94	p 60A$^{1-2}$	|The faithfull/Brothers [G] ED: Cofone #73, Sargent #61.

95 | [LA BARRE: <u>Courante</u> (C)]
| A [C]orant
| p 60A³⁻⁴ $\frac{C}{3}|7|10|$ [$\frac{3}{4}$]$|8|10|$]

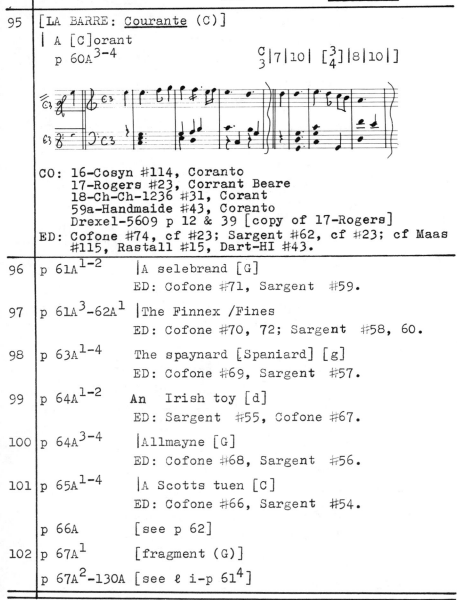

CO: 16-Cosyn #114, Coranto
    17-Rogers #23, Corrant Beare
    18-Ch-Ch-1236 #31, Corant
    59a-Handmaide #43, Coranto
    Drexel-5609 p 12 & 39 [copy of 17-Rogers]
ED: Cofone #74, cf #23; Sargent #62, cf #23; cf Maas
    #115, Rastall #15, Dart-HI #43.

96 | p 61A$^{1-2}$ |A selebrand [G]
                           ED: Cofone #71, Sargent #59.

97 | p 61A^{3}-62A^{1} |The Finnex /Fines
                           ED: Cofone #70, 72; Sargent #58, 60.

98 | p 63A$^{1-4}$ The spaynard [Speniard] [g]
                           ED: Cofone #69, Sargent #57.

99 | p 64A$^{1-2}$ An Irish toy [d]
                           ED: Sargent #55, Cofone #67.

100 | p 64A$^{3-4}$ |Allmayne [G]
                           ED: Cofone #68, Sargent #56.

101 | p 65A$^{1-4}$ |A Scotts tuen [C]
                           ED: Cofone #66, Sargent #54.

    | p 66A   [see p 62]

102 | p 67A^{1} [fragment (G)]
    | p 67A^{2}-130A [see ℓ i-p 61^{4}]

18-CH-CH-1236

Provenance: Oxford, ca. 1650-1674.

Location: Oxford; Christ Church College Library, Mus. Ms. 1236.

Description: 124 ℓ. (irregularly numbered by ℓ. and p. from both ends; originally 144: 16 ℓ. torn out); 19 quires (A^2, B^5, C-D^8, E^7, F-N^8, O^0, P-Q^7, R^8, S^4); oblong quarto format, 16.7 x 22.8 cm.(trimmed). Watermark #101. Original full leather, gilt-tooled binding, sprinkled edges, 17.5 x 23.5 cm.

Notation: Keyboard score (two 6-line staves, 3 systems per page, written page by page). Clefs: F^4, G^3.

Scribe: William Ellis (ca. 1620-1674).

Marginalia: Original numeration by pages to p. 34; modern numeration by leaves following; modern numeration by leaves from the back of the book. Two modern ℓ. pasted into front with incorrect index by Alays Hiff, 1917, with additions.

Summary:
Composers:

    BRYNE: #12.
    CHAMBONNIÈRES: #3.
    COLEMAN (Mark): #26.
    DUFAUT: #43.
    ELLIS: #36, 49-51, 68-75, 78, 81.
    FERRABOSCO (John): #28-30.
    LA BARRE: #1, 6(?), 8, 9, 31, 32(?), 33, 34, 47.
    LAWES (William): #80.
    LOOSEMORE: #14.
    MERCURE (John): #44-46.

PRICE (Robert): #76.
ROBERTS (John): #22, 23.
ROGERS: #35, 37-42, 48.
TRESURE: cf #1, 2, 2A, 4, 5, 6(?).

Contents: Miscellaneous harpsichord pieces, some
   in in suites.

<u>Inventory</u> from original front of book:

ℓ i	[blank, unruled]	
	[1 ℓ torn out]	
ℓ ii	[blank, unruled]	
p 1-2	[torn out]	

1 [**LA BARRE**: <u>Courante</u> (d)]
   [beginning lacking] ... Jonas Tresure
      p 3$^{1-3}$ 5|8|7| [$\frac{3}{4}$...6|8|8|]

CO: 4-Lynar #65, Courante de La Barre
    16-Cosyn #44, Coranto:- Mr Tresure
    18-Ch-Ch-1236 #8, Corant La bar
    19-Heardson #46, (coranto) Mr Gibbons
    27-Gresse #22, Courante
    29-Chigi #30, Corante de Monsu della Bara
    Oxford-IB

ED: Bonfils-58 #4; cf Maas #91, Curtis-MMN #69,
    Lincoln-II p 38, Bonfils-18 #23.

2   p 4$^{1-3}$ Courant. Jonas Tresure.[G]

2A p 5$^{1-3}$ Courant.variola |Jo. Tresure.[not Double
                          f #2 (G)]

3 | [CHAMBONNIÈRES: <u>Courante</u> (d)]

Corant |Mr Sambonier

  p 6^{1-3} $\frac{3}{1}$|13|17| [$\frac{3}{4}$|14|18|]

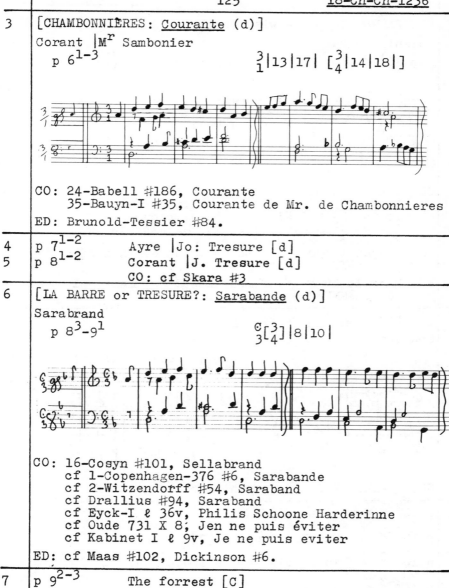

CO: 24-Babell #186, Courante
    35-Bauyn-I #35, Courante de Mr. de Chambonnieres

ED: Brunold-Tessier #84.

---

4 | p 7^{1-2}   Ayre |Jo: Tresure [d]
5 | p 8^{1-2}   Corant |J. Tresure [d]
  | CO: cf Skara #3

---

6 | [LA BARRE or TRESURE?: <u>Sarabande</u> (d)]

Sarabrand
  p 8^{3}-9^{1} $\substack{C\\3}$[$\frac{3}{4}$]|8|10|

CO: 16-Cosyn #101, Sellabrand
    cf 1-Copenhagen-376 #6, Sarabande
    cf 2-Witzendorff #54, Saraband
    cf Drallius #94, Saraband
    cf Eyck-I ℓ 36v, Philis Schoone Harderinne
    cf Oude 731 X 8; Jen ne puis éviter
    cf Kabinet I ℓ 9v, Je ne puis eviter

ED: cf Maas #102, Dickinson #6.

---

7 | p 9^{2-3}   The forrest [C]

8 | [LA BARRE: <u>Courante</u> with <u>Double</u> (d)]

Corant.|La bar

p 10$^{1-3}$ $\mathbf{C \atop 3}$|7|6|7|6| [$\mathbf{3 \atop 4}$|8|8|8|8|]

CO: 4-Lynar #65, Courante de La Barre
    16-Cosyn #44, Coranto:- Mr Tresure
    18-Ch-Ch-1236 #1, ... Jonas Tresure
    19-Heardson #46, (coranto) Mr Gibbons
    27-Gresse #22, Courante
    29-Chigi #30, Corante de Monsu della Bara
    Oxford-IB

ED: Bonfils-18 #23; cf Bonfils-58 #4, Maas #91,
    Curtis-MMN #69, Lincoln-II p 38.

9 | [LA BARRE: <u>Courante</u> with <u>Double</u> (d)]

Courant

p 11^{1}-12^{2} $\mathbf{C \atop 3}$|11|11|11|11| [$\mathbf{3 \atop 4}$|12| x 4]

CO: 19-Heardson #64, Corant Labar:

10 | p 12$^{2-3}$ Almaine [C]

11 | p 13$^{1-3}$ The Nightingale [C]

12 | p 14$^{1-2}$ **Tole Tole |Bryan finis [G]**

13 | p 14$^{2-3}$ A Coranto |finis [d]

14 | p 15$^{1-3}$ Courant. |Mr Loosemore [C]

15 | p 16^{1}-17^{3} An Almaine.[a]

16	p 18[1-3]	Corant.[a]
17	p 19[1-2]	Sarabrand |finis [a]
18	p 20[1]-21[3]	Almaine [d]
19	p 22[1-3]	Corant.[d]

20 | [Sarabande with Double (d)]

Sarabrand. |finis

p 22[3]-23[3] |8|8|7|7| [$\frac{3}{4}$|8|8|8|8|]

CO: 6-Munich-1511e #10, Sarrabande
    22a-Roper #56, Sarabande.
    cf 22a-Roper #56a, double

21	p 24[1-3]	An Ayre |finis [d]
22	p 25[1-3]	[untitled (d)] |M[r] Roberts
23	p 26[1]-27[3]	Coranto |Mr Roberts. [d]
24	p 28[1]-29[3]	[untitled (a)]
25	p 30[1-3]	Corant.|None [G]
26	p 31[1-3]	Corant.|Mark Coleman.,[C]
27	p 32[1-3]	Almonde. [C]
28	p 33[1-3]	Almond |John Ferabosco [D]
29	p 34[1-3]	Corant |Jo: Fer: [D]
		[original pagination stops here]
30	ℓ 34r[1-3]	Sarabrand |finis John Ferabosco [D]

31 | [LA BARRE: <u>Courante</u> (C)]

Corant
  ℓ 34v[1-3]

$\frac{C}{3}$|7|9| [$\frac{3}{4}$|8|10|]

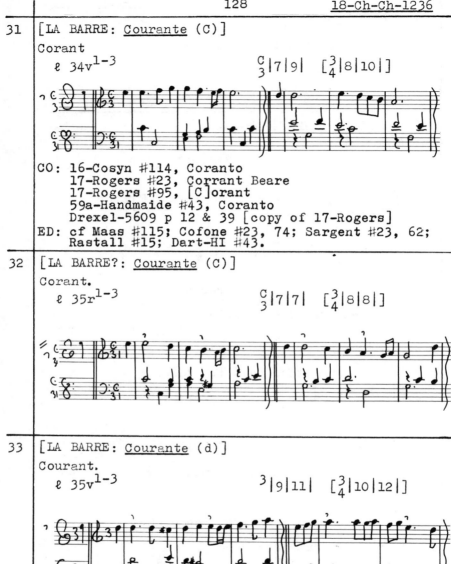

CO: 16-Cosyn #114, Coranto
    17-Rogers #23, Corrant Beare
    17-Rogers #95, [C]orant
    59a-Handmaide #43, Coranto
    Drexel-5609 p 12 & 39 [copy of 17-Rogers]
ED: cf Maas #115; Cofone #23, 74; Sargent #23, 62;
    Rastall #15; Dart-HI #43.

32 | [LA BARRE?: <u>Courante</u> (C)]

Corant.
  ℓ 35r[1-3]

$\frac{C}{3}$|7|7| [$\frac{3}{4}$|8|8|]

33 | [LA BARRE: <u>Courante</u> (d)]

Courant.
  ℓ 35v[1-3]

^{3}|9|11| [$\frac{3}{4}$|10|12|]

CO: 17-Rogers #21, Corrant Beare
    Drexel-5609 p 11 [copy of 17-Rogers #21
ED: cf Cofone #21, Sargent #21.

34 | [LA BARRE: <u>Sarabande</u> (d)]
Sarabrand
   ℓ 36r[1-3]

$^3[^3_4]|8|8|$

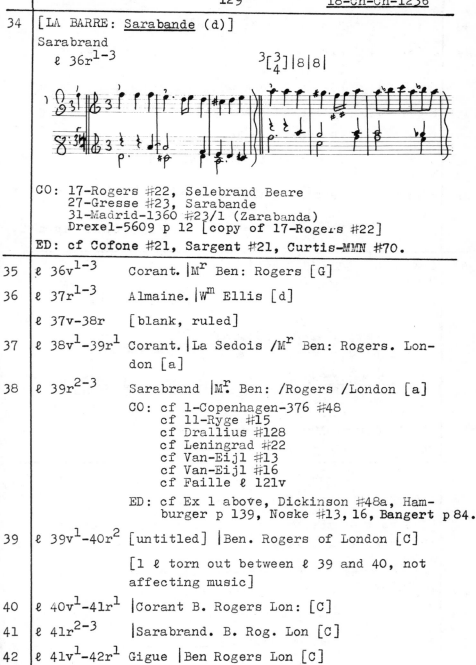

CO: 17-Rogers #22, Selebrand Beare
    27-Gresse #23, Sarabande
    31-Madrid-1360 #23/1 (Zarabanda)
    Drexel-5609 p 12 [copy of 17-Rogers #22]
ED: cf **Cofone** #21, **Sargent** #21, **Curtis-MMN** #70.

---

35 | ℓ 36v[1-3]   Corant. |M[r] Ben: Rogers [G]

36 | ℓ 37r[1-3]   Almaine. |W[m] Ellis [d]

   ℓ 37v-38r   [blank, ruled]

37 | ℓ 38v[1]-39r[1] Corant. |La Sedois /M[r] Ben: Rogers. London [a]

38 | ℓ 39r[2-3]   Sarabrand |M[r]. Ben: /Rogers /London [a]
                     CO: cf 1-Copenhagen-376 #48
                         cf 11-Ryge #15
                         cf Drallius #128
                         cf Leningrad #22
                         cf Van-Eijl #13
                         cf Van-Eijl #16
                         cf Faille ℓ 121v

                     ED: cf Ex 1 above, Dickinson #48a, Hamburger p 139, Noske #13, 16, **Bangert** p 84.

39 | ℓ 39v[1]-40r[2] [untitled] |Ben. Rogers of London [C]

                   [1 ℓ torn out between ℓ 39 and 40, not affecting music]

40 | ℓ 40v[1]-41r[1] |Corant B. Rogers Lon: [C]

41 | ℓ 41r[2-3] |Sarabrand. B. Rog. Lon [C]

42 | ℓ 41v[1]-42r[1] Gigue |Ben Rogers Lon [C]

43 | ℓ 42v[1]-43r[1] Corant |Du fault [e]

44 | ℓ 43v[1]-44r[3] Almaine |finis Almaine by Mercure.
      CO: 17-Rogers #66
      ED: cf Cofone #88, Sargent #74, Rollin p.74.

45 | ℓ 44v[1]-45r[1] |Mercure/Corant.[a]

      ED: Rollin p 108.

      Turn over to y[e] Sarabrand.

46 | ℓ 45v[1]-46r[1] Sarabrand |Mercure.[a]
      CO: 17-Rogers #69
      ED: cf Cofone #91, Sargent #76, **Rollin p 92.**

47 | [LA BARRE: _Courante_ (d)]
    Corant. |M[r] Bare.
       ℓ 46r[2-3] $^C_3$|8|6| [$^6_4$|5|5|]

    CO: 16-Cosyn #100, Coranto
    ED: Bonfils-18 p 27; cf Maas #101.

   | ℓ 46v-50r   [blank, ruled]
48 | ℓ 50v[1]-51r[1] Ayre |Ben Rogers, London [C]

    [The rest of the book is blank, ruled, except for
    the other end, ℓ 1A-19A:]

    | ℓ i-iv   [blank, unruled]
49 | ℓ 1Ar[1-2]   Almain |W Ellis [d]
50 | ℓ 1Ar[3]   Sarabrand |W Ellis [C]
51 | ℓ 1Av[1-2]   The Royallist |Willm Ellis [a]

52	ℓ 1Av^3	Madganacru [?] [G]
53	ℓ 2Ar$^{1-2}$	|Midsomer. [g]
54	ℓ 2Ar^3-v^3	The parson of y^e Parrish
55	ℓ 3Ar$^{1-3}$	Pembrook Colledge [a]
56	ℓ 3Av$^{1-2}$	Th. Capp of Maintainant [d]
57	ℓ 3Av^3-4Ar^1	A Sarabrand [F]
58	ℓ 4Ar$^{2-3}$	The Old man [a]
59	ℓ 4Av$^{1-2}$	A Pretty fancy [G]
60	ℓ 4Av^3-5Ar^3	The Picalominas March.[C]
61	ℓ 5Av$^{1-3}$	Corant [d]
62	ℓ 6Ar$^{1-2}$	A hedge or a Haycock [d]
63	ℓ 6Ar$^{2-3}$	A health in Canary [a]
64	ℓ 6Av$^{1-3}$	A lute lesson [C]
65	ℓ 7Ar$^{1-3}$	Corant. [D]
66	ℓ 7Av$^{1-3}$	|A Mask. [d]
67	ℓ 8Ar$^{1-3}$	A Mayds delight [G]
68	ℓ 9Av$^{1-3}$	Almaine |W: Ellis [d]
	ℓ 9Ar^1	[fragment (d)]
69	ℓ 9Av$^{1-3}$	Corant.|W: Ellis [d]
70	ℓ 10Ar$^{1-3}$	Corant.|W^m. Ellis [d]
71	ℓ 10Av^1-11Ar^1	Almaine. |W^m. Ellis [A]
72	ℓ 11Av$^{1-3}$	Corant |Will Ellis [F]
		[1 ℓ lacking]
	ℓ 12Ar	[blank, ruled]

73	ℓ 12Av^1- 13Ar^3	Bow Bells.set to y^e Virginall by W Ellis [C] ED: cf Dart-HI #30.
74	ℓ 13Av^1- 14Ar^1	Almond Mariae |W: Ellis [d]
75	ℓ 14Ar$^{2-3}$	Corant.|W: Ellis [d]
	ℓ 14Av	[blank, ruled]
76	ℓ 15Ar$^{1-2}$	Faire I would |Rob Price.[a]
77	ℓ 15Ar^3	The King's March.[F]
78	ℓ 15Av^1- 16Ar^2	Moulin's Sarabrand Set by Wi H Ellis [d]
79	ℓ 16Av$^{1-3}$	Vulcan e Venus [G]
80	ℓ 17Ar$^{1-3}$	Th: Goldon groue [LAWES (a)] ED: cf Dart-HI #45.
80A	ℓ 17Av$^{1-2}$	The Corant to y^e Golden Groue Corant [a]
80b	ℓ 17Av^3- 18Ar^1	The Contry dauce [a]
81	ℓ 18Ar$^{2-3}$	Molin's Corant. y^e Sarabrand 2 leaves Back- wards. [cf #78] [ELLIS (d)]
82	ℓ 18Av$^{1-2}$	Thomas yo^u Canott [G]
83	ℓ 18Av^3	Sarabrand [d]
84	ℓ 19Ar$^{1-2}$	The Irish Hay [G]
85	ℓ 19Ar$^{2-3}$	An Irish Jigg [F]
		[The rest of the book is blank, ruled, except for p 1-48 (see above).]

19-HEARDSON

Provenance: England, ca. 1664?

Location: New York City; The New York Public Library, Library and Museum of the Performing Arts, Research Division, Ms. Drexel 5611.

Description: 4 p.ℓ., 161 p. (i.e. 160: 124 omitted in numeration), 2 ℓ.; folio format, 28 x 18.5 cm. Watermarks #51, 71-72, 86-88. Contemporary full leather binding (tracing #107), gilt tooling, re-backed with binder's title on spine: Drexel 5611 Virginal Music MS English 17th Century, 29 x 19.5 cm.

Notation: Keyboard score (two 6-line staves, 4 systems per page, written page by page). Clefs: $F^{3,4,6}$, G^3, $C^{1,2,3}$; usually G^3, F^4.

Scribes: 2-3 hands which are difficult to differentiate:
A: #1-77, 79-82 (Thomas Heardson? fl. 1640-1679)
B: 78 (same as A?)
C: 88-90 and attributions of 84-85 (probably not Albertus Bryne)

Marginalia: Original numeration by pages, with later numbers from p. 126 correcting the original omission of p. 124 (Inventory below maintains original numeration). Doodles and marks on final end papers, including, "TAP" (monogram?) and "Danby P^h Brockham."

Summary:
Composers:
BRYNE: #81-90.
BULL: cf #66-67.
COBB: #49-54
COSYN: #74, 76.
FACY: #5, 6, 11-14, 28, 29, 31, 35, 70.

GIBBONS (Christopher): #38.

GIBBONS (Orlando): #40, 47, 48, 66-68.

GIBBS: #62.

HEARDSON: #1-2, 8, 15-16, 25-27, 30, 36-37, 39, 71.

LA BARRE: #46, 64, 65(?), 69(?).

LAWES (Henry): #75.

LOCKE: #78-80.

MERCURE: #41-45.

PHILIPS: #77.

ROBERTS (John): #3, 4, 7, 17-24.

ROGERS: #32-34.

TOMKINS: #55, 56.

TRESURE: #9-10, 57-63, 65(?), 69(?), 72-73.

Contents: Harpsichord pieces, generally grouped by key:

#1- 4 (G)	46-51 (d)
5-22 (d/D)	52-62 (a/d/)
23-34 (a)	63-64 (d)
35-38 (c/C/a)	65-77 (miscellaneous)
39-40 (F)	78-84 (D)
41 (d)	85-87 (a)
42-45 (a)	88-90 (d)

Inventory:

ℓ i^r   [blank, unruled]

ℓ i^v   [blank, unruled, but with portrait
            stubbed; engraved caption:] Christopher
            Gibbons /Mus. Doct. Oxon: MDCLXIV [1664]
            /From an original Painting in the Music-
            School, Oxford.

ℓ ii^r-iv^r [index by key, with headings (pieces 1-
            -77; 78-79 as later additions):] Key
            |Authurs |Lessons | Page [The index en-
            tries agree with the titles within the
            ms unless otherwise noted in parentheses

in the specific entries below.]

	ℓ iv^v	[blank, unruled]
1	p 1$^{1-4}$	Allmaine |Tho: Heardson:/ [G]
2	p 2$^{1-4}$	[untitled (G)] |T: H:
3	p 3$^{1-4}$	(Allmaine) M^r Jo: Roberts:/ [G]
4	p 4^1-5^1	(Allmaine) M^r. Roberts [G]
5	p 6^1-7^4	Hugh: Facy: |Voluntary [d]
6	p 8^1-9^4	Ave maris stella |M^r. Facy: [d]
	p 10	[blank, ruled]
7	p 11$^{1-4}$	Allmaine |M^r. Roberts:/ [D]
8	p 12$^{1-3}$	Allmaine |Tho: Heardson [D]
9	p 13$^{1-4}$	(Tresor) Corant [D]
10	p 14$^{1-2}$	(Tresor 2 Corant) Tresor: [D]
11	p 15^1-16^3	A Galliard |M^r. Facy: [d]
12	p 17$^{1-4}$	(1: a Toy) Mr Facy: [d]
13	p 18$^{1-3}$	(2: a Toy) M^r. Facy: [d]
	p 19	[blank, ruled]
14	p 20^1-21^4	(Lesson & hand) Mr Facy:/ [d]
	p 22·	[blank, ruled]
15	p 23$^{1-3}$	Allmaine |Tho: Heardson [d]
16	p 24$^{1-4}$	Corant:/ |Tho: Heardson:/ [d]
17	p 25$^{1-5}$	(Allmaine: division) M^r. Jo: Roberts:/ [d]
18	p 26^1-27^4	Allmaine | Mr Roberts: [d]
19	p 28$^{1-4}$	Sarabrand |M^r. Roberts:/ [d]
	p 29	[blank, ruled]
20	p 30^1-31^2	(1. Coranto) M^r. Jo: Roberts [d]

21	p 32^1-33^1	(2. Coranto) M^r Jo: Roberts:[d]
22	p 34^1-35^4	(3:) Corant |M$^r_.$ Roberts: [d]
	p 36-38	[blank, ruled]
23	p 39^1-41^3	(Allmaine division)|M$^r_.$ Roberts: [a]
24	p 42^{1-3}	(Allmaine) M$^r_.$ Roberts [a]
25	p 43^{1-3}	[untitled] Tho: Heardson:/ [a]
26	p 44^{1-4}	Corant |Tho: Heardson:/ [a]
27	p 45^{1-3}	Toy |T: H: [a]
28	p 46^1-47^4	(first) M$^r_.$ Facy [a]
29	p 48^1-49^4	(second) M$^r_.$ Facy [a]
30	p 50^1-51^2	Gerrards Tune |Tho: Heardson: [a]
31	p 52^1-57^1	(third)|M$^r_.$ Facy:[a]
32	p 58^{1-4}	(M$^r_.$ Ben: Rogers) Allmaine [a]
33	p 59^{1-4}	Corant: |M$^r_.$ Ben: Rogers: [a]
34	p 60^{1-4}	Sab: |Mr: Benjamin: Rogers: [a]
	p 61	[blank, ruled]
35	p 62^1-63^3	(a Lesson) M$^r_.$ Facy [c]
36	p 64^{1-4}	Allmaine |Tho: Heardson:/ [C]
37	p 65^{1-3}	Corant |T: H: [C]
38	p 66^1-67^1	(Allmaine)|Chr: Gibbons [a]
	p 68	[blank, ruled]
39	p 69^{1-4}	Corant |Tho: Heardson [F]
40	p 70^{1-4}	(Mr Gibbons Coranto) [F]
		CO: 17-Rogers #25
		ED: cf Hendrie #57, Cofone #25, Sargeant #25.
	p 71	[blank, ruled]
41	p 72^1-73^2	Corant:/ |Mercure: [d]
		ED: Rollin p 109.

| 42 | p 74[1-4] | (Allmaine) [MERCURE (a)] |
| | | ED: Rollin p 110. |

| 43 | p 75[1-4] | (Allmaine) Mercure: [a] |
| | | ED: Rollin p 111. |

| 44 | p 76[1-3] | Coranto: \|Mercure:/ [a] |
| | | ED: cf Rollin p 87. |

| 45 | p 77[1-4] | Sarab: \|Mercure: [a] |
| | | ED: Rollin p 112. |

46　[LA BARRE: <u>Courante</u> with <u>Double</u> (d)]

(1. Coranto) Mr Gibbons:

p 78[1-4]　　　　　　　　^{C}|6|6|5|5|　[$\frac{3}{4}$|8|8|8|8|]

CO: 4-Lynar #65, Courante de La Barre
　　16-Cosyn #44, Coranto Mr Tresure
　　18-Ch-Ch-1236 #1, ... Jonas Tresure
　　18-Ch-Ch-1236 #8, Corant La bar
　　27-Gresse #22, Courante
　　29-Chigi #30, Corante de Monsu·della Bara
　　Oxford-IB

ED: cf Hendrie #54, Maas #91, Bonfils-58 #4, Curtis-
　　MMN #69, Lincoln-II p 38, Bonfils-18 #23.

| 47 | p 79[1-2] | (Orlan: Gibbons 2 Coranto) [d] |
| | | ED: Hendrie #55. |

| 48 | p 80[1-4] | (3 Cor:) Mr Gibbons: [d] |
| | | ED: Hendrie #56. |

| 49 | p 81[1-4] | Allmaine: \|Mr Cobb: [d] |

| 50 | p 82[1-3] | (Allmaine) Mr Cobb:/ [d] |

| 51 | p 83[1-3] | (Mr: Cobb Coranto) [d] |

| 52 | p 84[1-3] | (Allmaine) Mr Cobb [a] |

53	p 85[1-3]	(M[r] Cobb: Allmaine) [a]
	p 86	[blank, ruled]
54	p 87[1-4]	(Corant) M[r] Cobb: [a]
	p 88-89	[blank, ruled]
55	p 90[1]-91[3]	Voluntary: |M[r] Tho: Tomkins:/ [d]
56	p 92[1]-93[4]	Voluntary |M[r] Tho: Tomkins: [a]
57	p 94[1-3]	Corant (Allmaine: Cora:) |M[r] Treser [a]
58	p 95[1-4]	Corant |Treser: [with Double (a)]
59	p 96[1]-97[2]	Corant (division) |Treser: [a]
60	p 98[1-3]	Corant: (Monsier Tresor) [a]
		CO: 24-Babell #161, Courante
61	p 99[1-3]	Corant |Treser [a]
62	p 100[1]-101[1]	Corant |M[r] Gibbs [a]
63	p 102[1-4]	Allmaine |Treser [d]

64 | [LA BARRE: Courante with Double (d)]
Corant |Labar:/
   p 103[1-4]   C[6/4]|6|6|6|6|

CO: 18-Ch-Ch-1236 #9, Courant

65 | [LA BARRE or TRESURE: Courante with Double (G)]
Corant: |Treser:
   p 104^1-105^2 $\mathbf{C}$ |7|8|7|8| [$\frac{3}{4}$|13|16|13|15|]

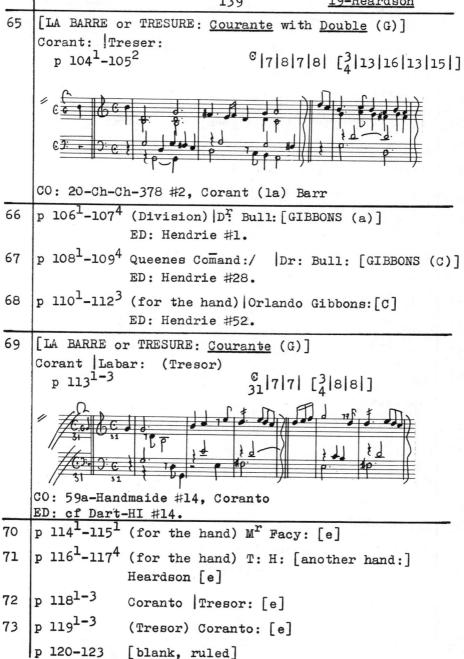

CO: 20-Ch-Ch-378 #2, Corant (la) Barr

66 | p 106^1-107^4 (Division) |D^r. Bull: [GIBBONS (a)]
        ED: Hendrie #1.

67 | p 108^1-109^4 Queenes Comānd:/ |Dr: Bull: [GIBBONS (C)]
        ED: Hendrie #28.

68 | p 110^1-112^3 (for the hand)|Orlando Gibbons:[C]
        ED: Hendrie #52.

69 | [LA BARRE or TRESURE: Courante (G)]
Corant |Labar: (Tresor)
   p 113$^{1-3}$ $\mathbf{C}$ |7|7| [$\frac{3}{4}$|8|8|]
        31

CO: 59a-Handmaide #14, Coranto
ED: cf Dart-HI #14.

70 | p 114^1-115^1 (for the hand) Mr Facy: [e]

71 | p 116^1-117^4 (for the hand) T: H: [another hand:]
        Heardson [e]

72 | p 118$^{1-3}$ Coranto |Tresor: [e]

73 | p 119$^{1-3}$ (Tresor) Coranto: [e]

    p 120-123   [blank, ruled]

[p 124 omitted in numeration]

74	p 125^1-126^4	Corant. |M^r. Benj. Coosens:[G]
	p 127	[blank, ruled]
75	p 128^{1-4}	Coranto: /Mr Lawes:[g]
76	p 129^1-130^3	[untitled]|Mr Benjamin Coosens [g]
77	p 131^1-139^3	Ground /by Phillips: |M^r. Phillipps [a]
78	p 140^{1-3}	[Allemande] Mr Locke:[D]
		ED: Dart-L #33.
79	p 141^{1-3}	Coranto: (Mr Lock) [D]
		ED: Dart-L #34.
80	p 142^{1-4}	Saraband |Mr Lock [D]
		ED: Dart-L #35.
81	p 143^{1-4}	Allmaine: |Mr Albertus Bryan [D]
82	p 144^{1-4}	Coranto |A. B: [D]
83	p 145^{1-3}	Sar: |Finis Mr Bryan:[D]
84	p 145^4-146^4	Allmaine |[in hand C?:] Albert Bryne [D]
	p 147-148	[blank, ruled]
85	p 149^1-150^1	Allmaine |[in hand C?:] Mr Bryne [a]
86	p 151^{1-4}	Corant [BRYNE (a)]
87	p 152^{1-4}	Sara: [BRYNE (a)]
	p 153-154	[blank, ruled]
88	p 155^1-156^4	Allmaine |A B [d]
89	p 157^1-158^2	[untitled] A:B:[d]
90	p 158^3-159^1	[untitled] A^t Bryan:[d]
	p 160-161	[blank, ruled]
		[2 end papers, blank; see "Marginalia"]

Provenance: England (Oxford?), ca. 1675-1710?

Location: Oxford; Christ Church College Library, Mus.
   Ms. 378.

Description: 4 p.ℓ., 28 ℓ.; 8 quires (A^3, B-G^4, H^5);
   oblong quarto format, 13 x 18.2 cm. (trimmed).
   Watermark #39. Contemporary grey paper boards,
   13.4 x 18.5 cm.

Notation: Keyboard score (two 6-line staves, 2 systems
   per page, written page by page). Clefs: F^4, G^3,
   C^{1,4,6}; usually F^4, G^3.

Scribe: One hand, probably Henry Aldrich (1647-1710).

Marginalia: Modern pencil numeration by leaves. Some
   original fingering. Modern table of contents pasted
   p ℓ ii^r.

Summary:
   Composers:
      GIBBONS (Orlando): #1.
      LA BARRE: #2(?), 3.
      TRESURE: #2(?).
   Contents: Miscellaneous pieces, often fragmentary,
      of English fantasy style; titles and composers may
      have been trimmed off.

Inventory:
   ℓ i-iii   [blank, unruled; see also "Marginalia"]
   ℓ iv^r [listing of keys, etc.; upside down]
1 ℓ iv^{v1}-3r^2 [GIBBONS: Prelude (a)]
             ED: Hendrie #1.

2 | [LA BARRE or TRESURE: <u>Courante</u> with <u>Double</u> (G)]
Corant (la[?]) Barr.[title partially trimmed off]
ℓ 3v^1-4v^2 $^C_3$1|13|11|22| [ie $\frac{3}{4}$|14|13|12|13|]

CO: 19-Heardson #65, Corant Treser

3 | [LA BARRE: <u>Allemande</u> (d)]
Almaine (de[?] Labar[?]) [title partially trimmed off]
ℓ 5r^1-8v^1 [$\frac{4}{4}$]|12|11|

CO: 35-Bauyn-III #32, Allemande de M^r De la barre
    35-Bauyn-III #66, Gigue de Mr De La barre
ED: cf Bonfils-18 p 25.

4 | ℓ 9r$^{1-2}$ [untitled (d)]
5 | ℓ 10r^1-v^2 [untitled (G)]
6 | ℓ 11r^1-v^1 [fragment (G)]
7 | ℓ 12r$^{1-2}$ [fragment? (d)]
8 | ℓ 12v$^{1-2}$ [fragment (part of #7?) (d)]
9 | ℓ 13r$^{1-2}$ [untitled (G)]
10 | ℓ 13v^1-14v^1 [untitled (fragment?) (d)]
11 | ℓ 15r^1-16r^2 [fragment (d)]
12 | ℓ 16v^1-17r^1 [untitled (fragment?) (a)]

13	ℓ 17v^1-18r^2	[untitled (fragment?) (C)]
14	ℓ 18v^1-19r^1	[untitled (d)]
15	ℓ 19v^1-20r^2	[untitled (g)]
16	ℓ 20v^1-21r^2	[untitled (d)]
17	ℓ 21v^1-22r^2	[untitled (C)]
	ℓ 22-27	[see ℓ 1A-6A]
		[The following pieces are written from the other end of the book:
	ℓ 1A-3A	[blank]
18	ℓ 4Ar^1	[untitled, 4-part, open score (G)]
19	ℓ 4Av$^{1-2}$	[untitled (F)]
20	ℓ 5Ar$^{1-2}$	[untitled (d)]
21	ℓ 5Ar^2-v^1	[untitled (d)]
22	ℓ 5Av^1-6Ar^2	[untitled (C)]

21-RÉS-1186bis

Provenance: England, post ca. 1680.

Location: Paris; Bibliothèque nationale, département de
   la musique, fonds conservatoire, Réserve 1186bis (1)
   (_olim_ Conservatoire de Musique 18570).

Description: 55 p. and/or ℓ. (i.e. 40 ℓ. numbered by
   pages to 31, then by leaves, plus modern end papers);
   folio format, 32 x 19.3 cm. Bound with another unrelated earlier English ms (Rés. 1186bis [2]) in
   modern half imitation vellum, 33 x 20.5 cm.

Notation: Keyboard score (two 6-line staves, 4 systems
   per page, written page by page). Clefs: F^4, G^3,
   $C^{1,6}$; usually F^4, G^3.

Scribes: Two closely related unidentified hands, the
   second finishing one piece begun by the first.
   A: #1-5[a]
   B: 5[b]-46

Marginalia: Miscellaneous library explanations and an
   index on the modern front end-papers; modern irregular numeration by leaves and pages in ink. Title for
   #4 in modern pencil.

Summary:
   Composers:
   BLOW: #22, 28.
   CROFT: #25, 34, 39, 40-41.
   FARINEL: #16.
   GIBBONS (Orlando): #3, 4.
   KING: #32.
   LEBÈGUE: #12.
   PRICE: #5.
   PURCELL: #29, 30.

Contents: Miscellaneous dance movements, including
   the following suites of 3 or more movements:
   #18-22 (G)
    29-31 (a)
    32-34 (A)
    43-45 (F)

<u>Inventory</u>:

1	p 1^1-2^3	Preludium [G]
2	p 3^{1-3}	[untitled (F)]
3	p 4^{1-4}	[GIBBONS: Fantasia (d)]
		ED: Hendrie #6.
4	p 5^1-9^3	[Prelude] by Orlando Gibbons |Orlando Gibbons [G]
		ED: Hendrie #2
5	p 10^1-17^2	Grou[n]d |M$^r_\cdot$ Price |M$^r_\cdot$ Price [d]
5A	p 17^3-21^4	A $3^d_\cdot$ Way [same ground melody]
6	p 22^1-23^3	[untitled (a)]
7	p 23^4-25^2	Old Symond y^e King [C]
8	p 25^{3-4}	A March [C]
9	p 26^{1-4}	The Old Man's wish [C]
10	p 27^{1-3}	A Ground [F]

11   [<u>Chaconne</u> (C)]

French Lesson: Chacone \|play y^e 1st Strain between/
ev'ry strain
   p 27^{3-4}

12 | [LEBÈGUE: <u>Gavotte</u> (C)]

Gavott
   p 28$^{1-2}$

CO: 10-Schwerin-617 #10, Gavotte
    13-Möllersche, [copy of 64-Lebègue-I #43]
    14-Schwerin-619 #91, Gavotte
    23-Tenbury #6, Gavotte Mr Le Begue
    24-Babell #60, Gavotte de Mr. le Begue
    30-Cecilia ℓ 47r, Gavotte
    35-Bauyn-III #54, (Gavotte) de Mr Lebegue
    36-Parville #68, Gauotte Mr le Begue
    45-Dart #22, [copy of 64-Lebègue-I #43]
    46-Menetou #102, Gavotte
    50-Paignon #11, Balet de Mr lebegue
    64-Lebègue-I #43, Gauotte

ED: cf Dufourcq-L p38, Brunold/Dart-Co #132.

---

13 | p 28^{3}-30^{2} Chacone |1st Strain /againe [C]

14 | p 30^{3}-31v^{3} The Spanish follyes [d]

15 | ℓ 31v^{4}-32v^{4} Ground [G]

16 | ℓ 33r^{1}-36r^{2} M^{r}. Faranella's Ground. D sol re |Finis [d]
               CO: cf RCM, Farranellas Ground

17 | ℓ 36r^{3}-v^{4} Upon y^{e} Bells [C]

18 | ℓ 37r$^{1-4}$ Hunting Allmand in gamut # [G]

19 | ℓ 37v$^{1-2}$ Corant [G]

20 | ℓ 37v^{3}-38r^{1} Saraband [G]

21 | ℓ 38r$^{2-3}$ Gavot [G]

22 | ℓ 38v^{1}-39v^{4} [Morlake's Ground] by D^{r}. Blow [G]
               ED: cf Fuller-Maitland 1:18

23 | ℓ 40r$^{1-3}$ Almand [F]

24	ℓ 40v$^{1-4}$	[Courante (F)]
25	ℓ 41r^{1}-42r^{3}	Ground [CROFT (c)]
		ED: Fuller-Maitland 3:10.
26	ℓ 42v$^{1-4}$	Almand [G]
27	ℓ 43r$^{1-4}$	Sar. Slow [d]
28	ℓ 43v$^{1-4}$	Almand [BLOW (g)]
		CO: Harpsichord-2 #1
29	ℓ 44r$^{1-4}$	Almand [PURCELL (a), Z. 663^{1}]
30	ℓ 44v$^{1-4}$	Corant [PURCELL (a), Z. 663^{2}]
31	ℓ 44v^{4}-45v^{2}	[Ground (a)]
32	ℓ 45v^{3}-46r^{2}	Almand [KING (A)]
		CO: 24-Babell #12
		ED: Fuller-Maitland 6:4.
33	ℓ 46r^{3}-v^{3}	[untitled (A)]
34	ℓ 46v^{4}-47r^{1}	Sar.^{d} [CROFT (A)]
		ED: Fuller-Maitland 3:16.
35	ℓ 47r^{2}-v^{2}	Almand [G]
36	ℓ 47v^{2}-49r^{4}	Ground /1st strain /again ǀEnd with the /first strain... [G]
37	ℓ 49v^{1}-50r^{3}	Slow Almand [d]
38	ℓ 50r^{4}-v^{4}	Corant ǀ1st ǀ2^{d} [d]
38a	ℓ 51r$^{1-4}$	[untitled (G)]
39	ℓ 51v$^{1-4}$.	Gavot ǀfirst strain /again [CROFT (e)]
		ED: Fuller-Maitland 4:17.
40	ℓ 52r$^{1-4}$	Corant [CROFT (E)]
		ED: Fuller-Maitland 3:23.
41	ℓ 52v$^{1-3}$	Sar. Slow ǀ1st strain again ǀEnd with y^{e} first strain [CROFT (E)]
		ED: Fuller-Maitland 3:24.
42	ℓ 52v^{4}-53r^{4}	Jigg [E]
43	ℓ 53v^{1}-54r^{1}	Almand [F]

44	ℓ 54r$^{1-4}$	Corant [F]
45	ℓ 54v$^{1-2}$	Sarabrand [F]
46	ℓ 54v^{3}-55r^{4}	Chacone [a]
	ℓ 55v	[blank, ruled]

[here is bound another unrelated ms of
earlier English music, Rés. 1186bis (2).]

<u>Provenance</u>: England, post ca. 1680.

<u>Location</u>: Oxford; Christ Church College Library, Mus. **Ms.** 1177.

<u>Description</u>: 41 ℓ. (originally 42: 1 ℓ. lacking); folio format, 32.8 x 20.5 (untrimmed). Watermark #20. Original vellum binding (32 x 25 cm) bound into modern full leather, gilt-tooled binding, 33.2 x 22 cm.

<u>Notation</u>: Keyboard score (two 6-line staves, 4-5 systems per page, written page by page). Clefs: F^4, G^3, C^4; usually F^4, G^3.

<u>Scribe</u>: One unidentified English hand.

<u>Marginalia</u>: Pieces numbered in modern ink; leaves numbered in modern pencil; two lists of contents are pasted inside the cover, the more complete by Howard Fergusson, dated 1963, with later additions. On original binding: "Mem -/ [illegible]/Mr Palman /had borrowed y /folio Book of /Lessons & Overturs /of my Fathers /William [?] & others / [crossed out, illegible] /R Coocson [?] Blacket." Inside the back original cover is a (modern?) brief list of contents. Outside the back original cover: "Mr Knight by /Lent Mr Blacket of S^{nt} Johns /the [illegible] book of Harmonia Sacra /Aug 28th 173(3[?])..." On ℓ. 1^r: "E.M. Richard You[ng?]" and in a later hand among miscellaneous writing, "you must send half a bushel of salt ..."

<u>Summary</u>:

Composers:

BLOW: #30-31, 36, 38, 39, 52, 53.
BRYNE: #10, 28a.
DIESSENER: #54.
DRAGHI: #34(?), 41.
GIBBS: #6, 7.
LA BARRE: #2.
LOCKE: #35.
LOWE: #4.
PORTMAN: #1.
PURCELL: #40, 42-45, 47(?), 48, 49, 51.
ROBERTS: #23, 25.

Contents: Miscellaneous dance pieces.

Inventory:

	ℓ 1r	[blank, ruled]
1	ℓ 1v^1-2r^1	Sarabrand|Rich Portman [C]

2 [LA BARRE: <u>Sarabande</u> with <u>Double</u> (e)]

Sarabrand\|La: Barr:
ℓ 2r$^{2-4}$ 　　^{31}|7|8|8|8| [$^3_4$|8|8|8|8|]

ED: Bonfils-18 p 29.

3	ℓ 2v$^{1-3}$	[untitled (G)]
4	ℓ 3r$^{1-2}$	[untitled] |M^r Ed: Lowe [d]
5	ℓ 3r$^{3-4}$	[untitled (a)]
6	ℓ 3v$^{1-3}$	**Allemaine** |R: Gibbs [a]
7	ℓ 4r$^{1-2}$	**Corant** |R: Gibbs [a]
8	ℓ 4v$^{1-3}$	The Kings ayre [F]

9	ℓ 5r$^{1-4}$	[untitled (F)]
	ℓ 5v	[blank, ruled]
10	ℓ 6r$^{1-2}$	Saraband |Alb: Bryan [F]
11	ℓ 6v$^{1-3}$	A [S]Cots Aire [C]
12	ℓ 7r$^{1-6}$	A horne pipe [d]
13	ℓ 7v^{1}	[untitled (C)]
14	ℓ 7v^{2}	[untitled (C)]
15	ℓ 7v^{3}	[untitled (C)]
16	ℓ 7v^{4}	Aire.[C]
17	ℓ 8r$^{1-3}$	[untitled (C)]
17a	ℓ 8v$^{1-2}$	[untitled (C/G)]
18	ℓ 8v$^{3-4}$	[untitled (G)]
19	ℓ 9r$^{1-3}$	Jigg [a]
20	ℓ 9r$^{3-4}$	Saraband [a]
21	ℓ 9v$^{1-3}$	Sar [Jigg?] [C]
22	ℓ 10r$^{1-3}$	[untitled (G)]
23	ℓ 10v$^{1-4}$	Almain Mr Roberts [d]
24	ℓ 11r$^{1-4}$	[untitled (d)]
25	ℓ 11v$^{1-4}$	Jigg |Mr John Roberts [d]
26	ℓ 12r$^{1-4}$	[Allemande (e)]
27	ℓ 12v$^{1-4}$	Ayre [G]
28	ℓ 13r^{1}-v^{4}	[untitled (G)]
28a	ℓ 14r$^{1-4}$	[untitled] Mr Bryan [a]
29	ℓ 14v$^{1-2}$	[untitled (d)]
29a	ℓ 14v^{3}	Jigg [C]
29b	ℓ 14v^{4}	Jigg [fragment (C)]

29c ℓ 15r$^{1-4}$ Jigg [d]

30   ℓ 15v^{1}-16r^{4} [Fugue] Dr Blow [g]
                    ED: Fuller-Maitland 2:1.

31   ℓ 16v$^{1-4}$ Prelude [BLOW (G)]
                    ED: Fuller-Maitland 2:3.
     ℓ 17r   [blank, ruled]
                    [1 ℓ lacking, stub remains]

     ℓ 17-41   [Written from other end of book, see
                    ℓ 1A-25A:]

     ℓ 1Ar   [blank, ruled]

32   ℓ 1Av^{1}-2Ar^{2} Almaine |Corant [ie #33] [d]
     (41r)

33   ℓ 2Av$^{1-4}$ Corant [d]
     (40r)

34   ℓ 3Ar$^{1-3}$ Sarabant |S^{gr} Batis [DRAGHI? (d)]
     (39v)

35   ℓ 3Av^{1}-4Ar^{2} Almand |Mr Mat Lock [G]
     (39r)   ED: cf Dart-L #31.

36   ℓ 4Av^{1}-5Ar^{3} Corant |Dr Blow [G]
     (38r)   ED: cf Fuller-Maitland 2:8,

37   ℓ 5Av^{1} [fragment (G)]
     (37r)

     ℓ 6Ar   [blank, ruled]

38   ℓ 6Av^{1}-7Ar^{2} Almaine |D^{r} Jo: Blow. [D]
     (36r)   ED: Fuller-Maitland 2:10.

     ℓ 7Av-8Ar   [blank, ruled]

39   ℓ 8Av^{1}-9Ar^{4} Almaine |D^{r} Jo: Blow [d]
     (34r)   ED: Fuller-Maitland 1:23.

     ℓ 9Av-10Ar   [blank, ruled]

40 | ℓ 10Av^1-11Ar^3 [PURCELL: Ground (C), Z. 681]
    (32r)

41 | ℓ 11Av^1-12Av^4 [DRAGHI: Ground scocca pur (c)]
    (30r)   ED: cf Dart-HII #20.

42 | ℓ 13Ar$^{1-5}$ Mr H. Purcell /Prelude [G] [Z. 662/1]
    (29v)

43 | ℓ 13Av^1-14Ar^3 Allmand |Mr Purcell [G] [Z. 662/2]
    (29r)

44 | ℓ 14Av^1-15Ar^3 Corant [PURCELL (G), Z. 662/3]
    (28r)

45 | ℓ 15Av^1-16Ar^1 [Sarabande] M^{r}H Purcell [a] [Z. 654]
    (27r)

46 | ℓ 16Av^1-17Ar^1 Trumpet Almond [D]
    (26r)

   | ℓ 17Av   [blank, ruled]

47 | ℓ 18Ar$^{1-4}$ Prelude [PURCELL? (a)]
    (24v)

48 | ℓ 18Av$^{1-4}$ Almand [PURCELL (a), Z. 663/2]
    (24r)

49 | ℓ 18Av$^{1-4}$ Corant [PURCELL (a), Z. 663/3]
    (23v)

50 | ℓ 19Av$^{1-3}$ [untitled (d)]
    (23r)

51 | ℓ 19Av^4-20Ar^1 Saraband /to the lessons before in A
    (23r)   [PURCELL (a), Z. 663/4]

52 | ℓ 20Av^1-21Ar^2 Morlake [Morlack's] Ground |Dr Blow [G]
    (22r)   ED: Fuller-Maitland 1:18, cf Dart-HII #23.

53 | ℓ 23Av^1-24Ar^1 Ground |Dr Blow [g]
    (20r)   ED: Fuller-Maitland 2:14.

54	ℓ 24Ar$^{2-4}$ (18v)	Ground Mr Disiner [C] ED: Fuller-Maitland 6:2.
55	ℓ 24Av^{1}-25Ar^{2} (18r)	[untitled (D)]
	ℓ 25Av-41A	[see ℓ 1-17]

Provenance: England, ca. 1691 (dated, ℓ. iA^V, "Elizabeth Roper her Booke 1691").

Location: Chicago; Newberry Library, Special Collections, Case MS VM 2.3 E58r.

Description: 1 p.ℓ., 115, 1 ℓ. (numbered [i], 1-67 from one end, and [i], 1-35 from the other; central 12 ℓ. blank and unnumbered); oblong quarto format, 19.1 x 26 cm. Watermark #62x. Contemporary well-worn full leather binding, faded sprinkled edges, 20 x 26.8 cm.

Notation: Keyboard score (two 5-line staves [except hand B: six-line staves], 3 systems per page, written page by page). Clefs: $G^{2,3}$, $F^{3,4}$, $C^{1,3}$. Also, some vocal score.

Scribes: 8-11 hands; one (H) probably that of an owner (Elizabeth Roper; cf. Marginalia, below); 3 primary hands (A, F & G), perhaps teachers of Mary and Elizabeth Roper:
A: #1-24, 27-29, 61.
B: #25-26, 35.
C: #30.
D: (same as C?) #31.
E: #32-34.
F: #39-51, ℓ. 49^V-50^r.
G: #52-59a, ℓ. 1A.
H: ℓ. 1A additions.
I: #60, 63-69.
J: (same as C?) #61 continuation, 62.
K: (same as H?) #70.

Marginalia: ℓ. i^V, "Mary Rooper her Booke," followed by miscellaneous numbers and library markings. ℓ. iA^V,

"Elizabeth Roper ÷ her Booke 1691 /is ueri proper,"
followed by ink scratchings. ℓ. 1A^r (smudged),
"chosen [?] very is very good ..." (illegible).
ℓ. 23^V, letter names of notes written above staff to
clarify a correction.

Summary:
  Composers:
    BYRON: #44, 46, 48.
    CAECILE, Sr. [?]: #35.
    CHAMBONNIÈRES: #58-59.
    CLARKE: #47, 48(?).
    ECCLES: #49.
    LEBÈGUE: #2-6, 9-12, cf 13, 17, 20-24, 57.
    LEGHI (?): #26.
    LULLY: #1, 19, 28, 51, 53.
    PURCELL: #39, 40, 42, 43, 70.
    SHORE: #47(?).
  Contents: Miscellaneous harpsichord pieces by French
    and English composers, with a few vocal works and
    one for organ:
    # 1-24   French (Lebègue, Lully, anon.)
      25-26   English (Leghi, anon.)
      27-34   French? (anon.)
      35-50   English (Purcell, Clarke, Byron, Caecile)
      51-59   French (Chambonnières, Lebègue, anon.)
      60-70   French vocal transcriptions, except:
        61   Offertoire (anon.)
        70   Ground (Purcell)

Inventory (letters in parentheses indicate scribes):
  ℓ i^r [blank, unruled]

  ℓ i^V [in an unsteady hand:] Mary Rooper her
                 Booke /2680145391716 /1243 [and library
                 markings and scribbles in pencil]

1   [LULLY, arr: _Air_ _de_ _trompettes_ from _Proserpine_ (1680)
     Prologue (C)]
     [untitled]
       ℓ 1r$^{1-3}$ ¢|5|8|

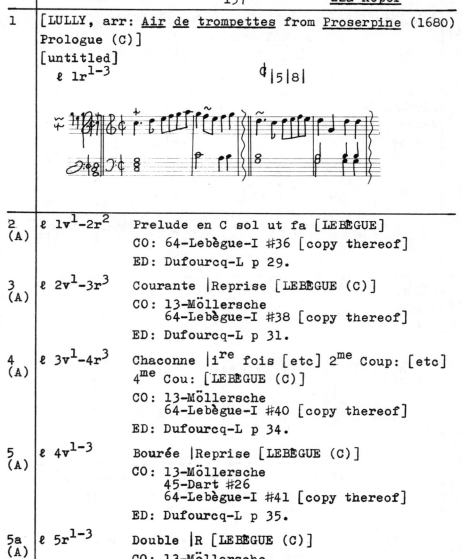

---

2   ℓ 1v^1-2r^2 Prelude en C sol ut fa [LEBÈGUE]
(A)
                       CO: 64-Lebègue-I #36 [copy thereof]
                       ED: Dufourcq-L p 29.

3   ℓ 2v^1-3r^3 Courante |Reprise [LEBÈGUE (C)]
(A)
                       CO: 13-Möllersche
                           64-Lebègue-I #38 [copy thereof]
                       ED: Dufourcq-L p 31.

4   ℓ 3v^1-4r^3 Chaconne |i^{re} fois [etc] 2me Coup: [etc]
(A)   4me Cou: [LEBÈGUE (C)]
                       CO: 13-Möllersche
                           64-Lebègue-I #40 [copy thereof]
                       ED: Dufourcq-L p 34.

5   ℓ 4v$^{1-3}$ Bourée |Reprise [LEBÈGUE (C)]
(A)
                       CO: 13-Möllersche
                           45-Dart #26
                           64-Lebègue-I #41 [copy thereof]
                       ED: Dufourcq-L p 35.

5a   ℓ 5r$^{1-3}$ Double |R [LEBÈGUE (C)]
(A)
                       CO: 13-Möllersche
                           64-Lebègue-I #41a [copy thereof]
                       ED: Dufourcq-L p 36.

     ℓ 6   [stubbed in]

6
(A)   ℓ 5v^1-6r^3   Gigue |i^re fois [etc] [LEBÈGUE (C)]

                   CO: 13-Möllersche
                       64-Lebègue-I #42 [copy thereof]
                       cf #13, below

                   ED: Dufourcq-L p 36.

7
(A)   [Menuet (C)]

      Menuet |Reprise
         ℓ 6v^1-3 $\frac{3}{4}$ 3 |8|10|

8
(A)   [Rigaudon (C)]

      Rigaudon
         ℓ 7r^1-3   ¢ |8|8|

9
(A)   ℓ 7v^1-8r^3   Prelude. En.a.my.la.re. [LEBÈGUE (a)]

                   CO: 64-Lebègue-I #28 [copy thereof]

                   ED: Dufourcq-L p 22.

10
(A)   ℓ 8v^1-9r^3   Allemande |i^re fois ...|Reprise...
                    [LEBÈGUE (a)]

                   CO: 13-Möllersche
                       28-Brussels-926 f 66r
                       64-Lebègue-I #29 [copy thereof]

                   ED: Dufourcq-L p 23.

11
(A) ℓ 9v^1-10r^3 Courante [LEBÈGUE (a)]

            CO: 13-Möllersche
                64-Lebègue-I #30 [copy thereof]

            ED: Dufourcq-L p 24.

12
(A) ℓ 10v^1-11r^3 Sarabande grave |Reprise ... [LEBÈGUE (a)]

            CO: 13-Möllersche
                45-Dart #11
                64-Lebègue-I #32 [copy thereof?]

            ED: Dufourcq-L p 25.

13
(A) [Double to LEBÈGUE: Gigue (C)]

Double de le gige en C sol-ut
     ℓ 11v^1-12r^3 ^{3}|14|16| [$^6_4$|14|17|]

CO: cf 13-Möllersche
    cf 22a-Roper #6
    cf 64-Lebègue-I #42
ED: cf Dufourcq-L p 36.

14
(A) [Chaconne (a)]
     [untitled]
         ℓ 12v^1-13r^3 ^{3}[$^3_4$]|4|6|8|16|8|

15
(A)

[Chaconne (D)]

chaconne

ℓ 13v¹-15v¹   ³[¾] |16|8|8|8|8|8|8|8|16|

16
(A)

[Prélude (D)]

[untitled]

ℓ 15v¹-16r³ |25|

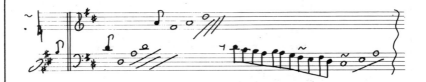

17
(A)

ℓ 16v¹-17r³ gigue |Reprise [LEBÈGUE (D)]

            CO: 13-Möllersche
                64-Lebègue-I #11 [copy thereof]

            ED: Dufourcq-L p 9.

18
(A)

[Variations on Folies d'Espagne (d)]

[untitled]

ℓ 17v¹-24r³   ³[¾] |16| x 21 [¾|336|]

19
(A)

[LULLY, arr: <u>La Mariéé</u> from <u>Roland</u> (1685) (unlocated)
(G)]

Air/ de L'opera |Reprise
    ℓ 24v^1-25r^2 ¢|14|12|

CO: cf 14-Schwerin-619 #62, La Mariee De Roland
    cf 36-Parville #122, La mariée
    cf 45-Dart #34, La Mariée
    cf 45-Dart #65, la marie de rolant

20
(A)

ℓ 25v^1-26r^3 Gigue d angleterre fort viste |i^{er} couplet
       ...4me [LEBÈGUE (G)]

CO: 12-Walther
    13-Möllersche
    64-Lebègue-I #24 [copy thereof]

ED: Dufourcq-L p 18.

21
(A)

ℓ 26v$^{1-3}$ Bourée |Reprise [LEBÈGUE (G)]

CO: 12-Walther
    13-Möllersche
    23-Tenbury #41
    24-Babell #85
    45-Dart #28
    64-Lebègue-I #25 [copy thereof]

ED: Dufourcq-L p 19.

21a
(A)

ℓ 27r$^{1-3}$ Double [LEBÈGUE (G)]

CO: 12-Walther
    13-Möllersche
    23-Tenbury #41a
    24-Babell #85a
    64-Lebègue-I #25a [copy thereof]

ED: Dufourcq-L p 20.

22
(A)

ℓ 27v^1-28r^3 Allemande [LEBÈGUE (G)]

CO: 65-Lebègue-II #35 [copy thereof]
    cf 11-Ryge #65 [similar allemande]

ED: Dufourcq-L p 79; cf Bangert p 13.

23
(A) ℓ 28v^1-29r^2 Courante En D# |Reprise [LEBÈGUE (D)]

                  CO: 13-Möllersche
                      64-Lebègue-I #9 [copy thereof]

                  ED: Dufourcq-L p 8.

24
(A) ℓ 29v^1-30r^3 Chaconne grave |3me ... [LEBÈGUE (D)]

                  CO: 13-Möllersche
                      64-Lebègue-I #12 [copy thereof]

                  ED: Dufourcq-L p 10.

25
(B) ℓ 30v$^{1-3}$ [Chaconne (g)] Pres [smudged and incom-
                  plete] |Persona [ie, autograph?]

26
(B) ℓ 31r$^{1-3}$ Allemande Mr Leghi [g]

     ℓ 31v-32r   [blank, ruled]

27
(A) [Gavotte (C)]

     gavotte |Reprise
        ℓ 32$^{1-3}$ ₵|4|8

28
(A) [LULLY, arr: Air (trompettes) from Isis (1677)
     Prologue-3 (C)]
     [untitled]
        ℓ 33r$^{1-3}$ ₵|4|8|

CO: cf 14-Schwerin-619 #74, Trompet Disis
    cf 40-Rés-476 #36, Trompette de l'opera
ED: cf Bonfils-LP p 103, Howell #3.

29
(A)

[__Menuet__ (C)]

Menuet |R
ℓ 33v[1-3]

$^3[\frac{3}{4}]|8|8|$

CO: 48-LaBarre-6 #34, Menuet

29a
(A)

[__Double__ (C)]

double |Reprise
ℓ 34r[1-3]

$[\frac{3}{4}]|8|8|$

CO: 48-LaBarre-6 #34a, Double

ℓ 34v-35r   [blank, ruled]

30
(C)

[Anon, arr: __Rigaudon__ (d) (fragment)]

Rigaudon |Reprise
ℓ 35v[1-2]

¢|5|4|

CO: cf 36-Parville #113, Rigaudon [g]
    cf 44-LaPierre p 59A, Rigaudon des Veissaux [g]
    cf 45-Dart #67, Rigaudon de la marine [g]
    cf 48-LaBarre-6 #27, Rigaudon

[1 ℓ cut out]

31
(D)

[Menuet (G)]

[untitled]

ℓ 36r[1-3]

ℓ 36v-37r   [blank, ruled]

32
(E)

[Courante (a)]

Courante

ℓ 37v[1]-38r[3]

33
(E)

[Sarabande (a)]

Sarabande

ℓ 38v[1]-39r[1]

33a
(E)

ℓ 39r[2]-v[3]   Double [a]

ℓ 40r   [blank, ruled]

34 (E)	[<u>Gigue</u> (a)] Gigue ℓ 40v^1-41r^3	$^3[{}^3_4]$ $|28|28|$

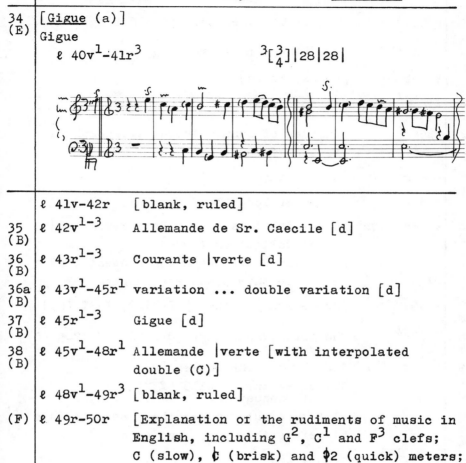

	ℓ 41v-42r	[blank, ruled]
35 (B)	ℓ 42v$^{1-3}$	Allemande de Sr. Caecile [d]
36 (B)	ℓ 43r$^{1-3}$	Courante |verte [d]
36a (B)	ℓ 43v^1-45r^1	variation ... double variation [d]
37 (B)	ℓ 45r$^{1-3}$	Gigue [d]
38 (B)	ℓ 45v^1-48r^1	Allemande |verte [with interpolated double (C)]
	ℓ 48v^1-49r^3	[blank, ruled]
(F)	ℓ 49r-50r	[Explanation of the rudiments of music in English, including G^2, C^1 and F^3 clefs; C (slow), $\mathbb{C}$ (brisk) and $\mathbb{C}$2 (quick) meters; ornaments: ╱ ╲ ✝ ╌✝ Rise Fall Beate preparing beat shake preparing shake turn shake slur
39 (F)	ℓ 50v^1-51r^3	Allemand by Mr Purcell [F] [Z 603/1a]
40 (F)	ℓ 51v^1-52r^3	Hornpipe [F] [PURCELL, Z 603/2b]
41 (F)	ℓ 52v$^{1-2}$	Prelude to be play'd before the two Lessons [F]
	ℓ 53r	[blank, ruled]

42 ℓ 53v^1-54r^2 Ayre by Mr H. Purcell [Z 570/6 (g)]
(F)

43 ℓ 54v$^{1-3}$ Jigg [PURCELL, Z 686/7 (g)]
(F)

    ℓ 55r   [blank, ruled]

44 ℓ 55v$^{1-3}$ Menuet by /My Lord Byron [B♭]
(F)

(F) ℓ 56r   Examples of Common |cords ... [Explana-
                     tions of figured bass]

45 ℓ 56v^1-57v^2 [untitled (C)]
(F)

    ℓ 58r   [blank, ruled]

46 ℓ 58v^1-59r^3 A Scottish tune by /My Lord Byron [B♭]
(F)   CO: cf Collection ℓ 9
                     [1 ℓ torn out between the present ℓ 58 &
                     59 before this piece was entered]

47 ℓ 59v$^{1-2}$ Shores Trumpet tune [CLARKE?, T437 (C)]
(F)

48 ℓ 60r$^{1-3}$ The Lord Byrons Jigg [CLARKE?, T312.9 (C)]
(F)

49 ℓ 60v^1-61r^3 Jigg by Mr John Eccles [g]
(F)   CO: cf 24-Babell #115 [f]
                         cf Banquet-2 ℓ 7
                     [1 ℓ torn out between the present ℓ 60 &
                     61 before this piece was entered]

50 ℓ 61v$^{1-3}$ Menuet [g]
(F)
                     [2 ℓ torn out]

    ℓ 62r   [blank, ruled]

(F) ℓ 62v-64v   [Explanations of figured bass, in English]

    ℓ 65r   [blank, ruled]

51
(D)
[LULLY, arr: <u>Air</u> from <u>Acis</u> <u>et</u> <u>Galathée</u> (1686)
Prologue (C) (fragment)]
La Rigaudoe
ℓ 65v[1]

CO: cf 22a-Roper #53, Le Rigodon
　　cf 36-Parville #67-67a, Rigaudon...Double...
　　cf 44-LaPierre p 14, 25A, Rigaudon
　　cf 45-Dart #37, Rigodon de Galatee
ED: cf Curtis-Co #32.

ℓ 66r-80v	[blank, ruled; 2 ℓ torn out after ℓ 67, 72 & 75; 4 ℓ torn out after ℓ 80; 1 staff with 6 notes laid in after ℓ 73]
ℓ 81r-115v	[Remainder of book written from the other end, numbered as ℓ 1A-35A (ℓ 81r is the same as ℓ 35Av]
ℓ iA[r]	[blank, unruled]
ℓ iA[v]	Elizabeth Roper + her Booke <u>1691</u> /is ueri proper [followed by ink scratch marks, seemingly in the same hand and ink]
ℓ 1A[r]	[solfege syllables written on the lines of 3 clefs: G[2], C[1], F[3] (hand G); sharps added in order, but with miscellaneous ones added, with smudged words (Hand H:)] roper [?] very is very good ... [illegible]

52
(G)

[Chaconne (C)]

[untitled]

  ℓ 1Av^1-2Ar^2 $^3[^3_4]$ |4| x 5

CO: cf 25-Bod-426 #2, Sarabande

53
(G)

[LULLY, arr: Air from Acis et Galathée (1686)
Prologue (C)]

Le Rigodon

  ℓ 2Av^1-3Ar^3 ^{C}|4|6|2|4|

CO: cf 22a-Roper #51, La Rigaudoe
   cf 36-Parville #67-67a, Rigaudon...Double...
   cf 44-LaPierre p 14, 25A, Rigaudon
   cf 45-Dart #37, Rigodon de Galateé

ED: cf Curtis-Co #32.

54
(G)

[Prélude]

prélude

  ℓ 3Av^1-4Ar^3 [unmeasured]

55
(G)

[Courante (d)]

Courante

ℓ 4Av¹⁻³   ³[⁶₄]|4|4|

CO: 5-Munich-1503ℓ #10, Courante
    7-Munich-1511f #12, Courante
    44-LaPierre p 12, Courante en d la re

55a
(G)

[Double (d)]

double

ℓ 5Ar¹⁻³   ³[⁶₄]|4|4|

56
(G)

[Sarabande (d)]

Sarabande

ℓ 5Av¹⁻³   ³[³₄]|8|8|

CO: 6-Munich-1511e #10, Sarrabande
    18-Ch-Ch-1236 #20, Sarabrand

56a [Double (d)]
(G) double
        ℓ 6Ar$^{1-3}$ $^3[{}^3_4]$|8|8|

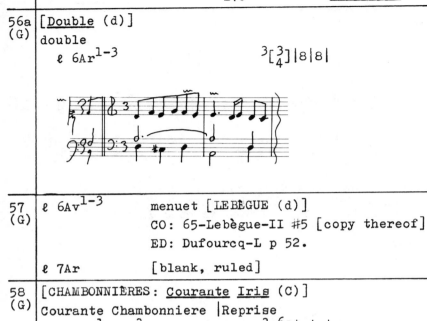

57   ℓ 6Av$^{1-3}$ menuet [LEBÈGUE (d)]
(G)   CO: 65-Lebègue-II #5 [copy thereof]
                             ED: Dufourcq-L p 52.

     ℓ 7Ar   [blank, ruled]

58   [CHAMBONNIÈRES: Courante Iris (C)]
(G) Courante Chambonniere |Reprise
        ℓ 7Av^1-8Ar^3 $^3[{}^6_4]$|8|8|

CO: 8-Hintze #15, Courante
    23-Tenbury #3, (courante chambonii)
    24-Babell #58, Courante de Mr. de Chambonniere
    33-Rés-89ter #2, Courante. Chambonnieres.
    35-Bauyn-I #9, Courante de Mr De Chambonnieres
    36-Parville #61, Courante Chanbonniere
    44-LaPierre p 18, p 34A, Courante Chambonniere
    47-Gen-2356 #12, Courante
    53-Oldham-2 p 107, Courante de Chamboniere
    55-Redon #23, Courante de Monsieur de Chambonniere
    62-Chamb-I #8, Courante Iris

ED: cf Dart-Ch #8, Brunold-Tessier #8, Gilbert p 148.

58a
(G) [Double (C)]

double |Reprise
ℓ 8Av^1-9Ar^3 $^3[^6_4]$|8|8|

CO: (cf?) 32-Oldham #17, Double de La Courante Iris
    cf 33-Rés-89ter #2, Double
    cf 44-LaPierre p 18, 34A, Double

59
(G) [CHAMBONNIÈRES: Courante (C)]

2me Courante |Reprise
ℓ 9Av^1-10Ar^3 $^3[^6_4]$|6|7|

CO: 33-Rés-89ter #3, 2. Courante Chambonnieres...Double
    35-Bauyn-I #23, Courante de Mr de Chambonnieres
    36-Parville #62, Courante Chanbonniere
    62-Chamb-I #9, Courante

ED: cf Dart-Ch #9, Brunold-Tessier #9, Gilbert p 150.

59a
(G) [Double (C)]

double |Reprise
ℓ 10Av^1-11Ar^3 $^3[^6_4]$|6|7|

CO: cf 33-Rés-89ter #3a, Double [d'Anglebert]
ED: cf Gilbert p 151, Brunold-Tessier p 117.

	ℓ 11Av	[blank, ruled]
60 (I)	ℓ 12Ar$^{1-3}$	une Ombre fortunée |Air [2 staves, text between (F)]
61 (A/ J)	ℓ 12Av^1-15Ar^3	Petitte Offertoire /P |grand jeu |P |Rd /RB ... [G] [in Hand A to ℓ 14Av^1, then original final chord changed by hand J which continues the piece]
62 (J)	ℓ 15Av^1-16Av^1	[untitled (F)]
63 (I)	ℓ 16Av-17Ar	Ayre, Soupire avec constance ... [on 3 staves, upper with text, using C^1; middle marked "violons," using G^1; lower using F^4 clef]
64 (I)	ℓ 17Av^1-18Ar^2	Vn Plaisir [text between staves:] Que de fleurs sur les bords vont paroitre... [clefs: C^3, F^4]
		[1 ℓ torn out between ℓ 17A & 18A before this piece was entered]

65 (I)	[Anon, arr: <u>Passacaille</u> (g)] Passacaille |Turn over quickly ...
	ℓ 18Av^1-21Ar^1 ^{3}[$\frac{3}{4}$]|121|

66 (I)	ℓ 21Av^1-22Ar^3	Vne des Graces [text between staves:] A l'Amour tout doit rendre les armes... [clefs: C^1, F^4]
67 (I)	ℓ 22Av-23Ar	Venus [text between staves:] Aymable vainqueur... [clefs: C^1, C^1, F^4]

68
(I)

[Anon, arr: <u>Air</u> <u>des</u> <u>vents</u> (B♭)]

Air des vents

ℓ 23Av^1-24Ar^2 ^{3}[$\frac{3}{4}$]|15|21|

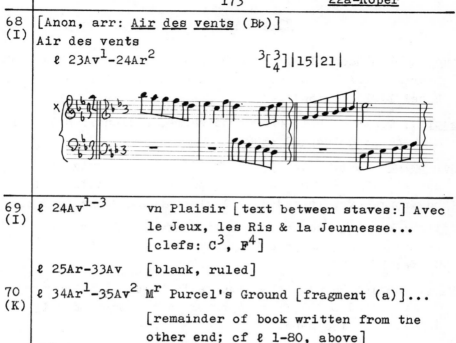

69
(I)

ℓ 24Av$^{1-3}$ vn Plaisir [text between staves:] Avec
                        le Jeux, les Ris & la Jeunnesse...
                        [clefs: C^3, F^4]

ℓ 25Ar-33Av   [blank, ruled]

70
(K)

ℓ 34Ar^1-35Av^2 Mr Purcel's Ground [fragment (a)]...

[remainder of book written from the
other end; cf ℓ 1-80, above]

Provenance: London, 1701 (dated inside front cover, "Ce
Liure Arpartient /a g^m [Guillaume, i.e. William]
Babel 1701 /London").

Location: Tenbury Wells (Worcestershire, England); St.
Michael's College MS 1508.

Description: 71 ℓ. (i.e. 69: ℓ. 1-2 lacking); irregular
format, 12 x 24 cm. Original paper boards with seal
on front cover in faded, illegible ink, 12.6 x 24.5 cm.

Notation: Keyboard score (two 5-line staves, 2 systems
per page, written page by page with red margin lines).
Clefs: F^4, G^2.

Scribe: Charles Babell, the same as in 24-Babell, Newberry,
Cummings and Bod-393; except #88, which was added by
an unidentified hand.

Marginalia: Original index inside front cover (see "Provenance"). Signature and notation on back cover in a
different hand, smudged and illegible, "James [?]
Madam /Is ..."

Summary:

Composers:
BARRETT: #34, 35, cf 88, 89, 91.
BRUININCKS (Hamel): #2.
BYRON: #20.
CHAMBONNIÈRES: #3, 40.
CLARKE: #16, 18, 19(?), 50, 66.
COLLASSE: #17.
COUPERIN (Louis): #12a.
DIEUPART: #30, 69, 93.
DRAGHI: #33.
ECCLES: #53, 59, 71, 78, 87.
FINGER: #43.

FORCER: #31.
HARDEL: #12.
KELLER: #14, 15, 21-23, 26, 44, 45, 54, 55, 60.
KING: #27-29, 32, 48, 72-74, 76, 83-86.
LEBÈGUE: #6, 41, 42.
LULLY: #17, 46, 49, 56, 67, 75, 79, 80.
MONNARD: #4.
MORGAN: #81.
OSSU: #8, 9.
PURCELL (Daniel): #77.
PURCELL (Henry): #7, 24, 25, 36-39, 51, 52, 61-64.
ROSSI: #11.
SHORE: #19(?).
STEFFANI: #70.
VALOIS: #10, 57.

Contents: 12 [i.e. 14] suites:

1	#1-6a	C		7	44-47	G
2	7-13	a		8	48-53	g
3	14-21	D		9	54-60	d
4	22-26	C		10	61-71	F/f
5	27-32	e		11	72-76	D
5a	33-35	b		11a	77-82	Bb
6	36-43	G		12	83-92	A

<u>Inventory</u> (information in parentheses is from the index):

ℓ 1-2   [lacking]

1   (prelude) [lacking]
               CO: 24-Babell #53?

2   (allemande de hamel [BRUININCKS; lacking])
               CO: 24-Babell #55?

3 | [CHAMBONNIÈRES: <u>Courante Iris</u> (C)]

(courante chambonii) [beginning lacking]

     -ℓ 3r^1 [$^3_2$] |7|

[incipit lacking]

CO: 8-Hintze #15, Courante
     22a-Roper #58, **Courante Chambonniere...double**
     24-Babell #58, Courante de Mr. de Chambonniere
     33-Rés-89ter #2, Courante. Chambonnieres...**Double**
     35-Bauyn-I #9, Courante de Mr De Chambonnieres
     36-Parville #61, Courante Chanbonniere
     44-LaPierre p 18, p 34A, Courante Chambonniere...**Double**
     47-Gen-2356 #12, Courante
     53-Oldham-2 p 107, **Courante de Chamboniere**
     55-Redon #23, Courante de Monsieur de Chambonniere
     62-Chamb-I #8, Courante Iris
     cf 32-Oldham #17, Double de La Courante Iris

ED: cf Brunold-Tessier #8, Dart-Ch #8, Gilbert p 148.

---

4 | [MONNARD: <u>Sarabande</u> (C)]

Sarabande |petite /Reprise

    ℓ 3r^2 ^{3}[$^3_4$]|4|8|

CO: 6-Munich-1511e #11, Sarrabande
     24-Babell #56, Sarabande
     30-Cecilia ℓ 48r, Sarabande ... redoublè
     31-Madrid-1360 #23/6, Sexta (Zarabanda)
     35-Bauyn-III #60, Sarabande De M. Monnard
     38-Gen-2348/53 #34, **Sarabande.**
     44-LaPierre p 2, [Sarabande]

ED: cf Ex 7 above; cf Bonfils-18 p 6.

---

5 | ℓ 3v^1-4r^2 Canaries |1 fois ... [C]

                  CO: 24-Babell #54

6   [LEBÈGUE: Gavotte (C)]
     Gavotte M^r /Le Begue
        ℓ 4v$^{1-2}$ ¢ |4|8|

     CO: 10-Schwerin-617 #10, Gavotte
         13-Möllersche, [copy of 64-Lebègue-I #43]
         14-Schwerin-619 #91, Gavotte
         21-Rés-1186bis #12, Gavott
         24-Babell #60, Gavotte de Mr. le Begue
         30-Cecilia ℓ 47r, Gavotte
         35-Bauyn-III #54, (Gavotte) de Mr Lebegue
         36-Parville #68, Gauotte Mr le Begue
         45-Dart #22, [copy of 64-Lebègue-I #43
         46-Menetou #102, Gavotte
         50-Paignon #11, Balet de Mr lebegue
         64-Lebègue-I #43, Gauotte

     ED: cf Dufourcq-L p 38, Brunold/Dart-Co #132.

6a   [LEBÈGUE: Double (C)]
     Double |Fin
        ℓ 5r$^{1-2}$ ¢ |4|8|

     CO: 13-Möllersche, [copy of 64-Lebègue-I #43a]
         24-Babell #60a, Double
         64-Lebègue-I #43a, Double
         cf 14-Schwerin-619 #91a, [Double]
         cf 35-Bauyn-III #54a, Double par Mr Couperin
         cf 36-Parville #68a, [Double]
         cf 36-Parville #146, Double de la Gavotte de Le
                              Bègue
         cf 50-Paignon #11a, la double
     ED: cf Dufourcq-L p 38, Brunold/Dart-Co #132[a].

    ℓ 5v   2me Suitte [a]

7   ℓ 5v$^{1-2}$ Prelude /H. Purcel /en A [a]

8   ℓ 6r$^{1-2}$ M^r. /Ossu /Courante [a]

9   ℓ 6v$^{1-2}$ Sarabande /M^r. Ossu [a]

10 ℓ 6v^2-7r^2 Courante M^r valois [a]

              CO: 24-Babell #153

11 ℓ 7v^1-8r^2 Passacaille /Sig^r. Loüisi [ROSSI (a)]

              CO: 24-Babell #166
                  35-Bauyn-III #91
                  36-Parville #57

              ED: **cf** Pierront p 6, Prunières p 18.

12 [HARDEL: Gavotte (a)]

Gavotte /M^r. Hardel
   ℓ 8v$^{1-2}$ ¢|4|8|

CO: 24-Babell #159, Gavotte
    25-Bod-426 #20, Gavotte d'Ardelle
    31-Madrid-1360 #41, Jabouste de Ardel
    35-Bauyn-III #50, (Gavotte) de Mr Hardel
    36-Parville #52, Gavotte de Mr Hardel
    45-Dart #60, Gauotte de Monsr Ardel
    49-RésF-933 #13, gavotte d ardellè
    St-Georges ℓ 51, Gavotte
    cf Saizenay-I p 61, Gavotte Ardelle [lute]
    cf Vm7-4867 p 52, Gavotte d'ardelle [violin]
    cf Saizenay-II p 17, Gavotte d'hardelle [lute]

ED: **cf Brunold/Dart-Co #131, Curtis-Co #11,**
    Quittard-H p 1.

12a [COUPERIN (L): Double (a)]

Double (du mesme)
  ℓ 9r[1-2]   ¢ |4|8|

CO: 24-Babell #159a, Double
    31-Madrid-1360 #41a [Double]
    35-Bauyn-III #50a, Double (de la gauotte) cy des-
                    sus Par Mr Couperin
    36-Parville #52a, Double de la gauotte fait par
                    Mr Couprin
    49-RésF-933 #13a, [Double]
    cf Vm7-4867 p 77, Double [violin]
ED: cf Brunold/Dart-Co #131[a], Curtis-Co #11a,
    Quittard-H p 2.

13	ℓ 9v[1]-10r[2] Gigue (angloise) |Reprise |pet Rep |Fin [a]
	ℓ 10v 3me Suitte [D]
14	ℓ 10v[1]-11r[2] Prelude /M[r] /Keller /en D#
15	ℓ 11v[1]-12r[2] Allemande /M[r]. Keller [D]
16	ℓ 12v[1-2] Air Lent. /M[r]. Clark [T 437 (D)]
17	ℓ 13r[1]-14r[2] Ouverture de Thetis /M[r]. Colasse [/LULLY]
	|Tournez viste |Reprise /Fugue |Lentement
	[Thétis et Pelée (1689) (D)]
	CO: cf 14-Schwerin-619 #42
	cf 48-LaBarre-6 #35
18	ℓ 14v[1]-15r[2] Marche /M[r]. Clark /Rondeau [T 435 (D)]
19	ℓ 15v[1-2] Scotch tune /M[r]. Shors [CLARKE?, T 434 (D)]
20	ℓ 15v[2]-16r[2] Gigue (mylord) M[r]. Byron [D]
21	ℓ 16v[1-2] Gigue /M[r]. Keller |Fin [D]

	ℓ 17r	4me Suitte [C]
22	ℓ 17r$^{1-2}$	Prelude en C. M^r. Keller.
23	ℓ 17v$^{1-2}$	Allemande /M^r. Keller [C]
24	ℓ 18r$^{1-2}$	Trumpett Tune M^r. H. Purcel [C]
25	ℓ 18v^1-19r^2	Imitation de /la descente /de Cybelle /H. Purcel [C] ⌊Z T678⌋ CO: cf **24-Babell** #208
26	ℓ 19v^1-21r^2	Trumpett /By Mr Keller |quick |Turn over quickli |Suitte /Slow |Fin ⌊C⌋
	ℓ 21v	5me. Suitte [e]
27	ℓ 21v$^{1-2}$	Prelude /M^r. King /en E. [e]
28	ℓ 22r$^{1-2}$	Sarabande (M^r. King) [e]
29	ℓ 22v^1-23r^2	Allemande |Reprise (Mr King) [e]
30	ℓ 23v^1-24r^2	Gavotte /M^r. Dieupart |P^{te} Reprise [e] CO: **24-Babell** #105
31	ℓ 24v^1-26r^2	Chaconne /M^r. Forcer |Tournez /viste [e]
32	ℓ 26v^1-27r^2	Gigue /M^r. King [e]
		[Suite 5a (b)]
33	ℓ 27v^1-28r^2	Gigue en B mineur |Reprise [DRAGHI] CO: **24-Babell** #38
34	ℓ 28v$^{1-2}$	Ecossoise /M^r. Barrett [b]
35	ℓ 29r$^{1-2}$	menuet (Rond. M^r. Baret) |fin |Fin [b]
	ℓ 29v	6me. Suitte [G]
36	ℓ 29v$^{1-2}$	Prelude /H Purcel /en G#
37	ℓ 30r$^{1-2}$	Allemande (Mr purcel) [G]
38	ℓ 30v$^{1-2}$	Courante /H. Purcell [G]
39	ℓ 31r$^{1-2}$	Sarabande (M^r purcel) [G]

40 | [CHAMBONNIÈRES: <u>Courante</u> (G)]

Courante /Chambonnie/re

ℓ 31v^1-32v^2 $\frac{3}{2}$|8|9|

CO: 24-Babell #87, Courante de Chre.
     32-Oldham #19, Courante
     33-Rés-89ter #34, Courante Chambonnieres ... Double
     35-Bauyn-I #92, Courante de Mr de Chambonnieres
     36-Parville #92, Courante chanbonniere
     63-Chamb-II #26, Courante

ED: cf Brunold-Tessier #56, Dart-Ch #56, Gilbert p 190.

---

41 | [LEBÈGUE: <u>Bourrée</u> (G)]

Bourée /de M^r /le Begue

ℓ 32v$^{1-2}$ ¢|4|8|

CO: 12-Walther, [copy of 64-Lebègue-I #25]
     13-Möllersche [copy of 64-Lebègue-I #25]
     22a-Roper #21 [copy of 64-Lebègue-I #25]
     24-Babell #85, Bouree de Mr. le Begue
     45-Dart #28, [copy of 64-Lebègue-I #25]
     64-Lebègue-I #25, Bourée

ED: cf Dufourcq-L p 19.

41a [LEBÈGUE: Double (G)]

Double (du mesme)
   ℓ 33r¹⁻²   ¢|4|8|

CO: 12-Walther [copy of 64-Lebègue-I #25a]
    13-Möllersche [copy of 64-Lebègue-I #25a]
    22a-Roper #21a [copy of 64-Lebègue-I #25a]
    24-Babell #85a, Double
    64-Lebègue-I #25a, Double

ED: cf Dufourcq-L p 20.

42 [LEBÈGUE: Menuet (G)]

Menuet /M^r. Le Begue /Serieux |a la 2me fois
   ℓ 33v¹-34r²   3[3/4]|16|8|

CO: 12-Walther, [copy of 64-Lebègue-I #26]
    13-Möllersche, [copy of 64-Lebègue-I #26]
    24-Babell #86, Menuet
    45-Dart #29, [copy of 64-Lebègue-I #26]
    64-Lebègue-I #26, 2me Menuet

ED: Dufourcq-L p 20.

43 ℓ 34v¹⁻²   Ecossoise /M^r. Finger |Fin [G]

   ℓ 35r   7me Suitte [G]

44 ℓ 35r¹⁻²   Prelude en G# M^r. Keller.

45 ℓ 35v¹-36r¹ Ecossoise /M^r. Keller [G]

46 | ℓ 36v^1-37r^2 La Discorde (Lully) [Air from **Proserpine** (1680) Prologue (G)]
CO: cf 14-Schwerin-619 #60

47 | ℓ 37v^1-38r^2 Gigue |Fin [G]
CO: 24-Babell #89

| ℓ 38v   8me Suitte [g]

48 | ℓ 38v^1-39r^2 Allemande /en G♭ (Mr King)

49 | ℓ 39v^1-40r^2 Air /d'Armide [LULLY: Second air (sourdines) II-4 (1686)] /Tendrement [g]
CO: cf 14-Schwerin-619 #64
    cf 24-Babell #124
    cf 36-Parville #115, 149
    cf 49-RésF-933 #2
    cf 68-d'Anglebert #33
ED: cf Gilbert p 115, Roesgen-Champion p 62.

50 | ℓ 40v^1-41r^2 (menuet en) Rondeau |fin [CLARKE, T 492 (g)]
CO: 24-Babell #141
    Clark-M678 p 27A

51 | ℓ 41v^1-42r^2 Air /H. Purcell [g]

52 | ℓ 42v$^{1-2}$ Gigue /H. Purcell [g]

53 | ℓ 43r$^{1-2}$ Menuet /M^r. J^n. **Eccles** |**Fin** [g]

| ℓ 43v   9me Suitte [d]

54 | ℓ 43v^1-44r^2 Prelude /By M^r. Keller /en D♭

55 | ℓ 44v^1-45r^2 Allemande /M^r. Keller [d]

56 | ℓ 45v^1-46r^2 Ouverture du Ballet de Flore [LULLY (1669) (d)]
CO: cf 24-Babell #143

57 | ℓ 46v$^{1-2}$ Courante /M^r. Valois [d]

58 | ℓ 47r$^{1-2}$ Menuet (la croise) |P. Reprise [d]
CO: 24-Babell #229

59	ℓ 47v$^{1-2}$	Air Sol. /Eccles /Slow [d]
60	ℓ 48r$^{1-2}$	Gigue M^r. Keller |Fin [d]
	ℓ 48v	10me Suitte [F]
61	ℓ 48v^1-49r^2	Allemande /H. Purcel /en F.
62	ℓ 49v^1-50r^2	Courante (H Purcel) [F]
63	ℓ 50v^1-51r^1	Air /H. Purcell [F]
64	ℓ 51r$^{1-2}$	Hornpipe (Henry purcel) [F]
65	ℓ 51v$^{1-2}$	Ecossoise [F]
66	ℓ 52r$^{1-2}$	Com Swet lass [CLARKE, T 336 (F)]

CO: 24-Babell #236
    Add-22099 ℓ 6v

67	ℓ 52v^1-53r^2	Les /Lutins [LULLY: Premier air from

Thésée (1675) III-6 (F)]

CO: cf 24-Babell #234˙
    cf 33-Rés-89ter #9

ED: cf Gilbert p 164.

68	ℓ 53v^1-54r^2	Gigue [F]

CO: 24-Babell #10

69	ℓ 54v$^{1-2}$	Sarabande /M^r. Dieupard [f]

ED: cf Brunold-D #39

70	ℓ 55r$^{1-2}$	Menuet (Stephani) [F]
71	ℓ 55v^1-56r^2	Gigue /M^r. Jo^n˙ /Eccles |Fin [F]
	ℓ 56v	11me Suitte [D]
72	ℓ 56v^1-57r^1	Allemande /M^r. King /en D#
73	ℓ 57v^1-58r^2	Courante /M^r. King [D]
74	ℓ 58v^1-59r^2	Sarabande /M^r. King [D]
75	ℓ 59v^1-60r^2	Chaconne /de /[Acis et] Galatée [LULLY,

II-5 (1686)] /Lentement [D]

CO: cf 14-Schwerin-619 #123
    cf 24-Babell #97

cf 36-Parville #29
cf 49-RésF-933 #4
cf 51-LaBarre-11 p 206
cf 68-d'Anglebert #55

ED: cf Gilbert p 106, Roesgen-Champion
p 112.

76 | ℓ 60v^1-61r^2 Gigue /M^r. King [D]

   [Suite 11a (Bb]

77 | ℓ 61v^1-62r^2 D. Purcel /Rondeau en B [Bb]

78 | ℓ 62v^1-63r^2 Air /M^r. Ecles [Bb]

79 | ℓ 63v$^{1-2}$ Les /mariez (lully) [Le Carnaval (1668/75)
   VII (Bb)]
   CO: cf 24-Babell #268

80 | ℓ 64r$^{1-2}$ Les Espagnols (lully) [Le Bourgeois Gentil-
   homme, Nations-3 (1670) (Bb)]
   CO: cf 24-Babell #269
       cf 36-Parville #130
       cf 50-Paignon #10
       cf Saizenay-I p 287 [lute]

81 | ℓ 64v$^{1-2}$ Gigue /M^r. Morgan [Bb]

82 | ℓ 65r$^{1-2}$ Bourée (Angloise [Bb]
   CO: 24-Babell #272

   ℓ 65v   12me. Suitte [A]

83 | ℓ 65v^1-66r^2 Allemande /M^r. King /en A#

84 | ℓ 66v$^{1-2}$ Courante (Mr King) [A]

85 | ℓ 67r$^{1-2}$ Sarabande (Mr King) [A]

86 | ℓ 67v^1-68r^2 Gigue (Mr King) [A]

87 | ℓ 68v$^{1-2}$ Hornpipe /M^r. Jo^n. /Eccles [A]

88 | ℓ 69r$^{1-2}$ Courante Mr Barrett [with key signature
   for A major, but the music was not filled
   in; in another hand:] Gavot [C]

89	ℓ 69v^1-70r^2	Bourée /M^r. Barett [A]
90	ℓ 70v$^{1-2}$	Gigue (angloise) [A]
91	ℓ 71r$^{1-2}$	Hornpipe M^r. Barrett [A]
92	ℓ 71v^1-	Air Champaistre [incomplete] [A]
		[ℓ lacking]
93		(Menuet Mr Dieupard) [lacking]

Provenance: London, 1702 (covers dated "1702").

Location: London; British Library [British Museum], Department of Manuscripts, Additional mss 39569.

Description: 3 p.ℓ., 360 p., 6 (modern) ℓ., 3 ℓ.; folio format, 33.5 x 26 cm. Watermark #40. Original gilt-tooled full leather binding, gilted edges, stamping on covers, "RECUEIL /DE PIECES CHOISIES /POUR LE CLAUESSIN /1702 /WILLIAM BABEL" (name lacking on back cover), 34.7 x 28.5 cm.

Notation: Keyboard score (two 5-line staves, 6-8 systems per page, written page by page, with red margin lines). Clefs: F^4, G^2, $C^{1,3}$; usually F^4, G^2.

Scribes: Charles Babell, the same as in 23-Tenbury, Cummings, Newberry and Bod-393, except for modern additions:
  B: #276
  C: #295
  D: #296

Marginalia: Bookplates: "W L H C" (Cummings, see below) and Shield (of Griffin?, see below). Then: "L. F. Selwyn /the gift of her dear Papa [William Selwyn] /July 25th, 1821"; in another hand: "William Babell, was born about 1680 (?) pupil of his father a professional Bassoon player, and afterward of Dr Pepusch – Babell was celebrated not only for his performances on the harpsichord, but also for his arrangements for that instrument and the spinet. He was a member of the Royal band and organist of All Hallows Bread St. He died at Canonbury 23 Sept. 1723 and was buried in All Hallows. /W.H.C." (W.H. Cummings; the information, except for the birth date, seems to be drawn from

Sir John Hawkins, A General History of the Science
and Practice of Music (author's ex: London, British Library
L.R.39a.6) s.v. "Babell"). Another note on the iden-
tity of   William Elwyn, signed "Ralph Griffin,"
who purchased the book at Sotheby's sale of the Cummings library on "17 May 1917 for Ŀ 7.50." Spine
stamping, "Presented [to the British Museum] by R.
Griffin ..." Original numeration by pages in red
through p. 249. Modern index on inserted ℓ. at the
end of the volume. Original numeration by suites
listed at the top of every page as running headings.
Modern pencil numeration by ℓ. (ignored here).

Summary:
 Composers:
  d'ANGLEBERT: #204.
  BACH (J.S.): cf #11.
  BARRETT: #16, 17, 190-195, 196(?).
  BLANKENBURGH: #119.
  BRUININCKS (Hamel): #55.
  BYRON: #238.
  CHAMBONNIÈRES: #58, 87, 184, 186, 200, 206, 220, 248.
  CHARPENTIER: #121.
  CLARKE: #99, 100, 141, 236, 270.
  CORELLI: #276 (hand B).
  COUPERIN (Louis): #159a, 222, 252, 254.
  CROFT: #65.
  DIEUPART: #18-26, 28-30, 32, 101-105, 109-113, 116, 172.
  DRAGHI: #34-42.
  ECCLES: #115.
  FIOCCO: #59.
  FORCER: #278.
  FROBERGER: #107.
  GAULTIER (E): #162, 226.
  GILLIER (P): #51, 163, 256, 257, 260.
  HANDEL: #295 (hand C).
  HARDEL: #147, 159, 219, 221.
  KING: #12-15, 70, 92, 93-95(?), 98(?).
  LA BARRE: #187, 223, 224.

LEBÈGUE: #8, 9, 60, 85, 86.
LULLY: #57, 97, 120, 123, 124, 128-136, 138, 143, 152,
    182, 183, 199, 209, 217, 218, 231, 233-235, 243, 247,
    258, 263, 268, 269, 280.
MARAIS: #240.
MONNARD: #56.
MUFFAT (Georg): #62, 274, 275, 283-294.
PAISIBLE: #125.
PEPUSCH: #277.
PURCELL (Henry): #2-4, 11, 63, 81-84, 208.
ROSSI: cf #11, 166.
SMITH (John Christopher): #296 (hand D).
TOLLET: #279.
TRESURE: #161.
VALOIS: #153.
ZIANI, #61.
Contents: 29 Suites:

1	#1-10	F		16	142-151	d
2	11-17	A		17	152-159	a
3	18-24	A		18	160-169	a
4	25-33	D		19	170-174	E
5	34-42	b		20	175-181	g
6	43-52	e		21	182-189	d
7	53-62	C		22	190-196	b
8	63-69	c		23	197-209	C
9	70-80	g		24	210-218	D
10	81-91	G		25	219-230	d
11	92-100	D		26	231-242	F
12	101-108	e		27	243-251	g
13	109-118	f		28	252-264	G
14	119-127	g		29	265-273	B♭
15	128-141	g				

#274-282: Miscellaneous pieces
  283-294: Muffat Toccatas

Inventory:

	p 1	P.^re Suitte en f- [F]
1	p 1^{1-6}	Prelude [F]
2	p 2^{1-2}	Allemande [PURCELL (F), Z 699/2]
3	p 2^{1-2}	Courante [PURCELL (F), Z 699/3]
4	p 3^{5-6}	Menuet [PURCELL (F), Z 699/4]
5	p 4^{1-3}	Sarabande [music not filled in]
6	p 4^{4}-5^{6}	Chaconne [F]
7	p 6^{1-3}	Ecossoise [F]

---

8 [LEBÈGUE: Menuet (F)]

Menuet de M.^r Le Begue, qui se joüe alternav^t /auec
le Suivant
         p 6^{4-6}   3[3/4]|8|16|

CO: 14-Schwerin-619 #23, [copy of 65-Lebègue-II #33]
    45-Dart #25, [copy of 65-Lebègue-II #33]
    65-Lebègue-II #33, Menuet

ED: cf Dufourcq-L p 75.

---

9 [LEBÈGUE: Menuet (F)]

2me /Menuet
         p 7^{1-2}   3[3/4] |8|8|

CO: 14-Schwerin-619 #22, [copy of 65-Lebègue-II #32]
    65-Lebègue-II #32, Menuet
ED: cf Dufourcq-L p 75.

10	p 7^{3-6}	Gigue [F]
		CO: 23-Tenbury #68
	p 8	2me Suitte en $A^{\#}_{\#}$
11	p 8^1-9^2	Prelude [A] [attr PURCELL (Z D229), JS BACH (S Anh 178) and ROSSI]
12	p 9^{3-6}	Allemande [KING (A)]
		CO: 21-Rés-1186bis #32 Clark-M678 p 10
		ED: Fuller-Maitland 6:4.
13	p 10^{1-4}	Courante [KING (A)]
		CO: Clark-M678 p 12
14	p 10^{5-6}	Sarabande [KING? (A)]
		CO: Clark-M678 p 13
15	p 11^{1-6}	Gigue |Maister King [A]
		CO: Clark-M678 p 15.
16	p 12^{1-2}	Hornpipe [BARRETT: Sarabande (A)]
		CO: Choice ℓ 15
17	p 12^{2-4}	Bourée [BARRETT: The St. Catherine (A)]
		CO: Choice ℓ 15
	p 12	3me Suitte en $A^{\#}_{\#}$
18	p 12^4-13^6	Ouverture [DIEUPART (A)]
		ED: Brunold-D #1.
19	p 14^1-15^1	Allemande [DIEUPART (A)]
		ED: Brunold-D #2.
20	p 15^{2-6}	Courante [DIEUPART (A)]
		ED: Brunold-D #3.
21	p 16^{1-3}	Sarabande [DIEUPART (A)]
		ED: Brunold-D #4.
22	p 16^{3-4}	Gavote [DIEUPART (A)]
		ED: Brunold-D #5.
23	p 16^{5-6}	Menuet [DIEUPART (A)]
		ED: Brunold-D #6.
24	p 17^{1-6}	Gigue |M^r. Deopard [A]
		ED: Brunold-D #7.

	p 18	4me Suitte en D$^{\sharp}_{\sharp}$
25	p 18$^{1-4}$	Ouverture [DIEUPART (D)]
		ED: cf Brunold-D #8.
26	p 19$^{1-4}$	Allemande [DIEUPART (D)]
		ED: cf Brunold-D #9.
27	p 19$^{5-6}$	Prelude [D]
28	p 20$^{1-4}$	Courante [DIEUPART (D)]
		ED: cf Brunold-D #10.
29	p 20^{5}-21^{1}	Sarabande [DIEUPART (D)]
		ED: cf Brunold-D #11.
30	p 21$^{2-3}$	Gavote [DIEUPART (D)]
		ED: cf Brunold-D #12.
31	p 21$^{4-6}$	Menuet [D]
32	p 22$^{1-5}$	Gigue [DIEUPART (D)]
		ED: cf Brunold-D #14
33	p 22^{6}-23^{6}	Chaconne |fin |on reprend /au comen^{nt}.
		|Jusqua a /ce mot fin. [D]
	p 24	5me Suitte en B mineur /Pieces de M^{r}.
		Baptiste [DRAGHI (?)]
34	p 24$^{1-4}$	[DRAGHI: Prelude (b)]
		CO: Clark-D173 p 2
35	p 24^{5}-25^{6}	Allemande [DRAGHI (b)]
		CO: Clark-D173 p 14
36	p 26$^{1-4}$	Courante [DRAGHI (b)]
		CO: Clark-D173 p 12
37	p 26^{5}-27^{1}	Tombeau [DRAGHI (b)]
		CO: Clark-D173 p 18
38	p 27$^{2-6}$	Gigue [DRAGHI (b)]
		CO: 23-Tenbury #33

39	p 28^{1-5}	Allemande [DRAGHI (b)]
40	p 28^{6}-29^{2}	Rondeau [DRAGHI (b)]
41	p 29^{3-6}	Autre Rondeau [DRAGHI (b)] CO: Clark-D173 p 20
42	p 30^{1}-31^{6}	[DRAGHI: Allemande (b)] CO: Clark-D173 p 4
	p 32	$6.^{me}$ Suitte en E mineur
43	p 32^{1-3}	Prelude [e]
44	p 32^{4-6}	$2.^{me}$ Prelude [e]
45	p 33^{1-6}	Allemandé [e]
46	p 34^{1-4}	Courante [e]
47	p 34^{5-6}	Sarabande [e]
48	p 35^{1-5}	Grond [e]
49	p 36^{1-4}	Gigue [e]
50	p 36^{4-6}	Sarabande [e]
51	p 37^{1-3}	[GILLIER:] Air [de violon] [e] CO: Gillier p 65
52	p 37^{4-6}	Courante [e]
	p 38	$7.^{me}$ Suitte en C
53	p 38^{1-3}	Prelude [C] CO: 23-Tenbury #1?
54	p 38^{4}-39^{1}	Canaries [C] CO: 23-Tenbury #5
55	p 39^{2-5}	Allemande /de M^{r} hamel Bruinincks CO: 23-Tenbury #2?

56 | [MONNARD: <u>Sarabande</u> (C)]

Sarabande

    p 39⁶ $\qquad$ $^3[\frac{3}{4}]$ |4|8|

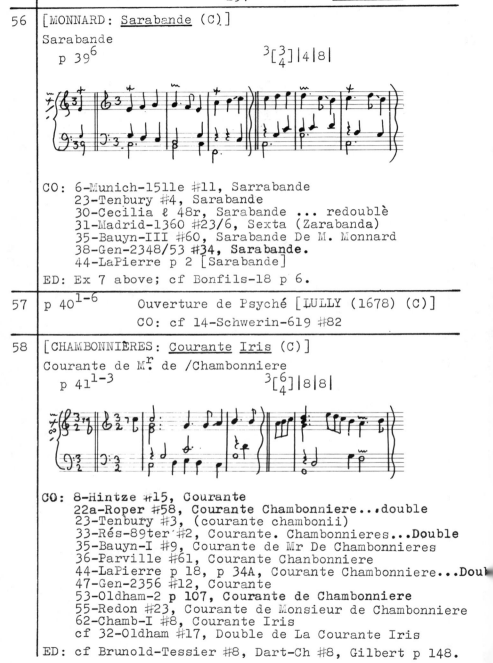

CO: 6-Munich-1511e #11, Sarrabande
     23-Tenbury #4, Sarabande
     30-Cecilia ℓ 48r, Sarabande ... redoublè
     31-Madrid-1360 #23/6, Sexta (Zarabanda)
     35-Bauyn-III #60, Sarabande De M. Monnard
     38-Gen-2348/53 #34, **Sarabande.**
     44-LaPierre p 2 [Sarabande]

ED: Ex 7 above; cf Bonfils-18 p 6.

---

57 | p 40¹⁻⁶   Ouverture de Psyché [LULLY (1678) (C)]

         CO: cf 14-Schwerin-619 #82

---

58 | [CHAMBONNIÈRES: <u>Courante Iris</u> (C)]

Courante de M^r de /Chambonniere

    p 41¹⁻³ $\qquad$ $^3[\frac{6}{4}]$ |8|8|

CO: 8-Hintze #15, Courante
     22a-Roper #58, Courante Chambonniere...double
     23-Tenbury #3, (courante chambonii)
     33-Rés-89ter #2, Courante. Chambonnieres...**Double**
     35-Bauyn-I #9, Courante de Mr De Chambonnieres
     36-Parville #61, Courante Chanbonniere
     44-LaPierre p 18, p 34A, Courante Chambonniere...**Doubl**
     47-Gen-2356 #12, Courante
     53-Oldham-2 **p 107, Courante de Chambonniere**
     55-Redon #23, Courante de Monsieur de Chambonniere
     62-Chamb-I #8, Courante Iris
     cf 32-Oldham #17, Double de La Courante Iris

ED: cf Brunold-Tessier #8, Dart-Ch #8, Gilbert p 148.

59 | p 41$^{4-6}$ Sarabande de M^r. Fiocco [C]

---

60 | [LEBÈGUE: Gavotte (C)]

Gavotte /de M^r. le Begue
   p 42$^{1-2}$ ¢|4|8|

CO: 10-Schwerin-617 #10, Gavotte
    13-Möllersche, [copy of 64-Lebègue-I #43]
    14-Schwerin-619 #91, Gavotte
    21-Rés-1186bis #12, Gavott
    23-Tenbury #6, Gavotte Mr Le Begue
    30-Cecilia ℓ 47r, Gavotte
    35-Bauyn-III #54, (Gavotte) de Mr Lebegue
    36-Parville #68, Gauotte Mr le Begue
    45-Dart #22, [copy of 64-Lebègue-I #43]
    46-Menetou #102, Gavotte
    50-Paignon #11, Balet de Mr lebegue
    64-Lebègue-I #43, Gauotte

ED: cf Dufourcq-L p 38, Brunold/Dart-Co #132.

60a | [LEBÈGUE: Double (C)]

Double
   p 42$^{3-4}$ ¢|4|8|

CO: 13-Möllersche, [copy of 64-Lebègue-I #43a]
    23-Tenbury #6a, Double
    64-Lebègue-I #43a; Double
    cf 14-Schwerin-619 #91a, [Double]
    cf 35-Bauyn-III #54a, Double par Mr Couperin
    cf 36-Parville #68a [Double]
    cf 36-Parville #146, Double de la Gavotte de Le
                  Bègue

cf 50-Paignon #11a, la double
ED: cf Dufourcq-L p 38, Brunold/Dart-Co #132[a].

61	p 42^5-43^6	M^r. /Ziani /Prelude /Adagio [C]
62	p 44^1-47^5	Nova /Cyclopeias /Harmonica /Aria |Ad Maleorum /Ictus Allusio [MUFFAT (C)]
		ED: cf Lange, p 72.
	p 48	**8me Suitte en C♭♭**
63	p 48^{1-6}	Prelude en Maniere /de Chaconne M^r. Purcel [c]
64	p 49^{1-6}	Allemande [c]
65	p 50^{1-3}	**[CROFT:] Courante** [c]
		ED: cf Ferguson #21.
66	p 50^{4-6}	Sarabande [c]
67	p 51^{1-3}	Maniere de Sarabande [c]
68	p 51^{4-6}	Gigue [c]
69	p 52^{1-6}	Allemande [c]
	p 53-55	[blank, ruled, headed]
	p 56	9me. Suite en G♭
70	p 56^{1-6}	Entrée M^r. King [g]
71	p 57^{1-6}	Allemande [g]
72	p 58^{1-3}	Courante [g]
73	p 58^{4-5}	Sarabande [g]
74	p 58^6-59^1	Gigue [g]
75	p 59^{2-3}	2me. Sarabande [g]
76	p 59^{4-6}	Bourée [g]
77	p 60^{1-5}	If Love's a Sweet /passion &c [**g**]
78	p 60^6-61^1	Menuet [g]
79	p 61^{2-4}	Air en Bourée [La Furstenburg (Air ancien) (g)]

CO: cf 42-Vm7-6307-2 #2
        cf 49-RésF-933 #16

80 | p 61$^{5-6}$ Gigue [g]

   | p 62   10me Suitte En G#

81 | p 62$^{1-2}$ Prelude. M^r. Purcel [G] [Z 660/1]

82 | p 62$^{2-4}$ Allemande [PURCELL (G), Z 660/2]

83 | p 62$^{5-6}$ Courante [PURCELL (G), Z 660/3]

84 | p 63$^{1-2}$ Sarabande [PURCELL (G), Z 660/4]

85 | [LEBÈGUE: Bourrée (G)]

Bouree /de /M^r. le /Begue
    p 63$^{3-4}$ ¢ |4|8|

CO: 12-Walther [copy of 64-Lebègue-I #25]
     13-Möllersche [copy of 64-Lebègue-I #25]
     22a-Roper #21 [copy of 64-Lebègue-I #25]
     23-Tenbury #41, Bourée de Mr. le Begue
     45-Dart #28, [copy of 64-Lebègue-I #25]
     64-Lebègue-I #25, Bourée
ED: cf Dufourcq-L p 19.

85a| [LEBÈGUE: Double (G)]

Double
    p 63$^{5-6}$ ¢ |4|8|

CO: 12-Walther, [copy of 64-Lebègue-I #25a]
     13-Möllersche, [copy of 64-Lebègue-I #25a]
     22a-Roper #21a, [copy of 64-Lebègue-I #25a]

23-Tenbury #41a, Double (du mesme)
64-Lebègue-I #25a, Double

ED: cf Dufourcq-L p 20.

86 | [LEBÈGUE: Menuet (G)]

Menuet
  p 64$^{1-3}$ $^3[^3_4]$ |16|8|

CO: 12-Walther, [copy of 64-Lebègue-I #26]
     13-Möllersche, [copy of 64-Lebègue-I #26]
     23-Tenbury #42, Menuet Mr. Le Begue Serieux
     45-Dart #29, [copy of 64-Lebègue-I #26]
     64-Lebègue-I #26, 2me Menuet

ED: cf Dufourcq-L p 20.

87 | [CHAMBONNIÈRES: Courante (G)]

Courante de Ch.^{re} |Reprise
  p 64$^{4-6}$ $^3_2$ |8|9|

CO: 23-Tenbury #40, Courante Chambonniere
     32-Oldham #19, Courante
     33-Rés-89ter #34, Courante Chambonnieres ... Double
     35-Bauyn-I #92, Courante de Mr de Chambonnieres
     36-Parville #92, Courante chanbonniere
     63-Chamb-II #26, Courante

ED: cf Brunold-Tessier #56, Dart-Ch #56, Gilbert p 190.

88 | p 65$^{1-2}$ Loin de Tircis /Je Languis, /Je Soupire [G]

89 | p 65$^{3-6}$ Gigue [G]
          CO: 23-Tenbury #47

90	p 66^1-67^4	Chaconne [G]
91	p 67^{4-6}	Gigue [G]
	p 68	11me Suitte en D#
92	p 68^{1-2}	Prelude Mr King [D]
93	p 68^{3-6}	Allemande [KING?] [D]
		CO: Clark-M678 p 18
94	p 69^{1-3}	Courante [KING?] [D]
		CO: Clark-M678 p 20
95	p 69^{3-6}	Sarabande [KING?] [D]
		CO: Clark-M678 p 23
96	p 70^{1-2}	Gavotte [D]
97	p 70^{2-6}	Chaconne de [Acis et] Galatée [LULLY, II-5 (1686) (D)]

CO: cf 14-Schwerin-619 #123
     cf 23-Tenbury #75
     cf 36-Parville #29
     cf 49-RésF-933 #4
     cf 51-LaBarre-11 p 206
     cf 68-d'Anglebert #55

ED: cf Gilbert p 106, Roesgen-Champion
     p 112.

98	p 71^{1-6}	Gigue [KING?] [D]
		CO: Clark-M678 p 25
99	p 72^{1-2}	grave [CLARKE, T 437 (D)]
100	p 72^{3-6}	Marche [CLARKE, T 435 (D)]
	p 73	12me Suitte en E. mineur
101	p 73^{1-6}	Ouverture [DIEUPART (e)]
		ED: cf Brunold-D #22.
102	p 74^{1-4}	Allemande [DIEUPART (e)]
		ED: cf Brunold-D #23.
103	p 74^5-75^1	Courante [DIEUPART (e)]
		ED: cf Brunold-D #24.

104	p 75$^{2-4}$	Sarabande [DIEUPART (e)]
		ED: cf Brunold-D #25.
105	p 75$^{5-6}$	Gavotte [DIEUPART (e)]
		CO: 23-Tenbury #30
105 a	p 76$^{1-2}$	Double dela Gavotte /precedente [e]
106	p 76$^{3-5}$	Menuet [e]
107	p 76^{5}-77^{3}	Gigue [FROBERGER (e)]
		CO: 35-Bauyn-III #10, cf #92
		36-Parville #33
		ED: cf Adler-II p 20 & 71, Bonfils-18
		p 15, Dufourcq-0 #7.
108	p 77$^{4-6}$	Allemande [e]
	p 78	[blank, ruled]
	p 79	13me Suitte en F$_b$♭
109	p 79$^{1-6}$	Ouverture [DIEUPART (f)]
		ED: Brunold-D #36.
110	p 80$^{1-5}$	Allemande [DIEUPART (f)]
		ED: Brunold-D #37.
111	p 80^{6}-81^{3}	Courante [DIEUPART (f)]
		ED: Brunold-D #38.
112	p 81$^{4-6}$	Sarabande [DIEUPART (f)]
		ED: Brunold-D #39.
113	p 82$^{1-2}$	Gavotte [DIEUPART (f)]
		ED: Brunold-D #40.
114	p 82$^{3-4}$	Menuet /serieux [f]
115	p 82^{5}-83^{2}	[Baloon's] Gigue [ECCLES] [f]
		CO: cf 22a-Roper #49
		cf Banquet-2 ℓ 7
117	p 83$^{3-6}$	Gigue [DIEUPART] [f]
		ED: Brunold-D #42.
117	p 84$^{1-2}$	Air graue [f]

118	p 84$^{3-6}$	Ground [f]
	p 85	[blank, ruled]
	p 86	14$^{\underline{me}}$ Suitte en G♭
119	p 86^{1}-87^{2}	Prelude /de Monsieur /Blankenburg [g]
120	p 87$^{3-6}$	Air p^{r} Le Printemps [LULLY: <u>Premier</u> <u>Air</u> from <u>Phaéton</u> (1683) IV-1 (g)] CO: cf 46-Menetou #107
121	p 88^{1}-89^{4}	Ouverture de Monsieur /Charpentier [g]
122	p 89$^{4-6}$	Menuet [g]
123	p 90^{1}-91^{1}	Preparons nous /pour la féste /Nouvelle [LULLY from <u>Le</u> <u>Temple</u> <u>de</u> <u>la</u> <u>paix</u> (1685) Prologue (g)] CO: cf 46-Menetou #40

124	p 91$^{2-6}$	Air d'Armide /Sourdines /tres doux [LULLY: <u>Second</u> <u>Air</u> (<u>Sourdines</u>) II-4 (1686) (g)]
		CO: cf 14-Schwerin-619 #64
		    cf 23-Tenbury #49
		    cf 36-Parville #115, 149
		    cf 49-RésF-933 #2
		    cf 68-d'Anglebert #33
		ED: cf Gilbert p 115, Roesgen-Champion p 62.

125	p 92^{1}-93^{2}	Passacaille /de M^{r}. Paisible [g]
126	p 93$^{3-4}$	Rigodon [g]
127	p 93$^{5-6}$	2$^{\underline{me}}$ Rigodon [g]
	p 94	15$^{\underline{me}}$ Suitte en G♭

128	p 94^{1}-95^{2}	Ouverture /D'Isis [LULLY (1677) (g)]
		CO: cf 14-Schwerin-619 #51
		    cf 33-Rés-89ter #42c
		    cf 36-Parville #42
		    cf 40-Rés-476 #35
		    cf 42-Vm7-6307-2 #5
		    cf 46-Menetou #85
		    cf 49-RésF-933 #24

cf Stoss ℓ 24v

ED: cf Bonfils-LP p 101, Howell #2, Gilbert p 199.

129 | p 95$^{2-6}$ Entrée d'Apollon [LULLY from Triomphe de
l'amour (1681) (g)]

CO: cf 14-Schwerin-619 #56
cf 30-Cecilia ℓ 52r
cf 36-Parville #43
cf 46-Menetou #100
cf 68-d'Anglebert #35
cf Stockholm-176 ℓ 14v
cf Saizenay-I p 222 [lute]

ED: cf Gilbert p 118, Roesgen-Champion p 64.

130 | p 96$^{1-3}$ Entrée /des Muses [LULLY: Premier Air pour
les muses from Isis (1677) Prologue-3 (g)]

CO: cf 42-Vm7-6307-2 #6
cf 45-Dart #52
cf 46-Menetou #61

131 | p 96$^{3-6}$ Les Songes Agreables [LULLY from Atys
(1676) III-4 (g)]

CO: cf 14-Schwerin-619 #53
cf 33-Rés-89ter #43
cf 36-Parville #117
cf 46-Menetou #114
cf 68-d'Anglebert #34

ED: cf Gilbert p 116, Roesgen-Champion p 63.

132 | p 97$^{1-6}$ Les zephirs Echo [LULLY: Entrée des zé-
phirs from Atys (1676) II-4 (g)]
CO: cf 14-Schwerin-619 #55

133 | p 98$^{1-2}$ Gavotte /d'Orithie [LULLY: from Le Tri-
omphe de l'amour (1681) (g)]
CO: cf 46-Menetou #112

134 | p 98$^{3-5}$ Entrée /D'Endimion [LULLY: Deuxieme Air
pour Endimion from Le Triomphe de l'amour
(1681) (g)]

135	p 98^5-99^2	[Premier] Air pour /la Jeunesse [LULLY from <u>Le Triomphe de l'amour</u> (1681) (g)] CO: cf 36-Parville #128
136	p 99^{2-4}	$2^{me}_{.}$ Air /Rondeau [LULLY: <u>Deuxieme Air pour les mesmes</u> from <u>Le Triomphe de l'amour</u> (1681) (g)]
137	p 99^{5-6}	Air grave [g]
138	p 100^1-102^5	Passacaille /D'Armide [LULLY (1686) V-2 (g)] CO: cf 14-Schwerin-619 #63 cf 31-Madrid-1360 #27 cf 49-RésF-933 #1 cf 68-d'Anglebert #37 **cf Minorite ℓ 44v** ED: **cf Gilbert p 108, Roesgen-Champion** **p 67.**
139	p 102^{5-6}	Menuet [g]
140	p 103^{1-3}	Mascarade [g]
141	p 103^{4-6}	Menuet Anglois Rondeau **[CLARKE, T 492 (g)]** CO: 23-Tenbury #50 Clark-M678 p 27A
	p 104	$16^{me}_{.}$ Suitte en D [d]
142	p 104^{1-4}	Prelude [d]
143	p 104^5-105^4	Ouverture /du Ballet /de Flore [LULLY (1669) (d)] CO: 23-Tenbury #56
144	p 105^{4-6}	Courante [d]
145	p 106^{1-3}	$2^{me}_{.}$ /Courante [d]
146	p $106^{4-6}_{.}$	Sarabande [d]

147 [HARDEL: _Gigue_ (d)]

Gigue
p 106⁶-107¹ $\frac{3}{8}$|7|13|

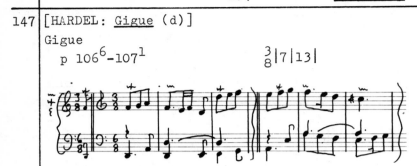

CO: 35-Bauyn-III #49, Gigue de Mr. Hardel
ED: cf Quittard-H p 8.

148	p 107²⁻⁶	Allemande [d]
149	p 108¹⁻³	Courante [d]
150	p 108⁴⁻⁶	**Sarabande** [d]
151	p 109¹⁻⁶	Air de violon [d]
	p 110	17ᵐᵉ Suitte en A [a]
152	p 110¹-111³	Ouverture /de Persée [LULLY (1682) (a)]
		CO: cf 14-Schwerin-619 #66 cf 46-Menetou #98
153	p 111³⁻⁶	Courante [VALOIS (a)]
		CO: 23-Tenbury #10
154	p 112¹⁻⁴	Allemande [a]
155	p 112⁵-113¹	Courante [a]
156	p 113²⁻³	Sarabande [a]
157	p 113⁴⁻⁶	Gigue [a]
158	p 114¹⁻⁶	Chaconne [a]

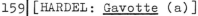
159 [HARDEL: Gavotte (a)]

Gavotte
   p 115$^{1-2}$ ¢ |4|8|

CO: 23-Tenbury #12, Gavotte Mr. Hardel
    25-Bod-426 #20, Gavotte d'Ardelle
    31-Madrid-1360 #41, Jabouste de Ardel
    35-Bauyn-III #50, (Gavotte) de Mr Hardel
    36-Parville #52, Gavotte de Mr Hardel
    45-Dart #60, Gauotte de Monsr Ardel
    49-RésF-933 #13, gavotte d ardelle
    St-Georges ℓ 51, Gavotte
    cf Saizenay-I p 61, Gavotte Ardelle [lute]
    cf Saizenay-II p 17, Gavotte d'hardelle [lute]
    cf Vm7-4867 p 52, Gavotte d'ardelle [violin]
ED: cf Brunold/Dart-Co #131, Curtis-Co #11, Quittard-H pl.

159 [COUPERIN (L): Double (a)]
a

Double
   p 115$^{3-6}$ ¢ |4|8|

CO: 23-Tenbury #12a, Double
    31-Madrid-1360 #41a [Double]
    35-Bauyn-III #50a, Double (de la gauotte) cy des-
             sus Par Mr Couperin
    36-Parville #52a, Double de la gauotte fait par
             Mr Couprin
    49-RésF-933 #13a, [Double]
    cf Vm7-4867 p 77, Double [violin]
ED: cf Brunold/Dart-Co #131[a], Curtis-Co #11a,
    Quittard-H p 2.

p 116   18me Suitte en A [a]

160 | p 116$^{1-5}$ Allemande [a]

161 | p 116^{6}-117^{1} Courante [TRESURE (a)]
                    CO: 19-Heardson #60

162 | p 117$^{2-4}$ 2me Courante [E. GAULTIER, arr: Courante
                    la belle homicide (d)]
                    CO: cf Stockholm-2 p 30
                        cf Stockholm-176 ℓ 10v
                    ED: cf Souris-G #19.

163 | p 117$^{4-6}$ [GILLIER, arr:] Sarabande [a]
                    CO: Gillier p 13

164 | p 118$^{1-3}$ Air grave [a]

165 | p 118$^{4-6}$ Rondeau [a]

166 | p 119$^{1-6}$ Passacaille [ROSSI (a)]
                    CO: 23-Tenbury #11
                        35-Bauyn-III #91
                        36-Parville #57
                    ED: cf Pierront p 6, Prunières p 18.

167 | p 120$^{1-6}$ Allemande [a]

168 | p 121$^{1-4}$ Courante [a]

169 | p 121$^{5-6}$ Gigue Italienne [a]

p 122   19me Suitte en E$^{\#\#\#}_{\#\#\#}$

170 | p 122^{1}-123^{2} Ouverture [E]

171 | p 123$^{2-6}$ Allemande [E]

172 | p 124$^{1-3}$ Courante [DIEUPART (E)]
                    ED: Brunold-D #31 [F]

173 | p 124$^{4-6}$ Sarabande [E]

174 | p 125$^{1-2}$ Gavotte [E]

p 125^{3}-127^{6} [blank, ruled]

	p 128	20me Suitte en Gb
175	p 128^1-129^3	Ouverture [g]
176	p 129$^{4-6}$	Courante [g]
177	p 130$^{1-2}$	Sarabande [g]
177 a	p 130$^{3-5}$	Double [g]
178	p 130^5-131^2	Rondeau /Gavote [g]
179	p 131$^{3-6}$	Air graue [g]
180	p 132^1-133^2	Bourée en Rondeau /redoublé [g]
181	p 133$^{3-6}$	Gigue en Rondeau [g]
	p 134	21me Suitte en D
182	p 134^1-135^4	Ouverture /de Roland [LULLY (1685) (d)]

CO: cf 14-Schwerin-619 #49
    cf 46-Menetou #27

| 183 | p 135$^{5-6}$ | Gavotte [LULLY: C'est l'amour from Roland |

(1685) Prologue (d)]

CO: cf 46-Menetou #28
    cf Lüneburg-1198 p 64
    cf Stockholm-228 ℓ 9v

---

184 | [CHAMBONNIÈRES: Allemande la loureuse (d)]

Allemande
    p 136^1-137^4 ¢ |7|12|

CO: 32-Oldham #23, Allemande La Loureuse
    35-Bauyn-I #30, Allemande la Loureuse de Mr de
                     Chambonnieres
    36-Parville #21, Allemande la loureuse Chanbonniere
    62-Chamb-I #11, Allemande la Loureuse
ED: cf Brunold-Tessier #11, Dart-Ch #11.

184 | [Double (d)]
a

Le Double
    p 136⁵-137⁴   ¢ |7|12|

185 | p 137⁵⁻⁶   Menuet [d]

186 | [CHAMBONNIÈRES: Courante (d)]

Courante
    p 138¹⁻³ $\frac{3}{2}$|7|9|

CO: 18-Ch-Ch-1236 #3, Corant Mr Sambonier
    35-Bauyn-I #35, Courante de Mr. de Chambonnieres
ED: cf Brunold-Tessier #84.

187 | [LA BARRE: Sarabande (d)]

Sarabande
    p 138⁴⁻⁶   ³[$\frac{3}{4}$]|8|20|

CO: 36-Parville #18, Sarabande la barre

188	p 139$^{1-3}$	Bourée Rondeau [d]
189	p 139$^{4-6}$	Menuet [d]
	p 140	22me Suitte en B mineur
190	p 140$^{1-5}$	Allemande /Mr Barett [b]
		CO: Harpsichord-2 #14
191	p 140^{6}-141^{2}	Courante [BARRETT (b)]
		CO: Harpsichord-2 #15
192	p 141$^{2-4}$	Sarabande [BARRETT (b)]
		CO: Harpsichord-2 #16
193	p 141$^{4-5}$	Ecossoise [BARRETT (b)]
		GO: Harpsichord-2 #20
194	p 142$^{1-3}$	Air [BARRETT (b)]
		CO: Harpsichord-2 #21
195	p 142$^{3-6}$	Gigue [BARRETT (b)]
		CO: Harpsichord-2 #22
196	p 142^{6}-143^{1}	Menuet en Rondeau [BARRETT? (b)]
		CO: Harpsichord-2 #17
	p 143^{2}-145^{6}	[blank, ruled]
	p 146	23me Suitte en C
197	p 146$^{1-2}$	Prelude [C]
198	p 146$^{3-6}$	Marche /Rondeau |Tromp |Tymb |violon |viol ... [C]
199	p 147$^{1-6}$	Ouverture de /Bellerophone [LULLY.(1679) (C)]

CO: cf 14-Schwerin-619 #83
        cf 27-Gresse #53
        cf 40-Rés-476 #26
        cf 46-Menetou #87
        cf Bod-576 p 54
ED: cf Bonfils-LP p 86, Howell #1.

200 [CHAMBONNIÈRES: *Allemande* *le* *moutier* (C)]

Allemande
   p 148$^{1-6}$ ^{C}|11|11|

CO: 32-Oldham #22, Le Moutie et la Mariée
    35-Bauyn-I #1, Allemande de Mr. Chambonnieres Le
                Moutier
    36-Parville #60, Allemande le moutier de Mr Chan-
                bonniere
ED: cf Brunold-Tessier #61, Curtis-Co #29, Brunold/
    Dart-Co #134.

200 [Double (C)]
 a
Le Double /de la Mesme
   p 148^6-149^6 ^{C}|11|11|

CO: cf 35-Bauyn-I #1a, Double du Moutier par Mr
                    Couperin
    cf 36-Parville #60a, Le Double du moutier fait par
                    Mr Couprin
ED: cf Brunold/Dart-Co #134, Curtis-Co #29a, Brunold-
    Tessier #61:

201 p 150$^{1-4}$ Courante [C]

202 p 150$^{4-6}$ Menuet /alternati ement [C]

203 p 151$^{1-2}$ 2.me menuet [C]

204 | [d'ANGLEBERT: <u>Chaconne</u> (C)]

Chaconne
  p 151$^{3-6}$ $^3[\frac{3}{4}]$ |36|

CO: 33-Rés-89ter #7, Chaconne. D'Anglebert
    36-Parville #65, Chaconne Danglebert
    45-Dart #39, Chaconne
    51-LaBarre-11 p 212, Chaconne de Mr D'anglebert
    51-LaBarre-11 p 229, Chaconne D'Anglebert
ED: cf Gilbert p 160, Roesgen-Champion p 148.

205 | p 152$^{1-2}$ Air [C]

206 | [CHAMBONNIÈRES: <u>La Sotise</u> (C)]

La Sotise
  p 152$^{3-6}$ $^3[\frac{3}{4}]$ |16|16|

CO: 35-Bauyn-I #7, Autre [Courante] du même Auteur
    36-Parville #148, [untitled]
ED: cf Brunold-Tessier #65.

207 | p 152^6-153^1 Menuet [C]

208 | p 153$^{2-6}$ Imitation de la descente de Cybelle
                        [PURCELL (C), Z T678]
                        CO: 23-Tenbury #25

209 | p 154^1-158^3 Chaconne /d'Amadis [LULLY (1684) V-5 (C)]
                        CO: cf 36-Parville #66

p 158⁴-159⁶ [blank, ruled]

p 160   24me Suitte en D$^{\#}$#

210 | p 160$^{1-5}$ Allemande [D]

211 | p 160^{5}-161^{2} Courante [D]

212 | p 161$^{3-6}$ Sarabande ou Tombeau [D]

213 | p 162^{1}-163^{1} Rondeau redoublé [D]

214 | p 163$^{2-4}$ Menuet [D]

215 | p 163$^{5-6}$ Gigue [D]

216 | p 164$^{1-3}$ Gavotte /en Rondeau [D]

217 | p 164^{4}-165^{1} La marche des /Insulaires [LULLY from Roland (1685) I-6 (D)]

218 | p 165$^{2-6}$ Second Air [LULLY: Entre-acte from Roland (1685) I-6 (D)]

p 166   25me Suitte en D

219 | [HARDEL: Allemande (d)]

Allemande
   p 166$^{1-4}$ ¢|13|15|

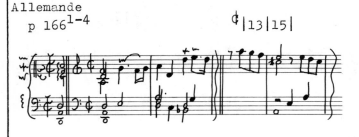

CO: 35-Bauyn-III #44, ALLemande de Mr hardel
    36-Parville #22, Allemande hardel
    44-LaPierre p 52, Allemande de Mr Hardel
ED: cf Quittard-H p 4.

220 | [CHAMBONNIÈRES: Courante (d)]

Courante
p 166⁵-167¹ $\frac{3}{2}$|6|9|

CO: 32-Oldham #13, 3me Courante
     35-Bauyn-I #37, Courante de Monsr. de Chambonnieres
     62-Chamb-I #14, Courante
ED: cf Brunold-Tessier #14, Dart-Ch #14.

221 | [HARDEL: Sarabande (d)]

Sarabande
p 167¹⁻³ $3[\begin{smallmatrix}3\\4\end{smallmatrix}]$|8|16|

CO: 35-Bauyn-III #48, Sarabande de Mr Hardel
ED: cf Quittard-H p 7.

222 | [COUPERIN (L): Courante (d)]

Courante
p 167⁴⁻⁶ $\frac{3}{2}$|8|16|

CO: 35-Bauyn-II #41, Courante de Monsr. Couperin
     36-Parville #5, Courante Couprain

cf 24-Babell #224, Courante
cf 36-Parville #16, Courante la Barre
ED: cf Brunold/Dart-Co #41, Curtis-Co #58.

223 │ [LA BARRE: Allemande (d)]

Allemande
p 168^{1-3}   C |8|7|

CO: 36-Parville #15, Allemande la Barre

224 │ [LA BARRE: Courante (d)]

Courante
p 168^{4-6}   3/2 |9|9|

CO: 36-Parville #16, Courante la Barre
cf 24-Babell #222, Courante
cf 35-Bauyn-II #41, Courante de Monsr Couperin
cf 36-Parville #5, Courante Couprain
ED: cf Brunold/Dart-Co #41, Curtis-Co #58.

225 │ p 169^{1-3}   Courante [d]

226 │ p 169^{4-6}   Courante L'Immortelle [E GAULTIER (d)]

CO: cf 33-Rés-89ter #29
cf 45-Dart #40
cf 66-Perine #1
cf Stockholm-176 ℓ 4v
cf Skara #20
cf Stockholm-2 p 32
cf Ottobeuren p 142
ED: cf Souris-G #81, 66, Gilbert p 182.

227 | p 170$^{1-3}$ | Rondeau Anglois |Rond. /again ... [d]

228 | p 170$^{4-6}$ | Autre [d]

229 | p 171$^{1-3}$ | Menuet [d]
CO: 23-Tenbury #58

230 | p 171$^{4-6}$ | Gigue [d]

p 172 | 26me Suitte en F

231 | p 172^{1}-173^{3} | Ouverture /du Triomphe /de L'Amour [LULLY (1681) (F)]
CO: cf 14-Schwerin-619 #84
cf 46-Menetou #94

232 | p 173$^{3-6}$ | Rondeau [F]

233 | p 174$^{1-3}$ | Prelude /de Thesée [LULLY (1675) III-3 (F)]

234 | p 174^{3}-175^{1} | Premier air /pour Les Lutins [LULLY from <u>Thésée</u> (1675) III-6 (F)]
CO: cf 23-Tenbury #67
cf 33-Rés-89ter #9
ED: cf Gilbert p 164.

235 | p 175$^{2-4}$ | Second Air [LULLY from <u>Thésée</u> (1675) III-6 (F)]
CO: cf 33-Rés-89ter #9a
cf Inglis ℓ 14r
ED: cf Gilbert p 165.

236 | p 175$^{5-6}$ | Gome Sweet Lass [CLARKE, T 336 (F)]
CO: 23-Tenbury #66
Add-22099 ℓ 6v

237 | p 176^{1}-177^{4} | Chaconne [F]

238 | p 177$^{5-6}$ | Ecossoise [BYRON, arr: <u>Scotch Tune</u> (F)]
CO: cf Clark-M678 p 21A
cf Add-52363 p 35

239 | p 178$^{1-4}$ | Loure en Rondeau [F]

240 | p 178^{4}-179^{2} | Air de M^{r}. Marais [F]

241 | p 179$^{3-4}$ | Gavotte [F]

242	p 179$^{5-6}$	Menuet [F]
	p 180	27me Suitte en G♭
243	p 180$^{1-6}$	Ouverture /d'Atys [LULLY (1676) (g)]
244	p 181$^{1-6}$	Allemande |variation pour la reprise [g]
245	p 182$^{1-3}$	Courante [g]
246	p 182$^{4-6}$	Sarabande [g]
247	p 183$^{1-2}$	2me Sarabande [LULLY: <u>Dieu des enfers</u> from

<u>La Naissance de Venus</u> (1665) II-6 (g)]

CO: cf 36- Parville #141
    cf 68-d'Anglebert #23

ED: cf Gilbert p 98, Roesgen-Champion p 45.

---

248   [CHAMBONNIÈRES: <u>Gigue</u> (g)]

Gigue
    p 183$^{3-6}$ $^{3}[\frac{3}{4}]$|26|20|

CO: cf 63-Chamb-II #21, Gigue
ED: cf Brunold-Tessier #51, Dart-Ch #51.

249	p 184$^{1-2}$	Bourée [g]
250	p 184$^{3-4}$	Menuet [g]
	p 184^{5}-185^{1}	[blank, ruled]
251	p 185$^{2-6}$	Gigue [g]
	p 186	28me Suitte en G#

252 | [COUPERIN (L): _Allemande_ (G)]

Allemande
p 186[1-4]   C |9|9|

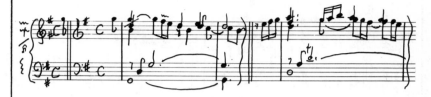

CO: 33-Rés-89ter #33, Allemande de Couperin ... Double
    35-Bauyn-II #82, Allemande du même Auteur
    36-Parville #88, Allemande Couprin
    47-Gen-2356 #5, Allemande du mesme Mr Couperin
ED: cf Brunold/Dart-Co #82, Curtis-Co #86, Gilbert p 186.

253 | [COUPERIN (L): _Courante_ (G)]

Courante
p 186[5]-187[1]   3/2 |8|8|2|

CO: 35-Bauyn-II #84, Courante du meme Auteur
    36-Parville #89, Courante Couprin
ED: cf Brunold/Dart-Co #84, Curtis-Co #87.

254 | [COUPERIN (L): <u>Sarabande</u> (G)]

Sarabande
   p 187$^{2-4}$ $^3[\frac{3}{4}]|8|16|$

CO: 35-Bauyn-II #87, Sarabande de Mr. Couperin
    36-Parville #98, Sarabande Couprin

ED: cf Brunold/Dart-Co #87, Curtis-Co #89.

255 | p 187$^{5-6}$ Menuet [G]

256 | p 188$^{1-3}$ Marche [GILLIER] [G]
                         CO: cf Gillier p 52

257 | p 188$^{3-6}$ Air [de violon]/de M^r. Giller [G]
                         CO: cf Giller p 54.

258 | p 189$^{1-6}$ Chaconne Italienne /p^r. les Triuelins et

                         les scaramouches [LULLY from <u>Le Bourgeois</u>

                         <u>Gentilhomme</u> (1670) Nations-4 (G)]

                         CO: cf 51-LaBarre-11 p 1

259 | p 190$^{1-3}$ Courante [G]

260 | p 190$^{4-6}$ Menuet [GILLIER] [G]
                         CO: cf Gillier p 58

261 | p 191$^{1-3}$ Bourée en Rondeau [G]

262 | p 191$^{4-6}$ Gigue [G]

263 | p 192^{1}-194^{4} Chaconne de Phaëton [LULLY (1683) II-5 (G)]

                         CO: cf 14-Schwerin-619 #61
                             cf 43-Gen-2354 #1
                             cf 44-LaPierre p 24, 45A
                             cf 46-Menetou #9
                             cf 68-d'Anglebert #15

                         ED: cf Gilbert p 100, Roesgen-Champion
                             p 30.

264 | p 194$^{5-6}$ Gigue [G]

    | p 195   29me Suite en B [Bb]

265 | p 195$^{1-4}$ Air [B♭]

266 | p 195$^{5-6}$ Marche [B♭]

p 196^{1}-197^{3} [blank, ruled]

267 | p 197$^{4-6}$ Ecossoise [B♭]

268 | p 198$^{1-3}$ Les Mariez [LULLY from Le Carnaval (1668/ 75) VII (B♭)]

CO: 23-Tenbury #79

269 | p 198$^{4-6}$ Les Espagnols [LULLY from Le Bourgeois Gentilhomme (1670) Nations-3 (B♭)]

CO: cf 23-Tenbury #80
     cf 36-Parville #130
     cf 50-Paignon #10
     cf Saizenay-I p 287 [lute]

270 | p 199$^{1-3}$ Ecossoise [CLARKE: The bonny Gray Ey'd Morn (B♭)]

CO: Harpsichord-1 #13.

271 | p 199$^{4-6}$ Gigue [B♭]

272 | p 200$^{1-3}$ Bourée Angloise [B♭]

CO: 23-Tenbury #82
     Harpsichord-1 #14

273 | p 200$^{4-6}$ Gigue [B♭]

p 201   [blank, ruled]

274 | p 202^{1}-203^{3} Chaconne |G. Muffat [G]

ED: cf Lange p 64.

275 | p 204^{1}-208^{4} Passacaille |Ad Majorem Dei Gloriam |Georg Muffat [g]

ED: cf Lange p 66.

p 209   [blank, ruled]

276 | p 210^{1}-211^{4} Corelli Sonata /Violoncello /Preludio ... |Augst 13th 1821. [Hand B, pencil]

p 211^{5}-235^{6} [blank, ruled]

277 | p 236^{1}-239^{1} Ground de M^{r}. Pepusch [B♭]

278 | p 240^{1}-241^{4} Chaconne de M^{r}. Forcer [e]

279 | p 242^{1}-234^{6} Ground M^{r}. Tollet [F]

280 | p 244^{1}-246^{6} Passacaille d'Achile [et Polixène]
     [LULLY (1687 I-5 (A)]

281 | p 247^{1-4} La St Jean est de retour [A]
282 | p 248^{1-6} Marche des Jeanissaires [G]
     CO: cf 42-Vm7-6307-2 #4
         cf 49-RésF-933 #20
     p 249   [blank, ruled; #283-294: cf ED: Lange p 1-63]

283 | p 250^{1}-252^{2} Toccata /Prima [MUFFAT (d)]

284 | p 252^{2}-254^{3} Toccata /Secunda [MUFFAT (d)]

285 | p 254^{4}-256^{6} Toccata /Tertia [MUFFAT (a)]

286 | p 257^{1}-259^{1} Toccata /Quarta [MUFFAT (e)]

287 | p 259^{2}-262^{1} Toccata /Quinta [MUFFAT (C)]

288 | p 262^{1}-264^{3} Toccata /Sexta [MUFFAT (F)

289 | p 264^{4}-270^{4} Toccata /Septima [MUFFAT (C)]

290 | p 270^{5}-273^{7} Toccata /Octtava [MUFFAT (G)]

291 | p 274^{1}-276^{7} Toccata /Nona [MUFFAT (e)]

292 | p 277^{1}-279^{7} Toccata /Decima [MUFFAT (D)]

293 | p 280^{1}-283^{2} Toccata Vndecima [MUFFAT (c)]

294 | p 283^{3}-286^{5} Toccata /Duo decima /et Ultima [MUFFAT (B♭)]

     p 286   Auctore Georgio Muffat /Il s'ensuit la
               Chaconne en G# pag 202 [#274] la Passa-
               caille en G♭ pag 204 [#275] et les Cy-
               clopes en C pag 44 [#62] [ie, the complete
               Apparatus musico-organisticus (1690)]
     p 287   [blank, ruled]
295 | p 288^{1}-289^{3} Arm, arm ye brave Judas Maccabeus [HANDEL;
               Hand C]

     p 289^{4}-291^{7} [blank, ruled]

296 | p 292^{1}-294^{5} Air from Smith's opera of the Fairies ...
               [Hand D]

p 295^1-360^7 [blank, ruled]

[here are stubbed 6 modern index ℓ]

[3 ℓ, blank]

25-BOD-426

Provenance: England, post 1708 (transcription from <u>Pyr-rhus</u> <u>et</u> <u>Demetrius</u>, English version by Haym).

Location: Oxford; Bodleian Library, Ms. Mus. Sch. E 426.

Description: 2 loose end papers, 5 p.ℓ., 40 ℓ., 2 loose end papers; oblong quarto format, 15.2 x 19.6 cm. (trimmed). Watermark #13 (same as Bod-425), 21 (back end papers), and 44 (front end papers). Contemporary full leather gilt-tooled binding, repaired, re-backed, 15.8 x 20 cm.

Notation: Keyboard score (two 5-line staves, 3 systems per page, written page by page). Clefs: F^4, G^2.

Scribes: 3 unidentified hands, the same as in Bod-425:
A: #1-24
B: 25-47
C: indexes

Marginalia: Original numeration by ℓ. (maintained below) and of pieces (incorrect; disregarded below). Modern numeration by ℓ. in pencil. Original stick counting and arabic numerals in front and back fly leaves. "André Roner a deux portes au dessus /de Blu post Tavern chez Mr Sharpless [in another ink:] in Martins Street. chez (Sharpless[?])," ℓ. i^v. Miscellaneous directions to a copyist (the scribe to himself?), cf. #13, 21. Hand B, ℓ. $iiiA^v$, "Mr Colin Music /Master living in plum /tree street Stockings Shop."

Summary:
Composers:
COLIN (Master): #29.
GODEAU: #42.

HARDEL: #20
LULLY: #7.
SCARLATTI (Alessandro), arr HAYM: #23.

Contents:

#1-14 Harpsichord pieces (C)
15-31 Miscellaneous harpsichord pieces
32-47 Vocal music (written from the back of the
       volume)

Inventory:

ℓ i-ii^r [blank, unruled; see "Marginalia"]

ℓ ii^v-iii^r Airs contenus de ce coté de livre ...
            [index in hand C of pieces #1-29]

ℓ iii^v-iv^r [blank, unruled]

ℓ iv^v-v^r [table of note values in hand A, with
            scale in hand B]

1   ℓ v^{v1}-1r^3 Prelude [unmeasured (C)]
2   ℓ 1v^1-2r^3 Sarrabande [C]
            CO: cf 22a-Roper #52
3   ℓ 2v^1-3r^3 Allemande [C]
4   ℓ 3v^1 1. Fanfares [C]
5   ℓ 3v$^{2-3}$ 2. Sarrabande |reprenez les /1ere Fan-
            fares |fin [C]
6   ℓ 4r^1 2. Fanfares |reprenez la Sarrabande [C]
7   ℓ 4r$^{2-3}$ Menuet [LULLY: Haubois from Thésée (1675)
            Prologue (C)]
            CO: cf 14-Schwerin-619 #71
                cf 36-Parville #132
                cf 44-LaPierre p 22A
8   ℓ 4v^1-6r^2 Les Ecchos [C]

            [1 ℓ, numbered 5, is incorrectly bound

		here; see #13-14]
9	ℓ 6v$^{1-3}$	Marche [C]
	ℓ 7r	[blank, ruled]
10	ℓ 7v^{1}-8r^{3}	Gigue [C]
11	ℓ 8v^{1}-9r^{3}	Marche [C]
12	ℓ 9v^{1}	Gavotte [C]
13	ℓ 5r$^{1-3}$	Menuet [music crossed out, stubbed note:] Ce menuet /marqué No 11 et /qui est rayé /ne doit pas /etre recrit.
14	ℓ 5v^{1}, 10r$^{1-2}$	Marche [C]
15	ℓ 10v^{1}-11r^{3}	Le Singe [a/E]
	ℓ 11v-12r	[blank, ruled]
16	ℓ 12v^{1}- 13Cr^{3}	folies d'espagne, Observer de les mettre suivant leur chifres [ie, 12 variations which are written out of order (d)]
17	ℓ 13Cv$^{1-3}$	Menuet [d]
18	ℓ 14r$^{1-3}$	Gavotte [d]
19	ℓ 14v^{1}-16r^{3}	Bourree [d]

20 | [HARDEL: <u>Gavotte</u> (a)]

Gauotte d'Ardelle
    ℓ 15v$^{1-3}$ ^{C}|4|8|

CO: 23-Tenbury #12, Gavotte Mr. Hardel
    24-Babell #159, Gavotte

```
31-Madrid-1360 #41, Jabouste de Ardel
35-Bauyn-III #50, (Gavotte) de Mr Hardel
36-Parville #52, Gavotte de Mr Hardel
45-Dart #60, Gauotte de Monsr Ardel
49-RésF-933 #13, gavotte d ardelle
St-Georges ℓ 51, Gavotte
cf Saizenay-I p 61, Gavotte Ardelle [lute]
cf Saizenay-II p 17, Gavotte d'hardelle [lute]
cf Vm7-4867 p 52, Gavotte d'ardelle [violin]
ED: cf Brunold/Dart-Co #131, Curtis-Co #11, Quittard-H pl.
```

	ℓ 16r	[blank, ruled]
21	ℓ 16v¹-17r³	La Cibelle qui ne doit pas **exerscrite** [a]
22	ℓ 17v¹-18r³	aimable vainqueur [D]
	ℓ 18v-19r	[written from the other end, see below]
23	ℓ 19v¹-20r³	Aria dell. opera de Pyrrhus et demetrius [text incipit:] Hast o Sun o quickly fly ... [SCARLATTI, arr HAYM from Pyrrhus et Demetrius (English version 1708) vocal/keyboard score]
	ℓ 20v-21r	[written from the other end, see below]
24	ℓ 21v¹⁻³	Leve le coeur [F]
	ℓ 22r	[blank, ruled]
25	ℓ 22v¹-23v³	Cibelle [a]
	ℓ 24r	[written from other end, see below]
26	ℓ 24v¹-25r³	Rigadoon [G]
27	ℓ 25v¹-26r³	Minuet [C]
28	ℓ 26v¹-27r²	Minuet [d]
29	ℓ 27v¹-27Ar²	Rigadoon /Composée by Master Colin [music crossed out (D)]
30	ℓ 27Av¹-28v¹	Trompett Tune [C]
31	ℓ 28v²-29r²	Minuet [C]

	ℓ 29r^3-40	[written from other end:]
	ℓ iA^r-iiA^r	[blank, unruled]
	ℓ iiA^v	Airs contenus de ce coté de livre [index in hand C of pieces 32-39]
	ℓ iiiA^{r-v}	[blank, unruled; see "Marginalia"]
	ℓ ivA^r	[miscellaneous notes on staves, giving the appearance of an unmeasured prelude, but without clefs or musical coherence]
32-42	ℓ ivA^v-8Av^1	[miscellaneous vocal pieces in French and Italian, including:] Psalm 2 [GODEAU]
	ℓ 8A^v-14A^r	[written from other end, see above]
42a	ℓ 14Av$^{1-5}$	psal. 2^e De Godeau La Basse ... [bass part of psalm]
	ℓ 15A^r-16A^v	[written from other end, see above]
43-44	ℓ 17Ar^1-20Ar^1	[sacred vocal music in French]
		[The remainder of the volume is written from the other end, see above.]

<u>Provenance</u>: Antwerp, ca. 1629 (many pieces dated, from
"anno 1621 in December," ℓ. 65v, to "19$^{\underline{a}}$ Octobris:-
1628," ℓ. 168r; most dates in chronological order;
no dates in latter section of ms).

<u>Location</u>: London; British Library [British Museum],
Department of Manuscripts, Additional mss 23623.

<u>Description</u>: 1 p.ℓ., 16-196 ℓ. (181 ℓ.: 1-15 lacking), 1
ℓ.; 24 quires (A^2, B-D^8, E^{10}, F-W^8, X^1); folio format,
23 x 19.6 cm. (trimmed). Watermark #30. Modern
(1972) cloth folder with remnant of original gilt-
tooled vellum binding (23 x 18.4 cm.) pasted inside.
Quires sewn onto modern stubs, leaves largely lami-
nated. Contemporary spine title, "TABLATVRE /DOCT
BVLL /1629."

<u>Notation</u>: Keyboard score (two 6-line staves, 3-4 systems
per page, written page by page). Clefs: F^{2,4}, G^3,
C^{1,4,6}; usually F^4, G^3, duplicated with C clefs.
Written in black ink with red numerals and titles;
measure lines in red in latter section of volume.

<u>Scribe</u>: Guliemus à Messaus (1585-1640), with marginalia
in 2 later hands.

<u>Marginalia</u>: Original numeration by ℓ. in ink (retained
below) and modern numeration by ℓ. in pencil (given
in parentheses below). Hand B, with additions by
hand C (in parentheses), ℓ. i^r: "Tablature Picturing
Mr Dr John Bull 1629 /Fantasia -&c. /by /Mr Dr John
Bull (temp queen /Elizabeth Esqr) /-1621- /-1628-
'&c. /Ex dono /Tho: James Mathias Queen' Tresyrer
(Charlotte) /Eliz = /Bohemia" with hand C noting on
same page, "Property /The Gift of Gabriel Mathias

/This Book once formed part of the /Library of Queen
Caroline (I Believe) consort /of King George 2^d /H:
Cocke /page 51. MS. of Mr Dr John Bull /I take it."
Also doodles on same page, sketch (caricature) of
Queen Elizabeth of Bohemia and light house. Various
notes in a later hand on ℓ. 23v, e.g. "then 5: then
15: or 13 ..." Section beginning with ℓ. 54 had
earlier numeration, "2-24," does not use any red ink
and originally had a fourth stave (trimmed off).
"Register ..." (heading mutilated) on final ℓ.$^{r-v}$ in
contemporary hand, listing contents, including ℓ. 1-
15.

Summary:
    Composers:
      BULL: #1, 3-4, 6-13, 15-34, 36, 45, 46a, 48,
           50a-62, 64-72.
      BYRD: #6(?), 50.
      CHAMPION (Jacques II): #17-19(?).
      CORNET: #47(?).
      FARNABY (Giles): #4(?).
      FERRABOSCO: #2.
      GIBBONS: #5, 35(?), 46.
      MACQUE: #49.
      SWEELINCK: #1(?), cf 21, 46a(?).
      TALLIS: #59-65(?), 72(?).
    Contents: Miscellaneous harpsichord and organ pieces,
      largely attributed or misattributed to Bull. **Free**
      forms, dances and variation forms are intermingled,
      except for the following groups:
        #11-14 Dances, anon.
        17-20 Chapel (CHAMPION?) pieces
        29-42 Courantes with French titles
        55-72 Keyboard pieces based on sacred tunes

Inventory (information from the "Register" is given in
in parentheses):

ℓ 1-15   [lacking]

                (11: salua Regina)

                (22: secundus versus)

                (93   Salue Regina transalue Regina)

                (¢14 Ad te Clamamus)

                (¢5 Eia ergo aduocata nostra 3)

                (¢56: O Clemens: a 4)

                (¢57 O dulcis virgo Maria a 5)

1   ℓ 16r^1-23v^1 Fantasia sopra re, re, re, /sol, vt, mi,
     (2v)   fa, sol /octaui toni /Du 'Jan Bull, /Doct^r
                 [BULL or SWEELINCK]
                 CO: cf 26-Bull #46a
                 ED: Dart-BI #14.

2   ℓ 23v^2-29v^3 Toccata di Roma /Sexti toni /Di hieronimo
     (9v)   Ferabosco

3   ℓ 29v^4-33v^3 Bonni well Robin /van /Doct^r. Jan Bull:
     (13v) |finis 18 /Jan: /1627.[d]
                 ED: Dart-BII #65.

4   ℓ 33v^4-35v^2 Rose a solis /van /Joan Bull Doct^r. |finis
     (17v)   [BULL or FARNABY (a)]
                 ED: Dart-BII #122.

5   ℓ 35v^3-37r^4 Praeludium octaui /Toni: van /Jan Bull Doct^r
     (19v) |finis [GIBBONS (G)]
                 CO: 26-Bull #46
                 ED: Hendrie #2.

6   ℓ 37v^1-38r^4 Praeludium van Doct^r./Jan Bull /Solfaut
     (21v) |finis [BYRD? (C)]
                 CO: cf 26-Bull #50

cf Parthenia #4
ED: cf Dart-BII p 221.

7   ℓ 38v^1-43v^2 Les Buffons van /Jan Bull: /Doct^r: |Finis
     (22v)   [C]
            ED: Dart-BII #101.

            [#8-24: an older quire, numbered also
            ℓ. 1-6, 2-24.   Pieces #9-13 do **not** appear
            in the "Register."]

8   ℓ 44r^1-49r^1 Den Lustelijcken meÿ /van Docto^r Bull
     (28r)   /quod fecit 30 meÿ /1622.
            ED: Dart-BI #52.

9   ℓ 49r^2-v^4 2 vers van Alma Redemptoris Septi toni
     (33r)   ED: cf Dart-BII p 222.

10   ℓ 50r^1-v^4 sexti toni 3 vers van Alma redemptoris
     (34r)   ED: cf Dart-BII p 222.

11   ℓ 51r$^{1-4}$ Courante la Reine [hand C:] Elizabeth of
     (35r)   Bohemia [C]
            ED: cf Dart-BII p 222.

12   ℓ 51r^4-v^4 [Bourrée (C)]
     (35r)   ED: cf Dart-BII p 222.

13   ℓ 52r$^{1-4}$ Canarie [C]
     (36r)   ED: cf Dart-BII p 222.

14   ℓ 52v$^{1-4}$ [Allemande (d)]
     (36v)

15   ℓ 53r^1-55v^2 fanta zia du Jan Bull: /super Vestiua i
     (37r)   /colli |finis [a]
            ED: Dart-BI #8.

16   ℓ 56r^1-58r^3 fanta zia secunda /super /Vestiua i /colli
     (40r)   Du Jan Bull. /Doct^r |finis
            ED: Dart-BI #9.

17 | [CHAMPION?: Fantasia (a)]
fantazia   3 /du Jan /Bull: |finis (Fantas: de Chappel)
ℓ 58v^1-61r^2 (42v)   ¢|77| [$\frac{2}{2}$|78|]

18 | [CHAMPION?: Pavane (D)]
Pauana sinfoniae |finis |Jan Bull /1622 (pauana simphoniae de Chappel)
ℓ 61v^1-63v^1 (45v)   ¢|16|16|16|16|

[meas. 49]

19 | [CHAMPION?: Galliard (D)]
Galiarde /du /Jan Bull /doct^r |finis (Gaillarde de Chappelle)
ℓ 64r^1-65r^2 (48r) ^{3}[$\frac{3}{2}$]|6|6|16|

[meas. 13]

20 | ℓ 65v^1-67v^3 Het Juweel /van Doctor /Jan Bull,
   | (49v)   quod fecit anno 1621 /i2 December
   | |finis (het Joweel voor cappelle
   | 162i) [BULL, dedicated to CHAMPION?]
   | ED: Dart-BII #142.

21 | ℓ 68r^1-70r^3 Fantasia op de fuge /van m. Jan
   | (52r)   Pieters [SWEELINCK] /faecit Doctor
   | Bull /1621: 15 Decemb |finis
   | ED: Dart-BI #4.

22 | ℓ 70v^1-72v^3 Pauana synfoniae /van Doct^r /Jan
   | (54v)   Bull: |finis
   | ED: Dart-BII #68á.

23 | ℓ 73r^1-74r^3 Galiarde voor de voorgaende pauane
   | (57r)   /van Doctor /Bull: |finis
   | ED: Dart-BII #68b.

24 | ℓ 74v^1-76v^3 Fantazia van Doctor /Jan Bull op de
   | (58v)   /fuge von La /Guamina
   | ED: Dart-BI #3.

   | (Rose a solis) [cf #4]

25 | ℓ 77r^1-79r^1 Een Kindeken /is vns gebo/ren. /van
   | (61r)   /Jan Bull: /Doct^r: |finis /hac 4^a.
   | April: /1628
   | ED: Dart-BI #54.

26 | ℓ 79r^2-80v^3 Een kindeken /is vns geboren /in D
   | (63r)   la sol re: /van /Jan Bull: /Doct:
   | |finis hac 5^a Aprilis /1628
   | ED: Dart-BI #55.

27 | ℓ 81r^1-v^2 Praeludium /voor /Laet vns /met
   | (65r)   hertzen /Reÿne /van Jan Bull D^r:
   | ED: Dart-BI #56.

27a | ℓ 81v^3-83v^3 Laet ons met harte̅ Reÿne: |Cornet
     | (65v) |cromhorne |cornet allée |voll Register
     | |finis [BULL]
     | ED: Dart-BI #56.

28 | ℓ 84r^1-86v^2 Het nieu /Bergomasco /van /Jan Bull
   | (68r)   /Doct^r: |finis hac 17^a. Aprilis. /1628
   | ED: Dart-BII #124.

29 | ℓ 86v^3-91v^1 Courante /Juweell:(alio modo) /van
   | (70v)   Jan Bull. /Doct^r |finis
   | ED: Dart-BII #141.

30 | ℓ 91v^2-92v^1 Courante /Battaille: /van /Jan Bull
   | (75v)   /Doct^r: |finis
   | ED: Dart-BII #106.

31 | ℓ 92v^2-95r^2 Courante: /Alarme: /van /Jan Bull: Doct:
   | (77v) |finis
   | ED: Dart-BII #80.

32 | ℓ 95r^3-96v^3 Courante: Joÿeuse: /van /Jan Bull:
   | (79r)   /Doct^r: |finis
   | ED: Dart-BII #136.

33 | ℓ 97r^1-98r^3 Courante /Brigante /van /Jan Bull /Doct^r
   | (81r) |finis
   | ED: Dart-BII #74.

34 | ℓ 98v^1-99v^1 Courante /The princes: /van /Jan Bull
   | (82v)   /Doct:- |finis.
   | ED: Dart-BII #98.

35 | ℓ 99v^2-100v^2 Courante /Adieu:- /off ^{te} /vaerwel:-
   | (83r)   van /Jan Bull:- /Doct:- |finis hac /5^a.
   | maÿ /1628 [GIBBONS?]
   | ED: Hendrie #40.

36 | ℓ 100v^3-101v^1 Courante:- /A Round /van /Jan /Bull:-
   | (84v)   /Doct:- |finis
   | ED: Dart-BII #137.

37   ℓ 101v^2-103v^3 Courante. /Kingston /van /Jan Bull:-
     (85v)   Doct |finis hac 13$^{\underline{a}}$ maÿ:- /1628
                    ED: Dart-BII #81.

38   ℓ 104r^1-105r^1 Courante /prima in /Alamire:- /van Jan
     (88r)   Bull /Doct:- |finis [d]
                    ED: cf Dart-BII p 222.

39   ℓ 105r^2-106r^1 Courante /Secunda /in Alamire /van /Jan
     (89r)   Bull:- /Doct |finis [d]
                    ED: cf Dart-BII p 222.

40   ℓ 106r^2-107r^1 Courante /Tertia:- /in Alamire:- /van
     (90r)   Jan Bull:- /Doct:- |finis [d]
                    ED: cf Dart-BII p 222.

41   ℓ 107r^2-108r^1 Courante Quarta /in /Alamire van /Jan
     (91r)   Bull:- /Doct:- |finis [d]
                    ED: cf Dart-BII p 223.

42   ℓ 108r^2-109r^1 Courante Quinta /in Alamire:- van /Jan
     (92r)   Bull:- /Doct:- |finis hac 17$^{\underline{a}}$ Maÿ /1628 [d]
                    ED: cf Dart-BII p 223.

43   ℓ 109r^2-112r^2 Boeren Dans: /van /Jan Bull: /Doct:- ...
     (93r)   ll /finis hac 13$^{\underline{a}}$ Julÿ:- /1628
                    ED: Dart-BII #111.

44   ℓ 112r^3-115v^3 Pauana /Secundi toni:- /van /Jan Bull
     (96r)   D$^{\underline{r}}$: |finis: hac 15$^{\underline{a}}$ /Julÿ: 1628
                    ED: Dart-BII #77.

45   ℓ 116r^1-116v^2 Præludium /voor de /fantasia octa/ui
     (100r)   toni /sopra, /Sol, vt, r, mi, /fa, sol
                    la:- /van /Jan Bull: Doct:-
                    ED: Dart-BI #2.

45a ℓ 116v^3-119v^3 fantasia:- |finis hac 18 Julÿ /1628
     (100v)   [BULL]
                    ED: Dart-BI #2.

46   ℓ 119r^1-121v^1 præludium /pour la /fantasia:- /Sopra
     (104r)   /Re, Re, Re, /Sol, vt, mi, /fa, Sol /Du
                    /Jan Bull: /D$^{\underline{r}}$:- [GIBBONS]
                    CO: 26-Bull #5

ED: Hendrie #2.

46a | ℓ 121v^2-129r^1 fantasia |finis /hac 19^a. /Augusti /1628
     (105v)   [SWEELINCK or BULL]
                  CO: cf 26-Bull #1
                  ED: Dart-BI #14.

47 | ℓ 129r^2-138r^3 fantasia, /Sexti toni. /A.4 /Du /Jan
     (113r)   Bull: /Doct:- |finis [BULL or CORNET]
                  ED: Dart-BI #13.

48 | ℓ 138v^1-142v^2 fantasia /Sexti toni /Sopra /A Leona,
     (122v)   /Du /jan Bull:- /Doct:. /A.4. |finis
                  hac /7^a. Septem/bris. /1628
                  ED: Dart-BI #7.

49 | ℓ 142v^3-144r^3 Ricerciar /Sexti toni, /A.4. |finis
     (126v)   [MACQUE (arr)]
                  ED: cf Dart-BII p 222.

50 | ℓ 144v^1-145r^3 Praeludium, /voor de /fantasia /Quinti
     (128v)   toni, /van /Jan Bull:- |torne La
                  /fantasia [BYRD]
                  CO: cf 26-Bull #6
                      cf Parthenia #4
                  ED: **cf Dart-BII p 221.**
50a | ℓ 145v^1-149r^3 fantasia quinti toni:- |finis hac 10^a.
     (129v)   Septembris /1628:- [BULL]
                  ED: Dart-BI #6.

51 | ℓ 149v^1-159v^3 fantasia Sopra /vt, Re, mi, /fa Sol,
     (133v)   la, /van /Jan Bull Doct:- /a.5. |finis
                  hac 11^a. /octobris 1628
                  ED: Dart-BI #19.

52 | ℓ 160r^1-161v^2 Ricerciar /primi toni /a.4. |finis
     (144r)   ED: cf Dart-BII p 223.

53 | ℓ 161v^3-165v^2 Ricerciar /Altra /primi toni, /A.4:-
     (145v) |finis
                  ED: cf Dart-BII p 223.

54	ℓ 165v^3-168r^3 (149v)	Ricerciar /Quinti toni /A.4. |finis: hac 19^a. octobris:- 1628 ED: cf Dart-BII p 223.
55	ℓ 168v^1-170r^3 (152v)	Vexilla Regis /prodeunt: /A.3. /van /Jan Bull D^r. /Vexilla Regis.1. |finis:- ED: Dart-BI #44.
56	ℓ 170v^1-172v^1 (154v)	Vexilla Regis /prodeunt:- /A.4. /van /Jan Bull:- /Doct:- /Vexilla Regis.2. |finis ED: Dart-BI #44(2).
57	ℓ 172v^2-174v^3 (156v)	Vexilla Regis /prodeunt. /van /Jan Bull, Doct:- /Vexilla Regis:- .3. |finis ED: Dart-BI #44(3).
58	ℓ 175r^1-177r^1 (159r)	Vexilla Regis /prodeunt:- /van /Jan Bull: D^r.: /A.4. /Vexilla Regis: -4. |finis ED: Dart-BI #44(4).
59	ℓ 177r^2-179r^2 (161r)	Jam Lucis orto /Sidere:- /van /Jan Bull. Doct^r. /A.3. /Jam Lucis .1. |finis [BULL or TALLIS] ED: Dart-BI #45(1).
60	ℓ 179r^3-181r^1 (163r)	Jam Lucis orto /Sidere:- /van /Jan Bull. Doct^r. /A.4. /Iam Lucis .2 |finis [BULL or TALLIS] ED: Dart-BI #45(2).
61	ℓ 181r^2-182v^1 (165r)	Te Lucis ante /Terminum /van /Jan Bull: D^r. /A.4. /Te Lucis:- |finis:- [BULL or TALLIS] ED: Dart-BI #46.
62	ℓ 182v^2-183r^2 (166v)	Alleluia: /van /Jan Bull /Doct^r. A.4. /Alleluia |finis [BULL or TALLIS] ED: Dart-BI #48.

63 | ℓ 183r³-185r¹ Veni Redemptor /genitum:- /van /Jan
   | (167r)   Bull: Doct.ᵣ /A.4. /Veni:- |finis
   | [TALLIS]
   | ED: cf Dart-BII p 222.

64 | ℓ 185r²-186v² Saluator /mundi Deus. /van /Jan Bull:
   | (169r)   Dᵣ /A.4. /Saluator mundi Deus: |finis
   | [BULL or TALLIS]
   | ED: Dart-BI #39.

65 | ℓ 186v³-188r¹ Telluris /Jngens Condi/tor. /v̂an /Jan
   | (170v)   Bull:- /A.4. /Telluris .1. |finis
   | [BULL or TALLIS]
   | ED: Dart-BI #47.

66 | ℓ 188r²-189r² Telluris /Jngens /Conditor, /van /Jan
   | (172r)   Bull /Dr. /A.4. /Telluris Jngens .2
   | |finis: hac 16ª nouem. 1628
   | ED: Dart-BI #47.

67 | ℓ 189r³-190r³ Telluris /Jngens Conditor /Canon. A.4
   | (173r)   /In Super Diatess /2. in. vna. /van
   | /Jan Bull: /Doct.ᵣ /Telluris ingens .3.
   | |finis
   | ED: Dart-BI #47.

68 | ℓ 190v¹-191v² Telluris /Jngens Conditor /van /Jan
   | (174v)   Bull:- /Canon a .4. /In Super Diatess.
   | /2. in vna: /Telluris ingens .4. |finis
   | ED: Dart-BI #47.

69. | ℓ 191v³-192v³ Telluris /Jngens Conditor: Canon A.4.
   | (175v)   In subdiatessa/ron 2. in vna /van /Jan
   | Bull: /Doct.ᵣ /Telluris: 5. |finis
   | ED: Dart-BI #47.

70 | ℓ 193r¹-194r³ Telluris In-/gens Conditor: /Canon.A.4.
   | (177r)   /In Super Dia-/pason, 2 in /vna. /van
   | Jan Bull Dᵣ /Telluris Ingengs Conditor:

6:- |finis
ED: Dart-BI #47.

71 | ℓ 194v^1-195v^2 Telluris Ingens Conditor /Canon A.4.
    (178v)   /Jn Sub diapason: /2 in vna /van /Jan
                    Bull D^r. /Telluris: 7 |finis
                    ED: Dart-BI #47.

72 | ℓ 195v^3-196v^3 Alleluia: /Canon.A.4. /2 in vna: /Jn
    (179v)   Diapen the /van /Jan Bull /D^r. [BULL or
                    TALLIS (incomplete)]
                    ED: Dart-BI #49.

                    [ℓ 198-23? lacking; contents from
                    Register:]

ℓ [1]98   (Preludium voor Fantasia Primi toni)

ℓ [1]98   (fantasia voor preludium)

ℓ [2]02   (Preludium p.. La fantasie]

                    (Tr... Pra... fou... [?] [bottom of ℓ.
                    mutilated]

[?]   (Fl... [?])

ℓ 20...   (La... su...e [?] [top of ℓ. mutilated]

ℓ 206   (fant Priuibur a 3...

ℓ 209   (gallardo Mussig [?])

ℓ 217   (fantasia)

ℓ 226   (Petru [?] Le Count)

ℓ 227   (fuga per gran Cappel)

ℓ 228   (fantasia cromatica Contra)

ℓ 233   (fantasia mit 3 fughas)

Provenance: The Netherlands, post 1669 (section 1: transcription from Ballet de flore); ca. 1680-1690 (sections
2-3 (transcription from Bellérophon).

Location: Utrecht; Instituut voor Muziekwetenschap der
Rijksuniversiteit te Utrecht, MS q-1.

Description: 85, 1 ℓ. (ℓ. 35v-85v: blank, ruled); 12
quires (in 8, except: E^6, F^6, I^6, K^6, L^5); folio
format, 31.7 x 19.2 cm. Watermarks: #16 and 43 (end
papers). Contemporary vellum binding, 32 x 20 cm.

Notation: Keyboard score (two 6-line staves, 5 systems
per page, written page by page. Clefs: F^4, G^3, duplicated with C clefs.

Scribes: 3 hands, the second associated with Gresse:
A: #1-15
B: 15a-35
C: 36-53

Marginalia: Scribbling and melody of #52 on ℓ. 34r.
Pencil corrections (accidentals, ornaments, notes,
chords) throughout, especially in section 2; pencil
sketch of dog, ℓ. 33r. Miscellaneous pencil numbers
on back end paper. Remnant of modern pencil pagina-
tion.

Summary:
Composers:
ARTUS: #4.
FROBERGER: #49.
GRESSE: #36, 41-43, 46-48, 51.
LA BARRE: #21-23.
LULLY: #9, 20, 29, 37, 38, 40, 52, 53.
SANDLEY: #24-27.
TRESURE: #17(-19?), cf 22, 31-32(?), 33, 34(?).

Contents:

#1-15   Simple dances, tunes (ARTUS, anon.)

15a-35   Suites and isolated dances (LA BARRE,
               TRESURE, LULLY, anon.)

36-53   Suites, isolated dances and free pieces
               (GRESSE, FROBERGER, anon.)

Inventory:

	ℓ 1r	[Illustrations of rudiments of music]
1	ℓ 1v$^{1-4}$	Bargamasko [G]
2	ℓ 2r$^{1-4}$	Stocken /Dans [d]
3	ℓ 2v$^{1-4}$	Tricoté [Air ancien (d)]

CO cf 7-Munich-1511f #2
   cf 8-Hintze #9
   cf Veron ℓ 21v

ED: cf MGG 13-661 (facsim).

| 4 | ℓ 3r$^{1-5}$ | La Bouré /Dartus [C] |

CO cf 7-Munich-1511f #24
   cf 8-Hintze #24 [D]
   cf 59a-Handmaide #22 [D]
   cf Celle p 18 [D]

ED **cf Dart-HI #22.**

| 5 | ℓ 3v$^{1-3}$ | Balet [**F/C**] |
| 6 | ℓ 4r$^{1-4}$ | La Moustarde [Air ancien (C)] |

CO: cf 3-Berlin-40623
   cf 7-Munich-1511f #20
   cf Veron ℓ 21v
   cf Add-16889 ℓ 99r
ED: cf Epstein #24.

| 7 | ℓ 4v$^{1-5}$ | La Moustarde /Reformé [G] |

CO: **cf 39-Vm7-6307-1 #14**
   cf 55-Redon #10
   cf Add-16889 ℓ 99r [lute]
   cf Celle p 140
   cf Terburg

| 8 | ℓ 5r$^{1-4}$ | La Gride /Liné [d] |
| 9 | ℓ 5v$^{1-4}$ | Leminuetté [LULLY from <u>Ballet</u> <u>de</u> <u>flore</u> (1669) XV (C)] |

CO: cf 9-Ihre-284 #88

cf 36-Parville #124

ED: cf Lundgren #39.

10	ℓ 6r$^{1-5}$	Herders /hij is /Geboren [C]
11	ℓ 6v$^{1-5}$	O Herders /Alsoetjes [G]
12	ℓ 7r$^{1-5}$	Welkom /kindeken /Jesu zoet [C]
13	ℓ 7v$^{1-5}$	La Coquille [Air ancien (G)]

CO: cf 3-Berlin-40623
cf Skara #34
cf Vat-mus-569 p 112

14	ℓ 8r$^{1-4}$	La Canari [D]
15	ℓ 8v$^{1-5}$	La Lande [G]
	ℓ 9r^{3}	[incipit of Psalm 50: Miserere]
16	ℓ 9v^{1}-10r^{3}	Praeludium. [G]

ED: Curtis-MMN #71.

| 17 | ℓ 10v^{1}-11r^{2} | Almande. J T. [TRESURE] |Verte [G] |

ED: Curtis-MMN #72.

| 18 | ℓ 11v^{3}-12r^{4} | Courante. |tourne. [TRESURE? (G)] |

ED: Curtis-MMN #73.

| 19 | ℓ 12v$^{1-4}$ | Sarabande. |Fin. [TRESURE? (G)] |

ED: Curtis-MMN #74.

| 20 | ℓ 13r$^{1-5}$ | Air /Dans un bois [LULLY from Trios pour le coucher du roi (C)] |

CO: cf 27-Gresse #52
cf 36-Parville #109
cf 51-LaBarre-11 p 205
cf 68-d'Anglebert #14

ED: cf Gilbert p 112, Roesgen-Champion
p 29.

21 | [LA BARRE: <u>Allemande</u> (d)]

Almande /LB
   ℓ 13v[1-4]

CO: cf 1-Copenhagen #39, Allamande [a]
    cf 3-Berlin-40623 #72, Allemande

ED: Ex 2 above, Curtis-MMN #68; cf Epstein #22a,
    Dickinson #39, Hamburger p 138.

---

22 | [LA BARRE: <u>Courante</u> (d)]

Courante
   ℓ 14r[1-3]

CO: 4-Lynar #65, Courante de La Barre
    16-Cosyn #44, Coranto:- Mr Tresure
    18-Ch-Ch-1236 #1, ... Jonas Tresure
    18-Ch-Ch-1236 #8, Corant La bar
    19-Heardson #46, (coranto) Mr Gibbons
    29-Chigi #30, Corante de Monsu della Bara
    Oxford-IB

ED: Curtis-MMN #69; cf Bonfils-18 #23, Bonfils-58 #4,
    Maas #91, Lincoln-II p 38.

23 [LA BARRE: Sarabande (d)]

Sarabande
    ℓ 14v^{1-4}

CO: 17-Rogers #22, Selebrand Beare
    18-Ch-Ch-1236 #34, Saraband
    31-Madrid-1360 #23/1, (Zarabanda)
    Drexel-5609 p 12 [copy of 17-Rogers #22]
ED: Curtis-MMN #70; cf Sargent #21, Cofone #21.

24 ℓ 15r^{1-4}   Almande [SANDLEY (G)]
                    ED: cf Dart-HI #3.

25 ℓ 15v^{1-4}   Courante [SANDLEY (G)]
                    ED: cf Dart-HI #4.

26 ℓ 16r^{1-4}   Sarabande [SANDLEY (G)]
                    ED: cf Dart-HI #5.

27 ℓ 16v^{1-5}   Jegg [SANDLEY (G)]
                    ED: cf Dart-HI #6.

28 ℓ 17r^{1-5}   Menuets du Dauphin [d]
                    ED: Curtis-MMN #80.

29 ℓ 17v^{1-4}   Air /Alcide [LULLY from Alceste (1674)
                    IV-1 (C)]

30 ℓ 18r^{1-6}   Praeludium [a]
                    ED: Curtis-MMN #75.

31 ℓ 18v^1-19r^1   Almande. in. a. [TRESURE?]
                    ED: Curtis-MMN #76.

32 ℓ 19v^{1-5}   Courante. [TRESURE? (a)]
                    ED: Curtis-MMN #77.

33 | ℓ 20r$^{1-4}$ Sarabande [TRESURE (a)]
      CO: 9-Ihre-284 #76
      ED: Curtis-MMN #78.

34 | ℓ 20v$^{1-5}$ Jigge [TRESURE? (a)]
      ED: Curtis-MMN #79.

35 | ℓ 21r$^{1-3}$ Sarabande /de la Royne [g]

36 | ℓ 21v$^{1-4}$ Allemande /J.b: gresse [D]
      ED: Curtis-MMN #61.

37 | ℓ 22r^{1}-22v^{2} Les plaisirs [LULLY from Isis (1677) II-7
      (d)]

38 | ℓ 23r$^{1-5}$ aij mez profitez [title in another hand]
      [LULLY from Isis (1677) II-7 (g)]

39 | ℓ 23v^{1}-24r^{5} Canzonna [G]
      ED: Curtis-MMN #59.

40 | ℓ 24v^{1}-25r^{1} Que ces lieux [LULLY from Isis (1677) II-7
      (g)]
      CO: cf 42-Vm7-6307-2 #10
      ED: Curtis-MMN #82.

41 | ℓ 25v^{1}-26r^{1} Allemande /Jb gresse [d]
      ED: Curtis-MMN #62.

42 | ℓ 26r^{2}-26v^{2} Courant J:b gresse [d]
      ED: Curtis-MMN #63.

43 | ℓ 26v$^{2-5}$ Sarabande jb: gresse [d]
      ED: Curtis-MMN #64.

44 | ℓ 27r$^{1-5}$ [untitled (g)]

45 | ℓ 27v^{1}-29r^{4} Canzon [a]
      ED: Curtis-MMN #58.

46 | ℓ 29v^{1}-30r^{1} Allemande /Jb: gresse [d]
      ED: Curtis-MMN #65.

47 | ℓ 30r$^{2-5}$ Courante /Jb: gresse [d]
                  ED: Curtis-MMN #66.

48 | ℓ 30v$^{1-4}$ Sarabande /Jb: gresse [d]
                  ED: Curtis-MMN #67.

49 | ℓ 31r^{1}-31v^{2} Preludium [FROBERGER (a)]
                  ED cf Adler-III p 22 [variant].

50 | ℓ 31v^{3}-32v^{3} Preludium [a]
                  ED: Curtis-MMN #57.

51 | ℓ 33r$^{1-4}$ Allemande J:B: gresse [A]
                  ED: Curtis-MMN #60.

52 | ℓ 33v$^{1-4}$ [**LULLY**: **Dans** **nos** **bois** from **Trios** **pour** **le** **coucher** **du** **roi** (C)]
                  CO: cf 27-Gresse #20
                      cf 36-Parville #109
                      cf 51-LaBarre-11 p 205
                      cf 68-d'Anglebert #14
                  ED: cf Gilbert p 112, Roesgen-Champion
                      p 29.

    | ℓ 34r   [miscellaneous writing, including some of #52, above]

53 | ℓ 34v^{1}-35r^{5} [LULLY: **Ouverture** to **Bellérophon** (1679) (C)]
                  CO: cf 14-Schwerin-619 #83
                      cf 24-Babell #199
                      cf 40-Rés-476 #26
                      cf 46-Menetou #87
                      cf Bod-576 p 54
                  ED: cf Bonfils-LP p 86, Howell #1

    | ℓ 35v-85v   [blank, ruled]

28-BRUSSELS-926

Provenance: Belgium, post 1670 (transcription from Les
Amants magnifiques).

Location: Brussels; Bibliothèque royale Albert 1er,
département de manuscrits, MS III 926.

Description: 121, 1 ℓ.; 16 quires (A-H^8, I^7, J-N^8, O^4,
P^6, Q^1; oblong quarto format, 15.2 x 22 cm. Watermark #63. Contemporary full leather, gilt-tooled
binding, gilted edges, holes for binding ties (ties
lacking), 15.5 x 22 cm.

Notation: Keyboard score (two staves: upper of 5-6 lines,
lower of 5 lines; 3 systems per page, usually written
on the recto only). Clefs usually F^4, G$^{2/3}$.

Scribes: 3-4 unidentified hands:
A: ℓ. 1-22 (usually on 6-line treble staves; post
1670)
B: ℓ. 22-75r (F^3 clef in left hand)
C: ℓ. 75v-99r (post 1685)
D: ℓ. 119v, 120v, 121v (same as B?)

Marginalia: Explanation in French of notation, including
use of double slash ornament for "tremblement," using
letter names (not solfege syllables) for notes, ℓ. 1r.
"Prie pour P. Braun," ℓ. 67v (owner?, scribe B?).

Summary:
Composers:
BEAUMON: cf ℓ 66v-75r.
BOYVIN: cf ℓ 66v-75r.
BRAUN: cf ℓ 66v-75r.
DAMANCE: cf. ℓ 66v-75r.
DUMANOIR: ℓ 2r.

LEBÈGUE: ℓ 66r, cf 66v-75r.

LULLY: ℓ 3r, 6r-8r, 11r-12r, 63v.

NIVERS: cf ℓ 66v-75r.

THOMELIN: cf ℓ 66v-75r.

Contents:

ℓ. 1-22　　Miscellaneous pieces, largely ballet
　　　　　　　transcriptions for harpsichord.

ℓ. 23-63r　Anon. organ pieces.

ℓ. 63v-66r　Harpsichord pieces by LEBÈGUE, LULLY
　　　　　　　(arr.).

ℓ. 66v-121v　Organ pieces by BEAUMON, BOYVIN, BRAUN,
　　　　　　　DAMANCE, LEBÈGUE, THOMELIN, anon.

<u>Inventory</u> (all versos are blank, ruled, unless otherwise
　　　　　　noted):

ℓ 1r	[blank; see "Marginalia"]
ℓ $2r^1$-v^1	Branles /de mons.^{r} /du manoir [1667 (C)] CO: cf Veron ℓ 50v
ℓ $3r^{1-3}$	grand /Courier |fin [LULLY: <u>Bel Iris</u> from <u>Ballet</u> <u>de</u> <u>l'impatience</u> (1661) (d)] CO: cf 3-Berlin-40623 #1 cf 11-Ryge #48 cf Skara #35 cf Terburg cf Van-Eijl #25 cf Rés-819-2 ℓ 72r cf Stockholm-228 ℓ 20v ED: cf Noske #25, Bangert p 78.
ℓ $4r^{1-3}$	Sara/band /Simple |Fin [d] CO: cf Vat-mus-569 p 98
ℓ $5r^{1-3}$	Sara/band /double |Fin [d]
ℓ $6r^{1-3}$	Les /Pescheurs /de Corailles |Fin [LULLY: <u>Danse</u> <u>des</u> <u>pêcheurs</u> from <u>Les</u> <u>Amants</u> <u>magni-</u> <u>fiques</u> (1670) I (F)]
ℓ $7r^{1-3}$	Neptune /pour le /Roÿ |Fin [LULLY: <u>Danse</u> <u>de</u> <u>Neptune</u> from <u>Les</u> <u>Amants</u> <u>magnifiques</u> (1670) I (F)]

ℓ 8r$^{1-3}$ Neptune /Pour le /même [LULLY: Les Suivants de Neptune (sarabande) from Les Amants magnifiques (1670) I (F)]

ℓ 9r$^{1-3}$ Allemande |Fin du Ballet du Roy danse a St. /Germain [F]

ℓ 10r$^{1-3}$ La Suiste |Fin [B♭]
CO: cf 31-Madrid-1360 #34.

ℓ 11r$^{1-3}$ Aire a /dancer |Fin [LULLY: Les Maîtrises à danser from Le Carnaval (1668) III (B♭)]

ℓ 12r$^{1-3}$ Canarie |Fin [LULLY from Le Carnaval (1668) III (B♭)]

ℓ 13r$^{1-3}$ Ballet |Fin [d]

ℓ 14r$^{1-3}$ Gauotte |Fin [d]

ℓ 15r$^{1-3}$ Menuet |Fin [B♭]

ℓ 16r$^{1-3}$ Gauotte |Fin [g]
CO: cf Babell-T p 11
ℓ 17r$^{1-3}$ Les /mousqué/taires |Fin [Air ancien (C)]
CO: cf Veron ℓ 9r

ℓ 18r$^{1-3}$ Allemande /St Nicolas |Fin [C]

ℓ 19r$^{1-2}$ Bouree /margo |Fin [Grand Bourée from Ballet royal (1654) (d)]
CO: cf Veron ℓ 2r
ED: cf Dart-HI #73.

ℓ 19v^{3} O Pupule |Pie nascernis [for organ]

ℓ 20r$^{1-3}$ Dorni Fili [for organ]

ℓ 21r$^{1-3}$ [untitled intonations for organ]

ℓ 22r$^{1-3}$ Gauotte des pois et des febures [?] [g]

ℓ 23r-63r   [unattributed organ pieces (hand B), including:]

ℓ 39r^{2} Allemande du 3. ton [beginning on G, ending on a] ℓ 63v^1-64r^3

Ouuerture |reprise [LULLY from Le Temple
de la paix (1685) Prologue (a)]
CO: cf 14-Schwerin-619 #68
    cf 46-Menetou #56

ℓ 64v^1-3

[Allemande (G)]
Allemande   ¢|6|9|

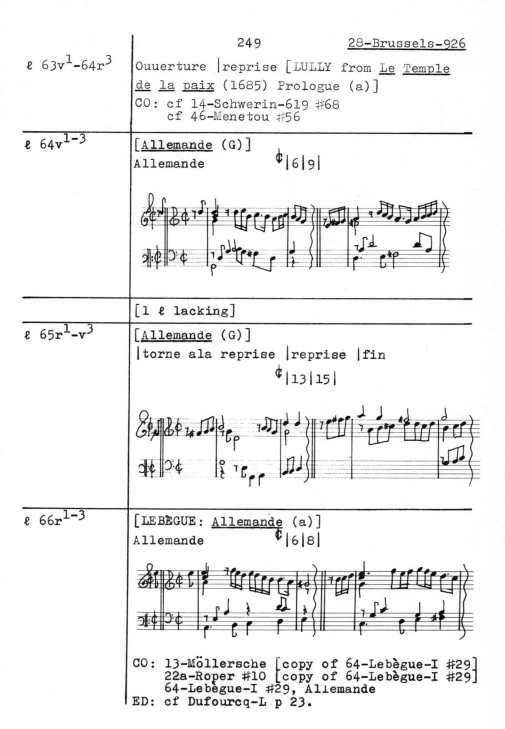

[1 ℓ lacking]

ℓ 65r^1-v^3

[Allemande (G)]
|torne ala reprise |reprise |fin
              ¢|13|15|

ℓ 66r^1-3

[LEBÈGUE: Allemande (a)]
Allemande   ¢|6|8|

CO: 13-Möllersche [copy of 64-Lebègue-I #29]
    22a-Roper #10 [copy of 64-Lebègue-I #29]
    64-Lebègue-I #29, Allemande
ED: cf Dufourcq-L p 23.

ℓ 66v-75r	[Organ pieces (hand B), including the following named composers: BEAUMON, BOYVIN, BRAUN DAMANCE, LEBÈGUE, NIVERS, THOMELIN]
ℓ 75v-99r	[Unattributed organ pieces (hand C)]
ℓ 99v-121v	[blank, ruled, except for organ fragments (hand D) on ℓ 119v, 120v, 121v]

..

29-CHIGI

Provenance: Italy, ca. 1650?

Location: Rome; Biblioteca **Apostolica** Vaticana, Chigi
Q IV 24.

Description: 56 ℓ.; oblong quarto format, 15.6 x 22.5 cm.
Watermarks #31-32. Original parchment binding, 17 x
22.5 cm.

Notation: Keyboard score (two staves: upper of 6 lines,
lower of 7 lines; 2 systems per page, written page
by page). Clefs usually C^1, F^4, duplicated with C^6.

Scribe: One unidentifed hand.

Summary:
Composers:
FRESCOBALDI: #6-7, 9-11, cf 34-36.
LA BARRE: #30-32.
Gio Batt[ist]a: #36.
Contents: Miscellaneous harpsichord pieces, largely
anonymous.

Inventory:

		[1 end paper stubbed in, blank]
1	ℓ $1r^1$-$4r^1$	T[o]cata sopra li pedali ⎮fuga [G]
		ED: Lincoln-II p 1.
2	ℓ $4r^2$-$5r^2$	[Ruggiero (G)]
		ED: Lincoln-III p 12.
3	ℓ $5v^1$-$6r^2$	[Ruggiero (G)]
4	ℓ $6v^1$-$7r^2$	[Ruggiero (G)]
5	ℓ $7r^1$-$8r^2$	Recercare [g]
		ED: Lincoln-I p 45.

6	ℓ $8v^1$-$9r^1$	Balletto [FRESCOBALDI (e)] ED: Pidoux p 72.
7	ℓ $9r^2$-v^2	Corente del'Baletto [FRESCOBALDI (e)] ED: Pidoux p 72.
8	ℓ $10r^1$-$11v^1$	Pasacagli [FRESCOBALDI (e)] ED: Lincoln-III p 23, Pidoux 3:72.
9	ℓ $11r^1$-v^1	Balletto 2° [FRESCOBALDI (e)] ED: Lincoln-II p 29, Pidoux 3:73.
10	ℓ $11v^2$-$12r^2$	Corente del Baletto [FRESCOBALDI (e)] ED: Lincoln-II p 36, Pidoux 3:74.
11	ℓ $12v^1$-$14v^2$	Pasagagli Primo Partes [FRESCOBALDI (d)] ED: Lincoln-III p 24, Pidoux 3:77.
12	ℓ $15r^1$-$16r^2$	Recercare [d] Lincoln-I p 46.
13	ℓ $16v^1$-$19r^2$	Canzone [d] ED: Lincoln-I p 19.
14	ℓ $19v^1$-$22r^1$	Canzone [g] Lincoln-I p 21.
15	ℓ $22r^2$-$23v^1$	Recercare [a] Lincoln-I p 47.
16	ℓ $23v^2$-$25v^2$	Sonare [?] Canzona [a] ED: Lincoln-I p 23.
17	ℓ $26r^1$-$28r^2$	[Toccata (d)] ED: Lincoln-II p 4.
18	ℓ $28v^1$-$30r^2$	Nelle feste della Madonna /Ave maris stella [d] ED: Lincoln-I p 1.
19	ℓ $30v^1$-$31v^2$	Nelle feste de' Confessori /Iste Confes- sor [G] ED: Lincoln-I p 2.

20 | ℓ 32r^1-34r^2 [Aria di Fiorenza] |2° Mod. [G]
                  ED: Lincoln-III p 41.

21 | ℓ 34v^1-35r^1 [Fiorenza variation 3 (G)]

22 | ℓ 35r^2-36v^2 Recercare [G]
                  ED: Lincoln-I p 49.

23 | ℓ 37r^1-37v^1 Tocata (per[?]) le levatione [fragment (G)]

24 | ℓ 38r$^{1-2}$ Kyrie delli Apostoli |Christe [d]
                  ED: Lincoln-I p 3.

25 | ℓ 38v^1-39r^2 [Corente (C)]
                  ED: Lincoln-II p 37, Pidoux 3:71.

26 | ℓ 39v^1-40r^2 [Recercare (G)]
                  ED: Lincoln-I p 51.

27 | ℓ 40v^1-42r^2 [Toccata (a)]
                  ED: Lincoln-II p 6.

28 | ℓ 42v$^{1-2}$ Balletto [e]

29 | ℓ 43r^1-46v^2 Balletto... [C][7 variations on More palatino]
                  ED: Lincoln-II p 30.

---

30 | [LA BARRE: Courante with Double (d)]
   Corente di Monsu della Bara
      ℓ 47r^1-v^2 ^{3}|6|4|7|5| [$\frac{3}{4}$|8|8|8|8|]

CO: 4-Lynar #65, Courante de La Barre
    16-Cosyn #44, Coranto:- Mr Tresure
    18-Ch-Ch-1236 #1, ... Jonas Tresure
    18-Ch-Ch-1236 #8, Corant La bar
    19-Heardson #46, (coranto) Mr Gibbons
    27-Gresse #22, Courante
    Oxford-IB

ED: Lincoln-II p 38; cf Bonfils-18 #23, Bonfils-58 #4, Maas #91, Curtis-MMN #69.

---

31 | [LA BARRE: <u>Courante</u> with <u>Double</u> (d)]

Nel Med.^{mo} |Altro modo

ℓ 48r^1-49r^2 ^{3}|11|9|10|9| [$\frac{3}{4}$|12|11|12|11|]

ED: Lincoln-II p 39.

---

32 | [LA BARRE: <u>Sarabande</u> (d)]

Sarabanda del mS.

ℓ 49v$^{1-2}$ ^{C}|6|9| [$\frac{3}{4}$|7|10|]

CO: cf 1-Copenhagen-376 #40, Sarabande
     cf Eyck-II ℓ 22v, Lossy

ED: Ex 3 above, Lincoln-II p 41; cf Dickinson #40, Hamburger p 138.

---

33 | ℓ 50r^1-v^2 Ciacona [C]
            ED: Lincoln-III p 26.

34 | ℓ 51r^1-52r^2 Canzona D. fr.[ancese?; Frescobaldi?][g]
            ED: Lincoln-I p 35.

35 | ℓ 52v^1-54r^2 fuga Di fr.[ancese?; Frescobaldi?][g]
            ED: Lincoln-I p 37.

36 | ℓ 54v^1-56r^1 Tocata di (Gio Batt[ist]a [?or:] Girolomo
                 [Frescobaldi] [followed by fragments]

   ℓ 56v   [fragments]

255   <u>29-Chigi</u>

[1 end paper stubbed in, blank]

Provenance: Italy, ca. 1700?

Location: Rome; Conservatorio di Musica Santa Cecilia,
A MS no 400.

Description: 1 p.ℓ., 78 ℓ.; 19 quires in 4; oblong quarto
format, 21.2 x 27.8 cm. Watermark #1. Contemporary
parchment-covered boards, green sprinkled edges,
22.4 x 28 cm.

Notation: 1: part (1 5-line stave, 8 staves per page).
2: Keyboard score (2 5-line staves, 4 systems per
page) clefs: $F^{3,4}$, G^{2-3}; usually F^4, G^2, duplicated
with C clefs (F^3 for French music).
3: Keyboard score (2 staves: upper of 6 lines, lower
of 8 lines; 2 systems per page); clefs: $F^{3,4,5}$,
$G^{1,2,4,5}$, $C^{1,3,4,5}$; usually F^4, G^2.

Scribe: One unidentified hand.

Marginalia: Modern pencil numeration by ℓ.

Summary:
Composers:
COUPERIN (François): ℓ 54r.
FRESCOBALDI: cf ℓ 61r-76r.
GRECO: cf ℓ 1r-16r.
LEBÈGUE: ℓ 47r.
LULLY: ℓ 52r.
MONNARD: ℓ 48r.
PASQUINI: cf ℓ 61r-76r.
STRADELLA: cf ℓ 61r-76r.
Contents: Miscellaneous Italian harpsichord and
organ pieces, largely anonymous, with French
group (ℓ. 40-54). Notations 1-2 to ℓ. 60v, then 3.

Inventory: For a complete thematic inventory see Lyle John
Anderson, "Cecilia A/400: Commentary, Thematic Index and
Partial Edition," (M.M. thesis, Univ. of Wisconsin, 1977).

ℓ $1r^1$-$16r^3$ | [untitled partimenti, notation 1, in part by
GRECO?]

ℓ $16r^5$-$39v^4$ | [short untitled Italian harpsichord pieces,

notation 2]

ℓ 40r^1-47r^2 [Anon. French organ pieces, grouped by tones; generic titles ("Recit de /Chromhorne /P^r. ton," etc; notation 2]

[LEBÈGUE: Gavotte (C)]

Gauotte

ℓ 47r^3-4   ¢|4|8|

CO: 10-Schwerin-617 #10, Gavotte
13-Möllersche, [copy of 64-Lebègue-I #43]
14-Schwerin-619 #91, Gavotte
21-Rés-1186-bis #12, Gavott
23-Tenbury #6, Gavotte Mr Le Begue
24-Babell #60, Gavotte de Mr. le Begue
35-Bauyn-III #54, (Gavotte) de Mr Lebegue
36-Parville #68, Gauotte Mr le Begue
45-Dart #22, [copy of 64-Lebègue-I #43]
46-Menetou #102, Gavotte
50-Paignon #11, Balet de Mr lebegue
64-Lebègue-I #43, Gauotte

ED: cf Dufourcq-L p 38, Brunold/Dart-Co #132.

ℓ 47v^1-2 Serrabande [C]

ℓ 47v^3-4 Menuet [C]

[MONNARD: Sarabande with Double (C)]

Sarabande |Suiue Redoublè
  ℓ 48r^1-4   ³[³₄]|8|4|8|4|

CO: 6-Munich-1511e #11, Sarrabande
    23-Tenbury #4, Sarabande
    24-Babell, #56, Sarabande
    31-Madrid-1360 #23/6, Sexta (Zarabanda)
    35-Bauyn-III #60, Sarabande De M. Monnard
    38-Gen-2348/53 #34, **Sarabande.**
    44-LaPierre p 2 [Sarabande]
ED: cf Ex 7 above, Bonfils-18 p 6.

ℓ 48v^1-2	Menuet [C]
ℓ 48v^3-49r^2	Menuet [with Double (G)]
ℓ 49r^3-4	Menuet [B♭]
ℓ 49v^1-2	Menuet [C]
ℓ 49v^3-4	Menuet [A]
ℓ 50r^1-2	Jeu de Cornet [B♭]
ℓ 50r^3-4	Menuet [D]
ℓ 50v^1-2	Menuet [b/e]
ℓ 50v^3-4	Menuet [g]
ℓ 51r^1-2	Menuet [c]
ℓ 51r^3-4	Jeù de cornet [F]
ℓ 51v^1-2	Menuet [C]
ℓ 51v^3-4	Jeù de cornet [D]
ℓ 52r^1-4	Dessante dopolon [LULLY: Entrée d'Apollon

from <u>Le Triomphe de l'amour</u> (1681) (g)]
CO: cf 14-Schwerin-619 #56
    cf 24-Babell #129
    cf 36-Parville #43
    cf 46-Menetou #100
    cf 68-d'Anglebert #35
    cf Stockholm-176 ℓ 14v
    cf Saizenay-I p 222 [lute]
ED: cf Gilbert p 118, Roesgen-Champion p 64.

ℓ 52v$^{1-4}$	Marche du /Prince d'orange [Gigue (G)] CO: cf 36-Parville #129
ℓ 53r$^{1-4}$	Courante de M. /La Dauphinè [d]
ℓ 53v$^{1-4}$	Gauotte [a]
ℓ 54r^{1}-v^{4}	Canaries |Redoublè [FR COUPERIN I-2 (d)]
ℓ 55r-60v	[Anon Italian harpsichord pieces, notation 2]
ℓ 61r^{1}-76r^{2}	[Italian pieces, including the following named composers: FRESCOBALDI, PASQUINI, STRA-DELLA, notation 3]
ℓ 76v	[blank, ruled]
ℓ 77r-78v	[blank, unruled]

Provenance: Spain, 1709 (Dated, ℓ. v, "Hverto ameno /de
/varias flores /de mussica /Recogidas de Ua/rios
Organistas /Por Fray Antonio /Martin /ano 1709 /de
Estevan Yusta Calvo."

Location: Madrid; Biblioteca nacional, M 1360.

Description: 245 ℓ., 29.5 x 20cm. Spine title, "Flores
de Música. T. IV."

Notation: Keyboard score (two 5-line staves, 5 systems
per page, written page by page). Clefs usually F^4,
G^2.

Scribe: One hand, probably that of Antonio Martin y Coll
(fl. 1706-1734); copied for Estevan Yusta Calvo?

Marginalia: "Al Ilustre Compositor Barbieri en prueba
de afecto su servidor y amigo, S. de Soto [Rubricado].
Labra 26 de Mayo de 1866," ℓ. iii. Original numeration
by ℓ.

Summary:
   Composers:
     AGUILLIERA DE HEREDIA: #1, 4.
     CABANILLES: #1, 6.
     CORELLI: #11.
     COUPERIN (Louis): #41a.
     FRESCOBALDI: #46-47.
     GAULTIER: #37.
     HARDEL: #41.
     LA BARRE: #23/1.
     LULLY: #24/7-9, 27, 31, 36, 38.
     MONNARD: #23/6.
   Contents: Miscellaneous harpsichord pieces, largely

grouped by **key**, sometimes by genre. Spanish
except for French pieces #24-41 (with possible
exceptions).

Inventory:

1	ℓ 1-37r	[11] Obras de lleno de Primer tono [AGUI-LIERA, CABANILLES, Anon]
2	ℓ 37v-48r	[4] Obras de 2° tono por Ge sol re/ut'
	ℓ 44v-48r	4ª De segundo tono por e la mi
3	ℓ 48r-53r	[2] Obras de 3° tono
4	ℓ 53v-72v	[5] Obras de 4° tono, de lleno [AGUILIERA, Anon]
5	ℓ 72v-111v	[8] Obras de quinto tono
6	ℓ 112r-149r	[11] Obras de sexto tono [CABANILLES, Anon]
7	ℓ 149v-157v	[3] Obras de Septimo tono.
8	ℓ 158r-176v	[6] Obras de octauo tono-
9	ℓ 177r-181v	Obra de primer tono/por B fa be mi blanco
10	ℓ 181v-185v	Otra de 2° tono por G sol re ut
11	ℓ 186r-199r	[3] Tocatas alegres de Coreli. [with figured bass]
12	ℓ 199v-200r	Otras tocatas alegres para violin y organo. /Zarabanda
13	ℓ 200r	Alamande
14	ℓ 200v	Un aire alegre
15	ℓ 200v-201v	Otro allegro
16	ℓ 201v-202r	Alamande
17	ℓ 202r	Bailo di Dame

18	ℓ 202r-202v	Zarabanda
		CO: cf Van-Eijl #5
		ED: cf Noske #5.
19	ℓ 203r-204r	El Villano
20	ℓ 204r-204v	Danza del acha
21	ℓ 204v-205r	Corrent
22	ℓ 205r-205v	Alamande
	ℓ 205v	Zarabandas

23/1 [LA BARRE: Sarabande (d)]

1.a
   ℓ 205r^4-206r^1 $^3[^3_4]$|8|9|

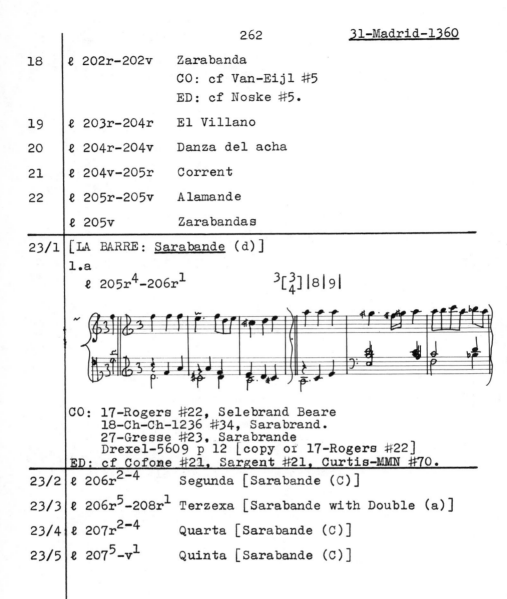

CO: 17-Rogers #22, Selebrand Beare
    18-Ch-Ch-1236 #34, Sarabrand.
    27-Gresse #23, Sarabrande
    Drexel-5609 p 12 [copy or 17-Rogers #22]
ED: cf Cofone #21, Sargent #21, Curtis-MMN #70.

23/2	ℓ 206r$^{2-4}$	Segunda [Sarabande (C)]
23/3	ℓ 206r^5-208r^1	Terzexa [Sarabande with Double (a)]
23/4	ℓ 207r$^{2-4}$	Quarta [Sarabande (C)]
23/5	ℓ 207^5-v^1	Quinta [Sarabande (C)]

23/6 | [MONNARD: <u>Sarabande</u> with <u>Double</u> (C)]

Sexta

     ℓ 207v$^{2-5}$ $^3[\frac{3}{4}]$ |4|4|4|4|4|4|

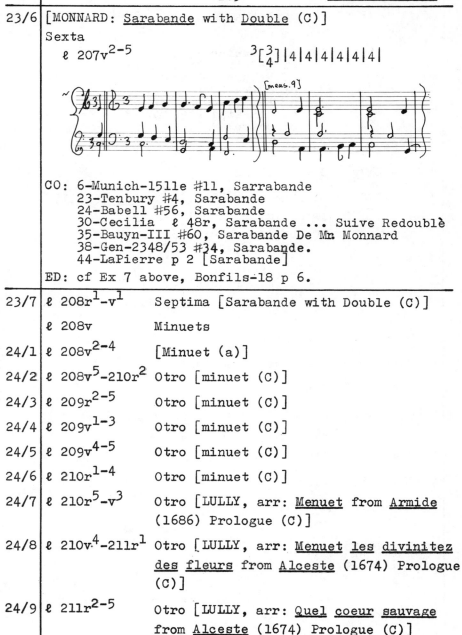

CO: 6-Munich-1511e #11, Sarrabande
       23-Tenbury #4, Sarabande
       24-Babell #56, Sarabande
       30-Cecilia ℓ 48r, Sarabande ... Suive Redoublè
       35-Bauyn-III #60, Sarabande De Mr Monnard
       38-Gen-2348/53 #34, Sarabande.
       44-LaPierre p 2 [Sarabande]

ED: cf Ex 7 above, Bonfils-18 p 6.

23/7 | ℓ 208r^{1}-v^{1} Septima [Sarabande with Double (C)]

     ℓ 208v   Minuets

24/1 | ℓ 208v$^{2-4}$ [Minuet (a)]

24/2 | ℓ 208v^{5}-210r^{2} Otro [minuet (C)]

24/3 | ℓ 209r$^{2-5}$ Otro [minuet (C)]

24/4 | ℓ 209v$^{1-3}$ Otro [minuet (C)]

24/5 | ℓ 209v$^{4-5}$ Otro [minuet (C)]

24/6 | ℓ 210r$^{1-4}$ Otro [minuet (C)]

24/7 | ℓ 210r^{5}-v^{3} Otro [LULLY, arr: <u>Menuet</u> from <u>Armide</u>
                          (1686) Prologue (C)]

24/8 | ℓ 210v^{4}-211r^{1} Otro [LULLY, arr: <u>Menuet</u> <u>les</u> <u>divinitez</u>
                          <u>des</u> <u>fleurs</u> from <u>Alceste</u> (1674) Prologue
                          (C)]

24/9 | ℓ 211r$^{2-5}$ Otro [LULLY, arr: <u>Quel</u> <u>coeur</u> <u>sauvage</u>
                          from <u>Alceste</u> (1674) Prologue (C)]

24/ 10	ℓ 211v^1-212r^1	Otro [<u>La Princesse</u> (Air ancien) with <u>Double</u> (d)]
		CO: cf 6-Munich-1511e #12
		cf 7-Munich-1511f #18
		cf 9-Ihre-284 #51
		cf Skara #26
		cf Berlin-40147
		cf Van-Eijl #12, 20
		cf Cassel "A"
25	ℓ 212r-215r	Las Folias [12 variations]
26	ℓ 215v-217v	Otras Folias
27	ℓ 217v-220v	La Chacona [LULLY, arr: <u>Passacaille</u> from <u>Armide</u> (1686) V-2 (g)]
		CO: cf 14-Schwerin-619 #63
		cf 24-Babell #138
		cf 49-RésF-933 #1
		cf 68-d'Anglebert #37
		cf Minorite ℓ 44v
		ED: cf Gilbert p 108, Roesgen-Champion p 67.
28	ℓ 220v- 221r	Las Vacas
29	ℓ 221r	Prado de S^n. Geronimo
30	ℓ 221r-v	Ruede la bola
31	ℓ 221v-222v	Canarios [LULLY, arr: <u>Canarie</u> from <u>Le Carnaval</u> (1668/1675) III (a)]
32	ℓ 222v	Otro genero de canarios
33	ℓ 222v-223r	Pasacalles
34	ℓ 223r-233v	Matassins CO: cf 28-Brussels-926 ℓ 10r
35	ℓ 223v-224r	Gigue
36	ℓ 224v	Entrada de Bretons [LULLY, arr: <u>Passe-pied</u> from <u>Ballet</u> <u>du</u> <u>temple</u> <u>de</u> <u>la</u> <u>paix</u> (1685) (C)]
37	ℓ 225r	La Marche de Gautier [C]

38	ℓ 225v	Obra de Pensie [LULLY, arr: <u>Gigue</u> from <u>Persée</u> (1682) IV-6 (C)]
		CO: cf 46-Menetou #99
39	ℓ 226r-v	Aire
40	ℓ 226v	Ballet

---

41   [HARDEL: <u>Gavotte</u> (a)]

Jaboste de Ardel

    ℓ 227r$^{1-5}$ ^{C}|4|8|

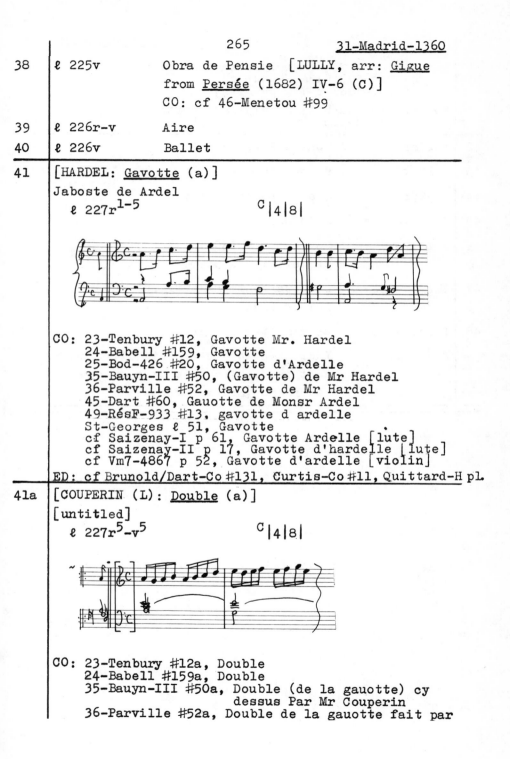

CO: 23-Tenbury #12, Gavotte Mr. Hardel
    24-Babell #159, Gavotte
    25-Bod-426 #20, Gavotte d'Ardelle
    35-Bauyn-III #50, (Gavotte) de Mr Hardel
    36-Parville #52, Gavotte de Mr Hardel
    45-Dart #60, Gauotte de Monsr Ardel
    49-RésF-933 #13, gavotte d ardelle
    St-Georges ℓ 51, Gavotte
    cf Saizenay-I p 61, Gavotte Ardelle [lute]
    cf Saizenay-II p 17, Gavotte d'hardelle [lute]
    cf Vm7-4867 p 52, Gavotte d'ardelle [violin]
ED: cf Brunold/Dart-Co #131, Curtis-Co #11, Quittard-H pl.

41a   [COUPERIN (L): <u>Double</u> (a)]

[untitled]

    ℓ 227r^5-v^5 ^{C}|4|8|

CO: 23-Tenbury #12a, Double
    24-Babell #159a, Double
    35-Bauyn-III #50a, Double (de la gauotte) cy
               dessus Par Mr Couperin
    36-Parville #52a, Double de la gauotte fait par

Mr Couprin
49-Rés-933 #13a, [Double]
cf Vm7-4867 p 77, [violin]

ED: cf Brunold/Dart-Co #131[a], Curtis-Co #11a,
    Quittard-H p 2.

42	ℓ 228r	Monica Forzata
43	ℓ 228v	El tatata
44	ℓ 229r	Quando podre lograrte
45	ℓ 229v-230v	Chinfonia [variations]
46	ℓ 231r-v	Corrent. [FRESCOBALDI (d)] ED: cf Pidoux 3:70.
47	ℓ 231v-232v	Otro Corrent [FRESCOBALDI (a)] ED: cf Pidoux 3:70.
48	ℓ 232v-243v	29 Minuetes al violin
	ℓ 244-245	Indice de lo que en este libro se contyne.... |Laudate Deum yn chordis et Organo |Estevan Yusta

Provenance: Paris (and Meudon, Toulouse?), ca. 1650-1661
  (many dates, not in chronological order, 1650-1659).

Location: London; private collection of Guy Oldham.

Description: 83 ℓ. (originally 96: 13 ℓ. lacking) oblong
  quarto format, 18.4 x 24 cm. Watermark #9. Contemporary full red morroco binding, gilt-tooled, gilted
  edges, 19 x 24.5 cm.

Notation: Keyboard score (two 5-line staves, 3 systems
  per page, written page by page); except #4 and 12:
  French letter score (cf. Ex. 7 in Commentary; cf.
  6-Munich-1511e, 7-Munich-1511f).

Scribes: Autograph of Louis COUPERIN (hand F), probably
  of d'ANGLEBERT (hand B) and possibly of CHAMBONNIÈRES
  (hand D), with 4 unidentified hands filling in the
  beginning and end of the book:
   A (Anon; Oldham "hand Aa"):
     1   Prélude (d)
     2   Courante (d)
     6   Sarabande (d)
     111 Courante (G)
   B (d'ANGLEBERT; Oldham "hand Bb"):
     3   MONNARD: Courante (a)
     4   d'ANGLEBERT: Courante (D)
     5   RICHARD: Sarabande (a)
     12 d'ANGLEBERT: Gaillarde (g)
   C (Anon; Oldham "hand Cc"):
     7-9 attributed CHAMBONNIÈRES pieces
   D (CHAMBONNIÈRES?; Oldham "hand Ch"):
     10-11, 13-16, 18-24a   unattributed CHAMBONNIÈRES
         pieces

E (Anon; Oldham "hand Dd"):

   17   Double de la Courante Iris (C)

F (Louis COUPERIN; Oldham "hand Co"):

   25-31   Harpsichord pieces by CHAMBONNIÈRES and
           HARDEL

   32-105 Organ and instrumental pieces by COUPERIN

   106-109 Harpsichord Suite by COUPERIN (a)

   110   Organ Fantaisie (C)

Marginalia: Extensive fingerings in pieces written by
hand A. No numeration.

Summary:

   Composers:

      d'ANGLEBERT: #4, 12.

      CHAMBONNIÈRES: #7-11, 13-16, cf 17, 18-30.

      COUPERIN (Louis): #32-110.

      FRESCOBALDI: #102.

      HARDEL: #31.

      MONNARD: #3.

      RICHARD: #5.

   Contents:

     1-31   Harpsichord pieces

     32-105   Organ and instrumental pieces (COUPERIN)

     106-109   Harpsichord Suite (COUPERIN)

     110   Organ Fantaisie (COUPERIN)

     111   Harpsichord Courante (Anon.)

Complete Inventory: For a title inventory which includes
the organ and instrumental pieces, see: Guy Oldham,
"A New Source of French Keyboard Music of the Mid
Seventeenth Century," Recherches 1 (1960): 51-60.

Inventory of Harpsichord Music (letters in parentheses
denote hands):

[2 ℓ lacking]

1
(A)
[Prélude (incomplete; beginning lacking) (d)]
(Prelude D) [mirror image of title visible on 1st ℓ] R
Oldham "a"   [unmeasured]

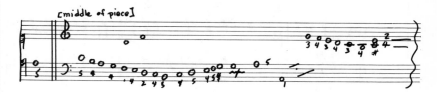

2
(A)
[Courante (d)]
Courante |R
Oldham "b"   [6/4] |5|5|

3
(B)
[MONNARD: Courante (a)]
Courante
Oldham "c"   3[6/4] |6|6|

CO: 35-Bauyn-III #72, Courante de Mr Monnard.
ED: cf Bonfils-18 p 7.

4   [d'ANGLEBERT: <u>Courante</u> (C)]
(B) Courante. |D'anglebert
         Oldham "d" ^{3}|8|8|

5   [RICHARD: <u>Sarabande</u> (a)]
(B) Sarabande
         Oldham "e" $^3[^3_4]$|8|12|

CO: 35-Bauyn-III #71, Sarabande de Mr Richard
ED: cf Bonfils-18 p 18, Dufourcq-0 #2.

6   [<u>Sarabande</u> (d)]
(A) Sarabande D |R
         Oldham "f" . $[^3_4]$|8|16|

CO: cf 5-Munich-1503ℓ #6, sarrabande
    cf 16-Cosyn #102, Sellabrand
    cf 17-Rogers #19, [Sarabande]
ED: cf Maas #103, Sargent #19, Cofone #19.

7   [CHAMBONNIÈRES: <u>Courante</u> (G)]

(C) Courante /de Monsieur /de chambonnieres |Reprise

      Oldham "A" $^3[^6_4]$|7|10|

CO: 33-Rés-89ter #35, Courante Chambonnieres...Double
      35-Bauyn-I #91, Courante de Mr. de Chambonnieres
      36-Parville #91, Courante Chanbonniere
      38-Gen-2348/53 #33, Courante
      63-Chamb-II #28, Courante

ED: cf Brunold-Tessier #58, Dart-Ch #58, Gilbert p 192.

---

8   [CHAMBONNIÈRES: <u>Sarabande jeunes zéphirs</u> (G)]

(C) Sarabande /de Monsieur /de Chambonnieres |Reprise

    |fin

    Oldham "B" $^3[^3_4]$|8|16|

CO: 5-Munich-1503ℓ #1, Sarrabande de Mons: Chambonnier
      33-Rés-89ter #36, Sarabande Chambonnieres ...
                 Double
      35-Bauyn-I #96, Sarabande de Mr de Chambonnieres
      36-Parville #93, Sarabande Chanbonniere
      44-LaPierre p 42, Les Zephirs de Mr de Chanboniere
      45-Dart #55, Sarabande de chambonniere
      63-Chamb-II #29, Sarabande Jeunes Zephirs
      cf Philidor p 22, Jeunes Zephirs (de Mr de chan-
                   boniere) [for instruments]

ED: cf Brunold-Tessier #59, Dart-Ch #59, Gilbert
    p 194.

9   [CHAMBONNIÈRES: <u>Courante</u> (G)]

(C) Courante /De Monsieur de /Chambonniere |Reprise |fin

     Oldham "C" $^3[^6_4]$ |9|8|

CO: 35-Bauyn-I #88, Courante de Mr de Chambonnieres
     36-Parville #90, Courante Chanbonniere
     38-Gen-2348/53 #36, Courante
     63-Chamb-II #27, Courante

ED: cf Brunold-Tessier #57, Dart-Ch #57.

10   [CHAMBONNIÈRES: <u>Courante</u> <u>la</u> <u>toute</u> <u>belle</u> (d)]

(D) Courante La Toute belle |fin

     Oldham "D" $^3[^6_4]$ |10|11|

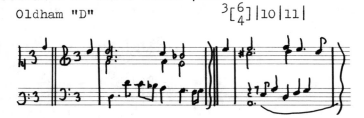

CO: 35-Bauyn-I #31, Courante La toute belle du même
              auteur
     36-Parville #19, Courante Chanbonniere dit la
              toute belle
     62-Chamb-I #12, Courante la toute belle

ED: cf Brunold-Tessier #12, Dart-Ch #12.

11
(D)

[CHAMBONNIÈRES: <u>Courante</u> <u>de</u> <u>madame</u> (d)]

Courante de Madame |Reprise |fin

Oldham "E" $^3[^6_4]$ |9|10|

CO: 35-Bauyn-I #34, Autre Courante du meme Auteur
    36-Parville #20, Courante chanbonniere
    62-Chamb-I #13, Courante de Madame

ED: cf Brunold-Tessier #13, Dart-Ch #13.

12
(B)

[d'ANGLEBERT: <u>Gaillarde</u> (<u>Sarabande</u>) (g)]

Sarabande, façon de Gaillarde. D'anglebert

Oldham "g" $^3[^6_4]$ |8|11|

CO: 68-d'Anglebert #26, Gaillarde Lentement

ED: cf Gilbert p 38, Roesgen-Champion p 49.

[1 blank page]

13
(D)

[CHAMBONNIÈRES: <u>Courante</u> (incomplete; 2nd strain lacking) (d)]

3me Courante

Oldham "F" $^3[^6_4]|6|$

CO: 24-Babell #220, Courante
    35-Bauyn-I #37, Courante de Monsr. Chambonnieres
    62-Chamb-I #14, Courante.

ED: cf Brunold-Tessier #14, Dart-Ch #14.

[2 ℓ lacking]

14
(D)

[CHAMBONNIÈRES: <u>Sarabande</u> (incomplete; 1st strain lacking)(d)]

... |R |fin

Oldham "G" $|19| [^3_4|20|]$

CO: 35-Bauyn-I #40, Sarabande de Monsr De Chambon-
                    nieres

ED: cf Brunold-Tessier #85.

15 [CHAMBONNIÈRES: <u>Le Printemps</u> (a)]

15A [15:] Le printemps |Reprise |Suite |trois fois Le

(D) petit Couplet

[15A:] Le printemps |Suite |trois fois Le dernier
Couplet

Oldham "H," "I" ^{3}|8|18| [$\frac{3}{4}$|12|19|

CO: 36-Parville #145, Le Printems de Chambonnieres
47-Gen-2356 #2, Paschalia de Mr Chambonnieres

ED: cf Brunold-Tessier #142.

16 [CHAMBONNIÈRES: <u>Sarabande</u> (incomplete?) (a)]

(D) Sarabande

Oldham "J" ^{3}[$\frac{3}{4}$]|8|14

17
(E)

[Double de la Courante Iris (CHAMBONNIÈRES) (C)]

Double de La Courante Iris |Reprise

Oldham "h" $^3[^6_4]$ |8|8|

CO: cf(?) 22a-Roper #58a, double
    cf 33-Rés-89ter #2a, Double [d'ANGLEBERT]
    (cf?) 44-LaPierre p 20, 36A, Double

ED: cf Brunold-Tessier #8, p 116; Dart-Ch #8 (original
    Courante); Gilbert p 149.

18
(D)

[CHAMBONNIÈRES: Gigue (incomplete) (a)]

gigue

Oldham "K" $^3[^3_4]$ |20|13|

19
(D)

[CHAMBONNIÈRES: Courante (G)]

Courante |fin

Oldham "L"

CO: 23-Tenbury #40, Courante Chambonniere
    24-Babell #87, Courante de Chre.
    33-Rés-89ter #34, Courante Chambonnieres ... Double
    35-Bauyn-I #92, Courante de Mr de Chambonnieres
    36-Parville #92, Courante chanbonniere

63-Chamb-II #26, Courante

ED: cf Brunold-Tessier #56, Dart-Ch #56, Gilbert p 190.

20 | [CHAMBONNIÈRES: <u>Sarabande</u> (G)]
(D) | Sarabande |fin

Oldham "M" ^{3}|8|22| [$^3_4$|8|24|]

21 | [CHAMBONNIÈRES: <u>L'Estourdie</u> (G)]
(D) | L'estourdie |fin

Oldham "N" ^{3}|7|15| [$^3_8$|8|20|]

22 | [CHAMBONNIÈRES: <u>Allemande</u> <u>le</u> <u>moutier</u> (C)]
(D) | Le Moutie et la Mariée |fin

Oldham "O" ^{C}|11|11|

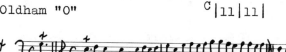

CO: 24-Babell #200, Allemande ... Double
    35-Bauyn-I #1, Allemande de Mr Chambonnieres Le
                    Moutier ... Double (Couperin)
    36-Parville #60, Allemande le moutier de Mr Cham-
                    bonniere ... Double (Couperin)

ED: cf Brunold-Tessier #61, Curtis-Co #29, Brunold/
    Dart-Co #134.

23
(D)

[CHAMBONNIÈRES: <u>Allemande</u> <u>la</u> <u>loureuse</u> (d)]

Allemande /La Loureuse |i fois 2 fois |pour recom-
mencer |fin

Oldham "P"   ^C|7|11|

CO: 24-Babell #184, Allemande ... Double
    35-Bauyn-I #30, Allemande la Loureuse de Mr de
                    Chambonnieres
    36-Parville #21, Allemande la loureuse Chanbonniere
    62-Chamb-I #11, Allemande la Loureuse

ED: cf Brunold-Tessier #11, Dart-Ch #11.

24
(D)

[CHAMBONNIÈRES: <u>Gaillarde</u> (Bb)]

Gaillarde b |fin

Oldham "Q"   ³[3/4]|8|16|

CO: 35-Bauyn-I #127, (Galliarde) de Mr. de Chambon-
                     nieres

ED: cf Brunold-Tessier #141.

24a [CHAMBONNIÈRES: Double (B♭)]
(D) Double |Reprise |Suitte |fin
     Oldham "R"

CO: 35-Bauyn-I #127a, Double dela (Gaillarde) par
                      led' Auteur
ED: cf Brunold-Tessier #141[a].

25   [CHAMBONNIÈRES: Sarabande (g)]
(F) Sarabande de Mons.r /de Chambonnieres |Suitte
     Oldham "S"   3[6/4]|4|11|

CO: 35-Bauyn-I #118, Sarabande de Mr de Chambon-
                      nieres [a]
    62-Chamb-I #26, Sarabande
ED: cf Brunold-Tessier #26, 133, Dart-Ch #26.

26   [CHAMBONNIÈRES: Courante (a)]
(F) Courante de Mr Chambre |Suitte |fin
     Oldham "T"   2/3|9|12| [3/4|18|21|]

27
(F)

[CHAMBONNIÈRES: <u>Courante</u> (a)]

Aultre Courante |Po^r la reprise |Po^r recommencer la

reprise |fin

    Oldham "U" $\frac{2}{3}[\frac{6}{4}]$ |7|9|

CO: 35-Bauyn-I #116, Courante du meme Auteur
    38-Gen-2348/53 #3, Courante
    62-Chamb-I #3, Courante

ED: cf Brunold-Tessier #3, Dart-Ch #3.

28
(F)

[CHAMBONNIÈRES: <u>Gigue la vetille</u> (<u>la coquette</u>) (a)]

La Vetille |Suitte dela /Vetille

    Oldham "V" $^3[\frac{6}{4}]$ |14|10|

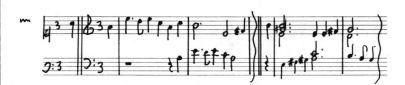

CO: 35-Bauyn-I #122, Gigue (la Coquette) de Mr de
                Chambonnieres
    47-Gen-2356 #8, Gigue de Monsr Chanbonnieres

ED: cf Brunold-Tessier #137.

29
(F)

[CHAMBONNIÈRES: Allemande la rare (a)]

Allemande la rare /de Mr Chamb.^re |Reprise |fin

Oldham "W"   ^C |10|13|

CO: 35-Bauyn-I #110, Allemande La rare de Mr de
                    Chambonnieres
    62-Chamb-I #1, Allemande la Rare

ED: cf Brunold-Tessier #1, Dart-Ch #1.

30
(F)

[CHAMBONNIÈRES: Courante (a)]

Courante |Reprise |fin

Oldham "X"   ^3[^6_4]|7|8|

CO: 35-Bauyn-I #112, Courante de Mr de Chambonnieres
    62-Chamb-I #2, Courante

ED: cf Brunold-Tessier #2, Dart-Ch #2.

30a | [CHAMBONNIÈRES: <u>Double</u> (a)]
(F) | Double dela Courante |Tournez po^r la Suitte /du double dela Courante |Suitte du double dela /Courante |j^{er} fois |j^{er} fois |derniere |fin

    Oldham "Y" $^3[^6_4]$|7|8|

CO: 35-Bauyn-I #112a, Double
    62-Chamb-I #2a, Double de la Courante
ED: cf Brunold-Tessier #2[a], Dart-Ch #2[a].

31 | [HARDEL: <u>Courante</u> (d)]
Courante /de M^r /hardel |fin

    Oldham "i" $^3[^6_4]$|7|8|

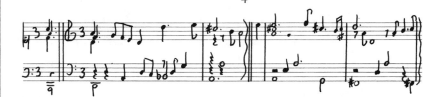

CO: 35-Bauyn-III #45, Courante de Mr Hardel
    44-LaPierre p 54, Premiere Courante
ED: Quittard-H p 3.

32- | [Organ and instrumental compositions by COUPERIN,
105 | many dated (1650-1659)]
(F) |

106 | [COUPERIN (L): <u>Allemande</u> (a)]
(F) | Allemande Couperin, d'ap[res au?....] |fin
     Oldham "j" ^{C}|10|10|

ED: Curtis-Co #14.

107 | [COUPERIN (L): <u>Courante</u> (a)]
(F) | Courante Coup^n
     Oldham "k" $^3[^6_4]$|10|10|

108 | [COUPERIN (L): <u>Courante</u> (a)]
(F) | Autre Courante Couperin |Reprise |fin
     Oldham "ℓ" $^3[^6_4]$|6|8|4|

109 [COUPERIN (L): <u>Sarabande</u> (a)]
(F) Sarabande Couperin |point céla |animez |reprise
|point |po^r les doubles passages de la basse
de la 4me mesure |Reprise

    Oldham "m"
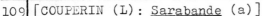

    CO: 35-Bauyn-II #110, Sarabande de Mr. Couperin
       36-Parville #50, Sarabande couprin
    ED: Curtis-Co #5; cf Brunold/Dart-Co #110.

110 fantaisie |Couperin a Meudon 1656 [for organ (C)]
(F)

111 [<u>Courante</u> (incomplete; 1st strain lacking) (G)]
(A) [untitled; written upside down from the back of the
book]

    Oldham "n"

[1 ℓ lacking]

Provenance: Paris, post 1677 (transcription from Isis);
probably 1677-1680.

Location: Paris; Bibliothèque nationale, département de
la musique, fonds conservatoire, Réserve 89ter (olim
Conservatoire de musique, 18223).

Description: 3 p.ℓ., 93 (i.e. 91: ℓ. 59-60 lacking), 1 ℓ.;
oblong quarto format, 17.7 x 23.2 cm. (trimmed).
Watermark #100. Contemporary gilt-tooled full red
morroco binding, marbled paste-downs and end papers,
gilted edges, 18.5 x 24 cm.

Notation: Keyboard score (two 5-line staves, 3 systems
per page, written page by page). Clefs: F^3, C^1, $G^{1,2}$;
usually F^3, C^1 or F^3, G^2.

Scribes: Jean-Henri d'ANGLEBERT (1628-1691) (hand A), with
3-4 later hands filling in formerly blank pages:
   B: #19
   C: ℓ. 29v-30v
   D: (same as C?) #19a, 19e, 20a-b, 23a
   E: #19b-d, 31

Marginalia: Numeration by ℓ. in modern pencil; numeration
of pieces in modern ink (maintained with adjustments
below). Small crosses at the tops of pages which
begin new pieces, in original ink (copyist's marks?).
Extra beam added in original hand, but later ink on
ℓ. 2v^3, meas. 1.

Summary:
  Composers:
    d'ANGLEBERT: #1-1a, 2a, 3a, 4a, 5a, 6-8, 20, 21, 22a,
      23, 24, 32, 33a, 34a, 35a, 36a, 37-40, 41a, 42a/e, 44.
    CHAMBONNIÈRES: #2, 3, 5, 22, 34, 35, 36.
    COUPERIN (Louis): #33.
    GAULTIER (D): #30.

GAULTIER (E): #11-13, 15-18, 25-29.

LAMBERT: #19 (hand E).

LULLY: #9-9a, 42b-d, 43.

MARAIS: #42.

MESANGEAU: #14.

PINEL: #4.

RICHARD: #41.

Contents (hand A only), 48 pieces & 12 doubles:
1-18   Suite (C)
  20-22   Miscellaneous pieces
  23-30   Suite (d)
  32-42   Suite (G)
  42a-44   Suite (g)

Inventory (hand A unless otherwise noted in parentheses):

| 1 | [d'ANGLEBERT: <u>Prélude</u> (C)] |

Prelude. /D'Anglebert
ℓ 1r$^{1-3}$ [unmeasured]

ED: Gilbert p 146, Roesgen-Champion p 143.

| 1a | [d'ANGLEBERT: <u>Allemande</u> (C)] |

Allemande. /D'Anglebert.
ℓ 1v^{1}-2r^{3} ^{C}|6|7|

ED: Gilbert p 147, Roesgen-Champion p 144.

2 | [CHAMBONNIÈRES: <u>Courante</u> <u>Iris</u> (C)]

Courante. /Chambonnieres.

ℓ 2v^1-3r^3 $^3[^6_4]$|8|8|

CO: 8-Hintze #15, Courante
    22a-Roper #58, **Courante Chambonniere**
    23-Tenbury #3, (courante chambonii)
    24-Babell #58, Courante de Mr. de Chambonniere
    35-Bauyn-I #9, Courante de Mr De Chambonnieres
    36-Parville #61, Courante Chanbonniere
    44-LaPierre p 18, p 34A, Courante Chambonniere
    47-Gen-2356 #12, Courante
    53-Oldham-2 p 107, **Courante de Chamboniere**
    55-Redon #23, Courante de Monsieur de Chambonniere
    62-Chamb-I #8, Courante Iris

ED: Gilbert p 148; cf Brunold-Tessier #8, Dart-Ch #8.

2a | [d'ANGLEBERT: <u>Double</u> (C)]

Double.

ℓ 3v^1-4r^3 $^3[^6_4]$|8|8|

CO: cf 22a-Roper #58a, **double**
    cf 32-Oldham #17 , Double de La Courante Iris
    cf 44-LaPierre p 20, 36A, Double

ED: Gilbert p 149, Brunold-Tessier p 116.

3 | [CHAMBONNIÈRES: <u>Courante</u> (C)]

2. /Courante. /Chambonnieres

ℓ 4v^1-5r^3 $^3[^6_4]$ |6|7|

CO: 22a-Roper #59, 2me Courante
    35-Bauyn-I #23, Courante de Mr. Chambonnieres
    36-Parville #62, Courante Chanbonniere
    62-Chamb-I #9, Courante

ED: Gilbert p 150; cf Brunold-Tessier #9, Dart-Ch #9.

3a | [d'ANGLEBERT: <u>Double</u> (C)]

Double

ℓ 5v^1-6r^3 $^3[^6_4]$ |6|7|

CO: cf 22a-Roper #59a, double
ED: Gilbert p 151, Brunold-Tessier p 117.

---

4 | [PINEL, arr d'ANGLEBERT: <u>Sarabande</u> (C)]

Sarabande. /Pinel

ℓ 6v^1-7r^2 $^3[^3_4]$ |8|12|

CO: cf 35-Bauyn-III #90, Sarabande de Mr. Pinel
    cf 36-Parville #64, Sarabande de Mr pignel
    cf 47-Gen-2356 #13, Sarabande
ED: Gilbert p 152.

4a | [d'ANGLEBERT: <u>Double</u> (C)]

Double.

ℓ 7v^1-8r^3

^{3}[$\frac{3}{4}$]|8|14|5|

ED: Gilbert p 153.

---

5 | [CHAMBONNIÈRES: <u>Gigue la verdinguette</u> (C)]

Gigue /La Verdinguette. /Chambonnieres.

ℓ 8v^1-9r^3

^{3}[$\frac{3}{4}$]|16|16|

CO: 35-Bauyn-I #22, Gigue du même Auteur
    63-Chamb-II #5, Gigue La Verdinguette

ED: Gilbert p 154; cf Brunold-Tessier #35, Dart-Ch #35.

5a | [d'ANGLEBERT: <u>Double</u> (C)]

Double.

ℓ 9v^1-10r^3

^{3}[$\frac{3}{4}$]|16|20|

ED: Gilbert p 155, Brunold-Tessier p 118.

6 | [d'ANGLEBERT: <u>Gaillarde</u> (C)]

Gaillarde. /D'Anglebert.

ℓ 10v^1-11r^3 ^{3}[$\frac{3}{2}$]|8|16|

CO: 35-Bauyn-III #63, Sarabande graue en forme (de
                gaillarde) de Mr D'anglebert
    cf 35-Bauyn-I #20, [Sarabande on similar theme]
    cf 63-Chamb-II #4 [Sarabande on similar theme]

ED: Gilbert p 157, Roesgen-Champion p 145; cf Brunold-
    Tessier #34, 75; cf Dart-Ch #34.

6a | [d'ANGLEBERT: <u>Double</u> (C)]

Double.

ℓ 10v^1-11r^3 ^{3}[$\frac{3}{2}$]|16|5|

ED: Gilbert p 158, Roesgen-Champion p 146.

7 | [d'ANGLEBERT: <u>Chaconne</u> (C)]

Chaconne. /D'Anglebert |Suitte dela /Chaconne.
ℓ 12v^1-14r^3 $^3[\frac{3}{4}|4|$ x 6]

CO: 24-Babell #204, Chaconne
    36-Parville #65, Chaconne Danglebert
    45-Dart #39, Chaconne
    51-LaBarre-11 p 212, Chaconne de Mr D'anglebert
    51-LaBarre-11 p 229, Chaconne D'Anglebert

ED: Gilbert p 160, Roesgen-Champion p 148.

8 | [**arr** d'ANGLEBERT: <u>Bourrée</u> <u>les</u> <u>Basques</u> (C)]

Boureé./Air de Ballet po.^{r} /Les Basques.[in a modern
hand:] Les Basques
ℓ 14v^1-15r^2 ¢|8|8|

ED: Gilbert p 162.

9 | [LULLY, arr d'ANGLEBERT: Premier Air from Thésée (1675)
III-6 (C)]
Les Demons./Air de Ballet./Viste.[in a modern hand:
Les Démons
ℓ 15v^1-16r^2 ¢|9|15|

CO: cf 23-Tenbury #67, Les Lutins [F]
    cf 24-Babell #234, Premier Air pour Les Lutins [F]
ED: Gilbert p 164.

9a | [LULLY, arr d'ANGLEBERT: Second Air from Thésée (1675)
III-6 (C)]
2e Air des Demons. /Viste.
ℓ 16v^1-17r^3 $^3[\frac{3}{4}]$|10|15|

CO: cf 24-Babell #235, Second Air [F]
    cf Inglis, ℓ 14r, [untitled] French Baptist [F]
ED: Gilbert p 165.

10 | [arr d'ANGLEBERT: <u>Marche</u> (<u>Air</u> <u>de</u> <u>ballet</u>) (C)]

Air de Ballet. /Marche.

  ℓ 17v¹-18r²   ¢|10|8|

ED: Gilbert p 163.

---

11 | [GAULTIER (E), arr d'ANGLEBERT: <u>Gigue</u> (C)]

Gigue du Vieux /Gautier.

  ℓ 18v¹-19r³   ¢|15|16|

ED: Gilbert p 172, Souris-G #84.

---

12 | [GAULTIER (E), arr d'ANGLEBERT: <u>Courante</u> (C)]

Courante du /Vieux Gautier.

  ℓ 19v¹-20r³   ³|12|15| [³/₄|13|16|]

ED: Gilbert p 169, Souris-G #75.

13 | [GAULTIER (E), arr d'ANGLEBERT: <u>Courante</u> (C)]
Courante du Vieux /Gautier.
  ℓ 20v^1-21r^3 ^{3}|9|8| [$^6_4$|7|8|]

ED: Gilbert p 167, Souris-G #79; cf Souris-G #40.

14 | [MESANGEAU, arr d'ANGLEBERT: <u>Sarabande</u> (C)]
Sarabande. /Megengeot
  ℓ 21v^1-22r^3 ^{3}[$^3_4$] |16|16|

CO: cf 35-Bauyn-III #51, Sarabande de Mr. Mesangeau
ED: Gilbert p 171, Souris-M p 56; cf Souris-M #12.

15 | [GAULTIER (E), arr d'ANGLEBERT: <u>Courante</u> (C)]
Courante du /Vieux Gautier.
  ℓ 22v^1-23r^3 ^{3}|16|15| [$^3_4$|16|16|]

ED: Gilbert p 168, Souris-G #76.

16 | [GAULTIER (E), arr d'ANGLEBERT: <u>Allemande</u> <u>la</u> <u>vestem-</u>
<u>ponade</u> (C)]

Allemande /du Vieux Gautier. [in a modern hand:] /La
Vestemponade

    ℓ 23v^1-24r^2 C|7|7|

ED: Gilbert p 166, Souris-G #74.

---

17 | [GAULTIER (E), arr d'ANGLEBERT: <u>Courante</u> (C)]

Courante du /Vieux Gautier.

    ℓ 24v^1-25r^3 $^3[^3_4]$|16|16|

ED: Gilbert p 170, Souris-G #77.

---

18 | [GAULTIER (E), arr d'ANGLEBERT: <u>Chaconne</u> (C)]

Chaconne du /Vieux Gautier. Suitte dela /Chaconne.

    ℓ 25v^1-27r^3 ^{3}|6|5|3|7|7|9| [$^6_4$|33|]

ED: Gilbert p 173 (with partial facsim),
    Souris-G #83.

19 (B)	ℓ 27v¹-28v²	air /De M. Lambert [for voice and figured bass; text incipit:] aimables habitans de ces naissant boc/cage ...
	ℓ 29r	[blank, ruled]
(C)	ℓ 29v	[scales, solfege and letter names of notes]
(C)	ℓ 30r-30v	[figured bass exercises]
	ℓ 31r	[blank, ruled]

19a [<u>Fugue</u> (fragment) (c)]
(D) [untitled]
   ℓ 31v¹⁻³   ᶜ|11|

	ℓ 32r-33v	[blank, ruled]
19b (E)	ℓ 34r	[treble melody (c)]
19c (E)	ℓ 34v	[treble melody (D)]
19d (E)	ℓ 35r	[treble melody (D)]

19e | [Chromatic Fantasy (C)]
(B) | [untitled]
  ℓ 35v¹-36r³   C|50|

20 | [d'ANGLEBERT: Gaillarde (a)]
Gaillarde. /D'Anglebert.
  ℓ 36v¹-37r³   ³[⁶₄]|24|

ED: Gilbert p 176, Roesgen-Champion p 150.

20a | [Gigue (C)]
(D) | [untitled]
  ℓ 37v¹-38v²   ⁶₈|21|36|

 ℓ 39r   [blank, ruled]

20b | [Fragment (C)]
(D) | [untitled]
  ℓ 39v¹⁻²
  ℓ 40r-43r   [blank, ruled]   C[⁴₄]|7|

21 | [d'ANGLEBERT: <u>Variations</u> <u>sur</u> <u>les</u> <u>folies</u> <u>d'Espagne</u> (d)]
Variations sur /les follies d'Espagne. d'Anglebert
... 22^e |fin.
    ℓ 43v^1-51r^3 $^3[\frac{3}{4}|16|$ x 22]

CO: 15-Berlin-30206, [copy of 68-d'Anglebert #49]
    68-d'Anglebert #49, Variations sur les folies
                    d'Espagne
ED: Gilbert p 64, Roesgen-Champion p 93.

22 | [CHAMBONNIÈRES: <u>Sarabande</u> <u>o</u> <u>beau</u> <u>jardin</u> (F)]
O beau Jardin /Sarabande.
    ℓ 51v$^{1-3}$ $^3[\frac{3}{4}]|8|12|$

CO: 35-Bauyn-I #80, Volte de Mr. de Chambonnieres
    36-Parville #80, Volte Chanbonniere
    cf Philidor p 23, O Beau Jardin de Mr de Chanbon-
               niere [for instruments (D)]
ED: Gilbert p 178, Brunold-Tessier p 119; cf Brunold-
    Tessier #110.

22a | [d'ANGLEBERT: <u>Double</u> (F)]

Double.

ℓ 52r$^{1-3}$ $^3[\frac{3}{4}]|9|13|$

ED: Gilbert p 179, Brunold-Tessier p 110.

---

23 | [d'ANGLEBERT: <u>Prélude</u> (d)]

Prelude. /D'Anglebert

ℓ 52v^1-55r^3 [unmeasured]

CO: 68-d'Anglebert #38, Prelude

ED: Gilbert p 204 (facsim); cf Gilbert p 45, 46; cf
     Roesgen-Champion p 71.

23a | ℓ 56v^1-58r^3 Concerto [written over hand A:] Courante
(D) | [treble solo part: allegro and adagio;
     | presto follows on ℓ 59v (D)] |([crossed
     | out:] Courante) |adagio

24 | [d'ANGLEBERT: <u>Sarabande</u> (d)]

Sarabande../d'Anglebert. |reprise

  ℓ 58v^1-59r^3 ^{3}[$^3_4$]|12|16|

CO: 12-Walther, [copy of 68-d'Anglebert #43]
    68-d'Anglebert #43, Sarabande

ED: Gilbert p 57, Roesgen-Champion p 82.

23a | ℓ 59v-60r   [continuation of Concerto:] presto [(incom-
(D)   plete)]

                [2 ℓ cut out between ℓ 59 and 60]

---

25 | [GAULTIER (E), arr d'ANGLEBERT: <u>Courante les larmes</u> (d)]

Courante du /Vieux Gautier.

  ℓ 60v^1-61r^3 ^{3}|16|15| [$^3_4$|17|16|]

CO: 36-Parville #17, Courante du Vieux gautier
    cf 66-Perrine #20, Courante du V.G. ou les Larmes
                [a]

ED: Gilbert p 180, Souris-G #78; cf Souris-G #51.

26 | [GAULTIER (E), arr d'ANGLEBERT: <u>Courante</u> <u>la</u> <u>petite</u> <u>bergère</u> (d)]
Courante du /Vieux Gautier
ℓ 61v¹-62r³   ³|16|15| [³/₄|16|16|

CO: cf 66-Perrine #28, Courante la petite bergère
ED: Gilbert p 181, Souris-G #80; cf Souris-G #33.

27 | [GAULTIER (E), arr d'ANGLEBERT: <u>Sarabande</u> (d)]
Sarabande du /Vieux Gautier.
ℓ 62v¹-63r³   ³|8|7|8|4| [³/₄|8|8|8|4|]

ED: Gilbert p 183, Souris-G #82; cf Souris-G #45.

28 | [GAULTIER (E), arr d'ANGLEBERT: <u>Gigue</u> <u>la</u> <u>poste</u> (d)]
Gigue du Vieux /Gautier.
ℓ 63v¹-64r³   C|9|9|

CO: cf 66-Perrine #7, 7a, Allemande du V.G.... Gigue
                          du v.G.
ED: Gilbert p 185, Souris-G #85; cf Souris-G #63.

29 | [GAULTIER (E), arr d'ANGLEBERT: Courante l'immortelle (d)]

Courante du /Vieux Gautier. /L'Immortelle.

ℓ 64v^1-65r^3 ^{3}|11|15| [$\frac{3}{4}$|12|16|]]

CO: cf 24-Babell #226, Courante L'Immortelle
    cf 45-Dart #40, Limortelle [g]
    cf 66-Perrine #1, l'jmmortelle du vieux Gaultier
    cf Stockholm-176 ℓ 4v, L'Immortelle Courante du V.
                              Gautier
    cf Skara   #20, Courant Monsr Gautier
    cf Stockholm-2 p 32, Courant immortele de Mons:
                              Gautie
    cf Ottobeuren p 142, L'Immortelle Courrante de
                              Suitte du mesme
ED: Gilbert p 182, Souris-G #81; cf Souris-G #66.

---

30 | [GAULTIER (D), arr d'ANGLEBERT: Sarabande (d)]

Sarabande. /Gautier le Jeune.

ℓ 66v^1-66r^3 ^{3}[$\frac{3}{4}$]|16|12|

CO: cf 66-Perrine #16, Sarabande du J.G.
ED: Gilbert p 184; Tessier-G p 125; cf Tessier-G #83.

31
(E) | ℓ 66v-67r   [Air for voice and figured bass; text
                    incipit:] non prin/temps tu n'est point
                    la saison des amours ...

32 | [d'ANGLEBERT: Prélude (G)]

Prelude./d'Anglebert.

   ℓ 67v^1-68r^3 [unmeasured]

CO: 68-d'Anglebert #1, Prelude

ED: Gilbert p 202 (facsim), Roesgen-Champion p 151;
    cf Gilbert p 2, Roesgen-Champion p 2.

---

33 | [COUPERIN (L): Allemande (G)]

Allemande../Couperin

   ℓ 68r^1-69r^3 ^{C}|9|9|

CO: 24-Babell #252, Allemande
    35-Bauyn-II #82, Allemande du même Auteur
    36-Parville #88, Allemande Couprin
    47-Gen-2356 #5, Allemande du mesme Mr Couperin

ED: Gilbert p 186; cf Brunold/Dart-Co #82, Curtis-Co
    #86.

33a | [d'ANGLEBERT: <u>Double</u> (G)]

Double.

  ℓ 69v^1-70r^3 ^{C}|9|9|

ED: Gilbert p 188, Curtis-Co #86A.

---

34 | [CHAMBONNIÈRES: <u>Courante</u> (G)]

Courante. /Chambonnieres.

  ℓ 70v^1-71r^3 $^3[^6_4]$|8|9|

CO: 23-Tenbury #40, Courante Chambonniere
   24-Babell #87, Courante de Chre.
   32-Oldham #19, Courante
   35-Bauyn-I #92, Courante de Mr de Chambonnieres
   36-Parville #92, Courante chanbonniere
   63-Chamb-II #26, Courante

ED: Gilbert p 190; cf Brunold-Tessier #56, Dart-Ch #56.

34a | [d'ANGLEBERT: <u>Double</u> (G)]

Double.

  ℓ 71v^1-72r^3 $^3[^6_4]$|8|9|

ED: Gilbert p 191, Brunold-Tessier p 120.

| 35 | [CHAMBONNIÈRES: <u>Courante</u> (G)] |

Courante. /Chambonnieres.
℮ 72v^1-73r^3 ^{3}[$^6_4$]|7|10|

CO: 32-Oldham #7; Courante de Monsieur de chambonnieres
35-Bauyn-I #91, Courante de Mr. de Chambonnieres
36-Parville #91, Courante Chanbonniere
38-Gen-2348/53 #33, Courante
63-Chamb-II #28, Courante

ED: Gilbert p 192; cf Brunold-Tessier #58, Dart-Ch #58.

| 35a | [d'ANGLEBERT: <u>Double</u> (G)] |

Double.
℮ 73v^1-74r^3 ^{3}[$^6_4$]|7|10|

ED: Gilbert p 193, Brunold-Tessier p 121.

| 36 | [CHAMBONNIÈRES: <u>Sarabande jeunes zéphirs</u> (G)] |

Sarabande. /Chambonnieres.
℮ 74v^1-75r^2 ^{3}[$^3_4$]|8|16|

CO: 5-Munich-1503℮ #1, Sarrabande de Mons: Chambonnier

32-Oldham #8, Sarabande de Monsieur de Chambon-
        nieres
35-Bauyn-I #96, Sarabande de Mr de Chambonnieres
36-Parville #93, Sarabande Chanbonniere
44-LaPierre p 42, Les Zephirs de Mr de Chanboniere
45-Dart #55, Sarabande de chambonniere
63-Chamb-II #29, Sarabande Jeunes Zephirs
cf Philidor p 22, Jeunes Zephirs (de Mr de chan-
        boniere) [for instruments]

ED: Gilbert p 194; cf Brunold-Tessier #59, Dart-Ch# 59.

36a [d'ANGLEBERT: <u>Double</u> (G)]

Double.

    ℓ 75v^1-76r^3 $^3[\frac{3}{4}]|8|20|$

ED: Gilbert p 195, Brunold-Tessier p 122.

---

37 [d'ANGLEBERT: <u>Gigue</u> (G)]

Gigue /D'Anglebert

    ℓ 76v^1-77r^3 $^3|16|16|3|$ $[\frac{3}{4}|16|16|5|]$

CO: 68-d'Anglebert #16, 2$^{\underline{e}}$ Gigue

ED: Gilbert p 18, Roesgen-Champion p 35.

38 | [d'ANGLEBERT: <u>Gaillarde</u> (G)]

Gaillarde./D'Anglebert.. |Reprise ·

 ℓ 77v^1-78r^3 ^{3}[$\frac{3}{2}$]|8|16|

CO: 68-d'Anglebert #8, Gaillarde

ED: Gilbert p 20, Roesgen-Champion p 18.

---

39 | [d'ANGLEBERT: <u>Gavotte</u> (G)]

Gauotte. /D'Anglebert.

 ℓ 78v^1-79r^2 ¢|4|8|

CO: 68-d'Anglebert #10, Gavotte

ED: Gilbert p 26, Roesgen-Champion p 24.

---

40 | [d'ANGLEBERT: <u>Menuet</u> (G)]

Menuet. /D'Anglebert.

 ℓ 79v^1-80r^3 ^{3}[$\frac{3}{4}$]|16|16|

CO: 68-d'Anglebert #11, Menuet

ED: Gilbert p 27, Roesgen-Champion p 25.

41 | [RICHARD: <u>Sarabande</u> (G)]

Sarabande. /Richard.
ℓ 80v^1-81r^3 ^{3}[$\frac{3}{4}$]|8|16|4|

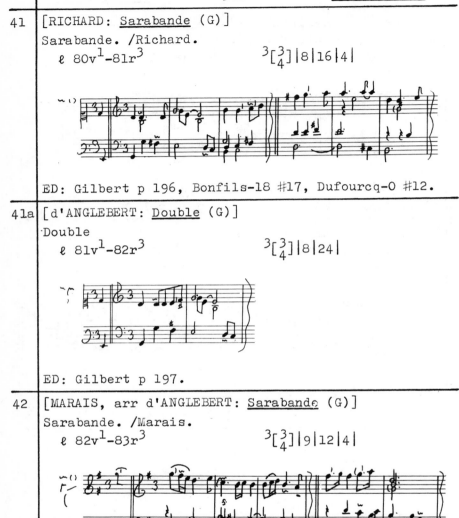

ED: Gilbert p 196, Bonfils-18 #17, Dufourcq-O #12.

41a | [d'ANGLEBERT: <u>Double</u> (G)]

·Double
ℓ 81v^1-82r^3 ^{3}[$\frac{3}{4}$]|8|24|

ED: Gilbert p 197.

42 | [MARAIS, arr d'ANGLEBERT: <u>Sarabande</u> (G)]

Sarabande. /Marais.
ℓ 82v^1-83r^3 ^{3}[$\frac{3}{4}$]|9|12|4|

ED: Gilbert p 198.

42A   [d'ANGLEBERT: Prélude (g)]

prelude. D'Anglebert.

   ℓ 83v^1-84r^1   [unmeasured]

CO: 68-d'Anglebert #17, Prelude

ED: Gilbert p 203 (facsim); cf Gilbert p 28, Roesgen-
     Champion p 36.

42b   [LULLY, arr d'ANGLEBERT: Ouverture from Le Carnaval

(1668, 1675) (g)]

Ouuertuor dela /Mascarade

   ℓ 84r^2-85r^3   [2/2] |13| [6/4] 10| [2/2] 27|

CO: 68-d'Anglebert #32, Ouuerture de la Mascarade

ED: Gilbert p 90, Roesgen-Champion p 60.

42c   [LULLY, arr d'ANGLEBERT: Ouverture from Isis (1677) (g)]

Ouuertuor /d'Isis.

   ℓ 85v^1-87r^3   ¢ |15| [3/4] 62|

CO: cf 14-Schwerin-619 #51, Ouverture Disis

cf 24-Babell #128, Ouverture D'Isis
cf 36-Parville #42, Ouuerture disis
cf 40-Rés-476 #35, Louuerture d'Isis
cf 42-Vm7-6307-2 #5, Ouuerture de Lopera disis
cf 46- Menetou #85, Ouuerture de lopera Disis
cf 49-RésF-933 #24, Ouuerture d isis
cf Stoss ℓ 24v

ED: Gilbert p 199; cf Bonfils-LP p 101, Howell #2.

42d │[LULLY, arr d'ANGLEBERT: <u>Courante</u> (g)]

Courante.

   ℓ 87v^1-88r^3 $^3[^6_4]|9|7|$

CO: 36-Parville #41, Courante de Mr Lully
    46-Menetou #117, Courante de Mr de lully
    68-d'Anglebert #21, Courante Mr. de Lully

ED: Gilbert p 95, (facsim), 96; Roesgen-Champion p 42.

42e │[d'ANGLEBERT: <u>Double</u> (g)]

Double dela /Courante.

   ℓ 88v^1-89r^3 $^3[^6_4]|9|7|$

CO: 36-Parville #41a, Double De La courante Lully
    68-d'Anglebert #21a, Double de la Courante

ED: Gilbert p 97, Roesgen-Champion p 43.

43 | [LULLY, arr d'ANGLEBERT Les Songes agréables from
Atys (1676) III-4 (g)]

Air de Ballet. /les Songes agreables.

ℓ 88v^1-90r^3 ^{3}[$^3_4$]|10|21|

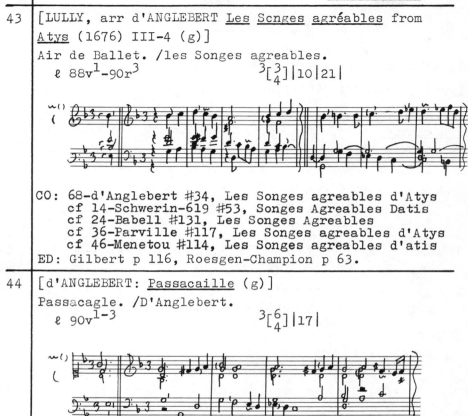

CO: 68-d'Anglebert #34, Les Songes agreables d'Atys
    cf 14-Schwerin-619 #53, Songes Agreables Datis
    cf 24-Babell #131, Les Songes Agreables
    cf 36-Parville #117, Les Songes agreables d'Atys
    cf 46-Menetou #114, Les Songes agreables d'atis
ED: Gilbert p 116, Roesgen-Champion p 63.

44 | [d'ANGLEBERT: Passacaille (g)]

Passacagle. /D'Anglebert.

ℓ 90v$^{1-3}$ ^{3}[$^6_4$]|17|

CO: 68-d'Anglebert #27, Passacaille
    cf Chigi-27 ℓ 36v [untitled]
ED: Gilbert p 40, Roesgen-Champion p 51.

Provenance: Paris, ca. 1690?

Location: Paris; Bibliothèque Sainte Geneviève, MS 2357, ℓ. 1-4.

Description: 4 ℓ. (i.e. 5: 1 ℓ. of another paper stubbed between ℓ. 1 and 2); oblong quarto format, 17.7 x 21.5 cm. Watermark #11 (same as 47-Gen-2356, but not the same ruling of staves). Modern full cloth binding, 17.5 x 23.5 cm. Bound with 8 ℓ. from the same original ms as MS 2350; cf 54-Gen-2350/57.

Notation: Keyboard score (two 5-line staves, 3 systems per page, written page by page). Clefs: F^3, G^2.

Scribe: One unidentified hand, similar to hand D of 47-Gen-2356; not the same as 54-Gen-2350/57.

Summary:

Composers:

Autograph of unidentified composer (?): "Couplett des folies d'espagnes de ma fasson," ℓ. 1Ar.

Contents:

Variations on <u>Folies d'Espagne</u>.

Inventory:

---

1 | [<u>11</u> <u>Variations</u> on <u>Folies</u> <u>d'Espagne</u> (incomplete) (d)]
folies d'espagnes |2 ... |ii
ℓ $1r^1-4v^3$

2 | [1 _Variation_ _on_ _Folies_ _d'Espagne_ (d)

Couplett des folies d'espagnes de ma fasson

ℓ 1Ar^1-v^3 [recto crossed out and same music re-
written on the verso; ℓ stubbed between
ℓ 1 and 2]

3 | ℓ 1Av$^{4-5}$ menuet [melody only]

35-BAUYN (I-III)

Provenance: France (Paris?), post 1658 (date, II ℓ. 74v, "1658").

Facsimile ed: Manuscrit Bauyn. Preface by François Lesure. Geneva: Minkoff, 1977.

Location: Paris; Bibliothèque nationale, département de la musique, Réserve Vm^7 674 and Réserve Vm^7 675$^{(1-2)}$ (olim Vm^7 1852 and Vm^7 1862$^{(1-2)}$.

Description: 2 v. (originally 3). V.1 (Rés Vm^7 674): 4 p. ℓ., 69, 33-64, 2 ℓ. (i.e. 2 p.ℓ., 69, 30 [2 ℓ. lacking], 2 ℓ.). V. 2 (Rés Vm^7 675): 6 p.ℓ., 76, 32, 4 ℓ. Both v.: folio format, 38.5 x 25 cm. Watermarks #58 and 59 (binding end papers). Matching original full leather bindings, added after mss were completed; stamped on front and back covers with the arms of Bauyn d'Angervilliers and N. Mathefelon (tracing #105); gilt-tooled, gilted edges; modern red leather spine label, "PIECES DE CLAVECIN."

Notation: Keyboard score (two 5-line staves, 6 systems per page, written page by page). Clefs: $G^{1,2}$, $F^{3,4,5}$, $C^{1,2,3}$; usually F^3, G^2.

Scribe: One unidentified professional hand.

Marginalia: Original numeration by ℓ. as 3 v., supplemented with modern pencil numeration by ℓ. to agree with bound order (see "Summary"). 35-Bayun-I ℓ 1r, at top, "Qui" (or meaningless marks?); 35-Bauyn-II ℓ. 1r, at top, "jost." Some pencil "x" marks and page numbers (added by one of the modern editors who have worked with the volumes?). Many words in titles and one entire piece carefully crossed out in contemporary (original?) hand.

Contents:

    35-Bauyn-I   Pieces by CHAMBONNIÈRES

    35-Bauyn-II Pieces by Louis COUPERIN

    35-Bauyn-III Miscellaneous pieces

Original order, as inventoried below:

    Rés Vm^7 674, ℓ. 1-69   35-Bauyn-I

    Rés Vm^7 675, ℓ. 1-76   35-Bauyn-II

    Rés Vm^7 675 end, ℓ. 1-32 35-Bauyn-III beginning

    Rés Vm^7 674 end, ℓ. 33-64 35-Bauyn-III end

Current order, as misbound:

    Rés Vm^7 674   35-Bauyn-I complete

                         35-Bauyn-III ℓ. 33-64

    Rés Vm^7 $675^{(1)}$ 35-Bauyn-II complete

    Rés Vm^7 $675^{(2)}$ 35-Bauyn-III ℓ. 1-32

Summary - 35-Bauyn-I:

Composers:

    CHAMBONNIÈRES: #1-127.

    COUPERIN (Louis): #1a, (18?).

Contents: Harpsichord pieces, grouped by key:

    #1-28 (C)   87-101 (G; 94 in C)

    29-43 (d)   102-109 (g)

    44-58 (D)   110-123 (a)

     59 (e)   124-124a (B♭)

    60-86 (F)

Summary - 35-Bauyn-II:

Composers:

    CHAMBONNIÈRES: #28?

    COUPERIN (Louis): #1-123.

Contents:

    #1-14 Préludes

    Pieces grouped by key:

15-29 (C)	92-99 (G)
30-34 (c)	100-112a (a)
35-57 (d)	113-115 (A)
58-62 (D)	116-118 (b)
63-65 (e)	119-120 (Bb)
66-81 (F)	121-123 Miscellaneous
82-91 (G)	

Summary - 35-Bauyn-III:

Composers:

d'ANGLEBERT: #63.

COUPERIN (Louis): #23-24, 27-31, 50a, 54a, 78(?), 78a.

DUMONT: #56-58, 81, 84-87, 94.

FRESCOBALDI: #19-20, 41.

FROBERGER: #1-15, 18, 67, 73-77.

GAULTIER: #64, 65.

HARDEL: #44-50.

LA BARRE: #32, 34, 55, 61, 66, 69.

LEBÈGUE: #54.

LORENCY: #43.

MESANGEAU: #51-52.

MONNARD: #53, 59, 60, 72.

PINEL: #90.

RICHARD: #21-22, 33, 40, 70-71, 82-83, 88-89, 92.

ROSSI: #91.

VINCENT: #93.

Contents:

#1-20 Pieces by FROBERGER, FRESCOBALDI, Anon.

21-31 Non-harpsichord pieces by RICHARD, COUPERIN.

32-34 Harpsichord pieces by LA BARRE, RICHARD.

35-43 Anon. Pavanes, miscellaneous pieces.

44-50 Pieces by HARDEL.

51-65 Pieces, mostly in C.

66-68 Pieces (d).

69-72 Pieces (a).

73-77   Pieces by FROBERGER.

78-94   Miscellaneous pieces.

Inventory - 35-Bauyn-I:

---

1 | [CHAMBONNIÈRES: <u>Allemande le moutier</u> (C)]

Allemande de M^r. Chambonnieres /Le Moutier |Reprise |fin

ℓ 1r$^{1-6}$ Minkoff p 1   ¢|11|11|

CO: 24-Babell #200, Allemande
    32-Oldham #22, Le Moutie et la Mariée
    36-Parville #60, Allemande le moutier de Mr Chambonniere
ED: Brunold-Tessier #61, Curtis-Co #29, Brunold/Dart-Co #134.

1a | [COUPERIN (L): <u>Double</u> (C)]

Double du Moutier par M^r. Couperin |Reprise |fin

ℓ 1v$^{1-6}$ Minkoff p 2   ¢|11|11|

CO: 36-Parville #60a, Le Double du moutier fait par
                     Mr Couprin
    cf 24-Babell #200a, Double de la mesme
ED: Brunold-Tessier #61, Curtis-Co #29a, Brunold/Dart-Co #134.

2   [CHAMBONNIÈRES: <u>Allemande</u> (C)]

Allemande de Mr de Chambonnieres. |fin

   ℓ 2r$^{1-5}$ **Minkoff** p 3 ^{C}|8|9|

ED: Brunold-Tessier #62.

---

3   [CHAMBONNIÈRES: <u>Allemande</u> <u>la</u> <u>Dunquerque</u> (C)]

Allemande La Dunquerque de Mr de Chambonnier.

   ℓ 2v$^{1-5}$ **Minkoff** p 4   ¢|12|8|

CO: 62-Chamb-I #7, Allemande la Dunquerque

ED: Brunold-Tessier #7, Dart-Ch #7.

---

4   [CHAMBONNIÈRES: <u>Allemande</u> (C)]

Allemande du même Auteur |fin

   ℓ 3r$^{1-5}$ **Minkoff** p 5   ¢|10|12|

ED: Brunold-Tessier #63.

5 | [CHAMBONNIÈRES: <u>Allemande</u> (C)]

Allemande de Mr de Chambonnieres |fin

　ℓ 3v$^{1-5}$ Minkoff p 6　　　^{C}|8|8|

CO: 63-Chamb-II #1, Allemande

ED: Brunold-Tessier #31, Dart-Ch #31.

6 | [CHAMBONNIÈRES: <u>Courante</u> (C)]

Courante de M^r. de Chambonnieres |Fin

　ℓ 4r$^{1-4}$ Minkoff p 7　　　$^3[^6_4]$|6|8|

CO: 35-Bauyn-I #94, Courante de Mr de Chambonnieres

ED: Brunold-Tessier #64.

7 | [CHAMBONNIÈRES: <u>La Sotise</u> (C)]

Autre de même Auteur |Fin

　ℓ 4v$^{1-5}$ Minkoff p 8　　　$^3[^3_4]$|16|16|

CO: 24-Babell #206, La Sotise
　　36-Parville #148, [untitled]

ED: Brunold-Tessier #65.

8 | [CHAMBONNIÈRES: <u>Courante</u> (C)]

Courante de Mr de Chambonnieres. |Fin

ℓ 5r$^{1-5}$ Minkoff p 8 $^3[^6_4]$|8|9|

ED: Brunold-Tessier #66.

9 | [CHAMBONNIÈRES: <u>Courante Iris</u> (C)]

Courante de M^r De Chambonnieres |Fin

ℓ 5v$^{1-5}$ Mindoff p 10 $^3[^6_4]$|8|8|

CO: 8-Hintze #15, Courante
    22a-Roper #58, Courante Chambonniere...double
    23-Tenbury #3, (courante chambonii)
    24-Babell #58, Courante de Mr. de Chambonniere
    33-Rés-89ter #2, Courante. Chambonnieres...Double
    36-Parville #61, Courante Chanbonniere
    44-LaPierre p 18, p 34A, Courante Chambonniere...Do▌
    47-Gen-2356 #12, Courante
    53-Oldham-2 p 107, **Courante de Chamboniere**
    55-Redon #23, Courante de Monsieur de Chambonniere
    62-Chamb-I #8, Courante Iris
    cf 32-Oldham #17, Double de La Courante Iris

ED: cf Brunold-Tessier #8, Dart-Ch #8, Gilbert p 148.

10 | [CHAMBONNIÈRES: <u>Courante</u> (C)]

Courante du même Auteur |fin

ℓ 6r$^{1-5}$ Minkoff p 11　　$^3[^6_4]$|7|7|

ED: Brunold-Tessier #67.

11 | [CHAMBONNIÈRES: <u>Courante</u> (C)]

Courante de Mr de Chambonnieres.|. |Fin

ℓ 6v$^{1-5}$ Minkoff p 12　　$^3[^6_4]$|7|10|

ED: Brunold-Tessier #68.

12 | [CHAMBONNIÈRES: <u>Courante</u> (C)]

Courante du même Auteur |Fin

ℓ 7r$^{1-4}$ Minkoff p 13　　$^3[^6_4]$|6|8|

ED: Brunold-Tessier #69.

13 | [CHAMBONNIÈRES: <u>Courante</u> (C)]

Courante de Mr de Chambonnieres .|. |Fin

ℓ 7v¹⁻⁵ Minkoff p 14   ³[⁶₄]|6|8|

CO: 63-Chamb-II #3, Courante

ED: Brunold-Tessier #33, Dart-Ch #33.

14 | [CHAMBONNIÈRES: <u>Courante</u> (C)]

Courante de Mr de Chambonnieres. |fin

ℓ 8r¹⁻⁵ Minkoff p 15   ³[⁶₄]|8|9|

ED: Brunold-Tessier #70.

15 | [CHAMBONNIÈRES: <u>Courante</u> (C)]

Courante de Mr Chambonnieres |fin

ℓ 8v¹⁻⁵ Minkoff p 16   ³[⁶₄]|7|6|

ED: Brunold-Tessier #71.

16 | [CHAMBONNIÈRES: <u>Courante</u> (C)]

Autre du même Auteur

ℓ 9r$^{1-5}$ **Minkoff p 17** $^3[^6_4]|7|9|$

ED: Brunold-Tessier #72.

---

17 | [CHAMBONNIÈRES: <u>Sarabande</u> (C)]

Sarabande de M^r. de Chambonnieres |fin

ℓ 9v$^{1-4}$ **Minkoff p 18** $^3|10|10|$ $[^3_4|12|12|]$

ED: Brunold-Tessier #73.

---

18 | [CHAMBONNIÈRES or COUPERIN (L): <u>Sarabande</u> (C)]

Sarabande.du même Auteur |Fin

ℓ 10r$^{1-4}$ **Minkoff p 19** $^3[^3_4]|8|16|$

CO: 35-Bauyn-II #28, Sarabande de Mr. Couperin
ED: Brunold-Tessier #74; cf Brunold/Dart-Co #28.

19 | [CHAMBONNIÈRES: <u>Sarabande de la reyne</u> (C)]

Sarabande dè Mr de Chambonnieres |fin
  ℓ 10v$^{1-6}$ Minkoff p 20 ^{3}|5|7| [$\frac{3}{4}$|8|29|]

CO: 62-Chamb-I #10, Sarabande de la Reyne
ED: Brunold-Tessier #10, Dart-Ch #10.

20 | [CHAMBONNIÈRES: <u>Sarabande grave</u> (C)]

Sarabande graue de Mr de Chambonnieres |Fin
  ℓ 11r$^{1-5}$ Minkoff p 21 ^{3}[$\frac{3}{4}$]|8|20|

CO: 63-Chamb-II #4, Galliarde
     cf 33-Rés-89ter #6 [Gaillarde on similar theme]
     cf 35-Bauyn-III #63 [Gaillarde on similar theme]
ED: Brunold-Tessier #75; cf Brunold-Tessier #34,
     Dart-Ch #34, Gilbert p 157, Roesgen-Champion p 145.

21 | [CHAMBONNIÈRES: <u>Gigue</u> (C)]

Gigue de M$^r_.$ de Chambonnieres |fin
  ℓ 11v$^{1-6}$ Minkoff p 22 ^{3}[$\frac{6}{4}$]|11|7|^{C}8|^{3}1|

ED: Brunold-Tessier #76.

22 | [CHAMBONNIÈRES: <u>Gigue</u> <u>la</u> <u>verdinguette</u> (C)]

Gigue du même Auteur |pour la 1re fois |pour le Refrain |Fin

ℓ 12r¹⁻⁵ Minkoff p 23   ³[$\frac{3}{4}$]|16|16|4|

CO: 33-Rés-89ter #5, Gigue la Verdinguette. Chambonnieres ... Double
    63-Chamb-II #5, Gigue La Verdinguette

ED: Brunold-Tessier #35, Dart-Ch #35; cf Brunold-Tessier p 118, Gilbert p 154.

23 | [CHAMBONNIÈRES: <u>Courante</u> (C)]

Courante de M^r. Chambonnieres |Fin

ℓ 12v¹⁻⁴ Minkoff p 24   ³|7|7| [$\frac{6}{4}$|6|7|]

CO: 22a-Roper #59, 2me Courante ... double
    33-Rés-89ter #3, 2. Courante Chambonnieres ...
                       Double
    36-Parville #62, Courante Chanbonniere
    62-Chamb-I #9, Courante

ED: Brunold-Tessier #9, Dart-Ch #9; cf Gilbert p 150.

24 | [CHAMBONNIÈRES: <u>Courante</u> (C)].

Courante de M^r. de Chambonnieres |fin
ℓ 13r¹⁻⁵ Minkoff p 25   ³[⁶₄]|6|8|

ED: Brunold-Tessier #77.

25 | [CHAMBONNIÈRES: <u>Courante</u> (C)]

Courante de M^r. de Chambonnieres |fin
ℓ 13v¹⁻⁵ Minkoff p 26   ³[⁶₄]|7|8|

ED: Brunold-Tessier #78.

26 | [CHAMBONNIÈRES: <u>Courante</u> (C)]

Courante du même Auteur |fin
ℓ 14r¹⁻⁵ Minkoff p 27   ³[⁶₄]|7|8|

ED: Brunold-Tessier #79.

27 | [CHAMBONNIÈRES: <u>Courante</u> (C)]

Courante de M^r De Chambonnieres |fin

   ℓ 14v$^{1-6}$ Minkoff p 28 $^3[^6_4]$|8|10|

ED: Brunold-Tessier #80.

28 | [CHAMBONNIÈRES: <u>Chaconne</u> (C)]

Chaconne de Mr Dela Chappelle dit Chambonnieres |fin

   ℓ 15r$^{1-5}$ Minkoff p 29 $^3[^3_4]$|4|9|18|

ED: Brunold-Tessier #81.

29 | [CHAMBONNIÈRES: <u>Allemande</u> (d)]

Allemande de M^r. de Chambonnieres |Fin

   ℓ 15v$^{1-5}$ Minkoff p 30 ^{C}|13|9|

CO: 38-Gen-2348/53 #39, [untitled]
    63-Chamb-II #6, Allemande
ED: Brunold-Tessier #36, Dart-Ch #36.

30 | [CHAMBONNIÈRES: <u>Allemande</u> <u>la</u> <u>loureuse</u> (d)]

Allemande la Loureuse de Mr de Chambonnieres |Fin
   ℓ 16r¹⁻⁵ Minkoff p 31   ¢|7|11|

CO: 24-Babell #184, Allemande ... Double
    32-Oldham #23, Allemande La Loureuse
    36-Parville #21, Allemande la loureuse Chanbonniere
    62-Chamb-I #11, Allemande la Loureuse
ED: Brunold-Tessier #11, Dart-Ch #11.

31 | [CHAMBONNIÈRES: <u>Courante</u> <u>la</u> <u>toute</u> <u>belle</u> (d)]

Courante La toute belle du même Auteur |fin
   ℓ 16v¹⁻⁶ Minkoff p 32   3[6/4]|10|11|

CO: 32-Oldham #10, Courante La Toute belle
    36-Parville #19, Courante Chanbonniere dit la
                     toute belle
    62-Chamb-I #12, Courante la toute belle
ED: Brunold-Tessier #12, Dart-Ch #12.

32 | [CHAMBONNIÈRES: <u>Courante</u> (d)]

Courante de Mr de Chambonnieres |fin

ℓ 17r$^{1-6}$ Minkoff p 33 $^3[^6_4]$|8|13|

ED: Brunold-Tessier #82.

---

33 | [CHAMBONNIÈRES: <u>Courante</u> (d)]

Courante de M$^r_.$ de Chambonnieres |fin

ℓ 17v$^{1-6}$ Minkoff p 34 $^3[^6_4]$|9|10|

ED: Brunold-Tessier #83.

---

34 | [CHAMBONNIÈRES: <u>Courante de madame</u> (d)]

Autre Courante du meme Auteur |fin

ℓ 18r$^{1-6}$ Minkoff p 35 $^3[^6_4]$|9|10|

CØ: 32-Oldham #11, Courante de Madame
    36-Parville #20, Courante Chanbonniere
    62-Chamb-I #13, Courante de Madame

ED: Brunold-Tessier #13, Dart-Ch #13.

35 | [CHAMBONNIÈRES: <u>Courante</u> (d)]

Courante de M![r] de Chambonnieres |fin

ℓ 18v[1-5] Minkoff p 36 $^3[^6_4]$|7|9|

CO: 18-Ch-Ch-1236 #3, Corant Mr Sambonier
     24-Babell #186, Courante

ED: Brunold-Tessier #84.

35a | [CHAMBONNIÈRES: <u>Double</u> (d)]

Double du meme Auteur |fin

ℓ 19r[1-5] Minkoff p 37 $^3[^6_4]$|7|9|

ED: Brunold-Tessier #84[a].

---

36 | [CHAMBONNIÈRES: <u>Les Barricades</u> (d)]

Courante de M![r] de Chambonnieres dit les barricades
|Fin

ℓ 19v[1-6] Minkoff p 38 $^3[^6_4]$|12|15|

CO: 52-Rés-2671 #14, Les Baricades
     62-Chamb-I #16, les Baricades
     cf 59-Dumont-1657 ℓ 31v, Allemande [by Dumont]

ED: Brunold-Tessier #16, Dart-Ch #16; cf Bonfils-13
     p 6, Cohen p 16.

37 | [CHAMBONNIÈRES: <u>Courante</u> (d)]

Courante de Monsr de Chambonnieres |fin

ℓ 20r¹⁻⁵ Minkoff p 39 $^3[^6_4]|6|9|$

CO: 24-Babell #220, Courante
    32-Oldham #13, 3me Courante
    62-Chamb-I #14, Courante

ED: Brunold-Tessier #14, Dart-Ch #14.

---

38 | [CHAMBONNIÈRES: <u>Sarabande</u> (d)]

Sarabande de Mr de Chambonnieres |Fin

ℓ 20v¹⁻⁴ Minkoff p 40 $^3[^3_4]|8|16|$

CO: 62-Chamb-I #15, Sarabande

ED: Brunold-Tessier #15, Dart-Ch #15.

---

39 | [CHAMBONNIÈRES: <u>Sarabande</u> (d)]

Sarabande du même Auteur |Finis

ℓ 21r¹⁻⁴ Minkoff p 41 $^3|5|9|$ $[^6_4|4|8|]$

CO: 63-Chamb-II #10, Sarabande

ED: Brunold-Tessier #40, Dart-Ch #40.

40 [CHAMBONNIÈRES: <u>Sarabande</u> (d)]

Sarabande de Monsr De Chambonnieres |Fin
ℓ 21v¹⁻⁴ Minkoff p 42 ^{3}|5|12| [$^6_4$|4|10|]

CO: 32-Oldham #14, [untitled]
ED: Brunold-Tessier #85.

---

41 [CHAMBONNIÈRES: <u>Sarabande</u> (d)]

Sarabande du même Auteur |Fin
ℓ 22r¹⁻⁴ Minkoff p 43 ^{3}|5|14| [$^6_4$|4|8|]

ED: Brunold-Tessier #86.

---

42 [CHAMBONNIÈRES: <u>Pavane</u> (d)]

Pauanne de Mr de Chambonnieres |Suitte |Fin
ℓ 22v¹-23r⁶ Minkoff p 44 ^{C}[$^4_2$]|17|16|4|^3[$^6_4$]|8|^{C}5|

ED: Brunold-Tessier #87.

43 | [CHAMBONNIÈRES: <u>Sarabande</u> (d)]

Sarabande de M^{r}. de Chambonnieres |Fin

ℓ 23v$^{1-5}$ Minkoff p 46 ^{3}|5|7|14| [$^{6}_{4}$|4|4|9|

ED: Brunold-Tessier #88.

44 | [CHAMBONNIÈRES: <u>Allemande</u> <u>la</u> <u>mignonne</u> (D)]

Allemande ([crossed out:] la mignonne) de M^{r} de
Chambonnieres |fin

ℓ 24r$^{1-6}$ Minkoff p 47 ^{C}|13|14|

ED: Brunold-Tessier #89.

45 | [CHAMBONNIÈRES: <u>Courante</u> (D)]

Courante de M^{r}. de Chambonnieres

ℓ 24v$^{1-5}$ Minkoff p 48 ^{3}[$^{6}_{4}$]|6|8|

CO: 38-Gen-2348/53 #27, Courante
ED: Brunold-Tessier #90.

46 | [CHAMBONNIÈRES: <u>Courante</u> (D)]

Courante du même Auteur |fin

ℓ 25r[1-6] Minkoff p 49 $^3[^6_4]$|8|8|

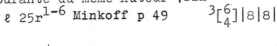

ED: Brunold-Tessier #91.

---

47 | [CHAMBONNIÈRES: <u>Courante</u> (D)]

Courante de Mr de Chambonnieres |1 fois |2[e] fois |fin

ℓ 25v[1-5] Minkoff p 50 $^3[^6_4]$|6|8|

CO: 38-Gen-2348/53 #32, Courante
ED: Brunold-Tessier #92.

---

48 | [CHAMBONNIÈRES: <u>Courante</u> (D)]

Courante du même Auteur |fin

ℓ 26r[1-5] Minkoff p 51 $^3[^6_4]$|7|8|

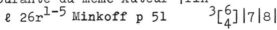

ED: Brunold-Tessier #93.

49 | [CHAMBONNIÈRES: <u>Courante</u> (D)]

Courante de Mr de Chambonnieres |Fin

ℓ 26v[1-5] Minkoff p 52   ³[⁶₄]|6|10|

CO: 38-Gen-2348/53 #31, Courante
ED: Brunold-Tessier #94.

---

50 | [CHAMBONNIÈRES: <u>Courante</u> (D)]

Courante du même Auteur

ℓ 27r[1-4] Minkoff p 53   ³[⁶₄]|6|8|

CO: 62-Chamb-II #14, Courante
ED: Brunold-Tessier #44, Dart-Ch #44.

---

51 | [CHAMBONNIÈRES: <u>Courante</u> (D)]

Courante de Mr de Chambonnieres |fin

ℓ 27v[1-5] Minkoff p 54   ³[⁶₄]|9|7|

ED: Brunold-Tessier #95.

52 | [CHAMBONNIÈRES: <u>Sarabande</u> (D)]

Sarabande du même Auteur |fin

ℓ 28r$^{1-5}$ Minkoff p 55 ^{3}|12|15| [$\frac{3}{4}$|12|14|

CO: 38-Gen-2348/53 #26, Sarabande

ED: Brunold-Tessier #96.

53 | [CHAMBONNIÈRES: <u>Sarabande</u> (D)]

Sarabande de Mr de Chambonnieres |fin

ℓ 28v$^{1-5}$ Minkoff p 56 ^{3}|8|15| [$\frac{3}{4}$|8|20|]

CO: 63-Chamb-II #15, Sarabande

ED: Brunold-Tessier #45, Dart-Ch #45.

54 | [CHAMBONNIÈRES, <u>Courante</u> (D)]

Courante du même Auteur |fin

ℓ 29r$^{1-5}$ Minkoff p 57 ^{3}[$\frac{6}{4}$]|6|8|

ED: Brunold-Tessier #97.

55 | [CHAMBONNIÈRES: <u>Courante</u> (D)]
Courante de Mr Chambonnieres |Fin
ℓ 29v¹⁻⁵ Minkoff p 58   ³|7|9| [$^6_4$|7|8|]

CO: 38-Gen-2348/53 #29, Courante
    63-Chamb-II #13, Courante
ED: Brunold-Tessier #43, Dart-Ch #43.

56 | [CHAMBONNIÈRES: <u>Gigue la madelainette</u> (D)]
Gigue ([crossed out:] La Madelainette) de M^r de
Chambonnieres |fin
ℓ 30r¹⁻⁶ Minkoff p 59   ³[$^6_4$]|10|15|

CO: 62-Chamb-I #17, Gigue
ED: Brunold-Tessier #17, Dart-Ch.#17.

57 | [CHAMBONNIÈRES: <u>Gigue bruscanbille</u> (D)]
Gigue Bruscanbille de Mr de Chambonnieres |fin
ℓ 30v¹⁻⁶ Minkoff p 60   ³[$^6_4$]|10|13|

ED: Brunold-Tessier #98.

58 | [CHAMBONNIÈRES: <u>Gigue</u> (D)]

Gigue du meme Auteur

ℓ 31r$^{1-6}$ Minkoff p 61 $^3[{}^6_4]$|14|14|

CO: 62-Chamb-I #18, Gigue

ED: Brunold-Tessier #18, Dart-Ch #18.

59 | [CHAMBONNIÈRES: <u>Gigue</u> (e)]

Gigue de Monsr de Chambonnieres |Suitte |fin

ℓ 31v^1-32r^4 Minkoff p 62 $^3[{}^3_4]$|32|28|

CO: 36-Parville #34, Gigue Chanbonniere

ED: Brunold-Tessier #99.

60 | [CHAMBONNIÈRES: <u>Allemande</u> (F)]

Allemande de Mr de Chambonnières. |fin

ℓ 32v$^{1-5}$ Minkoff p 64   ¢|9|8|

CO: 62-Chamb-I #19, Allemande

ED: Brunold-Tessier #19, Dart-Ch #19.

61 | [CHAMBONNIÈRES: <u>Allemande</u> (F)]

Allemande du même Auteur |fin

ℓ 33r$^{1-6}$ Minkoff p 65 ^{C}|10|10|

CO: 63-Chamb-II #16, Allemande

ED: Brunold-Tessier #46, Dart-Ch #46.

62 | [CHAMBONNIÈRES: <u>Courante</u> (F)]

Courante de Mr de Chambonnieres. |Fin

ℓ 33v$^{1-4}$ Minkoff p 66 $^3[^6_4]$|6|7|

CO: 38-Gen-2348/53 #18, Courante
    62-Chamb-I #22, Courante

ED: Brunold-Tessier #22, Dart-Ch #22.

63 | [CHAMBONNIÈRES: <u>Courante</u> (F)]

Courante du meme Auteur |fin

ℓ 34v$^{1-5}$ Minkoff p 67 $^3[^6_4]$|8|9|

CO: 35-Bauyn-I #64, Courante de Mr de Chambonnieres
    35-Bauyn-I #73, Courante du meme Auteur [duplicate]
    38-Gen-2348/53 #9, Courante

ED: Brunold-Tessier #100.

64 | [CHAMBONNIÈRES: <u>Courante</u> (F)]

Courante de Mr de Chambonnieres.

ℓ 34v[1-5] Minkoff p 68 $^3[^6_4]$|8|9|

CO: 35-Bauyn-I #63, Courante du meme Auteur
    35-Bauyn-I #73, Courante du meme Auteur
    38-Gen-2348/53 #9, Courante

ED: Brunold-Tessier #100.

65 | [CHAMBONNIÈRES: <u>Courante</u> (F)]

Courante du meme Auteur |Fin

ℓ 35r[1-5] Minkoff p 69 $^3[^6_4]$|8|10|

CO: 62-Chamb-I #20, Courante

ED: Brunold-Tessier #101; cf Brunold-Tessier #20;
    Dart #20.

66 | [CHAMBONNIÈRES: <u>Courante</u> (F)]

Courante de Mr de Chambonnieres |fin
  ℓ 35v$^{1-5}$ Minkoff p 70 $^3[^6_4]$|7|7|

CO: 62-Chamb-I #21, Courante
ED: Brunold-Tessier #21, Dart-Ch #21.

67 | [CHAMBONNIÈRES: <u>Courante</u> (F)]

Courante du meme Auteur |fin
  ℓ 36r$^{1-5}$ Minkoff p 71 $^3[^6_4]$|8|10|

ED: Brunold-Tessier #102.

68 | [CHAMBONNIÈRES: <u>Courante</u> (F)]

Courante de Monsr. de Chambonnieres. |fin
  ℓ 36v$^{1-4}$ Minkoff p 72 $^3[^6_4]$|6|8|

ED: Brunold-Tessier #103.

69 | [CHAMBONNIÈRES: Courante (F)]

Courante du meme Auteur |Fin

ℓ 37r$^{1-5}$ Minkoff p 73 $^3[^6_4]|7|9|$

CO: 38-Gen-2348/53 #14, Courante

ED: Brunold-Tessier #104.

70 | [CHAMBONNIÈRES: Courante (F)]

Courante de M^r. de Chambonnieres |fin

ℓ 37v$^{1-5}$ Minkoff p 74 $^3[^6_4]|7|10|$

71 | Courante de M^r. de Chambonnieres

ℓ 38r$^{1-5}$ Minkoff p 75 $^3[^6_4]|7|10|$

CO: 36-Parville #79, Courante Chanbonniere
    36-Parville #82, Courante chanbonniere

ED: Brunold-Tessier #105.

72 | [CHAMBONNIÈRES: <u>Courante</u> (F)]

Courante de Mr de Chambonnieres

ℓ 38v¹⁻⁴ Minkoff p 76   3[6/4]|6|7|

CO: 38-Gen-2348/53 #20, Courante
    63-Cham-II #18, Courante
ED: Brunold-Tessier #48, Dart-Ch #48.

---

73 | [CHAMBONNIÈRES: <u>Courante</u> (F)]

Courante du meme Auteur

ℓ 39r¹⁻⁵ Minkoff p 77   3[6/4]|8|9|

CO: 35-Bauyn-I #63 (qv, duplicate), Courante du meme
                                              Auteur
    35-Bauyn-I #64, Courante de Mr de Chambonnieres
    38-Gen-2348/53 #9, Courante
ED: Brunold-Tessier #100.

---

74 | [CHAMBONNIÈRES: <u>Rondeau</u> (F)]

Rondeau de Mr de Chambonnieres |fin

ℓ 39v¹⁻⁵ Minkoff p 78   ¢|4|8|8|

CO: 38-Gen-2348/53 #21, Rondeau
ED: Brunold-Tessier #106.

75 | [CHAMBONNIÈRES: <u>Courante</u> (F)]

Courante du même Auteur

ℓ 40r$^{1-4}$ **Minkoff** p 79 $^3[{6 \atop 4}]$ |6|9|

ED: Brunold-Tessier #107.

---

76 | [CHAMBONNIÈRES: <u>Courante</u> (F)]

Courante de Mr de Chambonnieres

ℓ 40v$^{1-5}$ **Minkoff** p 80 $^3[{6 \atop 4}]$ |7|8|

CO: 38-Gen-2348/53 #10, Courante
    63-Chamb-II #17, Courante
ED: Brunold-Tessier #47, Dart-Ch #47.

---

77 | [CHAMBONNIÈRES: <u>Courante</u> (F)]

Courante du même Auteur

ℓ 41r$^{1-4}$ **Minkoff** p 81 $^3[{6 \atop 4}[$ |6|8|

ED: Brunold-Tessier #108.

78 | [CHAMBONNIÈRES: <u>Sarabande</u> (F)]

Sarabande de Mr de Chambonnieres.

ℓ 41v$^{1-3}$ Minkoff p 82 ^{3}|4|11| [$^3_4$|4|12|]

ED: Brunold-Tessier #109.

79 | [CHAMBONNIÈRES: <u>Sarabande</u> (F)]

Sarabande du même Auteur

ℓ 42r$^{1-4}$ Minkoff p 83 ^{3}|5|7| [$^6_4$|4|12|]

CO: 36-Parville #81, Sarabande Chanbonniere
      62-Chamb-I #23, Sarabande

ED: Brunold-Tessier #23, Dart-Ch #23.

80 | [CHAMBONNIÈRES: <u>Volte</u> (<u>Sarabande</u>) <u>o beau jardin</u> (F)]

Volte de Mr de Chambonnieres

ℓ 42v$^{1-4}$ Minkoff p 84 ^{3}[$^3_4$]|8|12|

CO: 33-Rés-89ter #22, O beau Jardin.Sarabande...Double
      36-Parville #80, Volte Chanbonniere
   cf Philidor p 23, O Beau Jardin de Mr de Chanbon-
                        niere [for instruments]
ED: Brunold-Tessier #110, cf p 119; cf Gilbert p 178.

81 | [CHAMBONNIÈRES: <u>Sarabande</u> (F)]

Sarabande du même Auteur

ℓ 43r$^{1-4}$ **Minkoff p 85** ^{3}[$\frac{3}{4}$]|8|12|

CO: 38-Gen-2348/53 #16, Sarabande

ED: Brunold-Tessier #111.

---

82 | [CHAMBONNIÈRES: <u>Sarabande</u> (F)]

Sarabande de M^{r}. de Chambonnieres

ℓ 43v$^{1-5}$ **Minkoff p 86** ^{3}[$\frac{3}{4}$]|8|16|

ED: Brunold-Tessier #112.

---

83 | [CHAMBONNIÈRES: <u>Chaconne</u> (F)]

Chaconne du même Auteur

ℓ 44r$^{1-4}$ **Minkoff p 87** ^{3}[$\frac{3}{4}$]|8|4|8|

CO: 36-Parville #86, Chaconne Chanbonniere

ED: Brunold-Tessier #113.

84 | [CHAMBONNIÈRES: <u>Brusque</u> (F)]

Brusque de M^r. de Chambonnieres

ℓ 44v$^{1-6}$ Minkoff p 88 $^3[^6_4]$ |12|14|

CO: 38-Gen-2348/53 #12, Brusque

ED: Brunold-Tessier #114.

---

85 | [CHAMBONNIÈRES: <u>Brusque</u> (F)]

Autre brusque du même Auteur |fin

ℓ 45r$^{1-6}$ Minkoff p 89 $^3[^6_4]$ |12|16|

CO: 38-Gen-2348/53 #13, Brusque

ED: Brunold-Tessier #115.

---

86 | [CHAMBONNIÈRES: <u>Chaconne</u> (F)]

Chaconne de M^r. de Chambonnieres |fin

ℓ 45v$^{1-6}$ Minkoff p 90 $^3[^3_4]$ |12|8|12|9|

CO: 38-Gen-2348/53 #22, Chaconne

ED: Brunold-Tessier #116; Curtis-Co #75 (as "Louis Couperin?").

87 | [CHAMBONNIÈRES: Courante (G)]

Courante de Mr de Chambonnieres.

ℓ 46r$^{1-5}$ Minkoff p 91 $^3[^6_4]$ |8|10|

ED: Brunold-Tessier #117.

88 | [CHAMBONNIÈRES: Courante (G)]

Courante de Mr de Chambonnieres

ℓ 46v$^{1-5}$ Minkoff p 92 $^3[^6_4]$ |8|8|

CO: 32-Oldham #9, Courante De Monsieur de Chambonnieres
    36-Parville #90, Courante Chanbonniere
    38-Gen-2348/53 #36, Courante
    63-Chamb-II #27, Courante

ED: Brunold-Tessier #57, Dart-Ch #57.

89 | [CHAMBONNIÈRES: Courante (G)]

Courante du même Auteur

ℓ 47r$^{1-5}$ Minkoff p 93 $^3[^6_4]$ |8|10|

ED: Brunold-Tessier #118.

90 | [CHAMBONNIÈRES: Courante (G)]

Courante du meme Auteur

ℓ 47v[1-5] Minkoff p 94 ^{3}|10|9| [$^6_4$|10|6|$^4_4$1|$^6_4$2|]

ED: Brunold-Tessier #119.

91 | [CHAMBONNIÈRES: Courante (G)]

Courante de M[r]. de Chambonnieres

ℓ 48r[1-5] Minkoff p 95 ^{3}|8|10| [$^3_4$|14|20|]

CO: 32-Oldham #7, Courante de Monsieur de chambon-
          nieres
     33-Rés-89ter #35, Courante Chambonnieres ...
          Double
     36-Parville #91, Courante Chanbonniere
     38-Gen-2348/53 #33, Courante
     63-Chamb-II #28, Courante

ED: Brunold-Tessier #58, Dart-Ch #58; cf Gilbert p
     192.

92 | [CHAMBONNIÈRES: <u>Courante</u> (G)]

Courante de Mr de Chambonnières
    ℓ 48v¹⁻⁵ Minkoff p 96 $^3[^6_4]$ |8|9|

CO: 23-Tenbury #40, Courante Chambonniere
      24-Babell #87, Courante de Chre.
      32-Oldham #19, Courante
      33-Rés-89ter #34, Courante Chambonnieres ... Double
      36-Parville #92, Courante chanbonniere
      63-Chamb-II #26, Courante

ED: Brunold-Tessier #56, Dart-Ch #56; cf Gilbert p 190.

93 | [CHAMBONNIÈRES: <u>Sarabande</u> (G)]

Sarabande du même Auteur
    ℓ 49r¹⁻⁴ Minkoff p 97 $^3[^3_4]$ |10|12|

CO: 38-Gen-2348/53 #37, Sarabande
ED: Brunold-Tessier #120.

94 | [CHAMBONNIÈRES: <u>Courante</u> (C)]

Courante de Mr de Chambonnieres

ℓ 49v¹⁻⁴ Minkoff p 98 $^3[^6_4]|6|8|$

CO: 35-Bauyn-I #6, Courante de Mr de Chambonnieres
ED: Brunold-Tessier #64.

95 | [CHAMBONNIÈRES: <u>Sarabande</u> (C)]

Sarabande du même Auteur

ℓ 50r¹⁻⁴ Minkoff p 99 $^3[^3_4]|8|16|$

CO: 62-Chamb-I #28, Sarabande
ED: Brunold-Tessier #28, Dart-Ch #28.

96 | [CHAMBONNIÈRES: <u>Sarabande jeunes zéphirs</u> (G)]

Sarabande de Mr de Chambonnieres

ℓ 50v¹⁻⁴ Minkoff p 100 $^3[^3_4]|8|16|$

CO: 5-Munich-1503ℓ #1, Sarrabande de Mons: Chambonnier
  32-Oldham #8, Sarabande de Monsiur de Chambonnieres
  33-Rés-89ter #36, Sarabande Chambonnieres...Double
  36-Parville #93, Sarabande Chanbonniere

44-LaPierre p 42, Les Zephirs de Mr de Chanboniere
45-Dart #55, Sarabande de chambonniere
63-Chamb-II #29, Sarabande Jeunes Zephirs
cf Philidor p 22, Jeunes Zephirs (de Mr de chan-
                 boniere) [for.instruments]

ED: Brunold-Tessier #59, Dart-Ch #59; cf Gilbert p
    194.

---

97 | [CHAMBONNIÈRES: <u>Sarabande</u> (G)]

Sarabande du même Auteur

ℓ 51r$^{1-4}$ Minkoff p 101 $^3[^3_4]$|8|16|

CO: 36-Parville #94, Sarabande Chanbonniere
ED: Brunold-Tessier #121.

---

98 | [CHAMBONNIÈRES: <u>Gigue</u> <u>la</u> <u>villageoise</u> (G)]

Gigue La villageoise dudit Auteur

ℓ 51v$^{1-5}$ Minkoff p 102 ^{3}|16|14| [$^3_4$|16|$^6_4$14|]

CO: 38-Gen-2348/53 #38, Gigue La Villageoise De Mr.
                        Chambonnieres
    62-Chamb-I #29, Gigue la Vilageoise
ED: Brunold-Tessier #29, Dart-Ch #29.

99 | [CHAMBONNIÈRES: <u>Canarie</u> (G)]

Canaries de M^r. de Chambonnieres

    ℓ 52r¹⁻⁵ Minkoff p 103 $3[{6 \atop 4}]$|8|12|

CO: 36-Parville #96, Canaries Chambonniere
    38-Gen-2348/53 #25, Canaries
    62-Chamb-I #30, Canaris

ED: Brunold-Tessier #30, Dart-Ch #30.

100 | [CHAMBONNIÈRES: <u>Gigue</u> (G)]

Gigue de M^r. de Chambonnieres

    ℓ 52v¹⁻⁶ Minkoff p 104 $3[{6 \atop 4}]$|13|12|

CO: 36-Parville #95, Gigue chanbonniere

ED: Brunold-Tessier #122.

101 | [CHAMBONNIÈRES: <u>Chaconne</u> (G)]

Chaconne du même Auteur |fin

    ℓ 53r¹⁻⁶ Minkoff p105 3|5|7|5|9|6| [$3 \atop 4$|5|8|8|12|8|]

ED: Brunold-Tessier #123.

102 | [CHAMBONNIÈRES: <u>Allemande</u> <u>l'affligée</u> (g)]

Allemande dit l'affligée de Mr de Chambonniere /Lente-
ment

ℓ 53v$^{1-5}$ Minkoff p 106 ^{C}|8|7| [$^{2}_{1}$|7|6|]

ED: Brunold-Tessier #124.

103 | [CHAMBONNIÈRES: <u>Courante</u> (g)]

Courante du mesme Auteur

ℓ 54r$^{1-5}$ Minkoff p 107 ^{3}[$^{6}_{4}$]|8|10|

CO: 38-Gen-2348/53 #1, Courante
     63-Chamb-II #22, Courante
ED: Brunold-Tessier #52, Dart-Ch #52.

104 | [CHAMBONNIÈRES: <u>Sarabande</u> (g)]

Sarabande de Mr de Chambonnieres

ℓ 54v$^{1-4}$ Minkoff p 108 ^{3}|7|12| [$^{3}_{4}$|8|12|]

CO: 36-Parville #40, Sarabande Chanbonniere
ED: Brunold-Tessier #125.

105 | [CHAMBONNIÈRES: <u>Gigue</u> (g)]

Gigue du même Auteur

ℓ 55r$^{1-6}$ Minkoff p 109 $^3[^6_4]$|16|12|

ED: Brunold-Tessier #126.

106 | [CHAMBONNIÈRES: <u>Gigue</u> (g)]

Gigue de Mr de Chambonnieres |Suitte

ℓ 55v^1-56r^1 Minkoff p 110 $^3[^6_4]$|22|17|

ED: Brunold-Tessier #127.

107 | [CHAMBONNIÈRES: <u>Pavane</u> <u>l'entretien</u> <u>des</u> <u>dieux</u> (g)]

Pauanne de M^r /de Chambonnieres /[(crossed out: dit
l'Entrien des Dieux) |Reprise

ℓ 56r^3-v^6 Minkoff p 111   ¢|17|10|12| [$^4_2$|30|18|23|]

CO: 62-Chamb-I #24, Pauane /L'entretien des Dieux
ED: Brunold-Tessier #24, Dart-Ch #24.

108 | [CHAMBONNIÈRES: <u>Pavane</u> (g)]

Pauanne du même Auteur |Tournez |Suitte |fin

ℓ 57r[1]-v[3] Minkoff p 113 ¢|15|12|10 [$\frac{4}{2}$|29|25|20|

ED: Brunold-Tessier #128.

109 | [CHAMBONNIÈRES: <u>Pavane</u> (g)]

Pauanne de Mr de Chambonnieres |Suitte

ℓ 57v[4]-58r[5] Minkoff p 114 C|8|6|6| [$\frac{4}{2}$|16|14|13|]

CO: 63-Chamb-II #20, Pauanne
ED: Brunold-Tessier #50, Dart-Ch #50.

110 | [CHAMBONNIÈRES: <u>Allemande</u> <u>la</u> <u>rare</u> (a)]

Allemande La rare de Mr de Chambonnieres

ℓ 58v[1-5] Minkoff p 116 C|9|12| [$\frac{4}{4}$|10|13|]

CO: 32-Oldham #29, Allemande la rare de Mr Chambre
62-Chamb-I #1, Allemande la Rare
ED: Brunold-Tessier #1, Dart-Ch #1.

111 | [CHAMBONNIÈRES: <u>La Drollerie</u> (a)]

([crossed out:] La Drollerie du même Auteur)

ℓ 59r$^{1-5}$ Minkoff p 117 $\mathbb{C}$|9^3[$^6_4$]|8|$_{[2]}^2$5|

ED: Brunold-Tessier #129.

112 | [CHAMBONNIÈRES: <u>Courante</u> (a)]

Courante de Mr de Chambonnieres

ℓ 59v$^{1-4}$ Minkoff p 118 ^{3}[$^6_4$]|7|8|

CO: 32-Oldham #30, Courante
     62-Chamb-I #2, Courante

ED: Brunold-Tessier #2, Dart-Ch #2.

112 | [CHAMBONNIÈRES: <u>Double</u> (a)]
a
Double |fin

ℓ 60r$^{1-6}$ Minkoff p 119 ^{3}[$^6_4$]|7|8|

CO: 32-Oldham #30a, Double de la Courante
     62-Chamb-I #2a, Double de la Courante

ED: Brunold-Tessier #2[a], Dart-Ch #2[a].

113 | [CHAMBONNIÈRES: <u>Courante</u> (a)]

Courante de M.r de Chambonnieres

ℓ 60v$^{1-5}$ Minkoff p 120 $^3[^6_4]$|8|10|

ED: Brunold-Tessier #130.

---

114 | [CHAMBONNIÈRES: <u>Courante</u> (a)]

Courante du même Auteur

ℓ 61r$^{1-5}$ Minkoff p 121 $^3[^6_4]$|10|8|

ED: Brunold-Tessier #131.

---

115 | [CHAMBONNIÈRES: <u>Courante</u> (a)]

Courante de M.r de Chambonnieres |fin

ℓ 61v$^{1-6}$ Minkoff p 122 ^{3}|12|9| $[^6_4$|11|9|]

ED: Brunold-Tessier #132.

116 | [CHAMBONNIÈRES: <u>Courante</u> (a)]

Courante du meme Auteur

ℓ 62r¹⁻⁵ Minkoff p 123 $^3[^6_4]|7|8|$

CO: 32-Oldham #27, Aultre Courante
    38-Gen-2348/53 #3, Courante
    62-Chamb-I #3, Courante

ED: Brunold-Tessier #3, Dart-Ch #3.

117 | [CHAMBONNIÈRES: <u>Sarabande</u> (a)]

Sarabande de Mr de Chambonnieres |fin

ℓ 62v¹⁻⁴ Minkoff p 124 $^3[^3_4]|8|12|$

CO: 62-Chamb-I #5, Sarabande

ED: Brunold-Tessier #5, Dart-Ch #5.

118 | [CHAMBONNIÈRES: <u>Sarabande</u> (a)]

Sarabande de Mr de Chambonnieres |pour la fin

ℓ 63r¹⁻⁵ Minkoff p 125 $^3|8|16|3|$ $[^3_4|8|16|4|]$

CO: 32-Oldham #25, Sarabande de Monsr de Chanbonieres [g]
    62-Chamb-I #26, Sarabande [g]

ED: Brunold-Tessier #133; cf Brunold-Tessier #26,
    Dart-Ch #26.

119 | [CHAMBONNIÈRES: <u>Sarabande</u> (a)]

Sarabande de Mr de Chambonnieres

ℓ 63v$^{1-4}$ **Minkoff** p 126 $\frac{3}{2}$|8|16|

CO: 38-Gen-2348/53 #4, Sarabande
ED: Brunold-Tessier #134.

120 | [CHAMBONNIÈRES: <u>Sarabande</u> (a)]

Sarabande du même Auteur

ℓ 64r$^{1-5}$ **Minkoff** p 127 $^3[\frac{3}{4}]$|8|16|

CO: 38-Gen-2348/53 #6, Sarabande
ED: Brunold-Tessier #135.

121 | [CHAMBONNIÈRES: <u>Sarabande</u> (a)]

Sarabande de Mr de Chambonnieres

ℓ 64v$^{1-4}$ **Minkoff** p 128 $^3[\frac{3}{4}]$|12|13|

ED: Brunold-Tessier #136.

122 | [CHAMBONNIÈRES: <u>Gigue</u> <u>la</u> <u>vetille</u> (<u>la</u> <u>coquette</u>) (a)]

Gigue ([crossed out:] la Coquette) de Mr de Chambonnieres

ℓ 65r$^{1-6}$ **Minkoff p 129** $^3[{6 \atop 4}]$|14|10|

CO: 32-Oldham #28, La Vetille
     47-Gen-2356 #8, Gigue de Monsr Chambonnieres

ED: Brunold-Tessier #137.

123 | [CHAMBONNIÈRES: <u>Gaillarde</u> (a)]

([crossed out:] Gaillarde) de Mr de Chambonnieres

ℓ 65v$^{1-6}$ **Minkoff p 130** $^3[{3 \atop 4}]$|12|20|

CO: 62-Chamb-I #6, Gaillarde

ED: Brunold-Tessier #6, **Dart-Ch #6.**

124 | [CHAMBONNIÈRES: <u>Allemande</u> (B♭)]

Allemande du même Auteur

ℓ 66r$^{1-5}$ **Minkoff p 131** ^{C}|11|11|

ED: Brunold-Tessier #138.

125 | [CHAMBONNIÈRES: <u>Courante</u> (B♭)]

Courante de Mr de Chambonnières

  ℓ 66v$^{1-5}$ **Minkoff p 132** $^3[^6_4]$|7|8|

ED: Brunold-Tessier #139.

126 | [CHAMBONNIÈRES: <u>Sarabande</u> (B♭)]

Sarabande du même Auteur

  ℓ 67r$^{1-4}$ **Minkoff p 133** ^{3}|8|13| [$^3_4$|8|16|]

ED: Brunold-Tessier #140.

127 | [CHAMBONNIÈRES: <u>Gaillarde</u> (B♭)]

([crossed out:] Gaillarde) de Mr de Chambonnières

  ℓ 67v$^{1-5}$ **Minkoff p 134** ^{3}|8|15| [$^3_4$|8|16|]

CO: 32-Oldham #24, Gaillarde b
ED: Brunold-Tessier #141

127 [CHAMBONNIÈRES: Double (B♭)]
a
Double dela ([crossed out:] Gaillarde) par led' Auteur
   ℓ 68r[1-6] Minkoff p 135   ³|7|16| [³⁄₄|8|16|]]

CO: 32-Oldham #24A, Double
ED: Brunold-Tessier #141[a]

ℓ 68v-[69v] [blank, ruled]

[In the misbound v. 1 of Bauyn (Rés Vm⁷ 674) here
follows ℓ 33-62 of 35-Bauyn-III (qv for inventory)]

Inventory - Bauyn-II:

1 [COUPERIN (L): Prélude (d)]
Preludes de Mr. Couperin |Changement de mouuement
|Suitte
   ℓ 1r[1]-4r[1] Minkoff p 137 |-|³[⁶₄]38|-|

CO: 36-Parville #2, Prelude Coupprain
ED: Brunold/Dart-Co #1, Curtis-Co #45.

2 [COUPERIN (L): <u>Prélude</u> (D)]

Autre prelude de /Mr Couperin |Suitte |Fin

ℓ 4r^3-5v^4 Minkoff p 143 |-|

CO: 36-Parville #25, Prelude en D la.re grand becar

ED: Brunold/Dart-Co #2, Curtis-Co #39.

3 [COUPERIN (L): <u>Prélude</u> (g)]

Prelude de Mr Couperin.|. |Suitte /Changement **de mouuement**

ℓ 6r^1-7v^3 Minkoff p 147 |-|^3[$^6_4$]29|-|

CO: 36-Parville #35, Prelude couprin en g.re.sol. b
                    mol.

ED: Brunold/Dart-Co #3, Curtis-Co #92.

4 [COUPERIN (L): <u>Prélude</u> (g)]

Prelude de /Monsr Couperin .|. |Suitte |fin

ℓ 7v^5-8r^6 Minkoff p 150 |-|

ED: Brunold/Dart-Co #4.

5 [COUPERIN (L): Prélude (g)]
Prelude de Mons.ʳ Couperin |Suitte |fin
  ℓ 8v¹-9r³ Minkoff p 152 |-|

ED: Brunold/Dart-Co #5.

6 [COUPERIN (L): Prélude (a)]
Prelude de Mons.ʳ Couperin |Changement de mouuement
|Suitte |fin |Il faut retourner /au reuoy # |Fin
  ℓ 9r⁴-12r⁵ Minkoff p 153 |-|³[⁶₄]45|-|

CO: 36-Parville #45, Prelude de Mr Couprin a l'imita-
                    tion de Mr. froberger en a mi la
     cf 36-Parville #144 [untitled; identical opening]
ED: Brunold/Dart-Co #6 (omitting 3rd section, which
     is in Dart-Co App I); Curtis-Co #1 (cf #12).

7 [COUPERIN (L): Prélude (a)]
Prelude de Mons.ʳ Couperin |Fin
  ℓ 12v¹⁻⁵ Minkoff p 160 |-|

CO: 36-Parville #46, Prelude en a mi la
ED: Brunold/Dart-Co #7, Curtis-Co #7.

8 | [COUPERIN (L): <u>Prélude</u> (A)]
Prelude de M^r. Couperin |Fin
   ℓ 13r^1-v^5 Minkoff p 161 |-|

ED: Brunold/Dart-Co #8.

9 | [COUPERIN (L): <u>Prélude</u> (C)]
Prelude de M^r. Couperin |fin
   ℓ 14r^1-15r^6 Minkoff p 163 |-|

ED: Brunold/Dart-Co #9.

10 | [COUPERIN (L): <u>Prélude</u> (C)]
Prelude de M^r. Couperin |fin
   ℓ 15v^1-16r^{6}Minkoff p 166 |-|

CO: 36-Parville #58, Prelude en C Sol ut Couprin
ED: Brunold/Dart-Co #10, Curtis-Co #28.

11 | [COUPERIN (L): <u>Prélude</u> (C)]
Prelude de Mr Couperin |fin
    ℓ 16v^1-17r^3 Minkoff p 168 |-|

CO: 36-Parville #59, Prelude Couprin
ED: Brunold/Dart-Co #11, Curtis-Co #22.

12 | [COUPERIN (L): <u>Prélude</u> (F)]
Prelude de Mr Couperin |Suitte |Changement de mouue-
ment. |Suitte |fin
    ℓ 17r^4-18r^3 Minkoff p 169 |-|^3[$^6_4$]10|-|

CO: 36-Parville #75, Prelude du 6e en Et f. vt fa b:
                   mol Couprin
ED: Brunold/Dart-Co #12, Curtis-Co #76.

13 | [COUPERIN (L): <u>Prélude</u> (F)]
Prelude /De Mr Couperin .|. |fin
    ℓ 18r^5-19r^6 Minkoff p 171 |-|

CO: 36-Parville #76, Autre prelude du 6e
ED: Brunold/Dart-Co #13, Curtis-Co #68.

14 | [COUPERIN (L): <u>Prélude</u> (e)].
Prelude de Mr Couperin |fin
ℓ 19v¹-20r¹ Minkoff p 174 |-|

CO: 36-Parville #101, Prelude en E Si mi grand b♯
ED: Brunold/Dart-Co #14, Curtis-Co #64.

15 | [COUPERIN (L): <u>Allemande</u> (C)]
Allemande de Monsr Couperin |fin
ℓ 20r²⁻⁶ Minkoff p 175   ^C|10|11|

ED: Brunold/Dart-Co #15, Curtis-Co #23.

16 | [COUPERIN (L): <u>Courante</u> (C)]
Courante de Monsr Couperin |fin
ℓ 20v¹⁻⁵ Minkoff p 176   ³[⁶₄]|7|9|

ED: Brunold/Dart-Co #16, Curtis-Co #24.

17 | [COUPERIN (L): <u>Courante</u> (C)]
Courante de Monsr Couperin |fin
ℓ 21r¹⁻⁵ Minkoff p 177   ³[$^6_4$]|8|9|

ED: Brunold/Dart-Co #17.

18 | [COUPERIN (L): <u>Courante</u> (C)]
Courante de Monsr. Couperin |fin
ℓ 21v¹⁻⁵ Minkoff p 178   ³[$^6_4$]|8|10|

ED: Brunold/Dart-Co #18.

19 | [COUPERIN (L): <u>Courante</u> (C)]
Courante de Monsr. Couperin |pour la prem^{re} fois |fin
ℓ 22r¹⁻⁵ Minkoff p 179   ³[$^6_4$]|8|8|4|

ED: Brunold/Dart-Co #19, Curtis-Co #30.

20 | [COUPERIN (L): <u>Sarabande</u> (C)]

Sarabande de Mr Couperin |fin

ℓ 22v$^{1-3}$ Minkoff p 180 ^{3}|5|7| [$^6_4$|4|6|]]

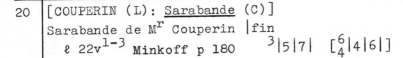

ED: Brunold/Dart-Co #20.

21 | [COUPERIN (L): <u>Sarabande</u> (C)]

Sarabande de M^r. Couperin |fin

ℓ 22v$^{4-6}$ Minkoff p 180 ^{3}|5|7| [$^6_4$|4|6|]]

ED: Brunold/Dart-Co #21.

22 | [COUPERIN (L): <u>Sarabande</u> (C)]

Sarabande de Monsr. Couperin |fin

ℓ 23r$^{1-3}$ Minkoff p 181 ^{3}|5|9| [$^6_4$|4|8|]]

ED: Brunold/Dart-Co #22, Curtis-Co #31.

23 [COUPERIN (L): <u>Sarabande</u> (C)]

Sarabande de Mr Couperin |fin

ℓ 23r$^{4-6}$ Minkoff p 181 ^{3}|5|7| [$^6_4$|4|6|]

ED: Brunold/Dart-Co #23.

24 [COUPERIN (L): <u>Sarabande</u> (C)]

Sarabande de Monsr Couperin |fin

ℓ 23v$^{1-3}$ Minkoff p 182 ^{3}[$^3_4$]|8|16|

ED: Brunold/Dart-Co #24.

25 [COUPERIN (L): <u>Sarabande</u> (C)]

Sarabande de Mr Couperin |fin

ℓ 23v$^{4-6}$ Minkoff p 182 ^{3}[$^3_4$]|8.|12|

ED: Brunold/Dart-Co #25, Curtis-Co #25.

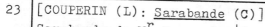
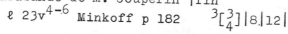

26 | [COUPERIN (L): <u>Chaconne</u> (C)]
Chaconne de Mons.[r] Couperin |Grand Couplet |fin |[ler]
... 4[e]
   ℓ 24r[1-6] Minkoff p 183 $^3[^3_4]$|8|8|12|8|12|

ED: Brunold/Dart-Co #26.

27 | [COUPERIN (L): <u>Passacaille</u> (C)]
Passacaille de M.[r] Couperin. |Grand couplet |fin |Se-
cond Couplet |4[e] Couplet |5[e] Couplet |3[e] Couplet
|Suitte |7[e] Couplet |8[e] Couplet |9[e] Couplet |10[e]
Couplet |par b mol /Grand Couplet |6[e] Couplet |Grand
Couplet &c
   ℓ 24v[1]-25r[6] Minkoff p 184 ^{3}|8|8|4|[etc] [$^6_4$|57|]

ED: Brunold/Dart-Co #27, Curtis-Co #26.

28 | [COUPERIN (L) or CHAMBONNIÈRES: <u>Sarabande</u> (C)]
Sarabande de Mr Couperin |fin
   ℓ 25v[1-3] Minkoff p 186 $^3[^3_4]$|8|16|

CO: 35-Bauyn-I #18, Sarabande du même Auteur [CHAM-

BONNIÈRES]

ED: Brunold/Dart-Co #28; cf Brunold-Tessier #74.

29 | [COUPERIN (L): <u>Menuet</u> (C)]

([crossed out:] Menuet de M^r) Couperin |fin

ℓ 25v$^{4-6}$ Minkoff p 186 ^{3}[$^3_4$]|8|20|

ED: Brunold/Dart-Co #29, Curtis-Co #27.

30 | [COUPERIN (L): <u>Allemande la précieuse</u> (c)]

Allemande de M^r. Couperin. |fin

ℓ 26r$^{1-5}$ Minkoff p 187 ^{C}|8|9|

CO: 36-Parville #70, La precieuse Suitte Allemande
ED: Brunold/Dart-Co #30, Curtis-Co #34.

31 | [COUPERIN (L): <u>Courante</u> (c)]

Courante de M̃^{r} Couperin |fin

ℓ 26v$^{1-5}$ Minkoff p 188 ^{3}[$^6_4$]|10|10|

CO: 36-Parville #71, Courante Couprin
ED: Brunold/Dart-Co #31, Curtis-Co #35.

32 | [COUPERIN (L): <u>Sarabande</u> (c)]

Sarabande de M^r. Couperin |Fin

ℓ 27r^{1-5} Minkoff p 189   ³[³₄]|8|16|

CO: 36-Parville #72, Sarabande Couprin
ED: Brunold/Dart-Co #32, Curtis-Co #36.

---

33 | [COUPERIN (L): <u>Gigue</u> (c)]

Gigue de Monsr. Couperin |fin |fin

ℓ 27v^{1-6} Minkoff p 190   ³[⁶₄]|12|16|

CO: 36-Parville #73, Gigue Couprin
ED: Brunold/Dart-Co #33, Curtis-Co #37.

---

34 | [COUPERIN (L): <u>Chaconne la bergeronette</u> (c)].

Chaconne de M^r. Couperin |fin |Fin

ℓ 28r^{1-4} Minkoff p 191   ³|8|8 [etc]   [³₄|8| x 4]

CO: 36-Parville #74, Chaconne Couprin dit la bergero-
                nette
ED: Brunold/Dart-Co #34, Curtis-Co #38.

35 | [COUPERIN (L): <u>Allemande</u> (d)]
Allemande de Monsr Couperin |fin
ℓ 28v¹⁻⁶ Minkoff p 192   C |12|11|

ED: Brunold/Dart-Co #35.

---

36 | [COUPERIN (L): <u>Allemande</u> (d)]
Allemande de Mr Couperin |Fin
ℓ 29r¹⁻⁵ Minkoff p 193   C |9|10|

CO: 36-Parville #4, Allemande Couprain
ED: Brunold/Dart-Co #36, Curtis-Co #46.

---

37 | [COUPERIN (L): <u>Pièce de trois sortes de mouvements</u> (d)]
Pieces de trois sortes de mouuements Par M. Couperin
|fin .|.
ℓ 29v¹⁻⁶ Minkoff p 194   ¢ |8| [3/4]12| [3/2]14|

ED: Brunold/Dart-Co #37, Curtis-Co #56.

38 [COUPERIN (L): <u>Courante</u> (d)]
Courante de Monsr. Couperin |Fin
ℓ 30r$^{1-5}$ Minkoff p 195 $^3[{}^6_4]$|9|9|

ED: Brunold/Dart-Co #38.

39 [COUPERIN (L): <u>Courante</u> (d)]
Courante de Monsr. Couperin
ℓ 30v$^{1-6}$ Minkoff p 196 $^3[{}^6_4]$|10|10|

CQ: 36-Parville #10, Courante Couprin
ED: Brunold/Dart-Co #39, Curtis-Co #57.

40 [COUPERIN (L): <u>Courante</u> (d)]
Courante de M^r. Couperin |fin
ℓ 31r$^{1-5}$ Minkoff p 197 $^3[{}^6_4]$|8|12|

ED: Brunold/Dart-Co #40.

41 [COUPERIN (L): <u>Courante</u> (d)]

Courante de Monsr Couperin |fin

ℓ 31v¹⁻⁵ Minkoff p 198 $^3[^6_4]$|8|10|

CO: 24-Babell #222, Courante
    36-Parville #5, Courante Couprain
    cf 24-Babell #224, Courante
    cf 36-Parville #16, Courante la Barre

ED: Brunold/Dart-Co #41, Curtis-Co #58.

42 [COUPERIN (L): <u>Courante</u> (d)]

Courante de Mr Couperin |fin

ℓ 32r¹⁻⁵ Minkoff p 199 $^3[^6_4]$|7|8|

ED: Brunold/Dart-Co #42, Curtis-Co #47.

43 [COUPERIN (L): <u>Courante</u> (d)]

Courante de Mr Couperin |fin |pour la derniere fois

ℓ 32v¹⁻⁵ Minkoff p 200 $^3[^6_4]$|8|10|

ED: Brunold/Dart-Co #43, Curtis-Co #48.

44 | [COUPERIN (L): <u>Sarabande</u> (d)]

Sarabande de Monsr Couprin |fin

ℓ 33r$^{1-3}$ **Minkoff p 201** $^3[\frac{3}{4}]$|8|16|

ED: Brunold/Dart-Co #44, Curtis-Co #60.

45 | [COUPERIN (L): <u>Sarabande</u> (d)]

Sarabande de Mr Couperin |fin

ℓ 33r$^{4-6}$ **Minkoff p 201** ^{3}|5|9| [$\frac{6}{4}$|4|8|]

ED: Brunold/Dart-Co #45.

46 | [COUPERIN (L): <u>Sarabande</u> (d)]

Sarabande de Monsr Couperin

ℓ 33v$^{1-3}$ **Minkoff p 202** ^{3}|4|10| [$\frac{3}{4}$|8|15|]

ED: Brunold/Dart-Co #46.

47 | [COUPERIN (L): <u>Sarabande</u> <u>en</u> <u>canon</u> (d)]

Sarabande en Canon de M.[r] Couperin |fin

ℓ 33v[4-6] **Minkoff** p 202   3[3/4] |8|16|

ED: Brunold/Dart-Co #47, Curtis-Co #50.

---

48 | [COUPERIN (L): <u>Sarabande</u> (d)]

Sarabande de Mr Couperin

ℓ 34r[1-5] **Minkoff** p 203   3[3/4] |32|

ED: Brunold/Dart-Co #48.

---

49 | [COUPERIN (L): <u>Sarabande</u> (d)]

Sarabande du même Auteur |fin

ℓ 34v[1-3] **Minkoff** p 204   3[3/4] |8|12|

CO: 36-Parville #6, Sarabande Couprain
ED: Brunold/Dart-Co #49, Curtis-Co #59.

50 | [COUPERIN (L): <u>Sarabande</u> (d)]
Sarabande de M^r. Couperin |fin
ℓ 34v$^{4-6}$ Minkoff p 204 $^3[^3_4]$|8|20|

ED: Brunold/Dart-Co #50.

51 | [COUPERIN (L): <u>Sarabande</u> (d)]
Sarabande de M^r. Couperin |fin
ℓ 35r$^{1-5}$ Minkoff p 205 $^3[^3_4]$|12|20|

ED: Brunold/Dart-Co #51, Curtis-Co #49.

52 | [COUPERIN (L): <u>Canarie</u> (d)]
Canaries de Monsr. Couperin. |fin
ℓ 35v$^{1-5}$ Minkoff p 206 $^3[^6_4]$|8|12|

CO: 36-Parville #8, Canaries Couprain
ED: Brunold/Dart-Co #52, Curtis-Co #51.

53 | [COUPERIN (L): <u>Volte</u> (d)]
Volte de Mr Couperin |fin
   ℓ 36r¹⁻³ **Minkoff** p 207 $\frac{3}{}[\frac{3}{4}]|8|16|$

ED: Brunold/Dart-Co #53, Curtis-Co #62.

54 | [COUPERIN (L): <u>La Pastourelle</u> (d)]
La ([crossed out:] Pastourelle) de M^r. Couperin
   ℓ 36r⁴⁻⁶ **Minkoff** p 207 $\frac{3}{}[\frac{3}{4}]|3|18|$

CO: 36-Parville #9, Pastourelle de Couprin
ED: Brunold/Dart-Co #54, Curtis-Co #52.

55 | [COUPERIN (L): <u>Chaconne</u> (d)]
Chaconne de M^r. Couperin |1er Couplet [etc] |4^e |fin
   ℓ 36v¹-37r³ **Minkoff** p 208 $\frac{3}{}|4|8|7|24|8|8|$ $[\frac{3}{4}|47|]$

CO: 36-Parville #12, Chaconne de Couprin
ED: Brunold/Dart-Co #55, Curtis-Co #54.

56 | [COUPERIN (L): <u>Sarabande</u> (d)]

Sarabande de Monsr Couperin |fin

ℓ 37r⁴⁻⁶ **Minkoff p 209**　　³[$\frac{3}{4}$] |8|24.|

ED: Brunold/Dart-Co #56.

---

57 | [COUPERIN (L): <u>Chaconne la complaignante</u> (d)]

Chaconne de Monsr Couperin |fin

ℓ 37v¹⁻⁶　**Minkoff p 210**　　³[$\frac{3}{4}$] |8|8|8|20|

CO: 36-Parville #13, La Complaignante Chaconne de
　　　　　　　　Couprin

ED: Brunold/Dart-Co #57, Curtis-Co #63.

---

58 | [COUPERIN (L): <u>Allemande</u> (D)]

Allemande de Mr Couperin |Il faut jouer cette piece

fort lentement.

ℓ 38r¹⁻⁶　**Minkoff p 211**　　^C|9|11|

CO: 36-Parville #26, Allemande Couprin

ED: Brunold/Dart-Co #58, Curtis-Co #40.

59 | [COUPERIN (L): <u>Courante</u> (D)]

Courante de M^r. Couperin |le dernier Couplet ne se re-
commence /point mais seulement Le Refrain

ℓ 38v$^{1-5}$ Minkoff p 212 $^3[^6_4]$|7|10|

ED: Brunold/Dart-Co #59, Curtis-Co #41.

60 | [COUPERIN (L): <u>Sarabande</u> (D)]

Sarabande de M^r. Couperin |fin

ℓ 39r$^{1-5}$ Minkoff p 213 $^3[^3_4]$|8|16|

CO: 36-Parville #28, Sarabande Couprin
ED: Brunold/Dart-Co #60, Curtis-Co #42.

61 | [COUPERIN (L): <u>Gaillarde</u> (D)]

([crossed out:] Gaillarde) de M^r. Couperin. |fin

ℓ 39v$^{1-6}$ Minkoff p 214 $^3[^3_4]$|8|20|

ED: Brunold/Dart-Co #61, Curtis-Co #43.

62 | [COUPERIN (L): <u>Chaconne</u> (D)]

Chaconne de Mr Couperin. |1.er Couplet |fin [etc] |4^e

ℓ 40r$^{1-5}$ Minkoff p 215 $^3[^3_4]$|8|9|8|9|

CO: 36-Parville #27, Chaconne couprin

ED: Brunold/Dart-Co #62, Curtis-Co #44.

63 | [COUPERIN (L): <u>Allemande de la paix</u> (e)]

Allemande de Mr Couperin |fin

ℓ 40v$^{1-5}$ Minkoff p 216 ^{C}|9|10|

CO: 36-Parville #30, Allemande de la paix Couprin
  cf 64-Lebègue-I #2 [similar Allemande]
  cf 13-Mollersche [similar Allemande]

ED: Brunold/Dart-Co #63, Curtis-Co #65; **cf Dufourcq-L p 2**.

64 | [COUPERIN (L): <u>Courante</u> (e)]

Courante de Mr Couperin. |fin première |pour la der-
nière fois |fin

ℓ 41r$^{1-5}$ Minkoff p 217 $^3[^6_4]$|8|7|3|

CO: 36-Parville #31, Courante couprin

ED: Brunold/Dart-Co #64, Curtis-Co #66.

65 | [COUPERIN (L): <u>Sarabande</u> (e)]

Sarabande de Monsr Couperin. |Fin

   ℓ 41v^1-5 Minkoff p 218   ³[3/4]|8|16|16|

CO: 36-Parville #32, Sarabande couprin
ED: Brunold/Dart-Co #65, Curtis-Co #67.

66 | [COUPERIN (L): <u>Allemande</u> (F)]

Allemande de Mr Couperin |fin

   ℓ 42r^1-5 Minkoff p 219   C|11|11|

ED: Brunold/Dart-Co #66, Curtis-Co #77.

67 | [COUPERIN (L): <u>Allemande grave</u> (F)]

Allemande graue de Mr Couperin |derniere fin |fin

pour la Reprise .|.

   ℓ 42v^1-6 Minkoff p 220   C|9|9|

CO: 36-Parville #77, Allemande graue Couprin
ED: Brunold/Dart-Co #67, Curtis-Co #69.

68 | [COUPERIN (L): <u>Courante</u> (F)]

Courante de Mr Couperin |pour la reprise |pour la derniere fois |fin

ℓ 43r¹⁻⁵ Minkoff p 221   ³[⁶₄] |6|7|2|

CO: 36-Parville #78, Courante Couprin
ED: Brunold/Dart-Co #68, Curtis-Co #70.

69 | [COUPERIN (L): <u>Courante</u> (F)]

Courante de Mr Couperin . |fin

ℓ 43v¹⁻⁵ Minkoff p 222   ³[⁶₄] |8|8|

ED: Brunold/Dart-Co #69, Curtis-Co #79.

70 | [COUPERIN (L): <u>Courante</u> (F)]

Courante du mesme Auteur |fin

ℓ 44r¹⁻⁵ Minkoff p 223   ³[⁶₄] |6|8|2|

ED: Brunold/Dart-Co #70.

71 | [COUPERIN (L): <u>Courante</u> (F)]
Courante de Mr Couperin
  ℓ 44v$^{1-5}$ Minkoff p 224 $^3[^6_4]$|8|8|

ED: Brunold/Dart-Co #71, Curtis-Co #78.

72 | [COUPERIN (L): <u>Sarabande</u> (F)]
Sarabande de Mr Couperin |fin
  ℓ 45r$^{1-3}$ Minkoff p 225 ^{3}|5|9| [$^6_4$|4|8|]

CO: 36-Parville #85, Sarabande couprin
ED: Brunold/Dart-Co #72, Curtis-Co #71.

73 | [COUPERIN (L): <u>Branle de Basque</u> (F)]
([crossed out:] branle de basque) de Mr Couperin |fin
  ℓ 45r$^{4-6}$ Minkoff p 225   ¢|8|8|

ED: Brunold/Dart-Co #73, Curtis-Co #72.

74 | [COUPERIN (L): <u>Sarabande</u> (F)]

Sarabande de Mr Couperin |fin

    ℓ 45v$^{1-5}$ **Minkoff p 226** ^{3}|9|9| [$^6_4$|8|8|]

ED: Brunold/Dart-Co #74, Curtis-Co #80.

75 | [COUPERIN (L): <u>Sarabande</u> (F)]

Sarabande du mesme Auteur |fin.

    ℓ 46r$^{1-5}$ **Minkoff p 227** ^{3}|9|13| [$^6_4$|8|8|]

ED: Brunold/Dart-Co #75.

76 | [COUPERIN (L): <u>Gigue</u> (F)]

Gigue de Mr Couperin |fin

    ℓ 46v$^{1-6}$ **Minkoff p 228** ^{3}[$^6_4$]|12|13|

ED: Brunold/Dart-Co #76.

77 [COUPERIN (L): <u>Gaillarde</u> (F)]

([crossed out:] Gaillarde) du même Auteur |fin

ℓ 47r$^{1-5}$ **Minkoff p 229** $^3[\frac{3}{4}]$|8|20|

CO: 36-Parville #84, Gaillarde Couprin

ED: Brunold/Dart-Co #77, Curtis-Co #74.

---

78 [COUPERIN (L): <u>Chaconne</u> (F)]

Chaconne de M^{r}. Couperin |fin |derniere mesure du 1.er

Couplet

ℓ 47v$^{1-6}$ **Minkoff p 230** $^3[\frac{3}{4}]$|4|8|8|8|18|

ED: Brunold/Dart-Co #78, Curtis-Co #81.

---

79 [COUPERIN (L): <u>Gigue</u> (F)]

Gigue de M^{r}. Couperin |pour recommencer |pour la

Reprise |Reprise |fin |Reprise pour la dernière fois

ℓ 48r$^{1-6}$ **Minkoff p 231** $^3[\frac{6}{4}]$|10|13|3|

ED: Brunold/Dart-Co #79, Curtis-Co #82.

80 | [COUPERIN (L): <u>Chaconne</u> (F)]
Chaconne de Mr Couperin |1er [etc] |fin
   ℓ 48v^{1-6} **Minkoff p 232** ^{3}|8|8|8|8|8| [$\frac{3}{4}$|40|]]

ED: Brunold/Dart-Co #80, Curtis-Co #83.

81 | [COUPERIN (L): <u>Tombeau de Mr. de Blancrocher</u> (F)]
([crossed out:] Tombeau de Mr de Blancrocher) Par
M^r. Couperin |plus viste |Tournez |Suitte |fin
   ℓ 49r^1-v^4 **Minkoff p 233** $^{¢}$|11|23|27|

ED: Brunold/Dart-Co #81, Curtis-Co #84.

82 | [COUPERIN (L): <u>Allemande</u> (G)]
Allemande du même Auteur |fin
   ℓ 50r^{1-5} **Minkoff p 235** ^{C}|9|9|

CO: 24-Babell #252, Allemande
   33-Rés-89ter #33, Allemande Couperin ... Double
   36-Parville #88, Allemande Couprin
   47-Gen-2356 **#5, Allemande Du mesme Mr Couperin**
ED: Brunold/Dart-Co #82, Curtis-Co #86;cf Gilbert p 186.

83 | [COUPERIN (L): <u>Allemande</u> (G)]

Allemande de Mr Couperin |fin

ℓ 50v^{1-5} Minkoff p 236   ^C |10|10|

ED: Brunold/Dart-Co #83.

84 | [COUPERIN (L): <u>Courante</u> (G)]

Courante du meme Auteur |fin |pour la derniere fois &c

ℓ 51r^{1-5} Minkoff p 237 $3[{6 \atop 4}]$ |8|8|

CO: 24-Babell #253; Courante
    36-Parville #89, Courante Couprin

ED: Brunold/Dart-Co #84, Curtis-Co #87.

85 | [COUPERIN (L): <u>Courante</u> (G)]

Courante de Monsr Couperin |fin

ℓ 51v^{1-5} Minkoff p 238 $3[{6 \atop 4}]$ |8|9|

ED: Brunold/Dart-Co #85.

86 | [COUPERIN (L): <u>Courante</u> (G)]
Courante du même Auteur |fin
ℓ 52r$^{1-5}$ **Minkoff p 239** $^3[^6_4]$|6|8|

CO: cf 68-d'Anglebert #3 [Courante on similar theme]
ED: Brunold/Dart-Co #86; cf Gilbert p 6, Roesgen-
    Champion p 6.

87 | [COUPERIN (L): <u>Sarabande</u> (G)]
Sarabande de M^r. Couperin |fin
ℓ 52v$^{1-5}$ **Minkoff p 240** $^3[^3_4]$|8|16|

CO: 24-Babell #254, Sarabande
    36-Parville #98, Sarabande Couprin
ED: Brunold/Dart-Co #87, Curtis-Co #89.

88 | [COUPERIN (L): <u>Gaillarde</u> (G)]
([crossed out:] Gaillarde) de M^r. Couperin |fin
ℓ 53r$^{1-5}$ **Minkoff p 241** $^3[^6_4]$|8|8|2|

CO: 36-Parville #100, Gaillarde de Monsieur Couperin
ED: Brunold/Dart-Co #88, Curtis-Co #90.

89 | [COUPERIN (L): <u>Chaconne</u> (G)]
Chaconne de M.r Couperin |Suitte |Tournez pour la
suitte .|. |Suitte |fin
ℓ 53v^1-54v^4 Minkoff p 242 ^{3}|4|4|16| [etc] [$^3_4$|99|]

CO: 36-Parville #99, Chaconne Couprin
ED: Brunold/Dart-Co #89, Curtis-Co #91.

90 | [COURANTE (L): <u>Courante</u> (G)]
Courante du même Auteur |fin
ℓ 55r$^{1-3}$ Minkoff p 245 ^{3}[$^6_4$]|6|7|

CO: 38-Gen 2348/53 #23, Courante
ED: Dart-Co #90; Brunold-Co #90 (1st strain only, with
35-Bauyn-II #90a).

90a | [COUPERIN (L): <u>Courante</u> (G)]
[untitled]
ℓ 55r$^{3-6}$ Minkoff p 245 ^{3}[$^6_4$]|7|8|

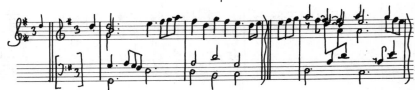

CO: 38-Gen-2348/53 #24, Courante
ED: Dart-Co #90bis, Curtis-Co #88; Brunold-Co #90 (after

1st strain of 35-Bauyn-II #90).

---

91 | [COUPERIN (L): <u>Courante</u> (G)]

Courante de Mr Couperin |fin

ℓ 55v^{1-5} **Minkoff p 246**   ^3[$^6_4$] |8|8|

ED: Brunold/Dart-Co #91.

---

92 | [COUPERIN (L): <u>Allemande</u> (g)]

Allemande de Mr Couperin |fin

ℓ 56r^{1-6} **Minkoff p 247**   ^C |12|14|

CO: 36-Parville #36, Allemande couprin
ED: Brunold/Dart-Co #92, Curtis-Co #93.

---

93 | [COUPERIN (L): <u>Courante</u> (g)]

Courante de Mr Couperin |fin

ℓ 56v^{1-6} **Minkoff p 248**   ^3[$^6_4$] |8|13|

CO: 36-Parville #37, Courante couprin
ED: Brunold/Dart-Co #93, Curtis-Co #94.

94 | [COUPERIN (L): <u>Sarabande</u> (g)]

Sarabande du même Auteur |fin

ℓ 57r$^{1-4}$ Minkoff p 249 ^{3}|5|9| [$^6_4$|4|8|]

CO: 38-Gen-2348/53 #2, Sarabande
ED: Brunold/Dart-Co #94, Curtis-Co #95.

95 | [COUPERIN (L): <u>Chaconne</u> (<u>Passacaille</u>) (g)]

Chaconne ou Passacaille de M^r. Couperin. |Suitte |fin

ℓ 57v^1-58r^6 Minkoff p 250 ^{3}|16|16|24|16|25| [$^3_4$|97|]

CO: 36-Parville #39, Passacaille Couprin
ED: Brunold/Dart-Co #95, Curtis-Co #96.

96 | [COUPERIN (L): <u>Sarabande</u> (g)]

Sarabande de M^r. Couperin |fin

ℓ 58v$^{1-4}$ Minkoff p 252 ^{3}[$^3_4$]|8|16|

CO: 36-Parville #38, Sarabande couprin
ED: Brunold/Dart-Co #96, Curtis-Co #97.

97 | ℓ 59r^1-v^3 Fantaisie Par Monsr. Couperin |Paris au
mois de Decembre,1656 [for organ] [g]
ED: Brunold-Co #97.

98 | ℓ 59v^4-60v^6 Duo. Par M^r. Couperin |Suite |fin [for
organ] [g]
ED: Brunold-Co #98.

99 | [COUPERIN (L): <u>Passacaille</u> (g)]
Passacaille de M^r. Couperin |Suitte |bemol |fin
    ℓ 61r^1-62v^5 Minkoff p 255 $^3[{3 \atop 4}]$|157|

ED: Brunold/Dart-Co #99, Curtis-Co #98.

100 | [COUPERIN (L): <u>Allemande</u> (a)]
Allemande de M^r. Couperin |fin
    ℓ 63r$^{1-5}$ Minkoff p 261 ^{C}|9|10|

ED: Brunold/Dart-Co #100, Curtis-Co #8.

101 | [COUPERIN (L): <u>Allemande</u> (a)]

Allemande de Mr Couperin |fin

ℓ 63v$^{1-6}$ **Minkoff** p 262 ^{C}|10|12|

ED: Brunold/Dart-Co #101, Curtis-Co #13.

102 | [COUPERIN (L): <u>Allemande</u> (a)]

Allemande de Mr Couperin |fin

ℓ 64r$^{1-6}$ **Minkoff** p 263 ^{C}|9|9|

CO: 36-Parville #47, ALLemande Couprin
    40-Rés-476 #29, **Allemande**
    47-Gen-2356 #3, L'aimable allemande de Mr Couperin
ED: Brunold/Dart-Co #102, Curtis-Co #2; cf Bonfils-LP
    p 94.

103 | [COUPERIN (L): <u>La Piémontoise</u> (a)]

La Piémontoise de Mr Couperin |fin

ℓ 64v$^{1-5}$ **Minkoff** p 264 ^{2}|8|24|

ED: Brunold/Dart-Co #103, Curtis-Co #6.

104 | [COUPERIN (L): <u>Courante</u> (a)]
Courante de Mr Couperin |Fin
  ℓ 65r¹⁻⁴ **Minkoff** p 265   3[6/4] |8|8|

ED: Brunold/Dart-Co #104, Curtis-Co #9.

105 | [COUPERIN (L): <u>Courante</u> (a)]
Courante de Mr Couperin |fin
  ℓ 65v¹⁻⁵ **Minkoff** p 266   3[6/4] |9|10|

ED: Brunold/Dart-Co #105, Curtis-Co #15.

106 | [COUPERIN (L): <u>Courante la mignonne</u> (a)]
Courante de Mr Couperin |pour la reprise |pour la
dern.^{re} fois
  ℓ 66r¹⁻⁵ **Minkoff** p 267   3[6/4] |6|8|2|

CO: 36-Parville #48, Courante Couprin dit la mignonne
    47-Gen-2356 #4, La mignonne Du Mesme Mr Couperin
ED: Brunold/Dart-Co #106, Curtis-Co #3.

107 | [COUPERIN (L): <u>Courante</u> (a)]

Courante de Mr Couperin |fin

    ℓ 66v$^{1-6}$ Minkoff p 268 ^{3}[$^{6}_{4}$]|10|16|

ED: Brunold/Dart-Co #107, Curtis-Co #4.

---

108 | [COUPERIN (L): <u>Sarabande</u> (a)]

Sarabande du même Auteur .|.

    ℓ 67r$^{1-3}$ Minkoff p 269 ^{3}|5|9| [$^{6}_{4}$|4|8|]

ED: Brunold/Dart-Co #108, Curtis-Co #17.

---

109 | [COUPERIN (L): <u>Sarabande</u> (a)]

Sarabande de Mr Couperin |fin

    ℓ 67r$^{4-6}$ Minkoff p 269 ^{3}[$^{6}_{4}$]|4|6|

ED: Brunold/Dart-Co #109, Curtis-Co #16.

110 | [COUPERIN (L): <u>Sarabande</u> (a)]

Sarabande de Mr Couperin |Fin

ℓ 67v¹⁻⁴   **Minkoff p 270** $^3[^3_4]$|8|16|

CO: 32-Oldham #109, Sarabande Couperin
    36-Parville #50, Sarabande couprin
ED: Brunold/Dart-Co #110, Curtis-Co #5.

111 | [COUPERIN (L): <u>Sarabande</u> (a)]

Sarabande du même Auteur |fin

ℓ 68r¹⁻⁵   **Minkoff p 271** ^{3}|8|15| [$^3_4$|8|16|]

ED: Brunold/Dart-Co #111, Curtis-Co #10.

112 | [COUPERIN?: <u>Menuet</u> <u>de</u> <u>Poitou</u> (a)]

([crossed out:] Menuet) de Mr Couperin

ℓ 68v¹⁻³   **Minkoff p 272** ^{3}|6|11| [$^3_4$|6|12|]

CO: 35-Bauyn-III #78, (Menuet) de Poitou
    36-Parville #53, Menüet de Poiètou
ED: Brunold/Dart-Co #112, cf #133; Curtis-Co #18.

112
a

[COUPERIN (L): <u>Double</u> (a)]

Double |fin

ℓ 68v[4-6] **Minkoff p 272** $^3[^3_4]$|6|12|

CO: 35-Bauyn-III #78a, Double par Mr Couperin
    36-Parville #53a, Double du menüet fait par Mr
                      Couperin

ED: Brunold/Dart-Co #112[a], cf #133[a]; Curtis #18A.

113

[COUPERIN (L): <u>Courante</u> (A)]

Courante de Mr Couperin |R |fin

ℓ 69r[1-6] **Minkoff p 273** $^3[^6_4]$|7|11|

ED: Brunold/Dart-Co #113.

114

[COUPERIN (L): <u>Sarabande</u> <u>en</u> <u>rondeau</u> (A)]

Sarabande de M[r] Couperin |fin

ℓ 69v[1-6] **Minkoff p 274** $^3[^3_4]$|8|15|7|8|

ED: Brunold/Dart-Co #114.

115 | [COUPERIN (L): <u>Gigue</u> (A)]

Gigue du meme Auteur |fin

ℓ 70r$^{1-6}$ **Minkoff p 275** $^3[^6_4]$|12|14|

ED: Brunold/Dart-Co #115.

---

116 | [COUPERIN (L): <u>Allemande</u> (b)]

Allemande de Mr Couperin |fin

ℓ 70v$^{1-5}$ **Minkoff p 276** ^{C}|9|9|

CO: 36-Parville #102, Allemande Couprin en E Si mi b #
ED: Brunold/Dart-Co #116, Curtis-Co #19.

---

117 | [COUPERIN (L): <u>Courante</u> (b)]

Courante du même Auteur |Pour recommencer. |Pour pas-
ser a la Reprise |fin

ℓ 71r$^{1-5}$ **Minkoff p 277** $^3[^6_4]$|8|8|

CO: 36-Parville #103, Courante Couprin
ED: Brunold/Dart-Co #117, Curtis-Co #20.

118 | [COUPERIN (L): <u>Sarabande</u> (b)]

Sarabande de M.r Couperin |fin

ℓ 71v[1-4] **Minkoff p 278** $^3[{3 \atop 4}]$|8|12|

CO: 36-Parville #104, Sarabande Couprin

ED: Brunold/Dart-Co #118, Curtis-Co #21.

119 | [COUPERIN (L): <u>Allemande</u> (B♭)]

Allemande de M.r Couperin |Fin

ℓ 72r[1-5] **Minkoff p 279** ^{C}|9|8|

ED: Brunold/Dart-Co #119.

120 | [COUPERIN (L): <u>Courante</u> (B♭)]

Courante du même Auteur |Fin

ℓ 72v[1-4] **Minkoff p 280** $^3[{6 \atop 4}]$|8|7|

ED: Brunold/Dart-Co #120.

121 | [COUPERIN (L): <u>Pavane</u> (f#)]

Pauanne de M^r. Couperin |pour recommencer |pour passer.

2^e. Partie |Suitte |pour la 2^e partie |pour passer.

3^e. partie |pour la 3^e. partie |fin

ℓ 73r^1-v^6 Minkoff p 281 ^{C}|19|12|21|

ED: Brunold/Dart-Co #121, Curtis-Co #100.

122 | [COUPERIN (L): <u>Chaconne</u> (g)]

Chaconne de M^r. Couperin |fin |Suitte |1658 |Fin

ℓ 74r^1-v^2 Minkoff p 283 $^3[\frac{3}{4}]$|8|8|12|16|

ED: Brunold/Dart-Co #122, Curtis-Co #98.

123 | [COUPERIN (L): <u>Gigue</u> (d)]

Gigue de Monsr. Couperin

ℓ 74v^3-75r^3 Minkoff p 284 $^3[\frac{6}{4}]$|12|14|

CO: 36-Parville #7, Gigue Couprain
    47-Gen-2356 #6, Gigue de Monsr Couperin
    cf Roberday #8, Fugue ... Caprice [on this theme]

ED: Brunold/Dart-Co #123bis, cf #123; Curtis-Co #61.

ℓ 75v-76v   [blank, ruled]

[here follows 35-Bauyn-III, ℓ 1-32, also
numbered in modern pencil as ℓ 77-108 (of
Rés Vm^7 675]

Inventory - Bauyn-III:

1	ℓ $1r^1$-$2r^6$ (77r)	Toccata del $Seig^r$ Gio Giacomo /Froberger [g] ED: Adler-III p 7.
2	ℓ $2v^1$-$3v^4$ (78v)	Tocade de M^r froberger [G] ED: Adler-I p 8.
3	ℓ $4r^1$-$5v^2$ (80r	Tocade de M^r froberger [a] ED: Adler-I p 1.
4	ℓ $5v^4$-$6v^6$ (81v)	Tocata /Di Gio Giacomo Froberger .|. [D] ED: Adler-III p 26.
5	ℓ $7r^1$-$8r^4$ (83r)	Toccata di Gio. Giacomo froberger /fatto a Bruxellis anno 1650 [d] ED: Adler-I p 5.
6	ℓ $8v^1$-$9v^6$ (84v)	Tocata di Gio Giacomo Froberger [F] ED: Adler-III p 16.
7	ℓ $10r^1$-$11r^6$ (86r)	Tocata del Seignor froberger [C] ED: **Adler-III p 28, cf p 10.**
8	ℓ $11v^{1-5}$ (87v)	Allemande di Gio Giacomo froberger [d] ED: Adler-II p 3.
9	ℓ $12r^{1-6}$ (88r)	**Allemande de M^r froberger fait a Paris [d]** ED: Adler-II p 36.
10	ℓ $12v^{1-6}$ (88v)	Gigue de M^r froberger [e] CO: 24-Babell #107 36-Parville #33 cf 35-Bauyn-III #92 ED: Adler-II p 71, cf p 20; cf **Bonfils-18** p 15, Dufourcq-O #7.
11	ℓ $13r^{1-6}$ (89r)	Allemande ti Gio Giacomo froberger [a] ED: Adler-II p 80.

12	ℓ 13v[1-6]	Gigue de M[r]. froberger [a]
	(89v)	ED: Adler-II p 82.

13	ℓ 14r[1-5]	Couranter ti Gio Giacomo froberger [d]
	(90r)	ED: Adler-II p 4.

14	ℓ 14v[1-4]	Sarabande di gio Giacomo froberger [a]
	(90v)	CO: 47-Gen-2356 #7
		ED: Adler-II p 81.

15	ℓ 15r[1]-16r[5]	fugue de M[r]. froberger fait a Paris
	(91r)	ED: Adler-I p 99.

16	ℓ 16v[1]-17r[2]	Fantaisie. Duo [d]
		ED: Adler-III p 105 (attr FROBERGER)

---

17 [Air italien (d)]
([title and piece completely crossed out:] Air Italien
|Tournez |Suitte)
   ℓ 17r[4]-v[4] (93r) Minkoff p 319 ^{3}|21|19|17| [$\frac{3}{4}$|22|19|17|]

ED: see Commentary, ex 11.

18	ℓ 18r[1-5]	Allemande ti Gio Giacomo froberger [D]
	(94r)	ED: Adler-II p 72.

18a	ℓ 18v[1-6]	Double de l'Allemande cy dessous [D]
	(94v)	ED: Adler-II p 72.

19	ℓ 19r[1-6]	Capricio del Seignor Girolamo frescobaldi
	(95r)	[G]
		ED: Shindle-II p 28.

19a	ℓ 19v[1]-20r[1]	Capricio del Seignor frescobaldi [G]
	(95r)	ED: Shindle-II p 29.

20 | ℓ 20r^2-v^3 Trio de frescobaldi [3 staves, open score]
   | (96r)   ED: Shindle-III p 72.

21 | ℓ 21r$^{1-6}$ Prelude de Mr Richard de s^t Jacques
   | (97r)   [a]
   | ED: Bonfils-18 p 16, Dufourcq-0 #9.

22 | ℓ 21v^1-22r^3 Prelude de Mr Richard [d]
   | (97v)   ED: Bonfils-18 p 8, Dufourcq-0 #10.

23 | ℓ 22r$^{5-6}$ Pseaume. Par Mr Couperin
   | (98r)   ED: Brunold-Co #124.

24 | ℓ 22v$^{1-2}$ **Pseaume.** de Mr Couperin
   | (98v)   ED: Brunold-Co #125.

25 | ℓ 22v^5-23r^6 Duo [g]
   | (98v)

26 | ℓ 23v^1-24r^4 Fantaisie [g]
   | (99v)

27 | ℓ 24v^1-25r^5 Fantaisie pour les Violes par Mr Couperin
   | (100v)   ED: Brunold-Co #126.

28 | ℓ 25v$^{1-6}$ Fantaisie de Violes par Mr Couperin
   | (101v)   ED: Brunold-Co #127.

29 | ℓ 26r$^{1-5}$ Simphonie par Mr Couperin
   | (102r)   ED: Brunold-Co #128.

30 | ℓ 26v$^{1-6}$ Simphonie par Mr Couperin
   | (102v)   ED: Brunold-Co #129.

31 | ℓ 27r$^{1-6}$ Simphonie par Mr Couperin
   | (103r)   ED: Brunold-Co #130.

32 [LA BARRE: <u>Allemande/Gigue</u> (d)]

Allemande de M^r De la barre

ℓ 27v¹⁻⁶ (103v) Minkoff p 340   ¢|12|11|

CO: 20-Ch-Ch-378 #3, Almaine (de Labar)
35-Bauyn-III #66, Gigue de Mr. De La barre

ED: Bonfils-18 p 25.

33 [RICHARD: <u>Allemande</u> (d)]

Allemande de Mr Richard

ℓ 28r¹⁻⁵ (104r) Minkoff p 341   C|11|8|

ED: Bonfils-18 p 10, Dufourcq-0 #8.

34 [LA BARRE, Joseph: <u>Allemande/Gigue</u> (C)]

Allemande de M^r De la barre

ℓ 28v¹⁻⁶ (104v) Minkoff p 342   ¢|11|11|

CO: 35-Bauyn-III #61, Gigue de Mr. Joseph De la barre
ED: Bonfils-18 p 23.

35 | [<u>Pavane</u> (e)]

Pauanne |fin

ℓ 29r¹⁻⁶ (105r)　Minkoff p 343　¢|14|12|15|

36 | [<u>Pavane</u> (e)]

Pauanne

ℓ 29v¹⁻⁶ (105v) Minkoff p 344　C|15|14|13|

37 | [<u>Pauane</u> (a)]

Pauanne |fin

ℓ 30r¹⁻⁶ (106r) Minkoff p 345　¢|11|12|12|

38 | [Pavane (a)]
Pauanne
   ℓ 30v$^{1-5}$ (106v) Minkoff p 346 ^{C}|11|13|

39 | ℓ 31r$^{1-4}$ Prelude [g]
   (107r)

40 | [RICHARD: Allemande (a)]
Allemande de M^r. Richard
   ℓ 31v$^{1-5}$ (107v) Minkoff p 348 ^{C}|7|10|

ED: Bonfils-18 p 17, Dufourcq-0 #11.

41 | ℓ 32r^1-v^4 Fantaisie du Seig^r. Hierosme frescobaldi
   (108r)   ED: Shindle-II p 31.

[4 end papers, blank, unruled]

[This concludes the misbound v 2 of Bauyn (Rés Vm^7 675). 35-Bauyn-III continues as the second half of v 1 (Rés Vm^7 674$^{(2)}$:]

42 [Pavane angloise (a)]

Pauanne Angloise |Suitte

   ℓ 33r^1-v^5 Minkoff p 351   ¢|24|22|25|

43 [LORENCY: Fantaisie (a)]

Faintaisie de Mr de Lorency

   ℓ 34r^1-v^2 Minkoff p 353   ¢|53|

44 [HARDEL: Allemande (d)]

ALLemande de M^r hardel |Suitte

   ℓ 34v^4-35r^4 Minkoff p 354 C|13|¢15|

CO: 24-Babell #219, Allemande
    36-Parville #22, Allemande hardel
    44-LaPierre p 52, Allemande de Mr Hardel

ED: Quittard-H p 4.

45 [HARDEL: <u>Courante</u> (d)]

Courante de M[r] hardel

   ℓ 35v[1-5] Minkoff p 356 $^3[^6_4]$ |7|8|

CO: 32-Oldham #31, Courante de Mr hardel
    44-LaPierre p 54, Premiere Courante

ED: Quittard-H p 3.

46 [HARDEL: <u>Courante</u> (d)]

Courante de M[r] hardel

   ℓ 36r[1-6] Minkoff p 357 $^3[^6_4]$ |8|9|

CO: cf 68-d'Anglebert #40, Courante [similar beginning]

ED: Quittard-H p 6; cf Gilbert p 52, Roesgen-Champion p 78.

47 [HARDEL: <u>Courante</u> (d)]

Courante de M[r] hardel

   ℓ 36v[1-5] Minkoff p 358 $^3[^6_4]$ |6|8|

ED: Quittard-H p 4.

48 | [HARDEL: <u>Sarabande</u> (d)]

Sarabande de M[r] Hardel

ℓ 37r[1-5] Minkoff p 359 $^3[^3_4]$|8|16|

CO: 24-Babell #221, Sarabande
ED: Quittard-H p 7.

49 | [HARDEL: <u>Gigue</u> (d)]

Gigue de M[r]. Hardel

ℓ 37v[1-4] Minkoff p 360 $^3_8$|7|13|

CO: 24-Babell #147, Gigue
ED: Quittard-H p 8.

50 | [HARDEL: <u>Gavotte</u> (a)]

([crossed out:] Gauotte) de M[r] Hardel

ℓ 38r[1-4] Minkoff p 361   ¢|4|8|

CO: 23-Tenbury #12, Gavotte Mr. Hardel
    24-Babell #159, Gavotte
    25-Bod-426 #20, Gavotte d'Ardelle
    31-Madrid-1360 #41, Jabouste de Ardel

36-Parville #52, Gavotte de Mr Hardel
45-Dart #60, Gauotte de Monsr Ardel
49-RésF-933 #13, gavotte d ardelle
cf St-Georges ℓ 51, Gavotte
 cf Saizenay-I p 61, Gavotte Ardelle [lute]
 cf Saizenay-II p 17, Gavotte d'hardelle [lute]
 cf Vm7-4867 p 52, Gavotte d'ardelle [violin]

ED: Brunold/Dart-Co #131, Curtis-Co #11, Quittard-H p 1.

50a | [COUPERIN (L): <u>Double</u> (a)]

Double ([crossed out:] de la gauotte) cy dessus /Par
Mr Couperin

 ℓ 38v$^{1-5}$ Minkoff p 362 ¢|4|8|

CO: 23-Tenbury #12a, Double
  24-Babell #159a, Double
  31-Madrid-1360 #41a [Double]
  36-Parville #52a, Double de la gauotte fait par
         Mr Couprin
  49-RésF-933 #13a, [Double]
  cf Vm7-4867 p 77, Double [violin]

ED: Brunold/Dart-Co #131[a], Curtis-Co #11a, Quittard-H p 2

---

51 | [MESANGEAU, arr: <u>Sarabande</u> (C)]

Sarabande de Mr Mezangeau

 ℓ 39r$^{1-5}$ Minkoff p 363 ^{3}[$^3_4$]|16|19|

CO: cf 33-Rés-89ter #14, Sarabande. Mezangeot
ED: cf Gilbert p 171, Souris-M p 56, Souris-M #12.

52 [MESANGEAU, arr: <u>Sarabande</u> (C)]

Sarabande de Mr Mezangeau

ℓ 39v¹⁻³ Minkoff p 364 $^3[^3_4]|8|8|$

ED: Souris-M p 57.

53 [MONNARD: <u>Courante</u> (C)]

Courante de Mr Monnard

ℓ 39v⁴⁻⁶ Minkoff p 364 $^3[^6_4]|6|6|$

CO: 35-Bauyn-III #59, Courante de Mr. Monnard
ED: Bonfils-18 p 5.

54 [LEBÈUGE: <u>Gavotte</u> (C)]

([crossed out:] Gauotte) de Mr Lebegue

ℓ 40r¹⁻³ Minkoff p 365 $¢|4|8|$

CO: 10-Schwerin-617 #10, Gavotte
   13-Möllersche, [copy of Lebegue-I #43]
   14-Schwerin-619 #91, **Gavotte**
   21-Rés-1186bis #12, Gavott
   23-Tenbury #6, Gavotte Mr Le Begue

24-Babell #60, Gavotte de Mr. le Begue
30-Cecilia ℓ 47r, Gavotte
36-Parville #68, Gauotte Mr le Begue
45-Dart #22, [copy of 64-Lebègue-I #43]
46-Menetou #102, Gavotte
50-Paignon #11, Balet de Mr lebegue
64-Lebègue-I #43, Gauotte

ED: cf Dufourcq-L p 38; Brunold/Dart-Co #132.

54a | [COUPERIN (L): <u>Double</u> (C)]

Double par Mr Couperin

 ℓ 40r$^{4-6}$ Minkoff p 365 ₵|7|14|

CO: 36-Parville #146, Double de la Gavotte de Le Bègue
 cf 13-Möllersche, [copy of 64-Lebègue-I #43a]
 cf 14-Schwerin-619 #91a, [Double]
 cf 23-Tenbury #6a, Double
 cf 24-Babell #60a, Double
 cf 36-Parville #68a, [Double]
 cf 50-Paignon #11a, la double
 cf 64-Lebègue-I #43a, Double

ED: Brunold/Dart-Co #132[a]; cf Dufourcq-L p 38.

---

55 | [LA BARRE: <u>Courante</u> (C)]

Courante de M.^{r} De la barre

 ℓ 40v$^{1-5}$ Minkoff p 366 ^{3}|13|16| [$^{3}_{4}$|14|16|]

ED: Bonfils-18 p 24.

56 | [DUMONT: <u>Allemande</u> (C)]

Allemande de Mr Dumont |fin

   ℓ 41r¹⁻⁶ **Minkoff** p 367   ^C|10|11|

ED: Bonfils-13 p 14.

57 | [DUMONT: <u>Allemande</u> (d)]

Allemande de M^r Du mont. |fin

   ℓ 41v¹⁻⁶ **Minkoff** p 368   ^C|11|12|

ED: Bonfils-13 p 15.

58 | [DUMONT: <u>Courante</u> (d)]

Courante de Mr Dumont. |fin

   ℓ 42r¹⁻⁵ **Minkoff** p 369 $^3[^6_4]$|6|8|

CO: 35-Bauyn-III #87, Courante de M^r. Du mont
ED: Bonfils-13 p 16.

59 | [MONNARD: <u>Courante</u> (C)]

Courante de Mr Monnard |fin

ℓ 42v$^{1-3}$ Minkoff p 370 $^3[{6 \atop 4}]|6|6|$

CO: 35-Bauyn-III #53 (qv, almost duplicate), Courante
de Mr. Monnard

ED: Bonfils-18 p 5.

60 | [MONNARD: <u>Sarabande</u> (C)]

Sarabande /De Mr Monnard |fin

ℓ 42v$^{5-6}$ Minkoff p 370 $^3[{3 \atop 4}]|4|8|$

CO: 6-Munich-1511e #11, Sarrabande
23-Tenbury #4, Sarabande
24-Babell #56, Sarabande
30-Cecilia ℓ 48r, Sarabande ... redoublé
31-Madrid-1360 #23/6, Sexta (Zarabanda)
38-Gen-2348/53 #34, Sarabande
44-LaPierre p 2 [Sarabande]

ED: Bonfils-18 p 6; cf Ex 7 above.

61 | [LA BARRE, Joseph: <u>Allemande/Gigue</u> (C)]

Gigue de Mr Joseph De la barre |fin

ℓ 43r$^{1-6}$ Minkoff p 371 $^{¢}|11|11|$

CO: 35-Bauyn-III #34, Allemande de Mr De la barre

ED: Bonfils-18 p 23.

62 | [Gavotte (C)]

([crossed out:] Gauotte) |fin

  ℓ 43v$^{1-5}$ Minkoff p 372   ¢|8|12|

63 | [d'ANGLEBERT: Gaillarde (Sarabande) (C)]

Sarabande graue en forme ([crossed out:] de gaillarde)
de M^r D'anglebert |1re fois |2e fois |fin

  ℓ 44r$^{1-6}$ Minkoff p 373 $\frac{3}{2}$|8|16|4|

CO: 33-Rés-89ter #6, Gaillarde. D'Anglebert.
    cf 35-Bauyn-I #20, [Sarabande on similar theme]
    cf 63-Chamb-II #4, [Sarabande on similar theme]
ED: Gilbert p 157, Roesgen-Champion p 145; cf Brunold-
    Tessier #34, 75; cf Dart-Ch #34.

64 | [GAULTIER, arr: Sarabande (C)]

Sarabande de Mr Gautier |fin

  ℓ 44v$^{1-5}$ Minkoff p 374 ^{3}|7|15| [$\frac{3}{4}$|8|20|]

65 | [GAULTIER, arr: <u>Canarie</u> (C)]

Canaries de M[r] Gautier |fin

ℓ 45r[1-5]   Minkoff p 375 $^3[^6_4]$|20|

---

66 | [LA BARRE: <u>Allemande/Gigue</u> (d)]

Gigue de M[r]. De La barre |fin

ℓ 45v[1-6]   Minkoff p 376   ¢|12|11|

CO: 20-Ch-Ch-378 #3, Almaine (de Labar)
35-Bauyn-III #32, Allemande de Mr De la Barre

ED: Bonfils-18 p 25.

ℓ 46-47   [cut out of volume]

67 | ℓ 48r[1-6]   Gigue de M[r] froberger [d]

ED: Adler-II p 38.

---

68 | [<u>Sarabande</u> (G)]

Sarabande

ℓ 48v[1-6]   Minkoff p 378 $^3[^3_4]$|16|16|

ED: Adler-II p 83 (attr FROBERGER).

69 | [LA BARRE: <u>Courante</u> (a)]

Courante de M^r De la barre

ℓ 49r$^{1-5}$ **Minkoff p 379** ^{3}|13|19| [$^3_4$|14|20|]

CO: 36-Parville #55, Courante de M. de la barre
ED: Bonfils-18 p 26.

70 | [RICHARD: <u>Courante</u> (a)]

Courante de M^r. Richard |Fin

ℓ 49v$^{1-5}$ **Minkoff p 380** ^{3}[$^6_4$]|7|8|

CO: 36-Parville #49, Courante Richard
ED: Bonfils-18 p 19, Dufourcq-O #1.

71 | [RICHARD: <u>Sarabande</u> (a)]

Sarabande de M^r. Richard |Fin

ℓ 50r$^{1-4}$ **Minkoff p 381** ^{3}[$^3_4$]|8|12|

CO: 32-Oldham #5, Sarabande
ED: Bonfils-18 p 18, Dufourcq-O #2.

72 | [MONNARD: <u>Courante</u> (a)]
Courante de M^r. Monnard. |Fin
   ℓ 50v¹⁻⁴ Minkoff p 382   ³[$^6_4$]|6|6|

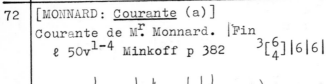

CO: 32-Oldham #3, Courante
ED: Bonfils-18 p 7.

---

73 | ℓ 51r¹⁻⁶   Gigue de M^r froberger [D]
             ED: Adler-II p 84.

74 | ℓ 51v¹⁻⁵   Allemande de M^r froberger   [g]
             ED: Adler-II p 51.

75 | ℓ 52r¹⁻⁵   Gigue de M^r. froberger [g]
             ED: Adler-II p 53.

76 | ℓ 52v¹⁻⁴   Courante   [FROBERGER (g)]
             ED: Adler-II p 52.

77 | ℓ 53r¹⁻⁴   Sarabande de M^r froberger   [g]
             ED: Adler-II p 52.

---

78 | [COUPERIN (L)?: <u>Menuet</u> <u>de</u> <u>Poitou</u> (a)]
([crossed out:] Menuet) de Poitou |fin
   ℓ 53v¹⁻⁴ Minkoff p 388   ³[$^3_4$]|6|12|

CO: 35-Bauyn-II #112, (Menuet) de Mr. Couperin
    36-Parville #53, Menuet de Poiètou
ED: Brunold/Dart-Co #133, cf #112; Curtis-Co #18.

78a [COUPERIN (L): <u>Double</u> (a)]

Double /par /Mr Couperin |fin

ℓ 53v$^{4-6}$ Minkoff p 388 $^3[^3_4]|6|12|$

CO: 35-Bauyn-II #112a, Double
    36-Parville #53a, Double du menüet fait par Mr
                     Couperin

ED: Brunold/Dart-Co #133[a], cf #112[a]; Curtis-Co
    #18A.

79 [<u>Pavane angloise</u> (a)]

Pauanne Angloise |Tournez |Suitte |fin

ℓ 54r^1-v^3 Minkoff p 389 ¢|19|22|20| [$^2_2$|20|22|21|]

80 [<u>Pavane italienne</u> (e)]

Pauanne Italienne |Suitte

ℓ 54v^4-55r^6 Minkoff p 390 ¢|10|7|9|

81 | [DUMONT: <u>Allemande</u> (d)]

Allemande de M.[r] Dumont |Fin

ℓ 55v[1-5] **Minkoff p 392**   ¢|10|12|

ED: Bonfils-13 p 17.

82 | [RICHARD: <u>Allemande</u> (d)]

Allemande de Mons.[r] Richard |fin

ℓ 56r[1-6] **Minkoff p 393**   C|13|12|

ED: Bonfils-18 p 11, Dufourcq-0 #3.

83 | [RICHARD: <u>Allemande</u> (G)]

Allemande de M.[r] Richard |Fin

ℓ 56v[1-4] **Minkoff p 394**   C|10|9|

ED: Bonfils-18 p 14, Dufourcq-0 #4.

84 | [DUMONT: <u>Allemande</u> (a)]

Allemande de M[r] Dumont |Fin

ℓ 57r[1-5] Minkoff p 395   ¢|8|11|

CO: 5-Munich-1503ℓ #12, belle allemande de mons. Du
                             mont

ED: Bonfils-13 p 18.

85 | [DUMONT: <u>Allemande</u> (C)]

Allemande graue de M[r.] Dumont

ℓ 57v[1-6] Minkoff p 396   C|18|17|

ED: Bonfils-13 p 19.

86 | [DUMONT: <u>Allemande grave</u> (C)]

Allemande du même Auteur |fin

ℓ 58r[1-6] Minkoff p 397   C|15|17|

CO: 58-Dumont-1652 ℓ 24, ALLEMANDA GRAVIS

ED: Bonfils-13 p 4..

87 | [DUMONT: <u>Courante</u> (d)]

Courante de M.^r Du mont |Fin

ℓ 58v^1-4 **Minkoff** p 398 $^3[^6_4]$|6|8|

CO: 35-Bauyn-III #58 (qv, almost duplicate), Courante
de Mr Dumont

ED: Bonfils-13 p 16.

---

88 | [RICHARD: <u>Courante</u> (d)]

Courante de Mr Richard |fin

ℓ 59r^1-5 **Minkoff** p 399 $^3[^6_4]$|8|9|

ED: Bonfils-18 p 12, Dufourcq-O #5.

---

89 | [RICHARD: <u>Gigue</u> (g)]

Gigue de Mr Richard |Derniere fois |fin |Refrain pour
la prem.^re fois |Cela Reprise

ℓ 59v^1-6 **Minkoff** p 400 $^3[^6_4]$|12|7|^C5|4|^31|

ED: Bonfils-18 p 13, Dufourcq-O #6.

90 | [PINEL, arr: <u>Sarabande</u> (C)]

Sarabande de M.[r] Pinel |fin

    ℓ 60r[1-5] **Minkoff p 401** ^{3}|5|7| [$^6_4$|4|6|]]

CO: **36**-Parville #64, Sarabande de Mr pignel
    47-Gen-2356 #13, Sarabande
    cf 33-Rés-89ter #4, Sarabande Pinel ... Double

ED: cf Gilbert p 152.

91 | ℓ 60v[1]-61r[1] Passacaille Del Seig.[r] Louigi [ROSSI]

    |Suitte [a]

        CO: 23-Tenbury #11
            24-Babell #166
            36-Parville #57

        ED: Pierront p 6, Prunières p 18.

92 | [RICHARD: <u>Gigue</u> (G)]

Gigue de Mr Richard |Fin

    ℓ 61r[2-5] **Minkoff p 403** ^{C}|6|8|

CO: cf 24-Babell #107, Gigue
    cf 35-Bauyn-III #10, Gigue de Mr. froberger
    cf 36-Parville #33, Gigue de Mr froberger

ED: Bonfils-18 p 15, Dufourcq-O #7; cf Adler-II p 20,
    71 (similar Froberger Gigues).

93 | [VINCENT: <u>Pavane</u> (a)]

Pauanne de M.ʳ Vincent |ˈfin

ℓ 61v¹⁻⁶ **Minkoff p 404**   ¢|7|8|8| [²⁄₂|9|8|8|]

94 | [DUMONT: <u>Pavane</u> (d)]

Pauanne de Monsʳ Dumont |Tournez |Suitte |Fin

ℓ 62r¹-v³ **Minkoff p 405**   ¢|9|8|10|

ED: Bonfils-13 p 21.

ℓ 62v³-64v [blank, ruled]

[2 end papers, blank, unruled]

[This concludes the second section of
the misbound v 1 of Bauyn (Rés Vm⁷ 674⁽²⁾;
v 2 (Rés Vm⁷ 675) begins with 35-Bauyn-II.]

<u>Provenance</u>: France (Paris?), post 1686 (transcription
from <u>Acis</u> <u>et</u> <u>Galathée</u>).

<u>Location</u>: Berkeley, California; University of California,
Music Library, MS 778.

<u>Description</u>: 350 p. (283 written; originally at least
354: 2 ℓ lacking); oblong quarto format, 19 x 26 cm.
Watermark #62. Contemporary (18th century?) full
leather, gilt-tooled binding, stamped on covers,
"M. DE /PARVILLE" (tracing #106), 20 x 27 cm.

<u>Notation</u>: Keyboard score (two 5-line staves, 3 systems
per page, written page by page). Clefs: $C^{1,2,3}$,
$G^{1,2}$, $F^{3,4,5}$; usually F^3, G^2.

<u>Scribes</u>: One unidentified primary hand (A), with 7-8
later hands completing volume:
A: # 1-104 (except #68a)
B: 105-109
C: 110-111
D: 112-137
E: 138-143
F: 144
G: 68a, 145-147
H: 148
I: 149 (hand of La Barre? the same as hand A of
48-LaBarre-6 and 51-LaBarre-11; and hand B
in 46-Menetou)

<u>Marginalia</u>: Numeration by pages in modern pencil. Pencil
number in front cover, "2 24." Red crayon number
inside back cover: "1203." Many original "x" marks
at the beginnings of pieces (copyist marks?).

Summary:

Composers:

d'ANGLEBERT: #17, 41, 65, 109, 141-143.

CHAMBONNIÈRES: #19-21, 34, 40, 60, 61-63, 79-82,
            86, 90-96, 145, 148.

COUPERIN (Louis): #1, 2, 4-13, 25-28, 30-32, 35-39,
            45-48, 50, 52a, 53(?), 58, 59,
            60a, 67a, 69-78, 84-85, 87-89,
            98-104, 144(?), 146, 148.

FROBERGER: #33, cf 45.

GAULITER (Ennemond): #17.

GAULITER (Pierre): #138, 140(?).

HARDEL: #22, 52.

LA BARRE: #3, 14-16, 18, 54-56, 83.

LEBÈGUE: #68, cf 146.

LULLY: #24, 29, 41-43, 66-67, 108-112, 115-118, 120-
        125, 127-128, 130-133, 141, 147, 149.

PINEL: #64.

RICHARD: #49, 97.

ROSSI: #57.

Contents: #1-104 (hand A) grouped by key:

#1-24	(d)	69-74	(c)
25-29	(D)	75-86	(F)
30-34	(e)	87-100	(G)
35-44	(g)	101	(e)
45-57	(a)	102-104	(b)
58-68	(C)		

#105-137: opera transcriptions

138-149: miscellaneous pieces

Inventory:

1 [COUPERIN (L)?: **Prélude** (d)]

Prelude en D La Re

p 1^{1}-5^{2} |-|^{C}23|-|

ED: Curtis-Co #55.

2 | [COUPERIN (L): Prélude (d)]
Prelude Coupprain |Suitte du prelude Couprain
   p 6^1-14^3 |-|^{3}39|-| [|-|$^3_2$38|-|]

CO: 35-Bauyn-II #1, Preludes de Mr. Couperin
ED: Curtis-Co #45; cf Brunold/Dart #1.

---

3 | [LA BARRE: Prélude (d)]
Prelude de Monsieur de la Barre
   p 15$^{1-3}$ ¢|12| [irregularly measured]

---

4 | [COUPERIN (L): Allemande (d)]
Allemande Couprain |Reprise
   p 16^1-17^1 C|9|10|

CO: 35-Bauyn-II #36, Allemande de Mr. Couperin
ED: Curtis-Co #46; cf Brunold/Dart-Co #36.

5 | [COUPERIN (L): <u>Courante</u> (d)]
Courante Couprain |Reprise
　　p 18¹-19¹　　　　　　　³[⁶₄]|8|10|

CO: 24-Babell #222, Courante
　　 35-Bauyn-II #41, Courante de Monsr. Couperin
　　 cf 24-Babell #224, Courante
　　 cf 36-Parville #16, Courante la Barre
ED: Curtis-Co #58; Brunold/Dart #41.

6 | [COUPERIN (L): <u>Sarabande</u> (d)]
Sarabande /Couprain
　　p 19²⁻³　　　　　　　[³₄]|8|12|

CO: 35-Bauyn-II #49, Sarabande du même Auteur
ED: Curtis-Co #59; cf Brunold/Dart #49.

7 | [COUPERIN (L): <u>Gigue</u> (d)]
Gigue Couprain
　　p 20¹-21³　　　　　　³[⁶₄]|12|14|

CO: 35-Bauyn-II #123, Gigue de Monsr. Couperin

47-Gen-2356 #6, Gigue de Monsr Couperin
   cf Roberday #8, Fugue ... Caprice [on this theme]
ED: Curtis-Co #61; cf Brunold/Dart-Co #123bis

---

8 | [COUPERIN (L): <u>Canarie</u> (d)]

Canaries Couprain
   p 22$^{1-3}$ $^3[^6_4]|8|12|$

CO: 35-Bauyn-II #52, Canaries de Monsr. Couperin
ED: Curtis-Co #51; cf Brunold/Dart-Co #52.

---

9 | [COUPERIN (L): <u>La Pastourelle</u> (d)]

Pastourelle de Couprin
   p 23$^{1-3}$ $^3[^3_4]|3|18|$

CO: 35-Bauyn-II #54, La (Pastourelle) de Mr. Couperin
ED: Curtis-Co #52; cf Brunold/Dart-Co #54.

10 | [COUPERIN (L): <u>Courante</u> (d)]

Courante Couprin |Reprise
p 24^1-25^1 $^3[{6 \atop 4}]$|10|10|

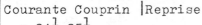

CO: 35-Bauyn-II #39, Courante de Monsr. Couperin
ED: Curtis-Co #57; cf Brunold/Dart-Co #39.

11 | [COUPERIN (L): <u>Gavotte</u> (d)]

Gauotte Couprin |Reprise
p 25^{2-3} $\mathcal{C}$|4|4|4|

ED: Curtis-Co #53.

12 | [COUPERIN (L): <u>Chaconne</u> (d)]

Chaconne de Couprin |1er Couplet [etc] |4^e Couplet
p 26^1-27^3 ^{3}|4|8|7|[etc] $[{3 \atop 4}$|4|8|8|24|8|5|]

CO: 35-Bauyn-II #55, Chaconne de Mr. Couperin
ED: Curtis-Co #54; cf Brunold/Dart-Co #55.

13 | [COUPERIN (L): <u>Chaconne la complaignante</u> (d)]

La Complaignante Chaconne de Couprin

p 28^1-29^3 ^{3}|6|8|8|8|15| [$^3_4$|8|8|8|8|16|]

CO: 35-Bauyn-II #57, Chaconne de Monsr. Couperin
ED: Curtis-Co #63; cf Brunold/Dart-Co #57.

14 | [LA BARRE: <u>Allemande</u> (d)]

Allemande /La Barre |Reprise

p 30^1-31^2 C|10|12|

15 | [LA BARRE: <u>Allemande</u> (d)]

Allemande la Barre |Reprise

p 32^{1-3} C|8|7|

CO: 24-Babell #223, Allemande

16 | [LA BARRE: <u>Courante</u> (d)]

Courante la Barre |Reprise
  p 33¹⁻³ $^3[^6_4]$|9|9|

CO: 24-Babell #224, Courante
    cf 24-Babell #222, Courante
    cf 35-Bauyn-II #41, Courante de Monsr. Couperin
    cf 36-Parville #5, Courante Couprain
ED: cf Curtis-Co #58, Brunold/Dart-Co #41.

---

17 | [GAULTIER (E), arr d'ANGLEBERT: <u>Courante les larmes</u> (d)]

Courante du Vieux gautier |Reprise
  p 34¹⁻³ $^3[^3_4]$|17|16|

CO: 33-Rés-89ter #25, Courante du Vieux Gautier
    cf 66-Perrine #20, Courante du V.G. ou les Larmes
                      [a]
ED: cf Gilbert p 180, Souris-G #78, Souris-G #51.

18 | [LA BARRE: <u>Sarabande</u> (d)]

Sarabande la barre |Reprise

p 35[1-3]   3[3/4] |8|20|

CO: 24-Babell #187, Sarabande

---

19 | [CHAMBONNIÈRES: <u>Courante la toute belle</u> (d)]

Courant Chanbonniere dit la toute belle |Reprise

p 36[1-3]   3 |10|11| [6/4|10|10|]

CO: 32-Oldham #10, Courante La Toute Belle
    35-Bauyn-I #31, Courante La toute belle du même
                                                Auteur
    62-Chamb-I #12, Courante la toute belle
ED: cf Brunold-Tessier #12, Dart-Ch #12.

---

20 | [CHAMBONNIÈRES: <u>Courante de madame</u> (d)]

Courante chanbonniere |Reprise

p 37[1-3]   3[6/4] |9|10|

CO: 32-Oldham #11, Courante de Madame
    35-Bauyn-I #34, Autre Courante du meme Auteur
    62-Chamb-I #13, Courante de Madame

ED: cf Brunold-Tessier #13, Dart-Ch #13.

---

21 | [CHAMBONNIÈRES: _Allemande_ _la_ _loureuse_ (d)]

ALlemande laloureuse chanbonnière

p 38$^{1-3}$ $\mathbb{C}$|7|11|

CO: 24-Babell #184, Allemande ... Double
    32-Oldham #23, Allemande La Loureuse
    35-Bauyn-I #30, Allemande la Loureuse de Mr. de
                    Chambonnieres
    62-Chamb-I #11, Allemande la Loureuse

ED: cf Brunold-Tessier #11, Dart-Ch #11.

---

22 | [HARDEL: _Allemande_ (d)]

Allemande hardel |Reprise

p 39$^{1-3}$ $\mathbb{C}$|13|15|

CO: 24-Babell #219, Allemande
    35-Bauyn-III #44, Allemande de Mr hardel
    44-LaPierre p 52, Allemande de Mr Hardel

ED: cf Quittard-H p 4.

23 | [Air italien à deux choeurs (d)]
Air /Air italien a deux Choeurs |Grand Choeur |Petit
Choeur |Grand Choeur
   p 40¹⁻³   ^C|4|4|9|11|

24 | [LULLY, arr: 2me Air pour les mesmes Jean Doucet from
L'Amour malade (1657) IX (d)]
Lamour malade |Reprise
   p 41¹⁻³   3|11|13 [$\frac{3}{4}$|12|14|]

CO: cf Veron ℓ 7v, L'amour malade

25 | [COUPERIN (L): Prélude (D)]
Prelude en D la re grand becar
   p 42¹-47¹ |-|

CO: 35-Bauyn-II #2, Autre prelude de Mr Couperin
ED: Curtis-Co #39; cf Brunold/Dart-Co #2.

26 | [COUPERIN (L): <u>Allemande</u> (D)]

Allemande Couprin |**Reprise**
  p 48^1-49^2   ^C|10|11|

CO: 35-Bauyn-II #58, Allemande de Mr Couperin ...
ED: Curtis-Co #40; cf Brunold/Dart-Co #58.

27 | [COUPERIN (L): <u>Chaconne</u> (D)]

Chaconne couprin
  p 50^1-51^1   ^3[$\frac{3}{4}$]|8|8|8|11|

CO: 35-Bauyn-II #62, Chaconne de Mr. Couperin
ED: Curtis-Co #44; cf Brunold/Dart-Co #62.

28 | [COUPERIN (L): <u>Sarabande</u> (D)]

Sarabande Couprin |Reprise
  p 51^2-3   ^3[$\frac{3}{4}$]|8|16|

CO: 35-Bauyn-II #60, Sarabande de Mr. Couperin
ED: Curtis-Co #42; cf Brunold/Dart-Co #60.

29 | [LULLY, arr: <u>Chaconne</u> from <u>Acis</u> <u>et</u> <u>Galathée</u> (1686)
II-5 (D)]

Chaconne de galatée

p 52^1-53^3 $^3[\frac{3}{4}]$ |41|

CO: cf 14-Schwerin-619 #123, Chaconne de Galothe
    cf 23-Tenbury #75, Chaconne de Galatée
    cf 24-Babell #97, Chaconne de Galatée
    cf 49-RésF-933 #4, [untitled]
    cf 51-LaBarre-11 p 206, Chaconne de Galatée de
                           Mr de lully
    cf 68-d'Anglebert #55, Chaconne de Galatée Mr de
                           Lullӯ

ED: cf Gilbert p 106, Roesgen-Champion p 112.

30 | [COUPERIN (L): <u>Allemande</u> <u>de</u> <u>la</u> <u>paix</u> (e)]

Allemande de la paix Couprin, en. E. si. mi. |Reprise

p 54^1-55^1 ^{C} |9|10|

CO: 35-Bauyn-II #63, Allemande de Mr. Couperin
    cf 64-Lebègue-I #2 [similar Allemande]
    cf 13-Möllersche [similar Allemande]

ED: Curtis-Co #65; cf Brunold/Dart #63, Dufourcq-L p 2.

31 | [COUPERIN (L): <u>Courante</u> (e)]

Courante couprin |Reprise |1.re fois, |d^{re} fois

   p 55$^{2-3}$ $^{3}[^{6}_{4}]$|8|9|

CO: 35-Bauyn-II #64, Courante de Mr Couperin
ED: Curtis-Co #66; cf Brunold/Dart-Co #64.

32 | [COUPERIN (L): <u>Sarabande</u> (e)]

Sarabande couprin |Reprise |2^{e} reprise

   p 56$^{1-3}$ $^{3}[^{3}_{4}]$|8|16|16|

CO: 35-Bauyn-II #65, Sarabande de Monsr. Couperin
ED: Curtis-Co #67; cf Brunold/Dart-Co #65.

33 | p 57^{1}-58^{2} Gigue de Mr Froberger |Reprise

        CO: 24-Babell #107
            35-Bauyn-III #10
            cf 35-Bauyn-III #92

        ED: cf Adler-II p·20, 71, Bonfils-18 p 15,
            Dufourcq-O #7.

34 [CHAMBONNIÈRES: Gigue (e)]

Gigue Chanbonniere
  p 58³-59³   ³|32|27| [³₄|33|29|

CO: 35-Bauyn-I #59, Gigue de Monsr de Chanbonnieres
ED: cf Brunold-Tessier #99.

35 [COUPERIN (L): Prélude (g)]

Prelude couprin en g. re. sol. b mol. |Changement de
mouuement
  p 60¹-64² |-|³[⁶₄]29|-|

CO: 35-Bauyn-II.#3, Prelude de Mr. Couperin
ED: Curtis-Co #92; cf Brunold/Dart #3.

36 [COUPERIN (L): Allemande (g)]

Allemande couprin |Reprise
  p 64³-65³   C|12|13|

CO: 35-Bauyn-II.#92, Allemande de Mr. Couperin
ED: Curtis-Co #93; cf Brunold/Dart-Co #92.

37 | [COUPERIN (L): <u>Courante</u> (g)]

Courante couprin |Reprise

p 66$^{1-3}$ ^{3}[$^6_4$] |8|13|

CO: 35-Bauyn-II #93, Courante de Mr Couperin

ED: Curtis-Co #94; cf Brunold/Dart-Co #93.

38 | [COUPERIN (L): <u>Sarabande</u> (g)]

Sarabande couprin |Reprise

p 67$^{1-3}$ ^{3}[$^3_4$] |8|16|

CO: 35-Bauyn-II #96, Sarabande de Mr. Couperin

ED: Curtis-Co #97; cf Brunold/Dart-Co #96.

39 | [COUPERIN (L): <u>Passacaille</u> (g)]

Passacaille Couprin

p 68^{1}-70^{3} ^{3}|8|8|16|24|8|9|25| [$^3_4$|98|]

CO: 35-Bauyn-II #95, Chaconne ou Passacaille de Mr.
                        Couperin

ED: Curtis-Co #96; cf Brunold/Dart-Co #95.

40 | [CHAMBONNIÈRES: Sarabande (g)]

Sarabande chanbonniere |Reprise
   p 71^1-3   ^3|7|12| [^3_4|8|12|]

CO: 35-Bauyn-I #104, Sarabande de Mr de Chambonnieres
ED: cf Brunold/Tessier #125.

41 | [LULLY, arr d'ANGLEBERT: Courante (g)]

Courante de Mr Lully |Reprise
   p 72^1-3   ^3[^6_4]|9|7|

CO: 33-Rés-89ter #42d, Courante
    46-Ménetou #117, Courante de Mr de lully
    68-d'Anglebert #21, Courante Mr. de Lully
ED: Gilbert p 96, cf p 95; cf Roesgen-Champion p 42.

41a | [d'ANGLEBERT: Double (g)]

Double De La courante Lully |Reprise
   p 73^1-3   ^3[^6_4]|9|7|

CO: 33-Rés-89ter #42e, Double dela Courante
    68-d'Anglebert #21a, Double de la Courante
ED: Gilbert p 97; cf Roesgen-Champion p 43.

42 | [LULLY, arr: <u>Ouverture</u> from <u>Isis</u> (1677) (g)]

Ouuerture disis |Reprise

p 74^1-76^2 ^{C}|15|$[^3_4]$60|

CO: cf 14-Schwerin-619 #51, Ouverture Disis
     cf 24-Babell #128, Ouverture D'Isis
     cf 33-Rés-89ter #42c, Ouuertuor /d'Isis
     cf 40-Rés-476 #35, Louuerture d'Isis
     cf 42-Vm7-6307-2 #5, Ouuerture de Lopera disis
     cf 46-Menetou #85, Ouuerture de lopera Disis
     cf 49-RésF-933 #24, Ouuerture d isis
     cf Stoss ℓ 24v

ED: cf Gilbert p 199, Bonfils-LP p 101, Howell #2.

---

43 | [LULLY, arr: <u>Entrée</u> <u>d'Apollon</u> from <u>Le</u> <u>Triomphe</u> <u>de</u>
<u>l'amour</u> (1681) (g)]

Entreé dapollon

p 76^3-77^3 ^{2}|9|21|

CO: cf 14-Schwerin-619 #56, Ouverture dapollon du
                              Triomphe de Lamour
     cf 24-Babell #129, Entrée d'Apollon
     cf 30-Cecilia ℓ 52r, Dessante dopollon
     cf 46-Menetou #100, entree dappollon
     cf 68-d'Anglebert #35, Air d'Apollon du Triomphe
                            de l'Amour de Mr de Lully
     cf Stockholm-176 ℓ 14v, Entreé d'Apollon
     cf Saizenay-I p 222, Entrée d'Apollon

ED: cf Gilbert p 118, Roesgen-Champion p 64.

44 | [Ah petite brunette (Air ancien) (g)]
ah petite brunette |Reprise
     p 78[1-3]   ¢|4|8|

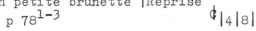

CO: cf Egerton-2514 p 213 (ℓ 107r), ah petit a petit

45 | [COUPERIN (L): Prélude à l'imitation de Mr Froberger
(a)]
Prelude de Mr Couprin alimitation de M[r]. froberger en
a mi la |Changement de mouuement
     p 79[1]-89[3] |-][3]46|-| [|-|[3/4]89|-|]

CO: 35-Bauyn-II #6, Prelude de Monsr. Couperin
    cf 36-Parville #144,[Prélude with identical be-
                         ginning]
ED: Curtis-Co #1; cf Brunold/Dart-Co #6 (lacking 3rd
    section), Dart-Co App I , Curtis-Co #12.

46 | [COUPERIN (L): <u>Prélude</u> (a)]

Prelude en a mi la
p 90^1-91^1 |-|

CO: 35-Bauyn-II #7, Prelude de Monsr Couperin
ED: Curtis-Co #7; cf Brunold/Dart-Co #7.

47 | [COUPERIN (L): <u>Allemande</u> (a)]

ALLemande Couprin |Reprise
p 92^1-93^3 ^{C}|9|9|

CO: 35-Bauyn-II #102, Allemande de Mr. Couperin
      40-Rés-476 #29, Allemande
      47-Gen-2356 #3, L'aimable allemande de Mr Couperin
ED: Curtis-Co #2; cf Brunold/Dart-Co #102, Bonfils-LP
      p 94.

48 | [COUPERIN (L): <u>Courante</u> <u>la</u> <u>mignonne</u> (a)]

Courante Couprin dit la mignonne |Reprise
p 94$^{1-3}$ ^{3}[$^6_4$]|6|8|

CO: 35-Bauyn-II #106, Courante de Mr. Couperin

47-Gen-2356 #4, La mignonne Du mesme Mr Couperin
ED: Curtis-Co #3; cf Brunold/Dart-Co #106.

---

49 | [RICHARD: <u>Courante</u> (a)]

Courante Richard |Reprise

p 95¹⁻³ $^3[{}^6_4]$|7|8|

CO: 35-Bauyn-III #70, Courante de Mr. Richard
ED: cf Bonfils-18 p 19, Dufourcq-O #1.

---

50 | [COUPERIN (L): <u>Sarabande</u> (a)]

Sarabande couprin |Reprise

p 96¹⁻³ $[{}^3_4]$|8|16|

CO: 32-Oldham #109, Sarabande Couperin
35-Bauyn-II #110, Sarabande de Mr. Couperin
ED: Curtis-Co #5; cf Brunold/Dart-Co #110.

---

51 | [<u>Gavotte</u> <u>le</u> <u>dieu</u> <u>qui</u> <u>nous</u> <u>engage</u> (a)]

Gauotte le Dieu qui /nous engage |Reprise

p 97¹⁻³   ¢|6|10|

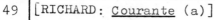

52 | [HARDEL: <u>Gavotte</u> (a)]

Gauotte de Mr Hardel |Reprise
  p 98^{1-3}   ¢|4|8|

CO: 23-Tenbury #12, Gavotte Mr. Hardel
    24-Babell #159, Gavotte
    25-Bod-426 #20, Gavotte d'Ardelle
    31-Madrid-1360 #41, Jabouste de Ardel
    35-Bauyn-III #50, (Gauotte) de Mr Hardel
    45-Dart #60, Gauotte de Monsr Ardel
    49-RésF-933 #13, gavotte d ardelle
    St-Georges ℓ 52, Gavotte
    cf Saizenay-I p 61, Gavotte Ardelle [lute]
    cf Saizenay-II p 17, Gavotte d'hardelle [lute]
    cf Vm7-4867 p 52, Gavotte d'ardelle [violin]
ED: Curtis-Co #11; cf Brunold/Dart-Co #131, Quittard-H p 1.

52a | [COUPERIN (L): <u>Double</u> (a)]

Double de la gauotte fait par Mr Couprin |Reprise
  p 99^{1-3}   ¢|8|15|

CO: 23-Tenbury #12a, Double
    24-Babell #159a, Double
    31-Madrid-1360 #41a, [Double]
    35-Bauyn-III #50a, Double (de la gauotte) cy dessus
                         Par Mr Couperin
    49-RésF-933 #13a, [Double]
    cf Vm7-4867 p 77, Double [violin]

ED: Curtis-Co #11A; cf Brunold/Dart-Co #131[a],
    Quittard-H p 2.

53 | [COUPERIN (L)?: <u>Menuet</u> <u>de</u> <u>Poitou</u> (a)]

Menüet de Poiètou |Reprise

p 100^{1-3} ^{3}|6|11| [$\frac{3}{4}$|6|12|]

CO: 35-Bauyn-II #112, (Menuet) de Mr. Couperin
    35-Bauyn-III #78 (Menuet) de Poitou
ED: Curtis-Co #18; cf Brunold/Dart-Co #112, 133.

53a | [COUPERIN (L): <u>Double</u> (a)]

Double du menüet fait par Mr Couperin |Reprise

p 101^{1-3} ^{3}[$\frac{3}{4}$]|6|12|

CO: 35-Bauyn-II #112a, Double
    35-Bauyn-III #78a, Double par Mr Couperin
ED: Curtis-Co #18A; cf Brunold/Dart-Co #112[a], 133[a].

54 | [LA BARRE: <u>Allemande</u> (a)]

Courante [sic] de M^r dela Barre |Reprise

p 102^1-103^1   ᶜ|8|10|

55 | [LA BARRE: <u>Courante</u> (a)]
([crossed out:] Gigue de M[r] delabarre [cf #56]) /Courante de M. de la barre |Reprise
p 104[1]-105[1] ^{3}|13|19| [$^3_4$|14|20|]

CO: 35-Bauyn-III #69, Courante de Mr De la barre
ED: cf Bonfils-18 p 26.

56 | [LA BARRE: <u>Gigue</u> (a)]
([crossed out:] Passacaille du Seigneur de Louigy [cf #57]) /Gigue de M[r] de la barre |Reprise
p 106[1]-107[3] ^{3}|25|30| [$^3_4$|26|31|]

57 | p 108[1]-109[3] Passacaille du Seigneur de Louigy [ROSSI (a)]
CO: 23-Tenbury #11
24-Babell #166
35-Bauyn-III #91
ED: cf Pierront p 6, Prunières p 18.

58 | [COUPERIN (L): <u>Prélude</u> (C)]

Prelude en C Sol vt Couprin
    p 110^1-113^2 |-|

CO: 35-Bauyn-II #10, Prelude de Mr. Couperin
ED: Curtis-Co #28; cf Brunold/Dart-Co #10.

59 | [COUPERIN (L): <u>Prélude</u> (C)]

Prelude Couprin
    p 114^1-115^3 |-|

CO: 35-Bauyn-II #11, Prelude de Mr. Couperin
ED: Curtis-Co #22; cf Brunold/Dart-Co #11.

60 | [CHAMBONNIÈRES: <u>Allemande le moutier</u> (C)]

Allemande le moutier de Mr Chambonniere |Reprise
    p 116^1-117^3 ¢|11|.11|

CO: 24-Babell #200, Allemande
     32-Oldham #22, Le Moutie et la **Mariée**
     35-Bauyn-I #1, Allemande de Mr Chambonnieres Le
           Moutier

ED: Curtis-Co #29; cf Brunold-Tessier #61, Brunold/
    Dart-Co #134.

60a | [COUPERIN (L): <u>Double</u> (C)]

Le Double du moutier fait par Mr Couprin |**Reprise**
  p 118[1]-119[3]   ¢ |11|11|

CO: 35-Bauyn-I #1a, Double du Moutier par Mr Couperin
    cf 24-Babell.#200a, Double de la mesme
ED: Curtis-Co #29A; cf Brunold/Dart-Co #134[a],
    Brunold-Tessier #61.

61 | [CHAMBONNIÈRES: <u>Courante Iris</u> (C)]

Courante Chanbonniere |Reprise
  p 120[1-3]   3[6 4] |8|8|

CO: 8-Hintze #15, Courante
    22a-Roper #58, Courante Chambonniere...double
    23-Tenbury #3, (courante chambonii)
    24-Babell #58, Courante de Mr. de Chambonniere
    33-Rés-89ter #2, Courante. Chambonnieres...Double
    35-Bauyn-I #9, Courante de Mr De Chambonnieres
    44-LaPierre p 18, p 34A, Courante Chambonniere...**Double**
    47-Gen-2356 #12, Courante
    53-Oldham-2 p 107, **Courante de Chamboniere**
    55-Redon #23, Courante de Monsieur de Chambonniere
    62-Chamb-I #8, Courante Iris
    cf 32-Oldham #17, Double de La Courante Iris

ED: cf Brunold-Tessier #8, Dart-Ch #8, Gilbert p 148.

62 | [CHAMBONNIÈRES: <u>Courante</u> (C)]

Courante Chanbonniere |Reprise

p 121$^{1-3}$ ^{3}|7|7| [$^6_4$|6|7|]

CO: 22a-Roper #59, 2me Courante...double
     33-Rés-89ter #3, Courante Chambonnieres ... Double
     35-Bauyn-I #23, Courante de Mr. Chambonnieres
     62-Chamb-I #9, Courante

ED: cf Brunold-Tessier #9, Dart-Ch #9, **Gilbert p 150.**

63 | [CHAMBONNIÈRES: <u>Courante</u> (C)]

Courante Chanbonniere |Reprise

p 122$^{1-3}$ ^{3}[$^6_4$]|6|7|

64 | [PINEL, arr: <u>Sarabande</u> (C)]

Sarabande de M^r pignel |Reprise

p 123$^{1-3}$ ^{3}|4|7| [$^6_4$|4|6|]

CO: **35-Bauyn-III** #90, Sarabande de Mr. Pinel
     47-Gen-2356 #13, Sarabande
     cf 33-Rés-89ter #4, Sarabande Pinel ... Double

ED: cf Gilbert p 152.

65 | [d'ANGLEBERT: <u>Chaconne</u> (C)]

1er couplet Chaconne Danglebert |2e [etc] 12^e

   p 124^1-125^3 ^{3}|4|4|[etc] [$\frac{3}{4}$|4| x 11]

CO: 24-Babell #204, Chaconne
    33-Rés-89ter #7, Chaconne. D'Anglebert
    45-Dart #39, Chaconne
    51-LaBarre-11 p 212, Chaconne de Mr D'anglebert
    51-LaBarre-11 p 229, Chaconne D'Anglebert

ED: cf Gilbert p 160, Roesgen-Champion p 148.

---

66 | [LULLY, arr: <u>Chaconne</u> from <u>Amadis</u> (1684) V-5 (C)]

Chaconne damadis |fin de la Chaconne

   p 126^1-137^3 ^{3}|295| [$\frac{3}{4}$|297|]

CO: cf 24-Babell #209, Chaconne d'Amadis

---

67 | [**LULLY, arr: Air from Acis et Galathée** (1686) **Prologue** (C)]

Riguaudon |Reprise |Suitte du Riguaudon |Reprise

   p 138^1-139^2 ¢|4|6|2|4|

CO: 22a-Roper #51, 53, La Rigaudoe, Le Rigodon
    44-LaPierre p 14, 25A, Rigaudon
    cf 45-Dart #37, Rigodon de Galateé

ED: Curtis-Co #32.

67a | [COUPERIN (L): <u>Double</u> (C)]

Double du Riguaudon fait par Mr Couprain |Reprise
|Suitte |Reprise
   p 140^1-141^3 ¢|4|6|2|4|

ED: Curtis-Co #32A.

68 | [LEBÈGUE: <u>Gavotte</u> (C)]

Gauotte M^r le Begue |Reprise
   p 142$^{1-3}$ ¢|4|8|

CO: 10-Schwerin-617 #10, Gavotte
    13-Möllersche, [copy of 64-Lebègue-I #43]
    14-Schwerin-619 #91, Gavotte
    21-Rés-1186bis #12, Gavott
    23-Tenbury #6, Gavotte Mr Le Begue
    24-Babell #60, Gavotte de Mr. le Begue
    30-Cecilia ℓ 47r, Gavotte
    35-Bauyn-III #54, (Gavotte) de Mr Lebegue
    45-Dart #22, [copy of 64-Lebègue-I #43]
    46-Menetou #102, Gavotte
    50-Paignon #11, Balet de Mr lebegue
    64-Lebègue-I #43, Gauotte

ED: cf Brunold/Dart-Co #132, Dufourcq-L p 38.

68a [Double (C)]
 [untitled; hand G]
   p 143^{1-3}   ¢|4|8|

CO: cf 13-Möllersche, [copy of 64-Lebègue-I #43a]
    cf 14-Schwerin-619 #91a [Double]
    cf 23-Tenbury #6a, Double
    cf 24-Babell #60a, Double
    cf 35-Bauyn-III #54a, Double par Mr Couperin
    cf 36-Parville #146, Double de la Gavotte de Le
                        Bègue
    cf 50-Paignon #11a, la double
    cf 64-Lebègue-I #43a, Double
ED: cf Dufourcq-L p 38, Brunold/Dart-Co #132[a].

69 [COUPERIN (L): Prélude (c)]
 Prelude en C Sol vt b.mol Couprain
   p 144^{1}-145^{3} |-|

ED: Curtis-Co #33.

70 | [COUPERIN (L): <u>Allemande la précieuse</u> (c)]

La precieuse Suitte Allemande en c Sol.vt b.mol

†Reprise

p 146^1-147^3 ^{C}|8|10| [$^4_4$|8|9|]

CO: 35-Bauyn-II #30, Allemande de M^r. Couperin

ED: Curtis-Co #34; cf Brunold/Dart-Co #30.

71 | [COUPERIN (L): <u>Courante</u> (c)]

Courante Couprin |Reprise

p 148^1-149^3 ^{3}[$^6_4$]|10|10|

CO: 35-Bauyn-II #31, Courante de M^r. Couperin

ED: Curtis-Co #35; cf Brunold/Dart-Co #31.

72 | [COUPERIN (L): <u>Sarabande</u> (c)]

Sarabande Couprin |Reprise

p 150^1-151^2 ^{3}[$^3_4$]|8|16|

CO: 35-Bauyn-II #32, Sarabande de Mr. Couperin

ED: Curtis-Co #36; cf Brunold/Dart-Co #32.

73 | [COUPERIN (L): <u>Gigue</u> (c)]
Gigue Couprin |Reprise
　p 152^1-153^3　　　　　　$^3[^6_4]$|12|16|

CO: 35-Bauyn-II #33, Gigue de Monsr. Couperin
ED: Curtis-Co #37; cf Brunold/Dart-Co #33.

74 | [COUPERIN (L): <u>Chaconne</u> <u>la</u> <u>bergeronette</u> (c)]
Chaconne Couprin dit la bergeronette
　p 154^1-155^3　　　　　　$^3[^3_4]$|8|8|8|8|8|

CO: 35-Bauyn-II #34, Chaconne de Mr Couperin
ED: Curtis-Co #38; cf Brunold/Dart-Co #34.

75 | [COUPERIN (L): <u>Prélude</u> (F)]
Prelude du 6e en Et f. vt fa b:mol Couprin
　p 156^1-159^1　　　　　　|-|$^3[^6_4]$10|-|

CO: 35-Bauyn-II #12, Prelude de Mr. Couperin
ED: Curtis-Co #76; cf Brunold/Dart-Co #12.

76 | [COUPERIN (L): <u>Prélude</u> (F)]

Autre prelude du 6ᵉ

    p 159¹-163² |-|

CO: 35-Bauyn-II #13, Prelude De Mr Couperin
ED: Curtis-Co #68; cf Brunold/Dart-Co #13.

---

77 | [COUPERIN (L): <u>Allemande</u> <u>grave</u> (F)]

ALlemande graue Couprin |Reprise |derniere fin |pour
la Reprise
    p 164¹-165³   ᶜ|9|9|

CO: 35-Bauyn-II #67, Allemande graue de Mr Couperin
ED: Curtis-Co #69; cf Brunold/Dart-Co #67.

---

78 | [COUPERIN (L): <u>Courante</u> (F)]

Courante Couprin |Reprise |po la rep: po La fin
    p 166¹⁻³   3[⁶₄]|6|9|

CO: 35-Bauyn-II #68, Courante de Mr Couperin
ED: Curtis-Co #70; cf Brunold/Dart-Co #68.

79 | [CHAMBONNIÈRES: <u>Courante</u> (F)]

Courante Chanbonniere |Reprise
   p 167$^{1-3}$ $^3[^6_4]$|7|10|

CO: 35-Bauyn-I #70, 71, Courante de Mr. de Chambon-
                                 nieres
    36-Parville #82, Courante chanbonniere
ED: cf Brunold-Tessier #105.

80 | [CHAMBONNIÈRES: <u>Volte</u> (<u>Sarabande</u>) <u>o beau jardin</u> (F)]

Volte Chanbonniere |Reprise
   p 168$^{1-3}$ ^{3}|6|7| [$^3_4$|8|12|]

CO: 33-Rés-89ter #22, O beau Jardin. Sarabande...Double
    35-Bauyn-I #80, Volte de Mr. de Chambonnieres
    cf Philidor p 23, O Beau Jardin de Mr de chan-
                                 bonniere [for instruments]
ED: cf Brunold-Tessier #110, p 119; cf Gilbert p 179.

81 | [CHAMBONNIÈRES: Sarabande (F)]

Sarabande Chanbonniere |Reprise
    p 169$^{1-3}$ $^3[\frac{3}{4}]$ |8|12|

CO: 35-Bauyn-I #79, Sarabande du même Auteur
    62-Chamb-I #23, Sarabande
ED: cf Brunold-Tessier #23, Dart-Ch #23.

82 | [CHAMBONNIÈRES: Courante (F)]

Courante chanbonniere |Reprise
    p 170$^{1-3}$ $^3[\frac{6}{4}]$ |7|8|

CO: 35-Bauyn-I #70, 71, Courante de Mr. de Chambon-
                                  nieres
    36-Parville #79, Courante Chanbonniere
ED: cf Brunold-Tessier #105.

83 | [LA BARRE: Courante (F)]

Courante la barre |Reprise
    p 171$^{1-3}$ $^3[\frac{6}{4}]$ |8|8|

84 | [COUPERIN (L): <u>Gaillarde</u> (F)]

Gaillarde Couprin |Reprise

   p 172^1-173^1 ^{3}[$^3_4$]|8|16|

CO: 35-Bauyn-II #77, (Gaillarde) du même Auteur

ED: Curtis-Co #74; cf Brunold/Dart-Co #77.

---

85 | [COUPERIN (L): <u>Sarabande</u> (F)]

Sarabande couprin |Reprise

   p 173$^{1-3}$ ^{3}|5|9| [$^6_4$|4|8|]

CO: 35-Bauyn-II #72, Sarabande de Mr Couperin

ED: Curtis-Co #71; cf Brunold/Dart-Co #72.

---

86 | [CHAMBONNIÈRES: <u>Chaconne</u> (F)]

Chaconne Chanbonniere |2^e |3^e

   p 174$^{1-3}$ ^{3}|9|4|7| [$^3_4$|9|4|8|]

CO: 35-Bauyn-I #83, Chaconne du même Auteur

ED: cf Brunold-Tessier #113.

---

p 175   [blank, ruled]

87 | [COUPERIN (L): <u>Prélude</u> (G)]

Prelude en g re Sol Couprin

    p 176^1-177^2 |-|

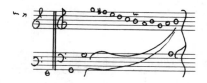

ED: Curtis-Co #85.

---

88 | [COUPERIN (L): <u>Allemande</u> (G)]

Allemande Couprin |Reprise

    p 178^1-179^3 C|9|9|

CO: 24-Babell #252, Allemande
     33-Rés-89ter #33, Allemande Couperin ... Double
     35-Bauyn-II #82, Allemande du même Auteur
     47-Gen-2356 #5, **Allemande Du mesme Mr Couperin**

ED: Curtis-Co #86; cf Brunold/Dart-Co #82, Gilbert p186.

---

89 | [COUPERIN (L): <u>Courante</u> (G)]

(ALLem [written over to read:]) Courante Couprin
|Reprise

    p 180$^{1-3}$ $^3[^6_4]$|8|8|

CO: 24-Babell #253, Courante

35-Bauyn-II #84, Courante du meme Auteur

ED: Curtis-Co #87; Brunold/Dart-Co #84.

90 | [CHAMBONNIÈRES: <u>Courante</u> (G)]

Courante Chanbonniere |Reprise

p 181$^{1-3}$ $^3[^6_4]$ |8|8|

CO: 32-Oldham #9, Courante De Monsieur de Chambonnieres
35-Bauyn-I #88, Courante de Mr de Chambonnieres
38-Gen-2348/53 #36, Courante
63-Chamb-II #27, Courante

ED: cf Brunold-Tessier #57, Dart-Ch #57.

91 | [CHAMBONNIÈRES: <u>Courante</u> (G)]

Courante Chanbonniere |Reprise

p 182$^{1-3}$ $^3[^6_4]$ |7|10|

CO: 32-Oldham #7, Courante de Monsieur de chambonnieres
33-Rés-89ter #35, Courante Chambonnieres ...
Double
35-Bauyn-I #91, Courante de Mr. de Chambonnieres
38-Gen-2348/53 #33, Courante
63-Chamb-II #28, Courante

ED: cf Brunold-Tessier #58, Dart-Ch #58, Gilbert p
192.

92 | [CHAMBONNIÈRES: <u>Courante</u> (G)]

Courante Chanbonniere |Reprise
    p 183$^{1-3}$ ^{3}[$^6_4$] |8|9|

CO: 23-Tenbury #40, Courante Chambonniere
    24-Babell #87, Courante de Chre.
    32-Oldham #19, Courante
    33-Rés-89ter #34, Courante Chambonnieres ... Double
    35-Bauyn-I #92, Courante de Mr. de Chambonnieres
    63-Chamb-II #26, Courante

ED: cf Brunold-Tessier #56, Dart-Ch #56, Gilbert p 190.

93 | [CHAMBONNIÈRES: <u>Sarabande jeunes zéphirs</u> (G)]

Sarabande Chanbonniere |Reprise
    p 184$^{1-3}$ ^{3}|8|15| [$^3_4$|8|16|]]

CO: 5-Munich-1503ℓ #1, Sarrabande de Mons: Chambonnier
    32-Oldham #8, Sarabande de Monsieur de Chambon-
                 nieres
    33-Rés-89ter #36, Sarabande Chambonnieres ...
                 Double
    35-Bauyn-I #96, Sarabande de Mr de Chambonnieres
    44-LaPierre p 42, Les Zephirs de Mr de Chanboniere
    45-Dart #55, Sarabande de chambonniere
    63-Chamb-II #29, Sarabande Jeunes Zephirs
    cf Philidor p 22, Jeunes Zephirs (de Mr de chan-
                 boniere) [for instruments]

ED: cf Brunold-Tessier #59, Dart-Ch #59, Gilbert p
    194.

94 | [CHAMBONNIÈRES: Sarabande (G)]

Sarabande Chanbonniere |Reprise

p 185[1-3]   3[3/4] |8|16|

CO: 35-Bauyn-I #97, Sarabande du même Auteur
ED: cf Brunold-Tessier #121.

95 | [CHAMBONNIÈRES: Gigue (G)]

Gigue chanbonniere |Reprise

p 186[1]-187[3]   3|13|13| [6/4|13|12|]

CO: 35-Bauyn-I #100, Gigue de Mr. de Chambonnieres
ED: cf Brunold-Tessier #122.

96 | [CHAMBONNIÈRES: Canarie (G)]

Canaries Chanbonniere |Reprise

- p 188[1]-189[1]   3[6/4] |8|12|

CO: 35-Bauyn-I #99, Canaries de Mr. de Chambonnieres
    38-Gen-2348/53 #25, Canaries
    62-Chamb-I #30, Canaris
ED: cf Brunold-Tessier #30, Dart-Ch #30.

97 | [RICHARD: <u>Courante</u> (G)]

Courante Richard |Reprise
   p 190$^{1-3}$ $^3[{}^6_4]|8|8|$

98 | [COUPERIN (L): <u>Sarabande</u> (G)]

Sarabande Couprin |Reprise
   p 191$^{1-3}$ $^3[{}^3_4]|8|16|$

CO: 24-Babell #254, Sarabande
    35-Bauyn-II #87, Sarabande de Mr. Couperin
ED: Curtis-Co #89; cf Brunold/Dart-Co #87.

99 | [COUPERIN (L): <u>Chaconne</u> (G)]

Chaconne Couprin |1er Couplet [etc] |10
   p 192^1-195^3 $^3|4|4|8|$[etc] $[{}^3_4|99|]$

CO: 35-Bauyn-II #89, Chaconne de Mr. Couperin
ED: Curtis-Co #91; cf Brunold/Dart-Co #89.

100 | [COUPERIN (L): <u>Gaillarde</u> (G)]

Gaillarde de Monsieur Couperin |Reprise

p 196^1-197^2 $^3[^6_4]$|8|8|3|

CO: 35-Bauyn-II.#88, (Gaillarde) de Mr Couperin
ED: Curtis-Co #90; cf Brunold/Dart-Co #88.

---

101 | [COUPERIN (L): <u>Prélude</u> (e)]

Prelude en.E Si mi grand b#

p 198^1-199^3 |-|

CO: 35-Bauyn-II #14, Prelude de Mr. Couperin
ED: Curtis-Co #64; cf Brunold/Dart-Co #14.

---

102 | [COUPERIN (L): <u>Allemande</u> (b)]

Allemande Couprin en E Si mi b# |Reprise

p 200^1-201^2 ^{C}|9|9|

CO: 35-Bauyn-II #116, Allemande de Mr Couperin
ED: Curtis-Co #19; cf Brunold/Dart-Co #116.

103 | [COUPERIN (L): <u>Courante</u> (b)]

Courante Couprin |Reprise
p 202¹-203¹ $^3[^6_4]$ |8|9|

CO: 35-Bauyn-II #117, Courante du même Auteur
ED: Curtis-Co #20; cf Brunold/Dart-Co #117.

104 | [COUPERIN (L): <u>Sarabande</u> (b)]

Sarabande Couprin
p 203²⁻³ $^3[^3_4]$ |8|12|

CO: 35-Bauyn-II #118, Sarabande de Mr. Couperin
ED: Curtis-Co #21; cf Brunold/Dart-Co #118.

105 | [<u>Prélude</u> (C)]

Prelude C. sol. ut |fin
p 204¹-205³ |-|

106 | [Prélude (F)]

Prelude f ut fa. |fin

p 206^1-207^3 |-|

107 | [Prélude (G)]

Prelude G re sol ♮ |fin

p 208^1-209^3 |-|

108 | [LULLY, arr: Passepied (unlocated) (G)]

Passepied de Lully |pr recom-/mencer |fin

p 210$^{1-3}$ $^3[\frac{3}{8}]$|8|8|

109 [LULLY, arr d'ANGLEBERT: <u>Menuet dans nos bois</u> from
<u>Trios pour le coucher du roi</u> (G)]

Menuet dans nos bois. Mr de Lully. |fin
 p 211$^{1-3}$ ^{3}[$^3_4$]|8|16|

CO: 51-LaBarre-11 p 205, Dans nos bois de Mr de lully
  68-d'Anglebert #14, Menuet. dans nos bois Mr de
            Lully
  cf 27-Gresse #20, Air Dans un bois
  cf 27-Gresse #52, [untitled]
ED: cf Gilbert p 112, Roesgen-Champion p 29.

110 [LULLY, arr: <u>Vous ne devez plus attendre</u> from <u>Amadis</u>
(1684) II-7 (g)]

Trio d'Amadis /vous ne devez plus attendre |fin
 p 212^1-213^3 ^{3}[$^3_4$]|6|30|

CO: cf 10-Schwerin-617 #19, Menuet
  cf 46-Menetou #20, vous ne deuez pas ...
  cf 46-Menetou #39, vous ne devez plus attandre
  cf 42-Vm7-6307-2 #8, Menuet de Lopera d'amadis
  cf 49-RésF-933 #23, vous ne devés plus attendre

[1 ℓ cut out of volume between p 212 & 213 before
#110 was entered]

111 | [LULLY, arr: <u>Aimons</u>, <u>aimons</u> from <u>Thésée</u> (1675) IV-7
(C)]
Trio de Theseé /aimons nous
    p 214$^{1-3}$ $^3[{}^3_4]$|13|12|

___

112 | [LULLY, arr: <u>Menuet</u> from **Proserpine** (1680) Prologue
(d)]
Menuet.
    p 215$^{1-3}$ $^3[{}^3_4]$|6|10|

___

113 | [Anon, arr: <u>Rigaudon</u> (g)]
Rigaudon
    p 216$^{1-3}$ ¢|8|12|

CO: cf 22a-Roper #30, Rigaudon [d]
    cf 44-LaPierre p 59A, Rigaudon des Veissaux
    cf 45-Dart #67, Rigaudon de la marine
    cf 48-LaBarre-6 #27, Rigaudon [d]

114 | [Anon, arr: <u>Rigaudon</u> (g)]

2^e Rigaudon

     p 217¹⁻³   ¢ |8|12|

CO: cf 44-LaPierre p 61A, Second Rigaudon
     cf 48-LaBarre-6 #28, 2e Rigaudon [d]

115 | [LULLY, arr: <u>Second</u> <u>Air</u> (<u>Sourdines</u>) from <u>Armide</u> (1686)

II-4 (g)]

Air d'Armide

     p 218¹-219² $\frac{6}{4}$ |7|12|

CO: cf 14-Schwerin-619 #64, Sourdinet damide
     cf 23-Tenbury #49, Air d'Armide
     cf 24-Babell #124, Air d'Armide Sourdines tres Doux
     cf 36-Parville #149, Sourdines de'Amide
     cf 49-RésF-933 #2, Sourdines d'Armide
     cf 68-d'Anglebert #33, Les Sourdines d'Armide
ED: cf Gilbert p 115, Roesgen-Champion p 62.

116 | [LULLY, arr: <u>Chaconne</u> from <u>Ballet des muses</u> (1666) II-2 (Bb)]

Air des Sorciers
  p 220^1-221^2 $^3[\frac{3}{4}]|30|$

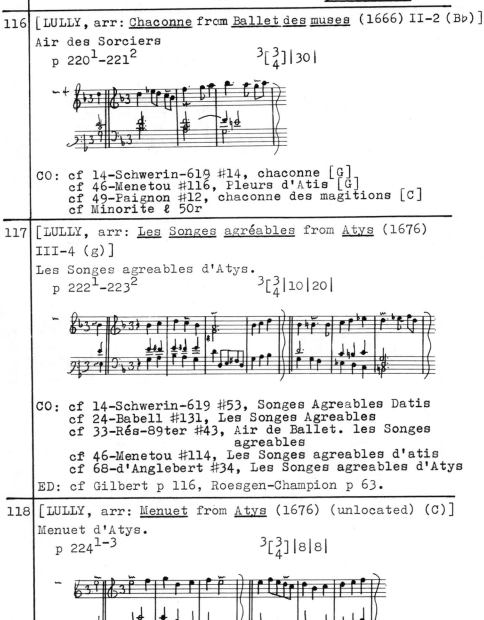

CO: cf 14-Schwerin-619 #14, chaconne [G]
   cf 46-Menetou #116, Pleurs d'Atis [G]
   cf 49-Paignon #12, chaconne des magitions [C]
   cf Minorite ℓ 50r

117 | [LULLY, arr: <u>Les Songes agréables</u> from <u>Atys</u> (1676)

III-4 (g)]

Les Songes agreables d'Atys.
  p 222^1-223^2 $^3[\frac{3}{4}|10|20|$

CO: cf 14-Schwerin-619 #53, Songes Agreables Datis
   cf 24-Babell #131, Les Songes Agreables
   cf 33-Rés-89ter #43, Air de Ballet. les Songes
           agreables
   cf 46-Menetou #114, Les Songes agreables d'atis
   cf 68-d'Anglebert #34, Les Songes agreables d'Atys
ED: cf Gilbert p 116, Roesgen-Champion p 63.

118 | [LULLY, arr: <u>Menuet</u> from <u>Atys</u> (1676) (unlocated) (C)]

Menuet d'Atys.
  p 224$^{1-3}$ $^3[\frac{3}{4}]|8|8|$

119 | [Les Sacrificateurs (a)]

Les Sacrificateurs.

p 225$^{1-3}$ $^3[\frac{3}{4}]|11|12|$

120 | [LULLY, arr: Haubois (passepied) from Persée (1682)
Prologue (a)]

Passepied de Persée

p 226^1-227^2 $\frac{3}{8}|32|$

CO: 46-Menetou #97, passepied

121 | [LULLY, arr: Ouverture from La Grotte de Versailles
(1668) (g)]

Ouuerture de la grotte de Versailles

p 228^1-229^3 $\mathcal{C}|10|[\frac{3}{4}]33|\mathcal{C}5|$

CO: cf 14-Schwerin-619 #121, Ouverture de La Grotte de
                                Versaille
     cf 46-Menetou #118, La grotte de Versaille
     cf 49-RésF-933 #3, Ouuerture de la Grote de Ver-

saille

cf Minorite ℓ 44r, De Mr Baptiste de Lulli Ouuer-
            ture La Grotte de Versaille
    cf Saizenay-I p 226, La Grotte de Versailles [lute]
ED: cf Strizich p 104.

---

122 [LULLY, arr: La Mariée from Roland (1685) (unlocated)
(G)]

La Mariée
     p 230[1]-231[2]   ¢|14|12|

CO: cf 14-Schwerin-619 #62, La Mariee De Roland
    cf 22a-Roper #19, Air de L'opera
    cf 45-Dart #34, La Mariée
    cf 45-Dart #65, la marie de rolant

---

123 [LULLY, arr: Premier Air pour les suivants de Mars
from Psyché (1678) V-4 (C)]

Les fanfares de Psiché |fin
     p 232[1-3]   ¢8|8|8|

CO: cf 36-Parville #147, Les Trompettes de Psiché
    cf 39-Vm7-6307-1 #12 Les grandes Trompettes a
                         Deux Choeurs en Rondeau

124 | [LULLY, arr: Menuet from Ballet de Flore (1669) XV (C)]

Menuet

   p 233$^{1-3}$ $^{3}[\frac{3}{4}]|8|12|$

CO: cf 9-Ihre-284 #88, Minoit InTavolat de Joh. Laurent
    cf 27-Gresse #9, Leminuetté
ED: cf Lundgren #39.

125 | [LULLY, arr: L'Amour plaist from Thésée (1675) IV-7
(C)]

Menuet

   p 234$^{1-3}$ $^{3}[\frac{3}{4}]|8|8|$

126 | [Anon, arr: Menuet en Rondeau (C)]

Menuet en Rondeau. |fin

   p 233$^{1-3}$ $^{3}[\frac{3}{4}]|8|8|4|$

CO: cf Lüneburg-1198 p 74, Menuet

127 [LULLY, arr: <u>Deuxieme</u> <u>Air</u> <u>pour</u> <u>les</u> <u>muses</u> from <u>Isis</u>
(1677) Prologue-3 (g)]

Menuet
   p 236^1-237^2 $^3[\frac{3}{4}]$|8|16|

CO: cf 40-Rés-476 #38, Menüet
ED: cf Bonfils-LP p 104, Howell #5.

128 [LULLY, arr: <u>Premier</u> <u>Air</u> <u>pour</u> <u>la</u> <u>jeunesse</u> from <u>Le</u>
<u>Triomphe</u> <u>de</u> <u>l'amour</u> (1681) (g)]

Air pour la Jeunesse
   p 238^1-239^3 $^3[\frac{3}{4}]$|33|

CO: cf 24-Babell #135, Air pour la Jeunesse

129 [Anon, arr: <u>Gigue</u> <u>du</u> <u>Prince</u> <u>d'Orange</u> (G)]

Gigue de prince d'Orange
   p 240$^{1-3}$ $\frac{6}{4}$|4|8|

CO: cf 30-Cecilia ℓ 52v, Marche du Prince d'orange

130 [LULLY, arr: 1er Air des Espagnols from Le Bourgeois
Gentilhomme (1670) Nations-3 (B♭)]

Les Espagnols |fin
   p 241¹⁻³ ${}^3[\frac{3}{4}]$ |5|4|8|

CO: cf 23-Tenbury #80, Les Espagnols (lully)
    cf 24-Babell #269, Les Espagnols
    cf 50-Paignon #10, Sarabande espagnol [C]
    cf Saizenay-I p 287, Entrée des Espagnols de Mr
                         de Lully

131 [LULLY, arr: Trompettes (Mars) from Thésée (1675)
Prologue (C)]

La descente de Mars |fin
   p 242¹⁻³ ${}^3[\frac{3}{4}]$ |6|8|5|3|

CO: cf 14-Schwerin-619 #69, Descente De Mars De Thesee
    cf 44-LaPierre p 44, 20A, Descente de Mars

132 [LULLY, arr: Haubois from Thésée (1675) Prologue (C)]

Menuet

   p 243[1-3] $^3[\frac{3}{4}]|7|12|$

CO: cf 14-Schwerin-619 #71, Menuet
    cf 25-Bod-426 #7, Menuet
    cf 44-LaPierre p 22A, menuet

---

133 [LULLY, arr: Marche from Thésée (1675) I-8 (C)]

La Marche de Theseé |fin |au commencem

   p 244[1]-245[2] $\mathsf{C}\!\!\!|\,|9|8|8|$

CO: cf 14-Schwerin-619 #72, Sacrifiee de Thesee
    cf 40-Rés-476 #42, La Marche
    cf 44-LaPierre p 23A, Marche
ED: cf Bonfils-LP p 109, Howell #9.

---

134 [Entrée (g)]

Entrée

   p 246[1]-247[2] $^3[\frac{3}{4}]|12|16|$

135 | [Entrée (g)]

Entrée
　　p 248[1]-249[2]　　　　　　　　　¢|10|10|

136 | [Gavotte (B♭)]

Gauotte
　　p 250[1-3]　　　　　　　　　²[4/4]|4|8|

137 | [Menuet en Rondeau (B♭)]

Menuet en Rondeau |fin
　　p 251[1-3]　　　　　　　　　³[3/4]|7|19|

138 | [GAULTIER (P), arr: **Les Plaisirs** (g)]

Les /plesirs /de /Gautier
p 252^1-253^1 $^3[\frac{3}{4}]$ |9|22|

CO: cf 14-Schwerin-619 #54, Les plaisirs de Gautier
    cf 14-Schwerin-619 #57, Les Plaisirs de Gautier
    cf 45-Dart #44, les plaisirs de Gautier
    cf Gaultier p 35, Les plaisirs [for instruments]

139 | [Rigaudon (g)]

Rigodon
p 254^{1-3}   ₵ |8|12|

140 | [GAULTIER (P?): Rigaudon (a)]

Rigodon /de Gautier
p 255^{1-3}   ₵ |8|16|

141 [LULLY, arr d'ANGLEBERT: <u>Sarabande</u>, <u>dieu</u> <u>des</u> <u>enfers</u>
from <u>Ballet</u> <u>de</u> <u>la</u> <u>naissance</u> <u>de</u> <u>Vénus</u> (1665) II-6 (g)]
Dieu /des /Enfers |1 fois |2 fois
   p 256^1-257^1 $^3[^3_4]$|8|16|

CO: 68-d'Anglebert #23, Sarabande Dieu des Enfers.
                     Mr de Lully
    cf 24-Babell #247, 2me. Sarabande
ED: cf Gilbert p 98, Roesgen-Champion p 45.

142 [d'ANGLEBERT: <u>La</u> <u>Bergère</u> <u>Anette</u> (Vaudeville) (g)]
La /Ber/gere /Anette.
   p 257$^{2-3}$ $^3[^3_4]$|6|18|

CO: 68-d'Anglebert #31, La Bergere Anette
ED: cf Gilbert p 122, Roesgen-Champion p 59.

143 [d'ANGLEBERT: <u>Menuet</u> <u>de</u> <u>Poitou</u> (Vaudeville) (g)]
Menuet /de /poitou |reprise
   p 258$^{1-3}$ $^3[^3_4]$|6|13|

CO: 68-d'Anglebert #36, Menuet de Poitou Vaudeville

ED: cf Gilbert p 123, Roesgen-Champion p 66.

p 259   [blank, ruled]

---

144 | [COUPERIN (L)?, Prélude (a)]
[untitled]
   p 260^1-273^2 |-|

CO: cf 35-Bauyn-II #6, Prelude de Monsr. Couperin
    cf 36-Parville #45, Prelude de Mr Couprin ...
ED: Curtis-Co #12; cf Curtis-Co #1, Brunold/Dart-Co
    #6, Dart-Co App I.

---

145 | [CHAMBONNIÈRES: Le Printemps (a)]
Le Printems de Chambonnieres:
   p 274^1-275^3 ^{3}|9|7|14| [$\frac{3}{4}$|10|12|15|]

CO: 32-Oldham #15, 15a, Le printemps
    47-Gen-2356 #2, Pasachalia de Mr Chambonnieres
ED: cf Brunold-Tessier #142.

146 | [COUPERIN (L): <u>Double</u> to LEBÈGUE: <u>Gavotte</u> (C)]

Double /dela /Gauotte /de le /Begue
   p 276^1-277^2 ¢ |4|8|

CO: 35-Bauyn-III #54a, Double par Mr Couperin
    cf 13-Möllersche [copy of 64-Lebèuge-I #43a]
    cf 14-Schwerin-619 #91a, [Double]
    cf 23-Tenbury #6a, Double
    cf 24-Babell #60a, Double
    cf 36-Parville #68a, [Double]
    cf 50-Paignon #11a, la double
    cf 64-Lebègue-I #43a, Double

ED: cf Brunold/Dart-Co #132[a]; cf Dufourcq-L p 38.

147 | [LULLY, arr: <u>Premier</u> <u>Air</u> <u>pour</u> <u>les</u> <u>suivants</u> <u>de</u> <u>Mars</u>
from <u>Psyché</u> (1678) V-4 (C)]

Les /Trompetes /de psiché.
   p 278^1-279^2 ¢ |8|8|8|

CO: cf 36-Parville #123, Les fanfares de Psiché
   cf 39-Vm7-6307-1 #12, Les grandes Trompettes a
                           Deux Choeurs en Rondeau

148 | [CHAMBONNIÈRES: La Sotise (C)]

[untitled]
p 280¹-281³   ³[³/₄]|16|16|

CO: 24-Babell #206, La Sotise
    35-Bauyn-I #7, Autre du même Auteur

ED: cf Brunold-Tessier #65.

---

149 | [LULLY, arr: Second Air (Sourdines) from Armide (1686)

II-4 (g)]

Sourdinnes de'Amide
p 282¹-283³   ³[³/₄]|14|24|

CO: cf 14-Schwerin-619 #64, Sourdinet damide
    cf 23-Tenbury #49, Air d'Armide
    cf 24-Babell #124, Air d'Armide Sourdines tres Doux
    cf 36-Parville #115, Air d'Armide
    cf 49-RésF-933 #2, Sourdines d'Armide
    cf 68-d'Anglebert #33, Les Sourdines D'Armide

ED: cf Gilbert p 115, Roesgen-Champion p 62.

---

p 284-350   [blank, ruled]